MW01596876

Waipi'o Valley

A Polynesian Journey from Eden to Eden

Volume 2

Jeffrey L. Gross

Copyright © 2017 by Jeffrey L. Gross. 539311

ISBN: Softcover   978-1-5245-3904-7
         Hardcover   978-1-5245-4626-7
         EBook   978-1-5245-3903-0

All rights reserved. No part of this book may be reproduced
or transmitted in any form or by any means, electronic
or mechanical, including photocopying, recording, or by
any information storage and retrieval system, without
permission in writing from the copyright owner.

Print information available on the last page

Rev. date: 06/13/2017

To order additional copies of this book, contact:
Xlibris
1-888-795-4274
www.Xlibris.com
Orders@Xlibris.com

ACKNOWLEDGMENTS

I would like to acknowledge the support and encouragement of my wife Christina during the years that it took me to produce this work, Jerold Adams and Daniel Moore whose computer assistance helped with the layout of the drawings, maps, and photographs and I would also like to thank my publisher Chris Orleans for his assistance.

CONTENTS

Waipi'o Valley
Photograph by Kirk Lee Aeder

"The Valley of Wai-pio may justly be termed the Eden of the Hawaiian Islands. Long before I saw it, I had heard it frequently spoken of in terms of the warmest admiration. On reaching the brink of the tremendous bank by which its southern limit was bounded, the scene was truly magnificent. The bed of the valley reposed at the depth of two thousand feet below . . . the dwellings of the natives dwindled away nearly to the size of ant hills. On the opposite bank . . . much higher than the one which I stood . . . glittering cascades were tumbling from rock to rock . . . the center of the valley was enlivened with two crystal rivers, winding . . . to meet the foaming surge that broke on the fair sand-beach at its mouth. There was something about that valley so lovely and undisturbed, that it pictured to the imagination the paradise in which the first man wandered with the first woman. It seemed to belong to another world or to be a portion of this into which sorrow and death had never entered . . . my explorations in this valley convinced me that it once teemed with a large and busy population. The boundaries of ancient fish-ponds, taro-beds, and village sites were very numerous. At different periods in its history there was not a single square rod which does not seem to have been well cultivated . . . The population is rapidly decreasing, in fact it is nearly extinct . . . this terrestrial paradise will be as desolate and forsaken as was Eden of old after the expulsion of its first tenants."

(From *Sandwich Island Notes by a Haole,* 1854, by George W. Bates)

The Valley of Waipi'o from the Sand Hills on the Beach

An etching by J. Archer from a drawing by Reverend William Ellis in the *Journal of William Ellis: A Narrative of a Tour through Hawaii or Owhyhee in 1823*. The first foreigner to visit the royal sites of Waipi'o Valley, Ellis "spent the morning making a drawing of the valley from the sand hills on the beach". In the foreground, located directly behind the ancient sand dune burial mounds at the mouth of Waipi'o Valley, are shown Ka Haunokama'ahala, the royal residence, and the Paka'alana Heiau with Hale o Liloa, the royal mausoleum, within its walls. Inland on the flat valley floor are taro pondfields, fishponds and the Wailoa River wandering across the valley floor emptying into Waipi'o Bay. Houses and agricultural fields are located below the cliffs on either side of the valley and the 1450 foot high double Hi'ilawe Waterfall along with the villages of Napo'opo'o and Koauka can be seen in the distance

PREFACE

On my wedding anniversary in January 2005, my wife and I stayed at a hotel along the Northern California Coast where we met an African musician from Timbuktu, Mali, West Africa. After my wife explained we had recently visited the Hawaiian Islands and that I had previously lived there in the late 1970s and early 1980s, he suggested I had unfinished business in the islands and should return, which my wife and I did in August 2005. That a book about Polynesia was the unfinished business never occurred to me. *Waipi'o Valley: A Polynesian Journey from Eden to Eden* recounts the sea voyages of the ancestors of the Polynesians across a third of the circumference of the earth; many in double-hull canoes built with Stone Age technology, perhaps the most remarkable migrations in human history. From the land of Sumer, Mesopotamia, the location of Kalana i Hau'ola, the Hawaiian name for the biblical "Garden of Eden", to ancient Egypt and the Indus River Valley of ancient India, through Island Southeast Asia and into the Pacific Ocean, the Proto-Polynesians resided in various "Gardens of Eden" along their journey to Waipi'o Valley on the island of Hawai'i of the Hawaiian Islands, the last Polynesian "Garden of Eden".

Included in the book are geological explanations for the formation of the Hawaiian Islands and the unique Waipi'o Valley that was a royal and religious center of great cultural and spiritual importance, home of the gods in mythological legends, entrance into the spirit world of the afterlife and historic home of ancient Hawaiian chiefs and their sacred temples or *heiau*. The ancient Polynesians lived in some of the most remote environments on earth where they were isolated for over 2000 years, yet they have complex societies indicating extensive interaction with ancient civilizations. Their cultural and religious beliefs contain elements from mankind's distant past nearer the beginning of human history.

Readying Canoes for a Voyage
A painting by Herb Kawainui Kane

They sailed in double-hull canoes built with Stone Age technology using tools of stone, bone, and shell. Canoe hulls were carved from tree logs, connected with crossbeams and a platform or *pola* lashed together with sennit or coconut fiber cords. Built on the platform was a movable structure or *hale lanalana* for long distance voyages and sails were made from woven pandanus leaves. Voyaging from the Marquesas Islands in Eastern Polynesia possibly as early as 25 BC to AD 125, they sailed north for more than 2000 miles through an unknown sea navigating by the stars of the night sky. Copyright; National Geographic Society

Eia Hawai'i! (Behold Hawai'i!)
Sighting Mauna Kea
A painting by Herb Kawainui Kane

Finally, after a month at sea a cloudbank appeared on the horizon with a mountain visible above the clouds. It was an island larger than they had ever seen. The gods delivered the Marquesas Islanders to a new home in the middle of the largest ocean on earth and when they landed the human history of the Hawaiian Islands began. Courtesy of Herbert K. Kane, LLC

INTRODUCTION TO VOLUME 2

Volume 1, Chapters 1 through 5, traced the epic migration routes and timeline of Proto-Polynesians from the steppes of Central Asia to the Black Sea and city-state of Aratta in Eastern Turkey. Proto-Polynesians migrated down the Euphrates River to the land of Sumer, Mesopotamia, along the shore of the Persian Gulf, location of Kahiki, land of the gods, the biblical "Garden of Eden" and the Hawaiian Flood of Nu'u or the biblical Flood of Noah. The Proto-Polynesians migrated across the Indian Ocean to the Indus River Valley of ancient Vedic India, around the Arabian Peninsula and up the Red Sea to the land of Egypt. After the biblical Flood, some Proto-Polynesians migrated inland up the Tigris/Euphrates River Valley then south eventually reaching the land of Canaan and Lower Egypt. Proto-Polynesians migrated to the islands of Sumatra and Java and through the Wallacea area of Island Southeast Asia establishing homelands in the Moluccas Islands and on the island of Gilolo or Halmahera. Proto-Polynesians sailed through the Makassar Strait settling on the northern outer islands of Melanesia along with Lapita settlers who originated from the Indus River Valley of ancient India. The Proto-Polynesian *ariki* reached Fiji, Tonga and Samoa, the islands of Western Polynesia, by migrating across the low islands and atolls of Micronesia. Polynesians voyaged north from the Marquesas Islands in double-hull canoes reaching Hawai'i Island, "land of raging fire", and the lush Waipi'o Valley. Later, Tahitians arrived in the Hawaiian Islands migrating from the sacred Taputapuatea Marae on Ra'iatea Island and established themselves as the ruling elite who remade Hawaiian society. Waipi'o Valley became a royal residence of the high *ali'i* chiefs of Hawai'i Island until 'Umi, first to unite Hawai'i Island, moved his royal residence to Kailua-Kona on Hawai'i Island's leeward side. Kamehameha the First, who spent his early years in the seclusion of Waipi'o Valley, eventually conquered and unified the Hawaiian Islands. After 20 years of waging war Kamehameha returned to Kamakahonu, Kailua-Kona, where he died in 1819 and then Hawaiian society changed. The oppressive religious *kapu* system was abolished and the carved *ki'i* idols and feathered gods of Hawaiian *heiau* were destroyed in what has been described as the "Hawaiian Cultural Revolution".

Volume 2 begins with Chapter 6, Culture And Religion: Rituals And The Gods. The Hawaiian creation prayer chant, the *Kumulipo,* describes the origins of the universe and mankind in *Po,* a realm of divine darkness before creation and the evolution of life on earth. In the Hawaiian theory of evolution organisms are transformed through reproduction into higher levels of complexity and into the spiritual realm of the divine. The legend of *Pele,* Hawaiian goddess of fire and volcanoes, and her sister or daughter *Hi'ilawe* illustrated the geological sequence of creation of the Hawaiian Islands through the route taken by the goddesses after their arrival; they moved in a progression from the older to the younger islands. Polynesian religion originated from their ancestral homelands of Sumer, Mesopotamia, the Indus River Valley of ancient Vedic India and ancient Egypt. Their temple traditions, sacrificial altars and pantheon of four major gods with numerous lesser deities represented by anthropomorphic images, originated from Sumer, Mesopotamia. Polynesian social structure, creation mythology, and concepts of *mana* and taboo originated from Vedic India. The major Polynesian gods were deified ancestors who navigated early Proto-Polynesian migratory voyages. The Polynesian concept of a Supreme Creator God as a sacred force goes back to the Near East, to ancient Egypt and the Israelites. Polynesians believed spirits of their righteous dead would set out on a westward journey to Kahiki, their ancestral homeland where in legend mankind was created and lived with the gods.

The ancient Hawaiian religion was animistic, believing divine spirits became manifest in features of the natural landscape and any natural object could represent a god. Hawaiians believed in immortality of the soul and the ancient Binary Soul Doctrine where man has two souls or spirits. In the Hawaiian version of the Binary Soul Doctrine man has two souls and a third created out of the union of the two souls and there is an invisible *aka* cord over which *mana* would flow connecting the universe, an idea going back to Vedic India, ancient Egypt and probably to the dawn of civilization. Hawaiian metaphysical knowledge known as *huna* originated in ancient Egypt and can be traced through religious beliefs of ancient India, the islands of Sumatra and Java, and the South Pacific islands of Samoa and Tahiti where *huna* traditions were preserved in Polynesia. In the Hawaiian Islands social ranking was determined by one's genealogy and there were different degrees of sacredness for high *ali'i* chiefs and the *mana* of the highest chiefs was considered equal to that of the gods. *Mana* together with *kapu* created a rigid system of social controls and regulations, protecting the sacred from the profane. Hawaiian *heiau* were sacred temples where sacrifices to the gods were conducted, where divine *mana* was concentrated and transferred to the realm of mankind during religious ceremonies. *Luakini heiau,* temples of human sacrifice, were the most important Hawaiian *heiau* and their dedication rituals were the most elaborate in all of Polynesia. The Polynesian cultural theme of conquering "stranger kings" ruling over the subjugated "native commoners" was illustrated in the Hawaiian Makahiki festival, a New Year and first-fruits celebration that began with the appearance of the Pleiades star cluster along the western horizon. Festivals similar to the Makahiki festival occurred throughout Polynesia and their origin goes back to annual harvest festivals in ancient Sumer, Mesopotamia. Hawaiian culture and religion developed from many ancient civilizations and Polynesian isolation on the islands of the Pacific Ocean for 2000 years has preserved many elements from mankind's ancient cultural past.

Waipi'o Valley with its fertile alluvial soil, perennial streams and luxurious tropical growth was the location of one of the initial settlements on Hawai'i Island. At first, settlers were dependent upon the sea for survival and their settlements expanded along the coastal strip. As their population increased they expanded inland relying on transplantation of food plants and domesticated animals brought by the original settlers to create a land-based economy. Extensive fishponds and a taro pondfield 'auwai irrigation system allowed expansion further up the valley to the forested uplands creating an *ahupua'a* land division. Waipi'o Valley evolved into a pyramidal genealogical social system with a small elite *ali'i* ruling class and became the residence of the first ruling chiefs of Hawai'i Island. Waipi'o Valley, site of the only undisturbed royal center in the Hawaiian Islands, contains many historic sites representing Hawaiian cultural heritage. Polynesian art and science reached its highest level of development in the Hawaiian Islands where Hawaiian *heiau* were the largest stone temples in Polynesia. Hawaiian canoes with *koa* wood dugout hulls were described as "the finest in the Pacific". Hawaiian feathered robes, capes and helmets represented the highest level of Polynesian featherwork.

There are many similarities between the biblical Israelite religion, customs and taboos, and those of Polynesians. The most sacred site in Polynesia, the Taputapuatea Marae on Ra'iatea Island, Tahiti, is where its holy ark was carried on the shoulders of four priests supporting two long poles and it had two carved representations of birds with their wings extended on top; clearly a replica of the Israelite Ark of the Covenant. Polynesian *ture* laws began in the Near East and the word *ture* for laws originated from the Hebrew word *torah* meaning laws. Hawaiian monthly taboo days resembled the Israelite Sabbath and Hawaiian *pu'uhonua* were related to biblical Israelite cities of refuge. In ancient Israel sacred pillars marked places where man had come in contact with the divine and the origin of the Hawaiian *Pohaku o Kane* was probably the biblical Bethel Stone. In ancient Israel the firstborn male child was dedicated to God and in the Hawaiian Islands the firstborn male child was consecrated to the gods. The layout and functions of the Paka'alana Heiau in Waipi'o Valley, both a *luakini heiau* and *pu'uhonua* or place of refuge and the most sacred site on Hawai'i Island, had many similarities to the Israelite Tabernacle at the base of Mount Sinai during the biblical Exodus. Located at the rear of the *luakina* or inner temple of the Paka'alana Heiau was the *lananu'u mamao* or oracle tower which had functions similar to the "Holy of Holies" which housed the Ark of the Covenant in the Israelite Tabernacle where man could communicate with God.

Kipuka in the Hawaiian Islands are oases of vegetation surrounded by a volcanic lava flow, "islands of life" that possess *mana,* the spiritual power of the gods, from which new growth is generated on barren lava. *Kipuka* represent the mythological struggle between *Pele,* goddess of fire, and *Hi'iaka,* goddess of plant growth. Waipi'o Valley that was of historic importance as a political, religious and royal center, and the sacred home of many high chiefs of Hawai'i Island is still considered sacred to native Hawaiians. Waipi'o Valley represents a cultural *kipuka,* an isolated island of traditional Hawaiian rural lifestyle where traditional Hawaiian customs and beliefs have continued into modern times. The Hawaiian Islands have the potential to regenerate the Hawaiian culture of the *kanaka maoli,* the indigenous Hawaiian people and are currently experiencing a rebirth of their ancient culture in support of *Ka Lahui Hawai'i,* The Hawaiian Nation.

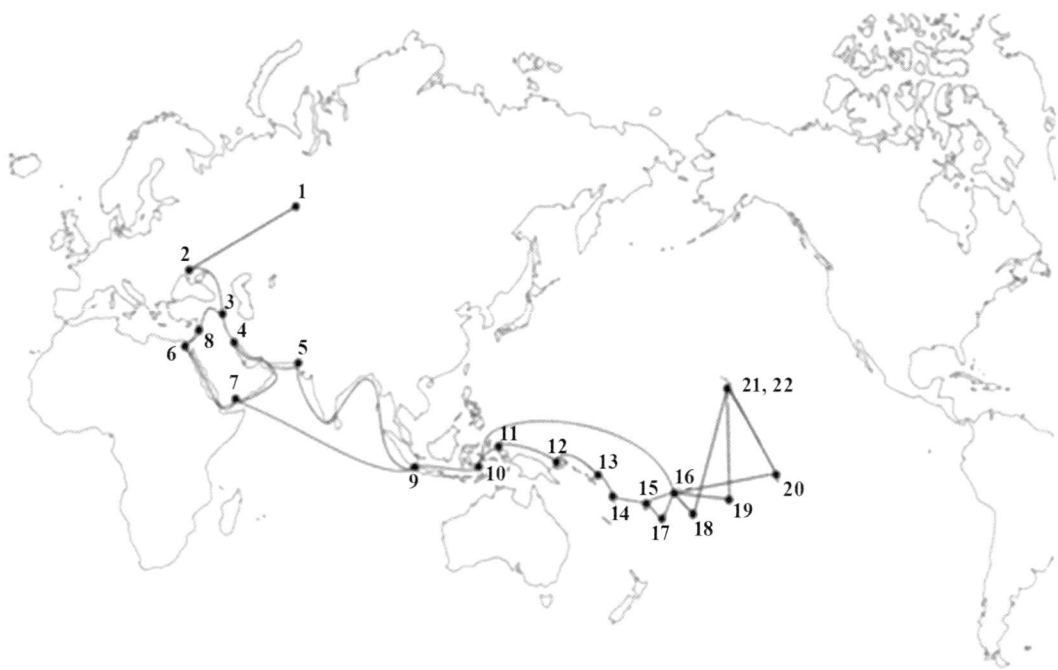

The Major Polynesian Migration Routes and
Timeline to the Hawaiian Islands

1. About 50,000 years ago, modern man migrated north out of Africa and reached the Ural Mountains and the steppes of Central Asia. This was from where Sumerian ancestors of the Polynesians originated.

2. Colder weather caused by a pole shift forced the Sumerian ancestors of Polynesians to migrate south where they established settlements along the shore of Lake Euxine, a freshwater lake in the Black Sea Basin. About 6700 BC, after the end of the last Ice Age, the earth became warmer and the vast glaciers began to melt flooding the Black Sea Basin.

3. After the Black Sea Flood the Sumerians founded Aratta, an urban city-state on the Anatolian Plateau of Eastern Turkey, located near the headwaters of the Tigris and Euphrates Rivers about 5500 BC.

4. Migrating down the Euphrates River on rafts and in small boats, the Sumerians entered the lower alluvial Mesopotamian Plain at the mouth of the Persian Gulf where they encountered the 'Ubaid civilization about 4500 BC. This was the location of the biblical "Garden of Eden" or the Hawaiian Kalana i Hau'ola where the biblical Flood, the Sumerian Flood of Ziusudra or the Hawaiian Flood of Nu'u occurred, probably about 2800 BC.

5. The Sumerians established a coastal trade route through the Persian Gulf across the Indian Ocean to the Indus River Valley of Vedic India as early as 4000 BC and after the biblical Flood Proto-Polynesians migrated east to the Indus River Valley. Later, after the fall of Sumer, Proto-Polynesians migrated by land up the Tigris/Euphrates River Valley becoming known as *manahune* or the people of Mana. The land of Mana or Manna was the name of their ancient homeland located near the city-state of Aratta.

6. There was another Sumerian coastal trade route around the Arabian Peninsula and after the biblical Flood, other Proto-Polynesians established settlements along the eastern coast of the Arabian Peninsula and eventually migrated up the Red Sea into Egypt.

7. Hawai'iloa was a legendary high chief and fisherman whose home was on the southeastern coast of the Arabian Peninsula, in what is now Yemen, and during his extensive fishing voyages he "discovered" the islands of Sumatra and Java about 3000 BC, there he was considered a founder of the Polynesian race.

8. At 2092 BC, after being commanded by God, Lua-nu'u or the biblical Abraham along with his wife, nephew and clan left the city of Haran in Northern Mesopotamia and migrated south to the land of Canaan and their descendants entered Lower Egypt at 1662 BC. The biblical Exodus probably occurred at 1447 BC, and included *ariki* ancestors of the Polynesians.

9. Proto-Polynesians of the islands of Sumatra and Java, thought to have been "discovered" by Hawai'iloa, became part of the Austronesian Nusantao Maritime Trading Network about 2400 BC. After Island Southeast Asia was invaded by Chinese and Malaysian warriors through the Malay Peninsula, the Proto-Polynesians migrated north by sea into the Wallacea area of Island Southeast Asia.

10. As Proto-Polynesians migrated through the Wallacea area of Island Southeast Asia, they established homelands in the Moluccas, Maluku, or Spice Islands and on the island of Gilolo or Halmahera. The Proto-Polynesians sailed north through the Makassar Strait, the "Gate of the Pacific", to the islands of Melanesia as early as 3800 BC, and by 1200 BC Proto-Polynesian *ariki* voyaged north into Micronesia.

11. The Sepik Coast of Northern Papua New Guinea, first settled by Papuans as early as 50,000 BC, was also settled about 3800 BC when Austronesian-speaking Proto-Polynesians arrived along the northern coast of Papua New Guinea.

12. The Bismarck Archipelago of Melanesia, first settled by Papuans about 37,500 BC who had been able to cross the Vitiaz Strait from the Huon Peninsula of Papua New Guinea by raft, was settled about 3000 BC when Austronesian-speaking Proto-Polynesians first migrated across the Vitiaz Strait to the Bismarck Archipelago. Lapita settlers who migrated from the Indus River Valley of Vedic India settled in the Bismarck Archipelago about 1900 BC.

13. The catastrophic WK-2 eruption of Mount Witori in the Bismarck Archipelago occurred about 1600 BC and initiated the rapid migration of Lapita settlers down the Melanesian Island chain as far as the Solomon Islands that had been the eastward extent of earlier Austronesian-speaking Proto-Polynesian migrations.

14. Due to their more advanced canoe technology and navigational ability, the migration of Lapita settlers was able to continue into Remote Oceania reaching the islands of Vanuatu.

15. The Fiji Islands of Western Polynesia were first reached by Lapita settlers sailing from the islands of Vanuatu about 1500 BC, and were followed by Austronesian-speaking Proto-Polynesians who arrived in the Fiji Islands about 1200 BC. The Proto-Polynesian *ariki,* who had migrated north from the Wallacea area of Island Southeast Asia and across the low islands and atolls of Micronesia, eventually reached the Manu'a Islands of Samoa about 900 BC.

16. Landing on the Manu'a Islands of Samoa, the Proto-Polynesians *ariki* found themselves under attack from Lapita settlers already on the islands who practiced human sacrifice. In the Samoan language the word *manu'a* means wounded and the *ariki* retreated to inland defensive positions.

17. The *ariki* rebuilt their forces, defeated the Lapita/Proto-Polynesians and halting their eastward expansion. They proceeded south conquering the Tonga Islands and then invaded the Fiji Islands where warfare raged for hundreds of years. The islands of Fiji, Tonga, and Samoa became the original "Polynesian Triangle" where the Polynesian language and culture first evolved and after an interruption lasting 500 to 1000 years Polynesian voyages of discovery resumed originating from the islands of Samoa.

18. The Cook Islands or kingdom of Rarotonga was probably first settled by expeditions of discovery leaving the islands of Samoa and Tonga arriving on the Cook Islands about 500 BC.

19. The islands of Tahiti or the Society Islands were probably first settled by migratory voyages of discovery originating from the islands of Samoa or directly from the Gilbert Islands of Micronesia also about 500 BC. Later, Ra'iatea Island in the leeward Tahitian Islands was settled by *ariki* from the Tuamotu Islands located to the east of the Tahitian Islands about AD 600.

20. Voyages of discovery leaving the islands of Samoa are thought to have first arrived on the Marquesas or Hiva Islands from 400 BC to 100 BC. Later, voyagers arrived from the islands of Tonga.

21. Marquesas Islanders, aware of the flight patterns of migratory birds, knew there was land to the north. They traveled north on a voyage of discovery over 1885 nautical miles, first reaching the Hawaiian Islands about AD 300 to AD 400, or possibly as early as 25 BC to AD 125.

22. There were later voyages to the Hawaiian Islands from the island of Rarotonga in the Cook Islands about AD 650, and from the islands of Tahiti about AD 1050 that continued until AD 1325. Then Hawaiian contact with the rest of Polynesia ceased.

A View of a Morai at O'whyhee
1782

An illustration by William Ellis engraved by William Walker of a row of images and a stone altar in the Hikiau Heiau, Kealakekua Bay, Hawai'i Island, where Captain James T. Cook was pronounced a divine incarnation of the god *Lono*

**A Representation of a Morai,
or Burial Place at O'whyhee**
circa 1788

A hand-colored version of an engraving of the Hikiau Heiau after a 1779 illustration by John Webber, artist on Captain James T. Cook's third voyage into the Pacific Ocean, with a row of carved anthropomorphic images behind a wooden fence and beyond a second fence are skulls mounted on posts. The Hikiau Heiau is located at Napo'opo'o Beach, Kealakekua Bay, Hawai'i Island. The image was published in *A New Royal Authentic and Complete System of Universal Geography Antient and Modern,* 1793, by Thomas Bankes

CHAPTER 6

CULTURE AND RELIGION: RITUALS AND THE GODS

1. *At the time that turned the heat of the earth,*
2. *At the time when the heavens turned and changed,*
3. *At the time when the light of the sun was subdued*
4. *To cause light to break forth,*
5. *At the time of the night of Makalii (winter)*
6. *Then began the slime which established the earth,*
7. *The source of deepest darkness.*
8. *Of the depth of darkness, in the depth of darkness,*
9. *Of the darkness of the sun, in the depth of night,*
10. *It is night,*
11. *So was night born.*

The first eleven lines of the epic Hawaiian creation chant *Kumulipo* as translated by the last Queen of the Hawaiian Islands, Queen Liliuokalani, while she was under house arrest at ʻIolani Palace in Honolulu. The first record of the *Kumulipo* chant was by composer Keaulumoku around 1700. *An Account of the Creation of the World According to Hawaiian Tradition,* Queen Liliuokalani's translation of the *Kumulipo* published in 1897, describes the evolutionary origin of species and ancestral genealogy of the Hawaiian royal family. It was the first complete English translation of the *Kumulipo* chant from the Hawaiian text written down by her brother King Kalakaua and published in 1889.

1. *At the time when the earth was turned*
   becoming hot with fire from inside.

2. *At the time when the heavens overturned*
   and were changed.

3. *At the time when the sun was but dawning,*
   the heavenly one first appeared.

4. *At first light broke forth faintly like the light of the moon,*
   then the bright one saw the light.

5. *During the winter season of growth when the Makaliʻi (Pleiades)*
   appears in the heavens.

6. *When the elements were mixed into the slime (walewale) with which the*
   earth was formed, when the divine seed was planted.

7. *In the primordial darkness, the deepest darkness, the spiritual*
    world began with the creation of the divine child of the royal dynasty.

8. *In the depth of the night, the deepest night, during*
    the time of the gods, a world of gods, the spiritual night began.

9. *In the darkness of the sun, in the depth of the night, in*
    the far distant past lost in remoteness.

10. *On a night long ago was the coming of the bright one*
    into the world of the gods.

11. *Born into a world of only gods.*

A composite translation of the first eleven lines of the *mele oli* or creation chant *Kumulipo* or "beginning in deep darkness" combining its "literal and underlying symbolic meaning" with the birth of the divine child, the "heavenly one". *Kumu* means origin, source or foundation; *lipo* means deep blue-black, color of the dark night of chaos and the deepest ocean. (Adapted from *The Kumulipo: A Hawaiian Creation Chant* by Martha W. Beckwith 1972 [1951])

THE KUMULIPO

The *Kumulipo* is a Hawaiian creation prayer chant or *mele oli,* a genealogical chant or *mele ko'ihonua,* a name chant or *mele inoa* and a prayer for the consecration of a chief or *pule ho'ola'a ali'i*. Referred to as the *Song of Creation*, it is an ancient account of the Hawaiian theory of creation of the universe and a genealogical chant tracing the ancestry of the divine, sacred royal child of pure Hawaiian *ali'i* descent back to the beginning of life on earth and the ancestral gods. Similar prayer chants were recited on the Marquesas and Tuamotu Islands during festivals on the occasion of birth of a chief's son.

The 2102 line *Kumulipo* divides the origin of the cosmos into two time periods each containing eight *wa* with each *wa* representing an age or eon of time. The first eight *wa* exist solely in *Po*, the divine darkness and primeval night of the spirit world, where the origin of the world and birth of the gods took place. In the first seven *wa,* lower forms of life belonging to the nonhuman world of *Po* are created. The eighth *wa* begins the time of the birth of man; it is the dawn of the age of light and begins the material world of *Ao*. The *Kumulipo* traces the divine genealogy of high chiefs, linking them back to the origin of the universe and major gods who began as deified chiefs born into the living world. The divine genealogy begins *mai ka Po mai* or "from the night of *Po*", from creation of the stars in the heavens and appearance of life on earth; night is considered a sacred continuation of *Po'ele'ele,* the "age of darkness".

In the creation mythology of Polynesia, both animate and inanimate objects are created through divine power spontaneously entering pairs of rocks that join and reproduce, "pairs of rocks suggesting the shape of male and female sex organs were worshipped as ancestral gods in old Hawai'i". (Beckwith 1972 [1951]) Pairs of male and female standing stone *massebah* have been found in ancient Israel. In a Tongan creation myth published by Catholic missionary Father P. Retter in 1907, *limu* or seaweed and *kele* or mud are intertwined and wash up on the shore of Pulotu, the mythical Polynesian paradise where they give birth to *Touiafutuna*, a large metallic stone that splits open and twins emerge, *Piki* a male and *Kele* a female. *Touiafutuna* gives birth to three other sets of twins and together they become the gods. The *'ili 'ili hanau o* Koloa or birthstones of Koloa are smooth waterworn stones located near Koloa Bay on Hawai'i Island, once the location of the Ninole fishponds along Punalu'u Beach, the black-sand beach of Ka'u, thought to have the supernatural ability to have sex and reproduce. Tahitian creation chants such as the *Creation of Man*, recorded by John Orsmond in 1822, contain concepts similar to those in the *Kumulipo*. They describe *Po* as the divine time of darkness and chaos and *Ao* as the time of light. In the Tahitian chant during the time of *Po*, mountains grew, rain fell, water rushed forth and then the Creator God *Ta'aroa* created a union between pairs of rocks that reproduced and were the first elements in the growth of living things.

In the *Kumulipo,* the world evolved as a product of active forces where continuous sexual creation produced successive mutations. (Beckwith 1972 [1951]) In a series of developmental stages, lower life forms evolved into more complex higher forms of life as a product of natural evolutionary forces with occasional help from the divine, such as when the god *Kane* separated the earth from the sky and when he created La'ila'i, the first woman, from the soil of the earth. The *Kumulipo* is Hawaiian oral literature passed on from generation to generation, preserved over centuries. A recital of the chant was a sacred formal affair; even knowledge of the *Kumulipo* was restricted to only the highest *ali'i*. The *Kumulipo* represents an ancient creation and genealogical prayer chant corresponding to other creation chants throughout Central and Eastern Polynesia. Sacred prayer chants recited at the birth of a high chief of ruling families representing their genealogy going back to the gods and beginning of life on earth have been found in the Samoa, Tahiti, Tuamotu, Cook and Marquesas or Hiva Islands and similar Maori creation chants have been found in New Zealand or Aotearoa.

The first written record of the *Kumulipo* was by Hawaiian scholar David Malo in the 1830s and 1840s, although it only included parts of the genealogy sections of the *Kumulipo* chanted by a Moloka'i *kahuna* of the *Hale Naua,* an ancient genealogical society, using a knotted cord or *hipu'u*, a Hawaiian system for calculating time representing the ancestors. The ancient Hawaiian *hipu'u* is an example of cultural diffusion. Knotted cords were used for navigation across the Indian Ocean to Island Southeast Asia, through Polynesia and as far as South America. The word *khipu*, meaning knot and a system of hanging knotted cords, originated from the pre-Inca Quechua language of the South American Andes and coastal Indians of Peru. In the Marquesas Islands, a long woven coconut sennit cord with hanging knotted cords or *ta'o mata* represent generations of their genealogy, each knot indicating an ancestor. The chant was recited by an *o'ono* or genealogist and their genealogies were said to go back to 2000 BC. On Easter Island, knotted cords were known by their Spanish South American name *quipu*.

In 1889, King Kalakaua had the *Kumulipo* published in the Hawaiian language to support his claim to the throne by tracing his family ancestry back to the origin of the universe. German anthropologist Adolf Bastian, after borrowing a copy from King Kalakaua, translated the first eleven lines into German which were published as early as 1881 and were then translated into English by Joseph Rock. Queen Liliuokalani translated the entire *Kumulipo* into English in *An Account of the Creation of the World According to Hawaiian Tradition* published in 1897 and in 1951, Martha Beckwith's translation of the *Kumulipo* was published. "The chant [is] a poetic symbol of the care for the sacred sparks in man from its inception to its maturity into a divinity, born as a human being on earth to carry on the family ruling line . . . Using ancient [cosmogony] beliefs [which were] common elsewhere in Polynesia as in Hawaii, in such a way as to trace the [royal] family back to the 'beginnings in deep darkness'". (Beckwith 1972 [1951])

In the *Kumulipo, Po* is a divine, heavenly realm of the supernatural where the spirit of the Supreme Creator God *'Io* is the one light in the cosmic darkness. In the beginning there was no sky, no sea, no earth, and no gods, only nothingness; a vast boundless time of intense total deep darkness that was totally divine. Then the Supreme Creator God, through his divine *mana*, formed the god *Kanenuiakea* or *Kane* of the wide expanse, "the great unseen god in the dark clouds of heaven" who shaped the world out of the chaos of *Po* with assistance from the gods *Ku* and *Lono*. This was the time of birth of the gods who were *akua hanau Po* or "gods born in the night of *Po*" an infinite realm of absolute nothingness, but in *Po* there was potential energy or *mana* from which all things are created. *Po* is "the realm of the gods" where "the god enters, man cannot enter". The *Kumulipo* is an account of creation of the universe from the initial movements of the earth and sky. In the beginning, in the time of darkness, heaven and earth were joined and then set into motion. The abrasive movement of the sky against the earth caused the earth to heat up and become productive, the rotation of the sky began time. After land rose out of the depths of the sea, life first appeared along its shore created by primitive slime or *walewale*, a combination of saltwater, air and earth, similar to the "primordial soup" of modern creation theory. "When life appears in the *Kumulipo,* it is the product of active, natural forces" and as each new life form appeared, it was more complex than its predecessor. Living things evolved through a process where new species were born as mutations and reproduction was "the realm of the gods".

During the second time period *Ao*, daylight gradually approached and the world of mankind began, it was a time of awakening when men multiplied on earth and were born by the hundreds. In the spirit world of *Po,* creatures were controlled by the gods alone and were beings without the light of reason. In *Ao* mankind emerged, now it was day and the gods existed within man, the divine had been transformed. The *Kumulipo* incorporates dualistic themes or *palua* such as *Po* passing into *Ao*, night into day and the spiritual into the material; earth and sky, land and sea, sun and moon, chaos and order, male and female, fire and water, life and death. In *Po*, born in the light possessing darkness is Kumulipo, positive male source of life, and Po'ele, negative female night. *Po* contains the divine male, sacred and life. *Ao* contains the human female, profane and death. Man is the strong generative power and woman is receptive and submissive. Born is "man for the narrow stream, woman for the broad stream", water passes through a narrow entrance with force and through a wide opening without struggle. The period of the existence of gods alone in *Po* ends with gods who are first born on earth as human beings. *Ao* is peopled by beings with consciousness, a world of living men created by the gods.

> "The time of the birth of the taboo chief,
> The time when the Heavenly One pushed his way out,
> The time when the bright one first saw the light,
> At first faintly like the light of the moon,
> At the season of Makali'i in the far past.
> From the slime of the mother the stock began,
> Began in the spirit world,
> Began in the time of the gods, in the world of gods,
> In the far distant past lost in remoteness,
> Long ago was the coming of the bright one into the world
>   of the gods,
> A world still peopled by gods alone."

(From *The Kumulipo: A Hawaiian Creation Chant,*
1972 [1951], by Martha Beckwith, page 49)

The *Kumulipo* is composed of ancient material transmitted over thousands of years, it records the ordered sequence of the development of life on earth, in agreement with ancient creation chants from many other Polynesian islands, with modern evolutionary theory and the "big bang theory" of modern physics. Evidence of the great antiquity of the *Kumulipo* is found in the fact some plants and animals it describes never existed in Polynesia, their origin was in the Near East. Perhaps, the *Kumulipo* was describing more ancient locations from early Proto-Polynesian homelands.

> Hawaiians understood the relationship between living organisms through their systematic observations of the natural environment. Their evolutionary concepts are in agreement with modern scientific thought and were assembled more than a century before Charles Darwin published *The Origin of Species by Means of Natural Selection* in 1859. In the *Kumulipo*, the earth was first covered with water and the gods drew the land out of

the fathomless depths of the sea. In the creation legend of Sumer, Mesopotamia, the god *Enki* lived along the shore of the primordial sea and *Enki's* word created order out of chaos beginning creation. In Egyptian creation mythology, before the gods came into existence there was only a dark, watery abyss whose chaotic potential energy contained the forms of all living things; the spirit of the creator existed in the primeval waters.

In the beginning God created the heaven and the earth.

And the earth was without form, and void; and darkness was upon the face of the deep. And the spirit of God moved upon the surface of the waters.

(Genesis 1:1, 2)

And God said, Let the waters under heaven be gathered together into one place, and let the dry land appear. And it was so.

And God called the dry land Earth: and the gathering together of the waters he called Seas. And God saw that it was good.

(Genesis 1:9, 10)

Born is the coral polyp, the simplest organism observable to Hawaiians. Coral begins life because reproductive power of the gods first entered stone and out of coral evolved the earliest forms of marine life, mollusks, sea urchins, starfish, and shellfish. During this time moss and small plants appear on the land, fish and eels appear in the sea. As the evolutionary progression continued, both land and sea birds appear and amphibious creatures swim out of the sea onto the shore as "those of the sea take to the land". Terrestrial warm-blooded mammals then appear; the pig, the rat, the dog and finally man, whose appearance marks the evolutionary passage from *Po* to *Ao*. The story of evolution found in the *Kumulipo* does not end with biological evolution and the ascent of man, but with spiritual evolution of the divine chiefs, the *akua ali'i*. Now, the Creator God has reproduced himself, spiritual evolution has advanced mankind into a higher state beyond the physical and into the realm of the divine. Jean-Baptiste Lamarck (1744-1829), a French soldier, botanist, naturalist, and a predecessor of Charles Darwin first proposed his theory of evolution in 1800. Lamarck believed an adaptive environmental force caused organisms to transform into higher levels of complexity with a progressive development toward human "perfection".

DIVINE INTERVENTION IN HAWAIIAN CREATION MYTHOLOGY

In the Polynesian evolutionary concept of the origin of man, the process was sometimes aided by deities, such as when the Hawaiian god *Ke-ali'i-wahi-lani*, "the chief who opens heaven", also known as the god *Kane*, looked down from the heavens and saw the beautiful woman La'ila'i dwelling in Lalowaia. He came down to earth and impregnated the beautiful La'ila'i who he had formed from the soil of the earth. In the myth of La'ila'i appearing in the *Kumulipo*, she becomes the mother of both gods and men establishing the divine into human life. The gods, being all male, create the first female from the soil of the earth; male is a descendant of the gods and female is of earthly origin. La'ila'i lived with her divine husband, the god *Kane*, in Nu'u-meha-lani, the "sacred raised place of the heavenly one", a land in the clouds. She gave birth to two daughters and one son with the god *Kane.* La'ila'i first slept with Ki'i, the first man, a mere mortal on earth and her eldest brother, a *ni'aupi'o* mating. The *Kumulipo* includes symbolic language and hidden meanings or *kaona* into its poetic imagery such as referring to La'ila'i as the "woman who sat sideways", an expression for a wife who takes another husband, her children were *po'olua* or with two fathers. La'ila'i had relations both with god and man, "she lived with Ki'i, she lived with Kane . . . she lived above and came bending down over Ki'i". La'ila'i first lived with Ki'i and his descendants were born first. She had five sons and three daughters with Ki'i and five of the eight survived. Her first son was with Ki'i and the god *Kane's* offspring became the younger line. The earth swarmed with La'ila'i's offspring who were half god and half man. The god *Kane* bears the name of man and man or *ki'i* is an anthropomorphic image of god. Now man and his gods became interrelated and dependent upon each other; the divine was not complete until it created mankind. In mythology of the islands of Tahiti, the Supreme God *Ta'aroa* created the first man, Ti'i, who took "the woman who ate before and behind" as a wife. In the Marquesas or Hiva Islands, La'ila'i is known as *Atanua*, goddess of the dawn, and on Easter Island or Rapa Nui, there is a myth where three males and a female known as Ra'ira'i populate the island. Theories of the evolutionary process occurring through sexual union, such as those found in the *Kumulipo* are consistent with creation mythologies found throughout Polynesia. To the Maori of New Zealand, *Rangi,* the sky god, mated with *Papa,* the earth goddess, during the time of *Po* when the earth was naked, *Rangi* creates plants covering the earth with forests of trees and then insects, shellfish, and reptiles appear, followed by birds, animals, and mankind.

A HAWAIIAN CREATION MYTH: THE COSMIC EGG

There is a Hawaiian legend where a great white bird creates the world. At first, there is only a dark featureless void where there is no life or land, only water. Then, the great white bird soars majestically on a mission of creation carrying an immense reddish brown egg with tongues of fire resting upon her back. The bird lets the egg fall and then ascends to the kingdom of the gods from where she had come, leaving a rainbow in her wake. When the egg crashes into the waters, clouds of steam rise into the air, huge pieces of flaming lava fly in all directions and the sea becomes a raging cauldron. Burning lava rains down upon the waters and is tossed about in the sea. When the lava cools, it anchors itself on the sea floor and islands are born.

> "Winging its way high above the vast waste of waters, far up under the blue vault of heaven, a great bird soared majestically, wheeling and dipping, now upon one wing and now upon the other, and then, sweeping downward, dropping an immense egg, which, falling upon the crested waves, burst into fragments and formed the archipelago known today as the Hawaiian Islands."
>
> (Hawaiian legend from *Under Hawaiian Skies,*
> 1922, by Albert P. Taylor, page 19)

The origin of the Hawaiian myth where a bird creates the world may have originated with the Haida Gwaii Indians of the coastal islands of Alaska and Western Canada believed to have been ancestors of Hawaiians. In the Haida creation myth, a raven that was originally a snow-white bird dropped a stone into the primordial sea forming land. In mythology of Western Polynesia, the Creator God *Tagaloa* of the Manu'a Islands of Samoa and *Tangaloa* of the islands of Tonga are the same god and each had *Tuli*, the divine messenger bird. In the Manu'a Islands, *Tagaloa* dwelt in the void and created the island of Tau so *Tuli* would have a place to land. In the islands of Tonga, *Tangaloa* sent *Tuli* over the primeval sea looking for a place to land and when *Tangaloa* cast down a rock, the first island was formed. 'Eua Island, located twenty-five miles southeast of the main Tonga island of Tongatapu, was where *Tuli* first landed on solid earth created by *Tangaloa*. Amazingly, the launch site of the Tonga Spaceport is located on a plateau along the southern tip of 'Eua Island. This "forgotten island", the Tongan mythological first land, is the oldest land of the Tonga Archipelago, perhaps in all of Polynesia dating to around 46 million years ago and will be a launch site for rockets going into outer space.

Another Polynesian cosmic egg legend can be found in the creation stories of the islands of Tahiti, where the Supreme Creator God *Ta'aroa* the parentless, ancestor of all the gods, floats adrift in his primeval egg shell, revolving in the impenetrable void and darkness of *Po*, where there was no land, no sky, no sea and no sun, moon or stars. The feathered god called out, but nothing replied and *Ta'aroa* lay in the solitude of his shell over eons of time. Then, the feathered god *Ta'aroa* began to stir, his shell cracked and when he emerged he began the act of creation. A piece of *Ta'aroa's* eggshell named *Rumia* fell onto the surface of the waters and became *te tumu nui o te fenua* or the great foundation of the earth, its rocks and soil, and another piece of his shell became the dome of the heavens. When *Ta'aroa* emerged from his shell, he shook off some of his red and yellow feathers that fell to earth and became trees and plants, he was *Te Tumu* or The Source. *Ta'aroa* mated with *Papa*, the earth goddess, and she gave birth to *Hina*. *Ta'aroa* slept incestuously with *Hina*, the moon goddess, who gave birth to the great god *'Oro* in *Po*. *Ao*, the realm of humans, was empty so *Ta'aroa* created the god *Tu*, whose son the god *Tane,* propped up the dome of the sky on pillars allowing light to enter into the world of *Ao*. Then *Tane* created Ti'i, the first man who he molded from the earth. Ti'i also slept with *Hina* and then *Ao,* the world of light, became filled with life as man multiplied. *Tane* raised the layers above their heads creating three levels of the earth and nine levels of heaven, then created the stars, sun, and the moon to adorn the highest heaven where he resides. *Ta'aroa* came down to earth in a valley on the 'Opoa Peninsula on Ra'iatea Island and where his foot touched ground the Vaeara'i Marae was later built. In the creation myth of the Tuamotu Islands, the universe begins as an egg containing *Te Tumu*, the foundation, and *Te Papa*, the stratum rock. The egg bursts producing three layers, *Te Tumu* and *Te Papa* remain on the lowest level where their mating produces mankind, animals, and plants. When people multiply they raise the level above them, strong men mounted on each other's shoulders lift the sky. In the Caillet Creation Chart of the Tuamotu Islands, the universe begins with an egg that bursts creating three levels of creation, the later Paiore Creation Chart increased the number of levels of creation from three to ten (Figs. 48 (1&2)). In the creation story of Mangaia Island in the Cook Islands, the universe begins not as an egg, but in the "hollow of a vast coconut shell" named Avaiki. The top has an opening allowing access to the upper world where mankind lives and the bottom is a thick stem representing the source of all things. At the lowest level of the coconut shell of Avaiki lived *Vari-te-takere* or the very beginning. She was a spirit being in human form that climbed up and out into the light of the upper world, created the land, and gave birth to the gods and mankind. In the creation myth of the Maori of New Zealand, *Rangi*, the heavenly father, and *Papa*, the earth mother, exist inside a cosmic egg floating on the sea of nothingness. *Rangi* and *Papa* are together within the egg, but after emerging from the egg they become separated, *Rangi* becomes the heavens and *Papa* the earth. In the creation legend of the Fiji Islands their ancient serpent god *Degei* or *Ndengei* lives with Turukawa, the hawk of creation, and while searching for Turukawa *Degei* comes across her nest with two abandoned eggs. *Degei* nurtures the eggs and they hatch giving birth to the first human couple and mankind is born.

The universal mythological motif of the cosmic egg often occurs in connection with a sacred bird. Proto-Polynesian Iban or Sea Dayaks of the island of Borneo have a creation myth where two primordial creator spirits, in the form of the birds *Ara* and *Irik*, glide over the vast waters of creation at the beginning of time. They gather two eggs from the primal waters, *Ara* makes the sky from his egg, and *Irik* makes the earth from hers. Then, they shape bits of earth into the first man and woman awakening them with their bird cries. In creation mythology of ancient Egypt, *Nun* is god of the primordial waters who in the form of a bird, lands on a mound emerging from the watery darkness of the primeval ocean of chaos, then lays an egg from which *Ra*, the sun god, hatches illuminating the universe, bringing light into the darkness. The sun god *Ra* begins creation and all other Egyptian gods are forms of *Ra*. The religious scripture of ancient Vedic India, the *Rig Veda,* depicts the Creator God as the sun god *Mitra* and in the Hindu cosmological creation myth of *Indra*, the spirit of the god *Brahma*, Creator God of the universe, forms the waters into which he deposits his seed which then grows into a golden cosmic egg that has the splendor of the sun. *Brahma* splits the egg into two halves that become the heaven and the earth. An exploding egg creating the universe corresponds to the "big bang theory" of modern physics where the universe begins as a tiny single point or "singularity" and then expands. According to modern physics, at the instant of creation, the universe became a formless sea of chaos and intense heat and pressure from which all things are created, similar to the Polynesian concept of *Po*.

> "The creation of heaven, the creation of earth, the earth is solid, firm
>   and enduring.
> The earth is thick set, its molecules are compressed together.
> Every particle firmly adheres with one another; and then it
>   bursts and shoots in the air.
> The crust of the earth flies into space,
>
> The sky is lighted up, is illuminated.
> The thunder roared in the heavens, electrified and shaken.
> Lightning flashes; the heavens trembled and thunder rumbled,
>   the thunder rolled, the lighting flashed, and behold the domes
>   of heaven tremblingly arose out of the chaos,
>
> The heavens have risen upward, the heavens are formed,
> The thunder clapped twice, its repeated claps
>   shook the heavens . . .
> The voice of the thunder trembles, it rumbles and cracks,
> The heavens are in tumult."

> (From *The Ancient History of Hookumu Ka Lani & Hookumu Ka Honua,*
> an ancient chant of the beginning of the creation of heaven and
> earth written by Solomon L.K. Peleioholani, 1903, and
> translated by J.M. Poepoe. Courtesy of Bishop
> Museum Manuscript Collection HI. L. 1.3 #1)

ANCIENT HAWAIIAN MO'O GODS

The earliest Hawaiian religious gods were lizard or dragon gods known as *mo'o, moio,* or *moko* that appear in legends throughout Polynesia. The ancient *mo'o* gods were brought to the Hawaiian Islands from the islands of Tahiti. In the Hawaiian Islands, *mo'o* gods were powerful, supernatural, amphibious lizards, black in color with thrusting tongues, terrifying in appearance and were believed to be as large as five *anana* in length or about thirty feet, an *anana* is the distance between the fingertips of outstretched arms, or approximately six feet. In the Hawaiian Island, *mo'o* water lizards or "water spirits" inhabited waterfalls, fishponds and even the sea, they could be seen when fires were lit on *ko'a* or sacred altars beside their watery homes.

(Kamakau 1964) Living in caves, they guarded damp marshlands and ponds of water and were almost always female. When in human form, *aumakua mo'o* were often beautiful women seen combing their long black hair in the sun beside a waterfall. Dangerous to men due to their power of seduction, they often drowned their human lovers rather than sharing them with another woman.

Worshipped by female chiefs, there were *waihau heiau* in the Hawaiian Islands for female *aumakua mo'o* deities such as *Kihawahine*, a famous half woman and half dragon *mo'o* goddess who guarded Mokuhinia, the royal fishpond surrounding the islet of Moku'ula at Lahaina, Maui. (Malo 1951 [1898]) *Kihawahine* was once a female chiefess deified after death and venerated by Kamehameha the Great. Since there are no large reptiles in the Pacific, the origin of the *mo'o* must have been from an earlier Polynesian Asiatic homeland where such reptiles existed and the memory of these reptiles remained with the Polynesian people. In the Hawaiian Islands, there is a legend of *Mo'oinanea*, the self-reliant dragon that dwelt on Kuaihelani, the floating island of the gods and hidden land of *Kane,* in the ancient far western homeland of the Polynesians. In Sumer, Mesopotamia, there were divine serpent gods, symbols of life energy that appeared in Kalana i Hua'ola or the "Garden of Eden". The snake was worshipped in ancient India and Sumer, Mesopotamia, as the symbol of rebirth and immortality, worship of water serpents such as lizards and crocodiles goes back to the Indus River Valley of ancient India. An ancient snake god was thought to have created Dilmun, the Sumerian Eden and paradise of the gods, and there were battles between King Nimrod and the serpent Kur. In ancient Egypt, there was a crocodile god named *Sobek* who was thought to have risen from the primeval waters, the Nile River having been created from his sweat. References to *mo'o* lizard gods are found in the Marquesas or Hiva Islands and in Mangaia Island, the southernmost of the Cook Islands, where the god *Rongo* or *Rono* defeated the *moio*, a lizard incarnation of the god *Matarau*. (Gill 1977) To the *manahune* of the islands of Tahiti the ancient lizard gods were demons, to the *ari'i* they were angels. As ancestors of the Polynesians migrated along the islands of Sumatra and Java, they encountered dangerous crocodiles and probably came in contact with the famous Komodo dragons or *ora* that grow up to ten feet long and weigh 150 pounds or more. Their last refuge consists of the remote Komodo Island and as of 1986 a United Nations World Heritage Site has been established including three nearby islands between the islands of Sumbawa and Flores in the Lesser Sunda Islands about 200 miles east of the island of Bali. In ancient times Komodo dragons had a much larger habitat, their remains have been found on Timor and Flores Islands dating back two million years, and they crossed the Wallace Line to the islands of Bali and Java. These monsters would certainly qualify as *mo'o* or lizard gods, although they are on the verge of extinction since human settlement. Terrestrial crocodiles once existed on New Caledonia Island of Melanesia and iguana lizards existed on the Fiji and Tonga Islands. In mythology of the Fiji Islands, the Creator God was a sacred serpent named *Degei*, or *Ndengei*. Throughout Polynesia *mo'o* gods were both worshipped and feared.

In Hawaiian mythology, a great *mo'o* reptile known as Mo'opeloa was the serpent of lies and deceiver of mankind in Kalana i Hua'ola or the "Garden of Eden". In Hawaiian mythology, the god *Kanaloa* revolted against the other gods by making his own human image of clay, but after being unable to breathe life into his man, *Kanaloa* resolved to destroy the man made by the god *Kane*. The god *Kanaloa* secretly entered the "Garden of Eden" as a *mo'o,* tricked the human couple to sin against the god *Kane* and they were expelled from *Eden*. Lizard gods or *mo'o* appear on a wooden image of *Kalaipahoa*, poison god of the island of Moloka'i, carved from wood of a *nioi, a'e* or *'ohe* tree from the Maunaloa Grove. Lizards with four legs and a long tail are painted over both eyebrows with one on each cheek facing the nose and one on each side of the chin. When the goddess *Kapo* entered the Maunaloa Grove, the wood became poisonous. *Kapo* was one of the sorcery and poison gods brought to the Hawaiian Islands by Pa'ao and the Ra'iateans from the islands of Tahiti. Scrapings from the wooden images were thought to be able to ward off evil, but when placed in food or drink could kill an enemy and were kept in hollow cavities in the back of the wooden images. Fatal to eat or touch, the spirit of death resided in the wooden images of the poison god that were both male and female.

LEGEND OF PELE, THE FIRE GODDESS, AND HI'IAKA:
THE FORMATION OF THE HAWAIIAN ISLANDS

In the legend of *Pele* and *Hi'iaka*, *Pele* or *Pelehonuamea*, fire goddess of the Hawaiian Islands, was born from divine parents. Her mother *Haumea* and her father *Kanehoalii* were from the land of Kuaihelani, a beautiful and mysterious floating island paradise of Kahiki and it was the mythological flood of *kai a ka hulu manu* or sea of the bird feathers, when birds lost all their feathers after a great tidal wave that submerged the land assisting *Pele* on her journey from island to island. (Emerson 1915) The fire goddess of the islands of Samoa is named *Fe'e* and in the islands of Tahiti she is known as *Pere* or consuming heat. *Pele* journeyed from the islands of Tahiti to the Hawaiian Islands. The first section of the legend illustrates the volcanic evolution of the Hawaiian Islands, *Pele* and her family voyage down the Hawaiian Archipelago from the northwest to the southeast, a route coinciding with the progression of the archipelago's volcanic formation. Clearly, ancient Hawaiians were aware of the volcanic chronological order of their islands and eventually *Pele* reached Halema'uma'u Crater at Kilauea Volcano on the island of Hawai'i, the youngest and most southeastern of the Hawaiian Islands, where she still resides. As a child *Pele* carefully observed her uncle *Lonomakua*, god of flames and her mother's "caretaker of fire", who taught her all the secrets of fire. *Pele's* conflict and rivalry with her older sister *Namaka o Kaha'i*, goddess of the sea, is symbolic of the opposition between fire and water. According to Abraham Fornander, *Pele* and her family were historical persons who left their ancestral homeland of Kahiki, the Polynesian place of origin in the Near East, later referred to as the islands of Tahiti, and traveled north to the Hawaiian Islands on a mystical canoe with red sails named *Honua ia kea* taking her youngest sister, *Hi'iaka* or *Hi'iakaikapoliopele*, with her on her voyage in the form of an egg *Pele* carried in her armpit in order to keep it warm. (Emerson 1915) It is possible armpit was a euphemism for another part of the body and *Hi'iaka* may actually have been the daughter of *Pele*. (From *Hawaiian Goddesses* by Serge Kahili King)

> "We stood to sail with my beloved siblings
> To an unknown land below the horizon;
> We boarded, – my kinsmen and I, – our canoe,
> Our pilot was the well skilled Ka-moho-alii [god
>   and elder brother of Pele]
> Our craft sailed over the waves.
> The sea was rough and choppy but the waves
>   bore us to surely on to our destined shore.
> The rock Nihoa, the first land we touched;
> Gladly we landed and climbed up its cliffs."

(From *Pele and Hiiaka: A Myth from Hawaii,* 1915, by
Nathaniel B. Emerson, page 11)

Pele and her family traveled the islands searching for a home in which she could keep her fires burning. *Pele* first sighted Mokupapapa Island, meaning low flat island, probably French Frigate Shoals in the Northwest Hawaiian Islands, although some have concluded Mokupapapa Island referred to a submerged seamount located southwest of Ka'ula Island called Five Fathom Pinnacle and this was what *Pele* first sighted, then sailed back to Mokumanamana or Necker Island. They moved on to Mokumanu or Nihoa Island their first stop. After landing on the islands of Ka'ula and Lehua, *Pele's* fires were extinguished by the sea. Landing on Ni'ihau Island, *Hi'iaka* rested while *Pele* attempted to build a fire pit at Halali'i, but it was extinguished with water by her angry older sister *Namaka o Kaha'i*, goddess of the sea, who pursued *Pele* to the Hawaiian Islands because she seduced her husband. *Pele* departed Ni'ihau Island from Point Papaa heading for the island of Kaua'i. (Emerson 1915)

> "Kamohoali'i [Pele's elder brother and king of the sharks]
>   turns now his prow,
> He will steer for the fertile Niihau.
> He sets out the wizard staff Paoa,
> To test if Kauai is to be their home;
> But they found it not there."

(From *Pele and Hiiaka: A Myth from Hawaii,* 1915,
by Nathaniel B. Emerson, page 12)

Pele arrived at the eastern end of the Na Pali Coast, along the northern coast of Kaua'i Island at Ke'e Beach near the village of Haena, but her fire pit found water just as they had on the islands of Ka'ula, Lehua, and Ni'ihau. She then moved to the western coast Kaua'i voyaging along the Na Pali Coast. *Pele* stopped at Waialeale Volcano, but it too was flooded and she created *Pu'u ka Pele* or the Hill of *Pele* located on the west side of Waimea Canyon, east of the Sands of Mana or Barking Sands. *Namaka*, seeing *Pele's* fire on Kaua'i Island, flooded it with water and attacked, "*Pele* was broken and smashed and left for dead", but *Pele* survived and left Kaua'i Island for the island of O'ahu. On her journey, *Pele* had taken with her a magic digging stick, *o'o*, or divining rod given to her by *Lonomakua*, god of flames. When she struck the earth with the divining rod called *Pa'oa*, it made a fire pit and *Pele* went from island to island digging along the beaches, but her fires were always extinguished by water. (Emerson 1915)

> "Once more the captain sails on with the rod,
> To try if Oahu is the wished for land:
> They thrust in the staff at Salt Lake Crater,
> But that proved not to be the land of their promise.
> We went to seek for abiding place.
> And found it, we thought, in Pele-ula;
> Found it in the sacred cape, Maka-pu'u;
> The limit of our journey by land."

(From *Pele and Hiiaka: A Myth from Hawaii,* 1915, by
Nathaniel B. Emerson, page 13)

Pele arrived on the island of O'ahu at Ka'ena Point and dug a fire pit at a hill near Kapolei, but it was soon filled with water. After stopping at Mount Ka'ala, the highest point on O'ahu, and Pu'u Konahuanui, the highest peak of the Ko'olau Mountains, *Pele* dug fire pits at Pele'ula within the present day city of Honolulu, at Kealiapaakai along the heights of Moanalua, at 'Aliapa'akai or Salt Lake, Puowaina or Punchbowl Hill, Le'ahi or Diamond Head, Hanauma Bay, Kohelepelepe or Koko Crater and lastly at Makapu'u Point, but nowhere proved satisfactory. *Pele* left the island of O'ahu from Makapu'u Point heading for the island of Moloka'i. (Emerson 1915)

> "Farewell to thee, Oahu!
> We press on to lands beyond,
> In search of a homing place."

(From *Pele and Hiiaka: A Myth from Hawaii,* 1915, by
Nathaniel B. Emerson, page 14)

Pele dug a fire pit in Kauhako Crater at the summit of Pu'u'uao, on the Kalaupapa Peninsula of the island of Moloka'i, but found water instead. Upon reaching the island of Lana'i *Pele* rested on the shore of Ka'a and dug a fire pit at Palawai, but it too was extinguished by *Namaka o Kaha'i* and fire pits on the island of Kaho'olawe dug by *Pele* were also flooded by the sea. (Emerson 1915)

> "The sea! O the sea!
> The sea is breaking,
> Breaking on Kanaloa [Kaho'olawe],
> At the cliffs is the grave of the sea,
> Passed is the quietness of the sea;
> It is breaking double,
> It is breaking triple,
> It is a sea carried on the back of Pele.
> The sea turned around and smote the earth,
> The sea is rising, . . .
> The sea of Pele is growing larger, . . .
> It is the sea of Pele the goddess!"

(From *Fornander Collection of Hawaiian Antiquities and Folk-lore,*
Volume V, Part III, 1916-1920, by Alexander Fornander, page
524. Courtesy of Bishop Museum Press, Honolulu)

Pele moved on to the island of Maui where she arrived at Pu'u Laina north of Lahaina Town, formed Pu'u Keka'a or Black Rock at the north end of Ka'anapali Beach, a jumping off place where souls of the dead departed for the afterlife. She moved on to Pu'u Kukui, a mountain peak in the Lihau section of Mauna Kahalawai or the West Maui Mountains. *Pele* moved to the summit of Haleakala Volcano, the "House of the Sun", where she hollowed out a great crater believing she had found a home because she was not driven out by water. *Pele* sent lava flowing north of La Perouse Bay, in the district of Honua'ula, to Pohaku Paea or the Rock of Paea, where she chased Paea into the sea. According to legend, *Pele* transformed herself into a beautiful woman in order to seduce the handsome Paea but realizing she was the goddess Pele, Paea refused her advances and was turned into stone. When *Pele's* sister *Namaka o Kaha'i*, saw smoke rising from the top of Haleakala Volcano along with red glowing clouds *Namaka* realized she had caught up with *Pele* and an epic battle ensued ending near Hana, Maui, where Pele was torn apart limb from limb with her bones remaining on an eroded red cinder hill known as *Ka Iwi o Pele* or The Bones of *Pele*. Just off the coast of Hana, Maui, is 'Alau Islet created when *Pele* broke open the side of *Ka Iwi o Pele.* Upon her death, *Pele* continued her journey south but in spirit form, leaving the island of Maui and its cluster of islands or "Big Maui" for the island of Hawai'i. (Emerson 1915)

> "Farewell to thee, Maui, farewell!
> Farewell to thee, Moloka'i, farewell!
> Farewell to thee, Kaho'olawe, farewell!
> We all stand girded for travel:
> Hawaii, it seems, is the land

On which we shall dwell evermore."

(From *Pele and Hiiaka: A Myth from Hawaii*, 1915, by
Nathaniel B. Emerson, page 15)

Pele's spirit flew across the 'Alenuihaha Channel glowing in the heavens above the summit of Mauna Kea on Hawai'i Island, above the clouds over 13,000 feet high where she came back to life residing in numerous cinder cones such as Pu'u o Kukahau'ula or *Ku* of the red-tinted snow, the highest point on Mauna Kea at 13,796 feet, where her fires were quenched by *Poli'ahu*, the snow goddess of Mauna Kea. *Pele* moved on to Moku'aweoweo Crater, the summit caldera of Mauna Loa Volcano, where she again battled with *Poli'ahu*. Moku'aweoweo Crater is three and a half by two miles in size with walls 1000 feet high and an inner crater one-quarter mile in diameter. Molten, steaming lava filled the entire crater, its floor became a lake of fire with fire geysers shooting columns of lava 200 to 600 feet into the air and crashing back into the lava lake. Loud explosions occurred as snow fell on Moku'aweoweo Crater where *Pele*, the fire goddess, and *Poli'ahu*, the snow goddess, battled. *Poli'ahu* claimed the crater and currently lava outflows from Mauna Loa Volcano originating 100 feet below its summit have reached the ocean north of Kiholo Bay on Hawai'i Island's west coast, south to Ka Lae or South Point, east to within four miles of the city of Hilo and to Kealakekua Bay where submarine eruptions have occurred one mile off shore. *Pele* moved on to Waiapele Crater near Kapoho, but *Namaka o Kaha'i* flooded it forming *Ka Wai o Pele,* The Water of *Pele* or Green Lake. Finally, *Pele* moved to the active Halema'uma'u Crater that has been continually erupting since 1982. Halema'uma'u Crater is located within Kilauea Crater, a great bowl two and a half miles across and nine miles in circumference with walls from 500 to 1000 feet high rising above the crater floor. Halema'uma'u Crater, *Ka Lua o Pele* or The Pit of *Pele*, is about 2700 feet in diameter and 270 feet below the floor of Kilauea Crater. Halema'uma'u literally means "House of Ferns", long ago there were two pits inside Kilauea Crater and the walls of one of the pits was covered with 'ama'uma'u ferns. Halema'uma'u's present popular translation is "House of Everlasting Fire". In the recent past it has been a molten sea of boiling lava, a raging lake of liquid fire with cones throwing fiery lava into the sky. Great floods of lava have poured out over the rim of the volcanic Kilauea Crater, "overflowing its banks, and inundating the adjacent territory". Kilauea Volcano became *Pele's* place of fire where she built her new permanent home. *Pele* still sends lava and fire down the slopes of the two active volcanoes of Kilauea and Mauna Loa, but *Poli'ahu,* the snow goddess, now reigns over Mauna Kea Volcano. *Pele's* domain includes Pu'u 'O'o cinder cone, a secondary crater located several hundred yards from Kilauea Crater that has been continually erupting since 1983 and Kilauea Iki Crater adjacent to the eastern edge of Halema'uma'u Crater last erupted in 1959.

After *Pele* established her home in Kilauea Volcano, she transformed her sister *Hi'iaka* from an egg into human form and gave the nearby Pu'uonioni Crater to her. When *Pele ka wahine 'ai honua* or *Pele* the woman who eats the land first arrived at Kilauea Volcano she found an existing fire god named *'Aila'au*, the wood eater or one who devours forests, in possession of Kilauea, the lake of fire, and both claimed Kilauea as their home. *Pele* and *'Aila'au* battled, they threw fireballs at each other, volcanoes erupted, lava flowed shaking the earth and black smoke filled the sky. When the smoke cleared it was evident *Pele* had won. In defeat, *'Aila'au* retreated into caverns below the surface of the earth. *Pele*, who arrived from a foreign land, defeated the existing fire god and now *Pele* claimed her new home. Lo'ihi, an active seamount 20 miles south of Hawai'i Island, is currently over 9000 feet above the floor of the Pacific Ocean. Lo'ihi, Kilauea, and Mauna Loa share the Hawaiian "hotspot" and Lo'ihi will become *Pele's* next Hawaiian Island home.

The legend of *Pele* and *Hi'iaka* occurs in two sections; the first section demonstrates the geological evolution of the Hawaiian Islands as *Pele* travels across the island chain from the northwest to the southeast and the second section illustrates the introduction of a new culture and religion. *Pele* arrived in the Hawaiian Islands after they were previously settled by gods and man. The role of *Hi'iaka* during *Pele's* arrival had been minor, but in the second section she becomes the heroine instrumental in defeating the existing *mo'o* gods and establishing a new Hawaiian culture. (Westervelt 1998 [1932]) One night, *Pele* fell into a deep trance and her spirit left her body taking the form of a beautiful woman who followed the sound of an *'ohe hano ihu* or Hawaiian nose flute. *Pele's* spirit found itself at a *hula* dance ceremony at a *halau hula* above Ke'e Beach at Haena Point on the island of Kaua'i, where she became enamored with the handsome young *hula* dancer, Prince Lohiau. In an alternate version of the legend, *Pele* met Lohiau after she first arrived at the Kaulu Paoa Heiau on Haena Point overlooking Ke'e Beach. After hearing the sound of *hula* drums coming from Lohiau's *halau hula* dance platform, known as *Ke Ahu a Laka* or The Altar of *Laka*, *Pele* moved inland where she met Lohiau. The *hula* platform along with Lohiau's house platform still exist, *Pele* joined the *hula* dance and fell in love with Prince Lohiau who took her to his home for three days and nights. *Pele* left to continue searching for a new home, but promised to send for Lohiau when her task was completed. Upon reaching O'ahu Island, *Pele* looked longingly back to Kaua'i Island, the home of her lover, but Lohiau died of grief after *Pele's* departure. Reaching her new home at Kileaua Crater on Hawai'i Island, *Pele* wished for Lohiau's presence and selected her faithful youngest sister, *Hi'iaka*, to be accompanied by her beautiful friend, Wahine'oma'o, on the long and perilous journey to the island of Kaua'i, a voyage filled with dangerous *mo'o* gods, to escort Lohiau back to her. Out of loyalty *Hi'iaka* accepted, but being aware of *Pele's* volatile nature, *Hi'iaka,* goddess of new plant growth on lava fields, required *Pele* to guarantee protection of her beloved forest of red-blossomed *'ohi'a lehua* groves and her human companion Hopoe while she was away. *Pele* agreed, but warned *Hi'iaka* not to become romantically involved with Lohiau.

On *Hi'iaka's* journey to Kaua'i Island to retrieve Lohiau, she defeated many evil *mo'o* spirits as she traveled from island to island with help from the supernatural *pa'u* or skirt given to her by *Pele* for protection. On Hawaii Island, *Hi'iaka* destroyed the *mo'o* witch Pana'ewa, who blocked her way with fog and rain in the forest above Hilo, and the *mo'o* sisters Piliamo'o and Nohoamo'o at the Wailuku River in Hilo. *Hi'iaka* slayed *Maka'u-kiu*, shark god at the mouth of Waipi'o Valley, who seized swimmers crossing the bay and subdued the fierce gang of giant dragon lizard *mo'o* intent on causing destruction along the Mahiki Trail above Waipi'o Valley when *Hi'iaka* destroyed Mo'olau, leader of the ferocious horde.

> "As I [Hi'iaka] journeyed above Wai-pi'o
> Mine eyes drank in that valley –
> The whole long march as far as from
> The sea-fight at Maka'u-kiu
> Till the trail climbs Ka-pu-o'a. . . .
> I entered the land of Mahiki;
> I counter the head-hunting witch. . . .
> See me tear out her very heart,
> Till her blood surges round me in waves . . .
> Mine is the common right of way,
> The traveler's right of way!"

(From *Pele and Hiiaka: A Myth from Hawaii,* 1915, by
Nathaniel B. Emerson, pages 50, 51, 52)

On the island of Moloka'i, *Hi'iaka* killed the bloodthirsty *mo'o* chiefess Kikipua and on O'ahu Island she slayed the huge *mo'o* dragon Moko-lii, leaving only his tail remaining as the islet of Mokoli'i or Chinaman's Hat. Then, *Hi'iaka* and Wahine'oma'o were welcomed to an *'awa* ceremony of purification. When *Hi'iaka* finally reached Ha'ena, Kaua'i, home of the mythological Prince Lohiau, she discovered he died from his longing for *Pele* or as the result of a romantic affair with two beautiful women who were actually *mo'o* witches in disguise. Lohiau's body had been hidden in a cavern in an inaccessible mountainside guarded by the two *mo'o* witches, Ka-lana-mai-no'u and Kilioe-i-ka-pua, who *Hi'iaka* destroyed with a magical incantation. *Hi'iaka* captured Lohiau's spirit, forced it back into his body through one of his eye sockets, and sprinkled his body with water. For ten days *Hi'iaka* recited chants to restore Lohiau, then breath and life once more entered his body. They descended from the mountain upon a rainbow and purified themselves in the sea. Now *Hi'iaka* began her return voyage to Hawai'i Island to bring Lohiau to the bed of *Pele.*

When *Hi'iaka* and Lohiau reached the seaside village of Kou on the island of O'ahu, that later became the location of the entry to Honolulu Harbor, they were guests of the prophetess Pele'ula at her *halau* for a *hula kilu* courtship game at which Lohiau was a skillful master. Lohiau inexplicably missed his target, but won the heart of *Hi'iaka* who was overcome with desire to make love to Lohiau, although she was not about to violate her agreement with *Pele.* Their travels took forty days, so long *Pele* became suspicious believing sending the beautiful *Hi'iaka* to bring back the handsome Lohiau had been a mistake, that they had found each other irresistible and had already become lovers. In a jealous rage *Pele* violated her promise, she devastated *Hi'iaka's 'ohi'a lehua* forests with a flood of molten lava sacrificing *Hi'iaka's* dearest friend, the innocent and beautiful Hopoe. Around the year AD 1100, a devastating explosive eruption occurred at Kileaua Volcano when massive lava flows reached the ocean. Although this was during the same period as Tahitian migrations to Hawai'i Island, a more likely possibility is the destruction was caused by the 'Aila'au Volcanic Flow Field, a vast outpouring of lava about AD 1420 that drained the massive magma chamber below Kileaua Volcano, explaining formation of Kileaua Crater and would have covered the landscape of Puna destroying *Hi'iaka's* magnificent *'ohi'a lehua* forests.

Their journey back to Kilauea Volcano on Hawai'i Island ends with the tragic death of Lohiau. Upon her return, *Hi'iaka* saw the destruction of her beautiful forests from a ridge above Hilo with lava pouring into the ocean and swore revenge. In defiance, *Hi'iaka* took Lohiau as her lover in a passionate embrace right in front of *Pele,* near the location of Halema'uma'u Crater. Enraged, *Pele* unleashed a torrent of molten lava encircling the lovers. Being a goddess *Hi'iaka* was protected by her *mana,* but Lohiau being a mortal was consumed by the flames. *Hi'iaka* began frantically tearing up the molten lava searching for Lohiau's spirit in Halema'uma'u Crater, hoping a flood of water would enter the crater and destroy *Pele. Hi'iaka* in her outrage was no longer able to remain a part of *Pele's* court and decided to leave Hawai'i Island, site of her troubles. The island of Kaua'i is the most remote of the major Hawaiian Islands, the farthest from Hawai'i Island, and "it was toward Kaua'i Island that *Hi'iaka* and her loyal attendants turn the prow of their canoe". Upon reaching the island of O'ahu, *Hi'iaka* again found herself at the *halau* of Pele'ula's Court where *kilu* games were taking place and when *Hi'iaka* began singing a song of her own, a familiar voice from the crowd completed her song, miraculously it was Lohiau. While the body of Lohiau had been entombed in lava, his spirit returned to Kahiki, land of the afterlife, where his body had been restored to life a second time. It was no accident Lohiau arrived at the *kilu* games just as *Hi'iaka* was about to sing, it was divine intervention. Lohiau rushed into *Hi'iaha's* arms, they were reunited and lived happily on the island of Kaua'i, home of Prince Lohiau. (Emerson 1915)

On their journey from Hawai'i Island to Kaua'i Island to bring Lohiau back to *Pele* at Kilauea Volcano, *Hi'iaka* and Wahine'oma'o were constantly under attack from ancient lizard or dragon *mo'o* gods, which they destroyed in battle. New anthropomorphic gods replaced the earlier gods establishing a new religion. Personal family gods with their animal forms became reduced in importance and *mo'o* gods once worshipped were now considered an evil force, just as the snake god of Sumer, Mesopotamia, was transformed into the evil snake in the biblical "Garden of Eden".

ORIGIN OF HAWAIIAN RELIGION

Many Polynesian gods originated from Sumer, Mesopotamia, ancient Egypt, and the Indus River Valley of ancient India. The gods of Sumer were originally deified kings who became superior to humans, more powerful and immortal, represented by anthropomorphic images. Polynesian religious beliefs, their temple traditions with sacrificial altars, and their pantheon of gods originated from ancient Sumerians who believed in a pantheon of immortal living gods in human form with superhuman powers. Although invisible, these gods would guide and control the universe. The Sumerian's four major gods and their numerous lesser deities correlate with the gods of Polynesia. (Kramer 1981) The original Supreme God of heaven of ancient Sumer was *Anu*, similar to *ahu*, the name of the sacred mounds or platforms of early Polynesian temples. Polynesian cultural and religious ideas were also influenced by Indian Vedic beliefs, such as their creation mythology, concepts of *mana* and taboo, and their hereditary caste system.

Hawaiian religious concepts and beliefs, first brought to the Hawaiian Islands by Marquesas or Hiva Island settlers, were later altered during the period of Tahitian migrations. The Marquesas Islanders believed in a cult of ancestor worship where skulls were venerated and kept in temples or *me'ae,* open courtyards with terraced platforms that contained erect stones representing their deceased ancestors. Later, Tahitians brought to the Hawaiian Islands a class of sacred and divine *ari'i* chiefs with new social and political ideas; they had oracles, diviners, spirit mediums and venerated animal incarnations. The Polynesian gods *Tane*, *Tu,* and *Rongo* or *Rono* who had been transported to the Hawaiian Islands by Marquesan settlers became *Kane, Ku,* and *Lono*. The Polynesian gods were anthropomorphic divinities infused with human attributes and experiences. They represented early leaders and navigators, human ancestors deified after death who connected man directly to the gods through his genealogy. Tahitians added *Ta'aroa*, their ancestral sea god, to the Hawaiian pantheon of gods who became known as *Kanaloa,* but was relegated to the role of the evil outcast.

THE POLYNESIAN CONCEPT OF A SUPREME BEING

The concept of a Supreme Creator God was an ancient feature of Polynesian religions and can be traced back to ancient Sumer, Mesopotamia, where *Anu, Enlil,* and *Enki* were the triad of Supreme Gods of the Sumerian pantheon. The Polynesian Supreme God *Iao, Io* or *'Io*, creator of all things, was not a deified ancestor but a sacred force. It has been proposed the name *Io* was a contraction of *Iahoue* or *Iahveh* (From *History of the People of Israel* by Ernest Renan, 1888), a form of the name *Jehovah*, and the name *Io* originated from the Polynesian ancient homeland in the Near East. (Best 2005) *Aiu* or *Iu* was the name of the Supreme God of the Aaiu people of Lower Egypt, who later became known as the Ius or Israelites. The god *Aiu* or *Iu* existed in ancient Egypt as the god *Atum-lu* and may have gone back to 11,000 BC. The Polynesian Supreme God *Io* or *Iao* has a Near Eastern origin and the name of the Phoenician Supreme God was also *Iao*. *Amun-Re*, the spiritual manifestation of *Nun*, god of the primeval waters and Supreme God of ancient Egypt, showed similarities to the Polynesian Supreme God *Iao* or *Io*. Both were inactive, not becoming involved in the affairs of man after creation was completed.

According to linguist, anthropologist and Catholic priest Wilhelm Schmidt (1868-1954) in *The Origin of the Idea of God* published in 1912, primitive religions among almost all tribal hunter-gatherer people included belief in an original Supreme Creator God, usually a father god residing in the sky, before worshipping a number of other gods. Monotheism, belief in a Supreme God, preceded polytheism and the concept of monotheism appears in the earliest sacred text of ancient Vedic India, the *Rig Veda.*

To what is One, sages give many a title.

(*Book 1, Hymn 164:46* of the *Rig Veda* translated by Ralph T. H. Griffith, 1896)

There was no realm of air, no sky . . . [there] was unfathomed depth of water, . . . That One Thing, breathed its own nature: apart from it was nothing whatsoever: concealed in darkness . . . chaos . . . all that existed then was void and formless . . . He, the first origin of this creation . . . He formed it all.

(*Book 10, Hymn 129* of the *Rig Veda* translated
by Ralph T. H. Griffith, 1896)

Although Polynesians worshipped deified ancestors, they believed in a Supreme Creator God who had never been human, was not involved in man's everyday affairs, and was above the other gods. The Supreme God was known throughout Polynesia by many names such as *Io, 'Io* or *'Io-'Io, Iao, Uli* or *Io-Uli, Oi-e, Iho* or *Ihoiho, Uho, Ore, Kiho* and *Kio*. In the language of the islands of Tahiti, *iho* means pith or core, the essential substance or primal source, "God is the pith, core, or life of man". *Ihoiho* means the very core, the solid inner heart and was the name of the ancient self-created Tahitian Supreme Being who dwelt in the universal darkness of *Po* and was replaced by the Supreme God *Ta'aroa*. In 1789, Captain William Bligh described the Tahitian Supreme God as *Ore*. The primordial Creator Goddess of the Tuamotu Archipelago was known as *Kiho*, the "source of sources", who first dwelt in the void, in the cosmic darkness of night before creation. She had no parents there was none but her, it was *Kiho* who first created the dark primordial waters and rock foundation of Havaiki. *Kiho* made her eyes glow with flame transforming darkness into light, she created the land realm, and with her husband *Kio* created the sky realm.

"While the Supreme Goddess was, the heavens were not.
There was no land; there was no living thing.
Kiho, Eternal Sleeper, lay dreamless in the void of space.
At last the goddess awoke.
Then Kiho looked upward into the black gleamless night, saying:
"This is indeed the dark night of Havaiki!"

Began to stir the inner urge of the land,
The rock base of the Universe was sleeping
     beneath the non-existence of the land.
The radiant realm of the Sky Regent was sleeping.
Then Kiho conjured forth the Primordial waters,
They commenced to rise, flowing upward.
Now Kiho spoke to . . . Kio, her husband-brother, saying:
"Make thou violently to quake the very rock base of Havaiki
     so that I become aware of all existence . . .
     and all things be set in their rightful places."

And at once Kiho made her eyes to glow with fire
     red as the volcano's womb bringing forth the molten earth
     and the darkness became light.
Kiho created . . . an earth realm, it was below.
And Kio created . . . a sky realm, it was above.
Then Kiho created Havaiki the ancient homeland . . .
     an earth realm, it was below.
And Kio created the life seed of the sacred one . . .
     a sky realm, it was above.
And she [Kiho] took the red earth and heaped it into a mound,
     forming a womens' parts and Kiho blew into the mound
     of red earth her sacred, vitalizing breath and this
     red, cherished earth became imbued with life.
Then Kio, the divine giver of life, penetrated that red, cherished
     earth filling it wholly,
And immediately it was transformed into a sentient being.
This living being was slumbering,
Then it awoke."

(Part of John F. Stinson's translation of the creation myth
Tuamotuan Archipelago, A Psalm of Creation. In *Songs
and Tales of the Sea Kings*, 1957. Peabody
Essex Museum, Salem, Massachusetts)

Two legends attribute the origin of creation to female deities, the Creator Goddess *Kiho* of the Tuamotus Islands and the Creator Goddess *Vari-ma-te-takere* of the island of Mangaia in the Cook Islands, where *Vari* dwelt alone at the beginning of creation in darkness at the base of the underworld of Avaiki, the Mangaia Island *Po*. Avaiki was like the inside of a coconut shell divided into spaces for *Vari's* six children. A common feature of Polynesian mythology is the unnatural births of children of the gods and *Vari's* children were plucked from her body. (Gill 1977) In the uppermost space dwelt *Vatea* or Watea who climbed out of the coconut shell into the light with *Papa* and the two gave birth to the primeval gods. In Aotearoa or New Zealand the Maori believed *Io*, the Supreme Being, created the universe, "*Io* dwelt within [the] breathing space of immensity; the universe was in darkness with water everywhere". Knowledge of *Io* was limited to the highest order of their ancient priesthood; the public knew nothing of *Io*. The name *Io* was so sacred only high priests could utter his name and only at certain times and places, no image was constructed and no form of temple was ever erected to *Io*, which was also true for *Amun*, Supreme Creator God of ancient Egypt, whose essence and physical appearance were unknowable. The name *Io* was never mentioned under a roof and worship of *Io* was conducted out in the open, in forest clearings with only the initiated in attendance. No sacrificial offerings were ever made to *Io* and two levels of heaven were added to the original ten levels in Maori cosmology with *Io* residing in the uppermost twelfth level. The site of teachings of *Io* was *tapu* or taboo, taking place in a sacred *marae* where no outsiders were allowed entry; the existence of *Io* was hidden behind a cover of secrecy. The Supreme God *Io* was also known as *Io nui* or *Io* the great god over all, *Io roa* or *Io* the eternal, *Io matua* or *Io* the parent of all things, *Io matua kore* or *Io* the parentless, indicating he was the very beginning, *Io mata ngaro* or *Io* of the hidden face, due to the fact his priesthood was forbidden to reveal knowledge of their sacred Supreme Being to the uninitiated, *Io mata aho* or *Io* only seen in a flash of light and *Io tikitiki o Rangi* or *Io* the exalted one of heaven. *Io* was also known as *Io taketake* or *Io* the eternal and unchanging, *Io te waiora* or *Io* the source of life and *Io te wananga* or *Io* the source of all knowledge.

> "Io [the Supreme Being] dwelt in the open space of the world,
> The world was dark, water was everywhere.
> There was no day, no light, no place of light.
> Only darkness and water everywhere.
> And it was he who first pronounced this word
> 'Night! Become Day-possessing Night!'
> Behold! The Day broke forth.
> Then he spoke in these words in the same way
> "Day! Become Night-possessing Day!"
> Behold! The great period of darkness returned."

(From the translation of a Maori Creation Chant in *Studies in
Maori Rites and Myths* by J. Prytz-Johansen, 1958)

The origin of the Polynesian word *atua, akua, etua,* or *otua* for god originated in the Polynesian's distant past. In ancient India, the word *tua* meant age, strength, superiority or an elder among family members and it came to express the idea of lord, master, or god. In the Fiji Islands, *tua* means grandfather, very old and immortal, by adding an *'a'* to *tua* making it *atua* it means supernatural, spirit or god. (Fornander 1996 [1878]) *Atua* or *akua* is a divine spiritual consciousness existing both in living beings and inanimate objects. Humans could be *akua* having divine power, although they were not considered a god until after death. In the Hawaiian Islands, the self-created Supreme Being and primeval creator *'Io,* also known as *Keawe,* was the source of all things in heaven and earth. *'Io* created the light possessing darkness that first appeared before the land, sea, and sky emerged. It was *'Io* who sent his *mana* across *Po*, creating the god *Kanenuiakea* or *Kane* of the wide expanse, who brought the world into existence. In the *Kumulipo*, the Hawaiian creation chant, *'Io* is associated with a bird and an egg and is the name of the exalted Hawaiian hawk soaring in the heavens (Fig. 49), a symbol of royalty and an *ali'i 'aumakua* representing the Supreme God *'Io* (Handy 1941), "the angel of God is a hawk". The hawk god of the Dayaks or Dyaks of the island of Borneo, *Laki Neho*, was a messenger of their Supreme Being *Laki Tenangan*. Worship of the hawk goes back to ancient Egypt where *Ra*, the Egyptian sun god, and *Horus*, the sky god, were represented with the body of a man and the head of a hawk. The Egyptian sun god *Ru* was known in the islands of Tahiti, their word for the sun and sun god was *Ra*.

In the Hawaiian Islands, as in Aotearoa or New Zealand, knowledge of the existence of the sacred Supreme Being was limited to the highest chiefs and priests, only they were allowed to learn of the rituals pertaining to the Supreme Being.

Information about such a sacred thing was hidden from the majority of the population and the name *'Io* was never mentioned outside the inner circle of his priesthood. In the Hawaiian Islands, no image was ever made of *'Io* and no sacrifice was ever offered to him, even his name was not to be spoken. In ancient Israel, the name of their Supreme Being *Yahweh*, meaning "I am" or "the one who is", was considered too holy to be spoken. The Polynesian concept of the Supreme Being appears to resemble *Yahweh*, the biblical monotheistic God of the Israelites, an unseen Creator God who was mysterious, intensely taboo or *kapu* and could not be portrayed by any image. In ancient Israel and Polynesia, the firstborn male of a high-ranking family was dedicated to their Supreme God. (Best 2005) *'Io,* Supreme God of the Hawaiian Islands, was considered the source of all existence. *'Io* was the cosmic force of creation and from his throne in *Po* ruled over the world he had yet to create, his divine "potential energy" was the one light in the universal darkness of *Po.* The god *'Io* the parentless was superior to all other deities and established the divine family creating a daughter *Na wahine* and the god *Kanenuiakea* or *Kane* of the wide expanse. When they mated, they gave birth to the gods *Ku, Lono,* and *Kanaloa,* sons of *Kane* and together they became the four major gods with great *mana,* who came out of the darkness of *Po.* The god *Kane* was the deity who pushed up the sky at the dawn of creation allowing shafts of light to separate heaven and earth, so space could come between them. In Indian mythology, it was *Indra* who separated the sky from the earth. In the ancient Sumerian concept of creation, the universe began as a watery abyss and then the gods separated heaven and earth forming a flat disc earth floating upon the primeval sea enclosed within the vault of the sky, a dome-shaped lid upon which the stars, planets, sun, and moon moved. Between the earth and the lid of the sky was the air and wind, beneath the earth was the land of the dead.

> In mythology of the islands of Tahiti, the Supreme Being was originally called *Ihoiho.* Later, with the arrival of the *ari'i,* the name of the Supreme Being was changed to *Ta'aroa* who cast down a piece of his shell that fell upon the primeval waters and became the land of Putotu, home of the gods. *Ta'aroa* was considered the source of all life who created the other gods and man out of the darkness of *Po.* "*Ta'aroa* was the ancestor of all the gods; he made everything. . . . He was his own parent, having no father or mother. . . . *Ta'aroa* sat in his shell in darkness for millions of ages. . . . The shell was like an egg revolving in endless space, with no sky, no land, no sea, no moon, no sun, and no stars. All was darkness, it was continuous thick darkness. . . . At last Ta'aroa caused [his shell to] crack . . . he slipped out and stood upon his shell, he looked and found that he was alone. There was no sound, all was darkness. The shell . . . became his house, the dome of god's sky, which was a confined sky, enclosing the world . . . Ta'aroa dwelt on for ages within the closed sky [named] Rumia; . . . he conjured forth gods, and they were born to him in darkness. For this reason the sky was called the sky of gods. It was much later that man was made."
>
> (From *Ancient Tahiti*, 1971 [1828], Bishop Museum
> Bulletin 48, by Teuira Henry, pages 336, 337, 338.
> Courtesy of Bishop Museum Press, Honolulu)

In the creation mythology originating from the Manu'a Islands of Samoa, the Supreme God was *Tagaloa,* creator of all things who dwelt alone in the void, the nothingness where there was no sky, no sea, and no earth. *Tuli,* the divine messenger bird of *Tagaloa* descended from heaven only to find water everywhere. *Tagaloa* created the island of Tau in the Manu'a Islands of Samoa so *Tuli* would have a place to land. A rock grew, *Tuli* landed and *Tagaloa* split the rock causing the earth, sea, and sky to form. At first, the sky lays flat upon the land, then *Tagaloa* propped up nine vaults of heaven residing in the ninth and highest level. Finally, mankind was created from maggots appearing on a vine brought down from heaven, but man was without spirit. *Tagaloa* created *Po* and *Ao,* night and day, in the first heaven where mankind resided and then added thought, heart, will, and spirit to man who became an intelligent living being. The concept of a Supreme Creator God is also found throughout Island Southeast Asia among Proto-Polynesians. The Supreme Creator God of the Batak of Sumatra Island was *Mulajadi na Bolon,* on the islands of Mentawai and Nias off the coast of the island of Sumatra he was known as *Luo Zaho* and to the Tana Toradja of the island of Sulawesi, the Supreme Creator God was *Puang Matua.* The Supreme God of the Proto-Polynesian Dayaks of the island of Borneo was *Laki Tenangan* who was referred to as *Iaoah, Iaouah,* or *Yahuwah,* suggesting a connection to the Israelites and ancient Egyptians. The Dayaks also had a story of an ancestor constructing a ladder to reach the heavens, but a worm ate into the foot of the ladder causing it to collapse, a variation of the biblical story of the Tower of Babel.

'IO, THE HAWAIIAN SUPREME GOD BEGINS CREATION

Within the deep, intense darkness of the great void of *Po,* the spirit of the Supreme God *'Io* or *Keawe* was the only source of the energy of creation. *'Io* sent his *mana* across *Po,* creating the god *Kanenuiakea* or *Kane* of the wide expanse who began creation. At first, the heavens lay flat upon the surface of the land and sea, leaving no space for life to exist. Then, the god *Kane* ascended to the heavens separating heaven from earth, allowing light to enter. *Kane* created a gourd from which he formed a calabash, he removed the cover of the great gourd calabash and threw it high into space where it formed the canopy of the sky. Reaching inside the calabash gourd, *Kane* brought forth from its inner core an orange disk, hung it in the sky and it became the sun. He drew out pulp from the gourd from which he formed the moon and clouds, a handful of seeds became the stars and planets, the juice became rain and from the bowl of the calabash, the god *Kane* fashioned the land and sea.

THE SACRED FOUR: THE PANTHEON OF POLYNESIAN GODS

Four was an ancient sacred number and is the smallest composite number; there are four seasons, four winds, four cardinal directions and the sacred number four was the smallest totality in the Polynesian numerical system. The pantheon of major gods varied only slightly from one Polynesian island group to another, the four major Polynesian deities were *Tangaroa, Tane, Tu* and *Rongo* or *Rono.* Below the Hawaiian Supreme Creator God known as *'Io* or *Keawe* were the four major Hawaiian gods, *Kane, Ku, Lono* and *Kanaloa.* The Vedic Indians and Sumerians of Mesopotamia used an ancient base-four numerical system. The ancient Polynesian numerical system was based on four; 4 was *ha*, 40 was *kanaka*, 400 was *lau*, 4000 was *manu*, 40,000 was *kini,* and 400,000 was *lehu.* The major gods of ancient Sumer were also four in number and were associated with different regions of the universe; the heavens, earth, air and water. Egypt had four major male creator deities correlating to the four cardinal directions, along with four female companions and protective goddess. Like the gods of ancient Sumer, the major gods of Polynesia were departmentalized with each having his own areas of responsibility or *kuleana* and since no one god could possibly attend to all the various demands placed upon him, Polynesians were able to consult the god in control of their particular need. Although the same four major gods were worshipped throughout Polynesia, they were not always associated with the same areas of responsibility. The Hawaiians believed a multitude of lesser supernatural deities filled the sea, sky and earth, that were counted in multiples of four; "the 40,000 deities, the 400,000 deities, the 4000 deities", although many were manifestations of the same individual deity. (Emerson 1965 [1909]) These many lesser gods or *kini akua* also had specific responsibilities, there was a class of gods watching over various professions, physical locations, and objects, such as canoes and houses. There were "a multitude of gods to respond to mankind's various requests and demands". With so many gods, no Polynesian ever felt abandoned, just as there had been many lesser gods in ancient Sumer, Mesopotamia.

The four major gods of the Polynesian pantheon were regarded as *akua 'aumakua,* they were divine ancestors deified after death who had been the commanders and skilled navigators who guided early Proto-Polynesian voyaging canoes on their remarkable migrations eastward from Kahiki, site of Kalana i Hau'ola or the biblical "Garden of Eden", across the Indian and Pacific Oceans. Over time they became the major Polynesian gods, "the daring mariners who had steered their ships through the unpierced horizon into the heart of the Pacific received the highest honor from their descendants by being elevated to the rank of gods." (From *Vikings of the Pacific*, first published as *Vikings of the Sunrise*, by Peter H. Buck, 1959 [1938]) The major gods of Polynesian religions first existed as living men deified after death and promoted to the status of gods due to their accomplishments in life. Only after death could a deified high chief be worshipped "as a real god". Throughout Polynesia, priests assembled their gods together into one family with the parentage of Wakea, the second son of Kahiko Lua Mea, the "very ancient and sacred one", and the goddess *Papa,* they were the sky-father and earth-mother. Wakea and *Papa* are the most widely known ancestors of the Polynesians and are worshipped throughout the Pacific Islands. According to Abraham Fornander, Wakea was chief of the Proto-Polynesians in Island Southeast Asia before their migrations across the Pacific Ocean into Polynesia. In mythology of the islands of Tahiti, Wakea is son of *Ta'aroa*, the Creator God. In the creation legends of the Hawaiian Islands, Wakea and *Papa* are ancestors of the Hawaiian people.

'AUMAKUA GODS

'Aumakua gods were ancestral deities, deceased family members who had not return to *Po,* the eternal timelessness existing before the universe was created, but had been transformed into guardian gods. *Ao 'aumakua* gods were a family's divine ancestors now spirits in the living world and there was a family male and female line. These *Ao 'aumakua* gods created a divine ancestral link going back to the creation of the universe, to the first humans and major gods. The first *'aumakua* were thought to have been the offspring of mortals who mated with the gods. The origin of the word *'aumakua* is from the Proto-Polynesian Austronesian language, *'au* is from *tua* meaning to travel distant seas generations back in time, *makua* is from *matu'a* meaning parent or ancestor. If a family had no *'aumakua* god, none being handed down from their ancestors, they were able to acquire one through a recently deceased relative, usually selected due to their achievements in life. Hawaiians believed in life after death, as did their ancient ancestors, and that the deceased were able to communicate with the world of the living. After death, *'aumakua*

were able to return to the world of the living and become guardian spirits for their living descendants. The spirits of the dead would hover around the family they had been separated from and were able to appear to the living and communicate with them through dreams. A *kahuna* performed the *kaku'ai* deification ceremony imparting divine power or *mana* to the deceased's bones that had been stripped of flesh transforming the deceased into an *'aumakua*. *'Aumakua* gods were personal family or *'ohana* guardian deities, ancestors whose spirits had been altered in *Po* after death, returned to the land of the living and were able to assume animal forms, such as a specific shark, lizard, owl, turtle or bird, a plant, mineral or even into a natural event, protecting and caring for their family members. The shark or *mano* and owl or *pueo* were considered the most important *'aumakua* animals due to their association with death. Hawaiians believed at death their soul would journey to *Po* and join their family *'aumakua*, personal ancestral gods family members would offer their allegiance to expecting divine protection and guidance, forgiveness of sins or wrongdoing, assistance in times of family trouble, victory in war, to acquire new lands or for agriculture abundance.

Every home had an altar erected to their *'aumakua* or family gods, these altars were a single upright stone as high as eight feet with greenery planted around it. Known as *Pohaku o Kane* or the Stone of *Kane*, they were "a gate to heaven" enabling men to speak with their family gods. The stones were selected by gods being revealed in a dream or vision and not chosen by man alone. (Kamakau 1964) The concept of a shrine to a family god located in the home goes back to ancient Sumer, Mesopotamia, and probably earlier. *'Aumakua* spirit gods were always referred to as the god *Kane* with an additional family name and unlike the major gods, *'aumakua* ancestral deities established a family kinship with the gods directly through their genealogical line. *'Aumakua* gods were thought to be able to counteract suffering or death sent by a sorcerer, offering "life from the *'aumakua*". Hawaiian *'aumakua* gods were similar to Tahitian *'orometua* gods and Maori *koromatua* gods that were also spirits of deceased relatives. On the island of Viti Levu in the Fiji Islands, ancestral spirits were thought to inhabit the *nanga*, sacred stone temples dedicated to the worship of ancestral spirits. The Nanga Society was limited to the western side of Viti Levu Island, suggesting it originated elsewhere and similar walled stone temple enclosures have been found in the Solomon and Vanuatu Islands of Melanesia.

In Melanesia ancestral spirits interacted with the living, death was only physical, man's spirit continued and was a source of *mana*. At Geelvink Bay in Papua New Guinea, Korwar or Karwar were images of deceased ancestors kept in the home and consulted by family members who were able to communicate with their souls. In the Proto-Polynesian cultures of Island Southeast Asia, souls of deceased ancestors were looked to for prosperity in life and help during periods of distress. In the Hawaiian Islands, after death the *'aumakua* of a recently deceased relative would linger over his place of death and around those they had been connected to during life. Hawaiian *'aumakua* spirit gods were capable of appearing as ghostly apparitions in human form inducing a trance in a living person, taking temporary possession of them and using the voice of the possessed to announce their presence. During this time, the possessed person was considered divine and was known as a *haka* or medium, as an *akua noho* or sitting god. *'Aumakua* gods, *na 'aumakua* or *'aumiikua* in plural, could act freely in the world, but the more powerful major deities required ceremonial invitations. Family *'aumakua* gods of the ruling high chief became of great importance and were prayed to at the national *luakini heiau*, the most important temples of Hawai'i Island. The gods, being invisible spirits manifest themselves in many plant and animal forms including inanimate objects ranging from natural stones and carved wooden figures to intricate feathered images. In the Hawaiian Islands, high *ali'i* ruling chiefs were considered gods due to their great power and the *kapu* observed toward them resembled those of the gods having the power of life and death, they were known as "gods that could be seen". (Beckwith 1932)

HAWAIIAN TREATMENT OF THEIR DEAD

In Hawaiian culture, dead physical remains were venerated, considered sacred and protected from desecration. After death, the body was cleaned, washed, and wrapped. "They would take the bones after the flesh was all gone, wrap the bones in red and black tapa". (Pukui 1983) Later, the bones were preserved and hidden in a way ensuring they would not be disturbed, burial in a secret place or *huna kele*. The bones were thought to retain a connection to the life spirit after death, especially the skull and long bones. Like the Sumerians, Hawaiians would bury their dead with offerings of food, clothing, tools, and ornaments for their journey into the afterlife. Some offerings placed in tombs were used by the soul as gifts for entry guardians to the lower world and for Milu, ruler of the underworld. Some bodies were laid out flat, while others had a rope tied around their legs and neck drawing the knees to the chest putting the body into a fetal position, then wrapped in a tapa cloth. These different burial customs are related to two different migration waves through Melanesia into Polynesia. (Rivers 1914) Sand dune and cave or lava tube burials were commonplace with some bodies being embalmed or *i'a loa*, their internal organs removed and the body cavity filled with salt and *pulu*, the silky fiber of the *hapu'u* tree fern, as a preservative. Several widespread Polynesian *ari'i* burial customs originated from ancient Egypt, such as preservation of the body by removal of its internal organs. In both the Marquesas and Tahitian Islands there were small temporary embalming houses, mummification consisted of drying by sun exposure, rubbing with coconut oil and removal of internal organs. In the Hawaiian Islands, those who remained with a corpse were considered unclean or *haumia,* after they took a ceremonial bath a *kahuna* performed the rite of *pi kai* upon all who attended a burial. They were sprinkled with seawater or saltwater with seaweed or *limu kala* and turmeric or *'olena* added to purify them of any harmful influences. Remains of the deceased were arranged in a bundle, the bones and hair were wrapped in tapa or *kapa* with the skull on top, then the deceased's spirit was believed to return to his bones that were often placed in boxes and kept in houses of his relatives. Family ancestral burial cave and lava tube sites were secret with their entrances hidden from view, families maintained land rights to the burial sites, and generally people remained living on lands of their ancestors.

The burial practices for a high *ali'i* chief culminated in his deification. After death of a chief, his body was wrapped in a "garment of leaves" or a *kapu lau* made of banana, *wauke* or paper mulberry tree, and taro leaves. Then, it was placed in a shallow pit in the shrine area of his *hale mua* or men's house lined with leaves and ferns, covered with about twelve inches of soil. A fire was lit along the ground above the full length the body and while a *kahuna* chanted the fire was kept burning for as long as ten days. When the body was exhumed, the *pela* or flesh and organs were easily removed from the bones or *iwi* and deposited in the ocean. The skull or *po'o* and long bones of the legs and arms including hair, teeth and fingernails were considered sacred containing the most *mana,* they were wrapped in *kapa* and covered with feathers. Then, the chief was deified and "worshipped as a real god". (Malo 1951 [1898]) Disposal in a secret cave was the most common method of burial during ancient times, some caves could only be reached by attendants being lowered by rope down the face of a cliff. Then the rope was cut with the servant falling to his death on the rocks below to prevent enemies from acquiring their *iwi* or bones and *mana.* Chiefly remains were sometimes placed on a *pu-o-a,* a high platform of sticks and stones, where the body lay in the sun for a day so its spirit might follow *la* or the sun and sometimes bones were cast into Halema'uma'u Crater of Kilauea Volcano so the deceased could be with *Pele,* the fire goddess. (Green 1926) Possessions of deceased leaders were kept in a family mausoleum, a wooden god house, along with carved wooden or stone images. Priests were buried within the *heiau* where they presided. (Linton 1925)

Individuals and social groups were conscious of the connection to their ancestors and believed ancestry of a deceased relative extended back to the origin of mankind, chiefly families derived their authority from their genealogical connection back to the beginning of the universe and the gods. Polynesians believed souls of their deified ancestors resided in Kahiki, their place of origin. The spirit world was always located far to the west and persisted in Polynesian memory over centuries as they migrated eastward. Kahiki was their mystical site of creation occupied in their remote past, the place of origin of their gods, their spirit realm and afterlife, place to where souls voyaged after death. Kahiki was located beyond the western horizon and the Polynesian word *raro* and Hawaiian word *lalo* mean west, down, below and also back in time. (Handy 1971 [1927])

HAWAIIAN BELIEF IN THE IMMORTALITY OF THE SOUL

Ancient Hawaiians believed in immortality of the soul, *'uhane* or *wailua,* that man's spiritual essence was not destroyed at death, but was set free from its physical body or *kino* in the afterlife. It was a common belief after death the newly released soul required assistance from surviving relatives to complete its journey into the next world. (Handy 1971 [1927]) A soul newly separated from its protective body just after death was weak and vulnerable to spirits of darkness and was met, protected and nourished by the deceased's *'aumakua,* spirits of his ancestors. A soul would enter the afterlife on a dangerous journey in which it could evolve into a god, but those unable to reach the next world would linger among the living becoming lost, wandering souls possibly being transformed into demons. Spirits were able to assume many forms in the afterlife; human, animal, plant, mineral, even weather events and were able to move freely between the supernatural and physical worlds.

Hawaiian religion included the concept of the Binary Soul Doctrine, an ancient belief that each individual has two souls or spirits occurring in different forms. In the Hawaiian Islands, they were the subconscious *'unihipili* and conscious *'uhane.* The *'uhane* or *wailua* spirit was able to leave the body during sleep and return, having an independent life of its own. It was thought to exit the living body through the inner angle of the eye, the tear duct was called the spirit hole, or *lau'uhane,* return to the body through the big toe, and the dreamer awoke. During dreams the *'uhane* was able to travel away from its living body, visit other wandering souls and deliver messages from *'aumakua,* visit souls in *Po,* the world of spirits and realm of the gods, and other living persons in dreams, *hihi'o,* or visions, *akaku,* while the person was awake. The *'uhane* would travel upward to a place of great light only to be denied entry and be returned to its physical body. In the *Rig Veda* of ancient Vedic India, *manas* were life spirits equivalent to the Hawaiian *'uhane.*

> "Thy spirit, that went far away to the four quarters of the world,
> Thy spirit, that went far away that visited the Sun and Dawn,
> Thy spirit, that went far away, away to the lofty mountain heights,
> Thy spirit, that went far away into this All, that lives and moves,
> Thy spirit, that went far away to distant realms beyond our ken
>   [awareness],

Thy spirit, that went far away to all that is and is to be,
We cause to come to thee again that thou mayst live and sojourn here."

(*Book 10, Hymn 58* of the *Rig Veda* translated
by Ralph T. H. Griffith, 1896)

After death, if the *'uhane* became separated from the *'unihipili*, it retained no memory and would wander in helpless confusion. Offerings of prayer, food, and drink would impart *mana* to the *'uhane* spirit through a process known as *ho'omanamana* and it would become deified. If these offerings were denied and rituals neglected, the *'uhane* would withdraw into the afterlife of *Po*. The *'uhane* spirit could be extracted or *unuhi* through a process known as *kahukahu*, then attached or *pili* into another body or object becoming a *'unihipili* that could be maintained and controlled by a *kahu* or caretaker. Many *'unihipili* were created from corpses of murdered infants or aborted fetuses becoming spirit demons endowed with evil, malignant powers causing sickness and disease, after having their lives on earth cut short they delighted in afflicting mankind. The population of the Polynesian Outlier of Ontong Java in the Solomon Islands believed the living also had two separate souls or spirits, one ceased to exist upon the person's death called *ngeinga*, another known as *kipua* grew old with man and was released upon a man's death becoming immortal. The *kipua* was able to reveal itself to the living, impart knowledge through their dreams and was believed to be able to affect the living by controlling births, illness, and death. (Hogbin 1961 [1934]) In the Hawaiian Islands *kupua* were demi-gods, supernatural beings with extraordinary powers, part human and part god they were able to appear in human, animal or plant form. Many were powerful, destructive ghost demons such as lizard dragons or *mo'o* that were the most feared.

THE HAWAIIAN SPIRITUAL WORLD

Hawaiians were deeply spiritual and every aspect of life was carried out with the belief each object in the universe possessed a divine spirit, therefore every undertaking was accomplished with religious or *haipule* rituals, prayers and feasts honoring their gods. They believed in two worlds, the material world or *Ao*, world of light and man, and the spirit world or *Po*, world of darkness and the gods. Spiritual life was as much a reality to Polynesians as was their physical existence. Almost every Hawaiian received communication from their *'aumakua*. Information from the spirit world could come in one's dreams when man's conscious mind was asleep and his spirit was able to move about freely. A priest sometimes slept near an idol expecting to receive knowledge in a dream. (Ellis 1969 [1829]) In the Hawaiian Islands, when a *kahuna kalai wa'a* was called upon to determine whether a tree was suitable for a canoe hull, this knowledge was revealed to him during a dream.

The purpose of Polynesian religious ritual was transformation of divine power of the gods into a state of usefulness for mankind. Rituals increased spiritual power or *mana* originating from the sacred realm of the gods creating a higher level of spiritual consciousness. Religion was the central authority in early Hawaiian society encompassing every aspect of life and every human activity was dependent upon favor of the gods. The Hawaiian religious world was crowded with divine beings, both in human form and in the natural world where all elements were manifestations of one of their major unseen supernatural gods. Hawaiian gods were thought of as powerful but unpredictable, they could take the form of storms, famine and sickness, as well as life-giving rain for the growth of crops. Hawaiian religious rituals, ceremonies and prayers were sacred drama attempting to establish a proper relationship with the divine, to maintain *pono* or the correct balance between the forces of nature, man and the gods. Man created gods representing various aspects of nature in order to establish relationships with the forces of nature. Hawaiians believed natural phenomena and man-made objects such as canoes, tools and weapons were filled with invisible *akua* or divine spirits that became animate with the temporary or permanent presence of their gods. These gods played an active role in human affairs, living in a "far away land" or in heaven, they were able to enter this world as a spiritual visitor affecting the affairs of daily life. At important festivals and religious ceremonies, the gods were believed to be present and religious rituals were an attempt to have some control over them. First, the appropriate god was requested to leave his customary home in *Po* and visit a place prepared for him. A *ho'omanamana* ceremony imparted *mana* to an idol or *ki'i* of the god making it *la'a* or sacred, enabling the god to enter. Afterward, the god or goddess was requested to return to his or her place of residence. These visitations were accompanied by sacrifices ranging from food to human beings. Sacrifice was a ritual action during which offerings of animal, vegetable, or manufactured items of symbolic value were consecrated to a deity. "The first food of the harvest was offered to the gods." (Kamakua 1961) The first fish caught on a fishing expedition was dedicated to fishing deities. (Valeri 1985) It was an obligation to offer for sacrifice the first portion of all things, from first-fruits, to the first fish caught and the body of the first enemy slain in war in the hope these offerings to the gods would bless the crops, fishing or the war effort. In early times, sacrifices were generally fruit from the land and fish from the sea, later human victims were more frequently included. The arrival of the gods on earth allowed man to acquire and increase his *mana* or divine power, but the gods could only be brought to earth through *heiau* rituals performed by priests or *kahuna*. Offerings were a requirement for the gods and *mana* was given in return, a generous gift enticed the gods to be generous in exchange and human sacrifice, the gift of human flesh was considered the greatest gift.

> "Although numerous variations may be found in different islands, Polynesians are unanimous in [the following beliefs]: that [most of] the gods inhabit a realm distinct from the physical world populated by human beings; that they are frequent visitors to the physical world; that the gods are responsible for a great deal of what happens in the physical world, including events both beneficial and detrimental to human beings; that humans may exercise, through properly executed ritual, some control over the visits of gods to the physical world and what they do here; and [what is one of the most distinctive feature of Polynesian religion] that the gods may be induced to withdraw from the physical world in circumstances where their influence is not welcome, or is no longer desirable."
>
> (From Polynesian Religion: An Overview, 1987, by F. Allan
> Hanson. In the *Encyclopedia of Religion* published by
> MacMillian Reference USA, New York)

Man's sacrifices were gifts to the gods, but the relationship between the gods and man was reciprocal, one of mutual benefit with obligations on both sides. Man was dependent upon the gods who sustained his existence and the gods were fed by man's offerings or *mohai,* the gods ate the food's "essence" before the sacrificer and his associates consumed it absorbing its divine *mana*. Polynesian and Hawaiian gods were created for the benefit of mankind and if a believer felt he had not received an adequate divine response, he was able to discharge the god who had failed him, but would only dismiss him at moments of extreme despair. Gods were sometimes replaced if they failed to provide victory in war or prevent sickness and death even after sacrifices were made to them. In the islands of Tahiti, a story is told about a priest or *tahuna* whose family was suffering illness going to the *marae* and chanting,

> "There is a casting off!
> I am casting thee off!
> Do not come to possess my spirit again.
> Let me not be a seat for thee again.
> Let me not know thee again.
> Go and seek some other medium for thyself in another home.
> Let it not be me, not at all!
> I am wearied of thee!
> I am terrified with thee!
> I am expelling thee!
> Return not again to me.
> Behold my family, stricken with sickness.
> Thou art taking them.
> Thou art a terrible man-devouring god!"
>
> (Polynesian Chant from *Voices on the Wind: Polynesian
> Myths and Chants* by Katharine Luomala, 1986 [1955],
> Bishop Museum Special Publication 75, page 65.
> Courtesy of Bishop Museum Press, Honolulu)

After the *marae* ceremony, the priest and his family would select new gods until their troubles ceased. In the islands of Tahiti, when illness afflicted followers of the god *Tane* they blamed their god for abandoning them, calling him "the god with yellow fangs who was eating his followers" and his symbolic image was set adrift in the sea. "The people made their own household gods and destroyed them when they failed to contribute to their success".

The Polynesians having created unseen spiritual gods needed material objects to represent them. When images of the gods were in human form, it was believed sacrifices would more likely appeal to them. In Sumer, Mesopotamia, Vedic India, and throughout Polynesia, it was not believed their divine images were gods, but representations their gods would inhabit. Polynesian gods were invisible spirits worshipped through carved anthropomorphic images known as *tiki* or *ki'i* in the Hawaiian Islands. In many Polynesian mythologies, *tiki* or *ti'i* represented the first man and were phallic fertility symbols of the god *Tane*. According to Thor Heyerdahl, author of *Early Man and the Ocean*, the name *tiki* originated from Con-Tici or Kon-Tiki Viracocha, the red-haired, bearded demigod who sailed from the coast of Peru settling on Easter Island from where the name spread throughout Polynesia.

In the Hawaiian Islands, *ki'i* is the term for sacred wooden images (Fig. 50). These were not gods, but receptacles for spirits of the deities who when requested would descend from the heavens during religious ceremonies, impart *mana* to the *ki'i* images which would become holy enabling man to communicate with his unseen gods. (Handy 1971 [1927]) Priests or *kahuna* would lead the rituals and the gods would temporarily reside in the sculptured images. "On the head [of the "ki'i" image was placed] a very fine feather, which drooped and streamed down to cover the head. When the god revealed his [presence], the feather stood straight up, twisting about and flew from its place and rested on the head of a person . . . these were signs that the god . . . would give his blessing." (From *Ke Au Okoa*, Vol. 5, no. 45, February 24, 1870 by Samuel M. Kamakau)

In the Hawaiian Islands, there were portable god images either hand-held or placed on top of poles and braced against a belt known as *akua ka'ai*. Stick gods could be placed into the ground for religious ceremonies and later stored away. Gods were also represented by anthropomorphic heads made of wickerwork frames covered with red and yellow feathers, eyes of mother of pearl and wide, gaping mouths in the form of a figure eight with shark's teeth and an overhanging crest on top of the head, they were placed on a wooden body wrapped with cloth or on top of a pole and were known as *akua hulu manu* (Fig. 46). Priests presided over ceremonies inducing a god to temporarily occupy the image giving man a means to communicate with the unseen deities allowing the gods to transmit their divine *mana*. In New Zealand, Maori "god sticks", wooden sticks about 18 inches long with a human head at the top wrapped with sennit bindings and red feathers were symbolic of the divine allowing the gods to enter. In the islands of Tahiti, there were decorative carved wooden slabs with attached feathers known as *unu* placed on the *marae* platform representing the gods (Fig. 35 (1)). In the Samoa and Tonga Islands, objects such as stones, whale teeth, bowls, or weapons were considered representations of the divine, wrapped in tapa they were stored in religious houses and only taken out during religious rituals. In the Marquesas Islands, stone images of the gods were wrapped and kept by priests until needed for temple ceremonies. In the islands of Tahiti, a cylindrical piece of wood covered with coconut sennit cord, known as a *to'o* containing suggestions of human features such as eyes, nose, hands and a navel with red feathers attached, represented *'Oro*, the Ra'iatean god of war (Fig. 37).

WAKEA AND PAPA

In most Hawaiian creation legends Wakea, an *'ehu* or one with reddish-brown hair, known throughout Polynesia as *Akea, Rangi* or *Tiki* and *Papa*, also known as *Hina*, are said to have been the first man and woman created by the god *Kanenuiakea* or *Kane* of the wide expanse. Wakea, the sky-father, represented male generative power and the heavens from where sunshine and rain descends upon the earth. *Papa*, the earth-mother/goddess who gave birth to the islands, represented the upper productive layer of earth where seeds are fertilized and growth occurs, "when the sky weeps, the earth lives". (Pukui 1972) According to the Kumuhonua genealogy the first man created by the gods was Kumuhonua, meaning earth beginning, and the first woman was Lalohonua, meaning earth below. According to the Kumu'uli genealogy recorded by Abraham Fornander, it was during the reign of Wakea's father, Kahiko Lua Mea, the "very ancient and sacred one" said to have been the first son of Lai'la'i and the first man, that a great flood occurred on the continent of *Ka Houpo o Kane* or The Bosom of *Kane* about 6000 BC. Fornander believed Wakea and *Papa* were actually ancestors of the Polynesians who migrated out of Island Southeast Asia into Polynesia and this occurred during the flooding of Sundaland. He thought Wakea had been a chief on Olalowaia, Gilolo or Halmahera Island, one of the Moluccas or Spice Islands of Island Southeast Asia, an earlier homeland of ancestors of the Polynesians, when a great exodus occurred caused by the flooding of Island Southeast Asia and Wakea's father, Kahiko Lua Mea, also resided on Olalo-i-mehani referring to Gilolo Island.

In mythology of the Hawaiian Islands, Wakea and *Papa* establish the separation of the sexes and *ali'i* from other men through their genealogy beginning with their child Haloa, the first *ali'i* having the divine ranking of *ni'aupi'o*. They were mythological ancestors of the Hawaiian people, the genealogies of all Hawaiian *ali'i* go back to this couple, the Kumu-uli genealogy leads to Wakea, the Kumuhonua genealogy leads to *Papa* and when they mate, the different lines of Proto-Polynesian ancestors are rejoined. In the story of Wakea and *Papa,* the Hawaiian sacrificial system became the origin of the separation of the sexes, the pure from the impure, *ali'i* from other men and the establishment of *ali'i* incest as a way to rulership. The creation theme of the sky-father and earth-mother occurs in India, the Near East and is also found throughout Proto-Polynesian Island Southeast Asia. In the Moluccas Islands, the female earth was impregnated by the male "sun lord of heaven". To the Dayaks of the island of Borneo, the sky-father and sea-mother gave birth to mankind and to the Tana Toradja of Sulawesi Island, the sky-father descended from the heavens to a mountain top and the water-woman rose out of a river pool.

Wakea and *Papa* had a daughter named Ho'ohokukalani, meaning "she who placed the stars of heaven". Wakea mated with his daughter creating the taro or *kalo* plant, *lau kapu lili* or the "quivering leaf" sustaining Hawaiian life. Their first child, Haloa-naka or "long waving stem", was born premature and deformed, a *keiki 'alu'alu.* (Malo 1951 [1898]) The child died and his body was buried at the east end of their house. Each day, Ho'ohokukalani tended and watered the burial site and out of the child's body grew the first taro plant, the Hawaiian staff of life thought to be an ancestor of the Hawaiian people. Taro is considered sacred and divine, a heavenly gift of their incestuous union and is propagated by cuttings, therefore all taro plants are direct descendants of Haloa-naka. Taro was the firstborn and mankind was second, making taro even more sacred and having more *kapu* than man. Myths of the origin of important plants that sustain mankind sprouting from the buried bodies of deified ancestors are common throughout the islands of the Pacific Ocean. In mythology of Melanesia, the kava plant arose from the body of a buried female deity. In mythology of Kirbati or the Gilbert Islands, when *Nei Tituabine,* goddess of vegetation, died from her grave grew three trees; a coconut tree from her head, a pandanus tree from her heels and an almond tree from her navel. In the islands of Samoa, kava or *'ava* grew out of the body of Ava, son of the god *Tagaloa,* who said from his grave would grow a plant of great value and Tuna, eel lover of Sina, knowing he was going to be killed by jealous suitors commanded Sina to cut off his head after he was dead and plant it in the ground, from his head grew the coconut palm. In mythology of the islands of Tahiti, after creation and the time of the god *Ta'aroa*, the human population became mortal and increased in numbers, many plant species sprang up from their dead bodies such as the breadfruit and coconut.

Wakea, with the assistance of his older brother, the priest Lehu'ula, instituted the sacrificial or taboo system establishing the separation of men and women, the pure from impure. Wakea had Lehu'ula set up taboos separating himself from his wife *Papa* for two nights and this separation enabled Wakea to realize his desire for incest. He had a second son with his daughter Ho'ohokukalani who was also named Haloa and was fed from the taro or *kalo* plant. The lineage of Haloa, their first divine high chief, was the origin of all Hawaiian *ali'i.* The Hawaiian dynasty of divine high chiefs began with a legendary incest between father and daughter. Wakea's refusal to give his daughter away in marriage to another line separated the *ali'i* high chief from other *ali'i.* Mythology where an incestuous father-daughter union occurs in the creation of mankind is common throughout Polynesia. In the creation myth of the islands of Tahiti, *Ta'aroa* and his wife *Haruru-papa*, had a daughter *Hina,* who *Ta'aroa* incestuously slept with and conceived the god *'Oro.* In legends of the Tuamotu Islands, *Tiki*, also known as *Atea*, seduced his daughter and in the Marquesas Islands, *Atea* or *Vatea* took his daughter *Atanua* or "goddess of the dawn" to be his wife and their children became the lesser gods and mankind. There is an equivalent Maori myth to the story of Wakea and *Papa* where the god *Tane* created Hineahuone from the sand of the earth and with the power of *Io*, the Supreme Being, breathed life into her. *Tane* and Hineahuone had a beautiful daughter, Hinetitama, the "dawn maiden", who had children with *Tane* becoming the mother of mankind, but when Hinetitama discovered *Tane* was her father she descended into the underworld in shame. In the Hawaiian Islands, a daughter destined to be mated with her father was removed at birth and raised separately so as not to create psychological problems. Mythology where mankind is restored through an incestuous father-daughter union goes back to ancient Vedic India, to the story of Manu who survived a great flood. It along with other incestuous creation unions between a divine father and daughter can be found in the text of the *Rig Veda,* the oldest literature of Vedic India.

In the Hawaiian Islands, high *ali'i* chiefs were considered to be like gods, perfect unto themselves and free from desire. Divine *ali'i* were forbidden to have sexual relations with women of lower rank remaining virgins until their marriage to a high-ranking woman. This royal sacrificial obligation produced a divine high-ranking heir, incestuous unions between brother and sister kept royal bloodlines pure, a ruling *ali'i* would marry an elder sister to increase his *mana.* Incest was not permitted in Hawaiian society except for a limited number of high-ranking *ali'i* and for them incest was a requirement. Another purpose of these incestuous marriages was to keep the size of the ruling *ali'i* group as small as possible. According to the priestly order of Kanalu, established after repeated catastrophes, "chiefs must increase their numbers and this can be done if brother would marry sister". *Ka nalu* means tsunami, early inhabitants were repeatedly almost wiped out and had to repopulate. (Namakaokeahi 2004) Founding colonies were small and went through a period where mating was inevitable between close relatives. In Sumer, Mesopotamia, incest was generally forbidden in society, but not among the gods. In ancient Egypt, marriage to a sister who was a daughter of your father was required for royalty and there was royal incest among the Inca of Peru. In the Hawaiian Islands, incest was also a political strategy to prevent rivals from increasing their genealogical ranking by monopolizing the sexuality of high-ranking women. For high chiefs, the choice of a first wife of high rank was necessary in order to secure a proper offspring for succession. "The *ali'i* is divine as long as he acts like a god . . . allowed to desire only a replica of himself [with] his sister or a woman of the same rank." (Valeri 1985)

Traditionally, a young Hawaiian *ali'i* of high rank would marry his sister so as to produce offspring of the highest possible ranking, "the very act of incest is proof of divinity". A *ho'ao* marriage ceremony was held whose purpose was to produce offspring of high-ranking whose *mana* was assured and in whom mental and physical perfection was expected. (Gutmanis 1983) Genealogical rank was inherited by the firstborn regardless of their sex, although political office was generally held by the male line. According to the priestly order of Kanalu, it was the youngest male child who inherited the priesthood position. (Namakaokeahi 2004) A child inherited rank from both parents and could claim a higher ranking than either one. Male *ali'i* often chose a spouse with a higher rank than their own to increase the ranking of their children.

THE HAWAIIAN 'AHA ALI'I

The purpose of the Hale Naua Society, first established about AD 1030 on the island of Maui by high chief Haho, son of Paumakua, was to examine and authenticate the genealogical credentials or *'ano* of *ali'i* desiring admittance to the *'Aha Ali'i* or Congregation of Chiefs. Genealogists or *ku'auhau* analyzed the applicant's rank, established their ancestral genealogical connection to high chiefs from the 'Ulu or Nana'ulu bloodlines going back ten generations and those with the most recent shared ancestry held the highest-ranking. (Hommon 1976) The purpose of the *'Aha Ali'i* was to record the rank of existing high chiefs under pressure due to the Tahitian settlement of the Hawaiian Islands. In 1886, King David Kalakaua established the Hale Naua II reviving the *'Aha Ali'i.* Before arrival of the Tahitian *ari'i,* the Hawaiian Islands were governed by *'aha* councils located on each island. The *'aha* was a woven cord composed of eight braided single *aho* strands representing individual council members. Later, the *'aha* cord became proof of high ancestry, of genealogical bloodlines descending from the ancestral gods of creation separating the chiefly *ali'i* class from the *maka'ainana* or commoners. Social status and political position depended upon one's genealogical ranking and was carefully presented by a professional genealogist or *ku'auhau* whose accuracy was essential, any mistake could bring misfortune to the *ali'i.* (Hommon 1976)

Before a *pi'o* mating, the young man and woman of high-ranking were placed in the charge of guardians, the woman was obligated to remain a virgin until they had sexual intercourse assuring with certainty their bloodline would produce an heir of proper ranking and afterward both became free. The female high *ali'i* was housed in a special pavilion where her virginity could be assured and then the male high *ali'i* came to her, setting an *akua ka'ai* or portable stick god outside her tent and a *kahuna* would pray their union would prove fruitful. After the wife of a high *ali'i* chief became pregnant, chants were composed in praise of the ancestry of the royal child and dances were performed in honor of the child throughout the land. The pregnant woman was placed in seclusion and guarded to prevent the child from being killed in her womb. The birth of a Hawaiian royal child or *keiki ali'i* was attended by high *kahuna* with their feathered gods. Drums were sounded announcing his birth and he was taken to a *waihau heiau* where his umbilical cord was cut. His body was *la'a* or sacred not to be defiled, his food and clothing were holy and his hair was left uncut. Throughout most of the islands of Polynesia, purity of the bloodline of the chiefly firstborn was protected by elaborate precautions. In the islands of Tahiti, the birth of a high *ari'i* occurred behind a *marae* inside a shelter of ferns. After delivery, mother and child were taken to a *fare hua* or house of the helpless and kept in strict seclusion. Young Tahitian *ari'i* chiefs were told, "Let not the blood of your parents be tainted by you – better were it for you to hide your shame in hell". (Handy 1971 [1927])

CLASSIFICATIONS OF HAWAIIAN ALI'I CHIEFS

There were four degrees of ranking of *kapu ali'i* or sacred chiefs in the Hawaiian Islands based upon genetic ancestry determining their sacredness; they were *pi'o, niau pi'o* or *naha, ho'i,* and *wohi.* The first three were known as *ni'aupi'o* rankings and they were considered descendants of the gods, *ali'i akua.* The highest marriage was between the brother and sister of a high-ranking *ni'aupi'o* father and mother, a marriage concentrating *mana* in their offspring. This union was called *ho'ao pi'o* or an arched marriage and a child born from this marriage was called *ninau pi'o* and was said to be born in the "arching of the rainbow", the pathway by which the gods ascended and descended from heaven symbolizing a divine *akua* chief. At the birth of a *pi'o* chief, there were flashes of lightning and the roll of thunder in the sky, these *ali'i* were direct descendants of the gods of *Po.* They had power over heaven and earth and were known as *hanau ka Po,* "born like the gods in the darkness of *Po*". Every birth of a *pi'o* child was regarded as a repetition of the first *ali'i* birth, of Haloa son of Wakea and his daughter Ho'ohokukalani. This union was so sacred a child born from it was equal to the gods, being born of "fire, heat, and raging blazes." (Kamakau 1992 [1961]) A *pi'o* child carried the *kapu moe* or prostration taboo and the *kapu wela* or burning fire taboo. Commoners were required to prostrate themselves with their faces touching the ground in the presence of a *pi'o* chief or any of his personal articles, even chiefs of lower rank were required to uncover their upper body. If a shadow fell on a high chief or upon his house the penalty was death, therefore it was common for chiefs of this highest divine ranking to only go out at night when no shadow could be cast upon them or in disguise. *Ali'i* with this supreme ranking became invisible sacred beings and when seen they appeared godlike wrapped in cloaks and helmets covered with red and yellow feathers. They owned the *'aha kapu ali'i* or sacred cord insignia and the *kahili,* a feathered standard symbolizing divine power made from a long bone of a sacrificed enemy chief. At its upper end were feathers of birds of prey, *kahili* always surrounded the high *ali'i* protecting them. Not subject to the *kapu moe* or prostration taboo, a *wohi* chief being permitted to remain upright would proceed in front of a *ni'aupi'o* high chief waving a ti or *ki* branch, a *kapu* stick or *pulo'ulo'u,* a tapa covered ball on a stick, indicating royalty was approaching and call out *kapu moe.* All in his or her presence were required to fall to the ground, face down in an attitude of worship, the taboo or *kapu* of *ni'aupi'o* high chiefs being equal to those of the gods. In the Hawaiian Islands, the most sacred high chiefs were carried on a litter or *manele* because their footsteps made the ground sacred and forbidden. In the islands of Tahiti, high *ari'i* chiefs were carried on the backs of servants.

The next highest sacred chiefs were known as *niau pi'o,* from a marriage between the brother and half-sister of a father and mother of *ni'aupi'o* ranking. Their union was called *naha* meaning split. If a male *pi'o* child married his half-sister, their child was a *naha* chief, also of *ni'aupi'o* ranking although not equal to a *pi'o* chief, *naha* chiefs carried only the *kapu noho* or sitting taboo. When both the father and mother were children of *ni'aupi'o* chiefs by secondary spouses, their children were *la'auli* or *kuhaulua*, secondary status chiefs. (Kamakau 1992 [1961]) If a mother of *ni'aupi'o* ranking had two husbands, also being of *ni'aupi'o* ranking, it was a mating known as *po'o lua* meaning "two headed" or *puna lua* meaning "two springs". When it was uncertain as to which of the men was the father and if acknowledged by both men, the child acquired status from both fathers and the mother. The chiefly *ho'i* ranking applied to union between brothers or sisters of *ni'aupi'o* ranking with nieces or nephews. The child of this marriage was also of *ni'aupi'o* ranking and was entitled to the *kapu noho* or sitting taboo. (Malo 1951 [1898]) The *wohi* chief was one whose father or mother was of *ni'aupi'o* ranking, *pi'o, naha,* or *ho'i*, but their union was with a spouse of lesser *ali'i* status, a cousin in the same family of the *ni'aupi'o* father or mother or a child of the *ni'aupi'o* chief or chiefess through secondary unions. These children were known as *wohi* chiefs and were excluded from either *kapu*. Many incestuous marriages were between half siblings where the women were the product of secondary unions resulting in unification of several high-ranking chiefly lines.

The *papa* ranking was the child of a mother of *ni'aupi'o* ranking with a cousin of lesser *ali'i* ranking. The *lokea* ranking was the child of a father of *ni'aupi'o* ranking with a mother of lesser *ali'i* ranking. *Kaukau* was a ranking produced by the union of a high *ali'i* father of *ni'aupi'o* ranking with an *ali'i* chiefess of lower-ranking but not a commoner, their children were known as *kaukau ali'i* chiefs. (Kamakau 1992 [1961]) There were *ali'i* chiefs who lived in the mountains and preserved their chiefly status, if a kingdom was without a high chief or if a high chief was without a wife one could be found in the mountains, such as the *lo ali'i* chiefs living in the mountains of O'ahu Island. Many chiefly families hid themselves in the back districts of the countryside where they were *ali'i maka'ainana*, unknown to the commoners keeping their status secret. (Kamakau 1992 [1961]) If a *ni'aupi'o* chief or chiefess lived in the country with a mate without ranking, their child would be a *noanoa* chief or chiefess without *kapu*, only recognized under special permission.

Political and social ranking in the Hawaiian Islands was determined by one's genealogical ancestry, the highest chiefs were *ali'i akua* due to their divine bloodline, they were considered equal to the gods because they were able to confirm their genealogy was directly from the gods. The highest-ranking *ali'i* were able to trace their ancestry back to Kahiki, the mythological Polynesian place of origin and location of Kalana i Hau'ola, the biblical "Garden of Eden". *Ali'i* ranking depended upon the combination of the rank of the father and mother, therefore high chiefs competed to monopolize high-ranking women and establish a genealogical line superior in rank to all others. To mate with a woman of high rank was to capture her *mana*, women became "signs of rank".

High-ranking sacred male *ali'i* practiced incestuous unions to continue their divine bloodline. They were required to first only have sex with women of high rank and this same taboo or *kapu* operated for women of royal blood, royalty was required to reproduce itself. A high-ranking sacred *ali'i* was divine desiring to mate with his sister or a woman of his same rank. (Valeri 1985) To keep their royal bloodlines pure, brothers married sisters, fathers married daughters, and mothers married sons, as was common among royal families of ancient Egypt. After a high *ali'i's* first union preserved their royal genealogy and ancestral line, they were free to take as many other partners as they wished, their obligation was complete. (Malo 1951 [1898]) The political wife of a high chief was called *wahine hoao*, others were known as *hai wahine*. Many male *ali'i* had beautiful young women of commoner class as mistresses, although if a low caste woman bore a child fathered by an *ali'i* or if an *ali'i wahine* gave birth to a child from a man of low status it might be killed, infanticide being practiced to assure purity of the *ali'i* bloodlines.

In history of the Hawaiian Islands status rivalry led to ritualized warfare. After the death of a high chief wars of succession invariably followed and although hereditary rank never lost its status, authority became exercised by militarily powerful chiefs. After defeat, high-ranking *ali'i* contenders were sacrificed and transformed into divine chiefs whose *mana* was transferred to the victor elevating him to divine status. These contenders were not only enemies, they were close relatives, and the fratricidal nature of the high chief's sacrifice is found in violent confrontations for succession in Hawai'i Island history including the sacrifice of enemy brothers. What began as fratricide ended with incest, the destruction of brothers and marriage to a sister led to the conception of a divine successor, incest manifest the high chief's divine power demonstrating his transcendent status. (Valeri 1985) In the Fiji, Tonga, and Samoa Islands, high chiefs would marry their sisters and daughters to chiefs on other islands, these high-ranking women would not marry local chiefs due to the fact they or their high-ranking offspring might become rivals.

MANA

Mana, a traditional term and concept used throughout Polynesia is sacred power, the universal divine spiritual energy of creation "given by the gods"; the primordial life force of the universe. The source of *mana* is the spirit world of *Po;* it was transmitted through one's ancestors going back to the gods enabling a person to achieve distinction. *Mana* is the means by which the divine manifests itself in the human world. To Hawaiians, man and nature are one and *mana* exists in both living beings and inanimate objects; it inhabits man, animals, plants and the natural landscape. Not only an inherited genealogical potential or potency, *mana* is also a quality, substance or action. (Mauss 1971) *Mana* is believed to be an invisible fluid material substance whose spiritual action is capable of working through contact or at a distance. *Mana* of the divine chief had been genetically passed on through his unbroken genetic hereditary line going back to the gods. The *mana* of the highest-ranking chiefs was so great it was "like that of a god." (Malo 1951 [1898]) Divine *mana* was transmitted to the first man and woman who received it directly from the gods and it has been transmitted through generations of firstborn males, giving high chiefs their supernatural power and authority. Those closest to the gods had the most *mana* correlating with their genealogical ranking. Ruling high chiefs, being direct descendants of the gods of *Po,* were able to transmit their *mana* across heaven and earth. "*Mana* manifest itself in the well-being of the community, in human knowledge and skills and in nature". (Buck 1939) A man's *mana* determined his social status and wealth. It was the source of his intelligence showing his power, strength, authority, skill, and the excellence he possessed. His effectiveness and success were proof of his *mana.* Religious ritual activities focused on controlling the relationship between the divine and human, on transferring divine *mana* into the realm of mankind.

Priests and men of learning, although of high birth, were less powerful than ruling chiefs having *mana* that was more dispersed. Whoever made a sacrificial offering, an *alana* or *mohai* to the gods received divine *mana,* therefore all were capable of acquiring *mana.* Warfare was a way of acquiring *mana,* those who were victorious gained *mana* from the defeated who were sacrificed to *Ku,* god of war. If a man was a successful warrior it was not thought to be due to his strength and quickness, but rather a result of *mana* contained in the spirits of warriors he had slain in battle. *Mana* existed in weapons, tools, and utensils; the war club of an ancestral warrior was powered by *mana* when wielded by his descendant in battle. It was believed the body absorbed psychic energy from food and when the flesh of a slain enemy was consumed, a warrior was able to incorporate his *mana.* Skilled craftsmen created products of visible effectiveness and like warriors gained *mana* through their successes. The *mana* of a canoe builder and his tools was manifest in his craftsmanship, that of a farmer by his crops and a fisherman by his catch. *Mana* is pragmatic, "it is what it does". After death, *mana* resides in bones of the deceased that family members would often hide in secret caves or pits protecting them from enemies who would otherwise make utensils and tools from them, causing the deceased's spirit to suffer. The *mana* of the spirit of the deceased could be increased by a *kahuna* through the *ho'omanamana* ceremony where over time the spirit would gain power enabling it to "travel on the wind". The concept of *mana* existed in remote antiquity, in Vedic India *mahat* meant universal divine consciousness or cosmic mind, and *parna* was the universal life force containing *mahat* or divine universal intelligence. The concept of *mana* is also found in Island Southeast Asia among Proto-Polynesians, Sea Dayak medicine men of the island of Borneo are called *manang.*

Georg Ernst Stahl (1660-1734), a German chemist and physician, proposed all matter contains a vital force and animal life has an immaterial soul. Emanuel Swedenborg (1688-1772), a Swedish scientist, theologian and philosopher, believed there is a divine life force existing in the natural world, in all living things and in material substances as well. Franz Anton Mesmer (1734-1815), a German physician who studied and practiced in Vienna, Austria, theorized there was a universal fluid he called "fluidum" able to transfer energy between animate or inanimate objects even at remote distances, similar to the Hawaiian concept of *aka.* It is a vital energy force permeating all forms of matter Mesmer referred to as "material magnetism" and "animal magnetism". Baron Karl Ludwig von Reichenbach (1788-1869), a chemist influenced by the work of Franz Mesmer, proposed an invisible cosmic fluid is a life force emanating from most objects, permeating and connecting all living things. Reichenbach called it the "odic force" or "od". Sigmund Freud (1856-1939), an Austrian neurologist and founder of psychoanalysis, introduced the concept of "libido", an instinctual psychic energy force contained within what Freud called the "id" or subconscious mind. Carl Gustav Jung (1875-1961), a Swiss psychiatrist and younger colleague of Freud, defined "libido" as an individual's psychic energy, similar to his *mana* or spiritual power, and Wilhelm Reich (1897-1937), an Austrian psychiatrist and psychoanalyst who was once a student of Sigmund Freud, studied energy in man and nature claiming to have discovered "orgone", a primordial divine life energy force similar to *mana* he though was a universal substance like the pervasive *aka* substance over which *mana* energy flows connecting everything in the physical universe. Serbian/American scientist, electrical engineer and inventor Nikola Tesla (1856-1943), discovered what he believed to be the source of all energies he called the "zero point energy field" or "tachyon energy field". The tachyon is a subatomic particle that travels faster than the speed of light creating an abundance of energy in the vacuum of space. Georges Lakhovsky (1869-1942), a Russian-born engineer residing in France, discovered all living cells radiate and receive electromagnetic life force energy from outside sources and exposure to high-frequency energy fields stimulates a cell's life force. Dr. Harold Saxton Burr (1889-1973), a professor of anatomy at Yale University School of Medicine, proposed the term L-field or "fields of life" for bioelectric fields controlling all living things. Modern physicists such as Albert

Einstein, Werner Heisenberg, and David Bohm have said all matter is actually various states of subatomic energy in a quantum energy field, making up everything and connecting everything in the universe in a vast invisible wave/particle energy stream capable of transmitting energy and consciousness across space and time. Consciousness exists within all matter in the form of electromagnetic energy and universal consciousness permeates all creation. This is the divine life force energy known as *mana* throughout Melanesia and Polynesia; the divine life force of the gods.

According to modern quantum mechanics, ordinary visible matter composed of atoms constitutes only 4.9 percent of the mass-energy density of the observable universe, 95.1 percent is composed of an invisible substance located in the vacuum of space known as dark matter, composing 26.8 percent, and dark energy, 68.3 percent. Dark matter was first hypothesized in 1933 by Swiss astrophysicist Fritz Zwicky (1898-1974) to account for the "missing mass" necessary to create the gravity necessary to hold galaxies together, the existence of the invisible dark matter is inferred by its ability to react to the force of gravity. The dark matter and dark energy dominating the universe could be considered a dark flow with similarities to the Hawaiian concepts of *mana* and *aka* cords, the divine life energy force capable of transmitting thoughts and emotions across remote distances, across time and space. *Mana* energy exists as a substance, an invisible fluid material of subatomic particles that form *aka* cords upon which the primordial *mana* energy flows. Both *mana* and dark matter/energy are dualistic in nature as indicated by Albert Einstein's equation $E = mc^2$ where matter and energy are different forms of the same substance; dark matter/energy and *mana* represent the same force.

TABOO OR KAPU IN THE HAWAIIAN ISLANDS

Hawaiian *kapu* was a code of conduct, a system of laws and regulations establishing separation of the sacred and divine from the secular and profane, controlling interactions between different classes of people and preserving *pono*, a state of order and balance between mankind, the natural environment and the gods. The idea of the sacred was derived from *mana*, sacred people and objects possessing *mana* required protection and were potentially dangerous, *mana* together with *kapu* created a rigid system of social controls affecting nearly every aspect of ancient Hawaiian life. *Kapu* or taboo was a state of contact with the divine controlling the flow and binding the potency of *mana* by establishing forbidden areas of protective sacredness around persons, places or objects with closeness to the divine; marking and setting them apart. The *mana* of *ali'i* chiefs accumulated through their ancestors going back to the gods presented a danger to commoners. The *ali'i* were *kapu* because they were intermediaries between the gods and society, they were divine *ali'i akua*. Commoners were *noa*, in a state of separation from the divine. *Ho'okapu* or "to make *kapu*" was the transformation from a *noa* state to a *kapu* state and *ho'onoa* or "to make *noa*" was to be free from *kapu* and return to a secular life free of restrictions, when the sacredness of persons, places or objects ended. (Valeri 1985)

> "Tabus varied greatly both in extent and duration. Sometimes a single tree, or a single animal only, would be made tabu . . . sometimes a single house or a piece of land, or fishing ground, at others a whole district, or even islands. Sometimes the tabu would be limited to a day, others would continue for weeks and months."

> (From the *Journal of a Residence in the Sandwich Islands, Vol. I*, 1830, by Rev. Charles Samuel Stewart, page 36)

Kanawai were sets of laws established to determine if something was *kapu*. *Kanawai* means "belonging to the freshwater" and was the word for law in the Hawaiian Islands, where freshwater meant life and was sacred to the god *Kane*. Early *kanawai* laws dealt with management and distribution of freshwater or *wai, waiwai* meant wealth. There were two kinds of *kanawai* laws; *kanawai kapu akua*, laws of the gods, and *kanawai kapu ali'i*, laws of the sacred *ali'i* chiefs. (Kamakau 1992 [1961]) The genealogical ranking or *kulana* of *ali'i* chiefs determined the *kanawai kapu ali'i* laws belonging to them; *ni'aupi'o* chiefs were equal to the gods and only *ni'aupi'o* chiefs could overrule a *kapu* of the gods. (Kamakau 1992 [1961]) "In the ancient days there were many *kapu* . . . and they were in the hands of the chiefs." (Kamakau 1992 [1961]) These laws controlled an individual's behavior, establishing order in the social, political, and physical environment of ancient Hawaiian society, protecting the sacredness of *mana* and conserving natural resources. In the Hawaiian Islands, *kapu* were placed on the land, crops, and species of fish for conservation purposes. There were lunar *kapu* periods regulating land use, planting and fishing, eating *kapu, kapu* on *heiau* worship and *kapu* protecting the *mana* and sanctity of the *ali'i*. Violation of a *kanawai kapu ali'i* law was punishable by death and the punishment for violation of a *kanawai akua* law was burnt sacrifice to the god *Ku*, although acquittal for either was possible if one were able to reach a *pu'uhonua* or place of refuge, be pardoned and absolved by a *heiau kahuna*. There were executioners who enforced sacred *kapu* of the gods and high chiefs known as *ko kanawai*. In the Marquesas Islands, taboo was known as *tahbu* and a strip of white cloth served as a sign of taboo. In Proto-Polynesian Austronesian languages *tampu* means sacred and forbidden and the concept of taboo is found throughout Melanesia and Island Southeast Asia. In the Solomon

Islands, two crossed sticks indicating *tampu* were similar to two crossed spears indicating *kapu* in the Hawaiian Islands. Proto-Polynesians of Island Southeast Asia had a custom called *pomali* similar to Polynesian *tabu*. The Proto-Polynesian Cham of Vietnam, originally from the island of Borneo, had a taboo system called *tabun* resembling Polynesian *tabu*. The taboo system went back to Sumer, Mesopotamia, ancient Egypt and the Indus River Valley of ancient India where sacred taboo strings were worn around the wrist to indicate the divine and taboo developed into the caste system of the Vedic culture of ancient India.

In the Hawaiian Islands, names of the major gods and high chiefs were *kapu* and forbidden to be spoken by commoners. *Kapu* surrounded high *ali'i* chiefs with their powerful *mana*, they were the embodiment of divine sacredness, *kapu* laws protected their divinity and that of their ancestors from a loss of *mana* due to contact with commoners. The highest chiefs possessed the prostration *kapu*, runners would precede the high chief shouting *kapu moe*, and people below a certain rank were required to fall flat, face down on the ground until the chief passed. High chiefs were the descendants of the gods and could not be looked upon. On January 21, 1778, on the island of Kaua'i, Captain James T. Cook and two members of his crew were escorted to a *heiau* a short distance up the Waimea River. "Our guide proclaimed our approach and every one whom we met fell on their faces and remained in that position till we had passed. This, as I afterwards understood, is done to their great chiefs". "The lowly commoner prostrated himself, face to the ground, in the position assumed by victims on the platforms of human sacrifice". (Sahlins 1985)

In the presence of a high chief, *ali'i* of lower rank were required to strip to their waist and no one of lesser rank was allowed to touch a high chief. It was even forbidden to touch a high chief's shadow because it was believed a man's shadow contained some of his *mana*. The personal space surrounding a high chief was regulated by *kapu*. Spatial distances among chiefs and the area of *kapu* space around a chief varied with his ranking. In the islands of Tahiti, people stripped to the waist as a high chief went by. In the Tonga Islands, upon entering the house of a sacred chief, his subjects would touch the soles of his feet with the back of their hands. Because high *ali'i* chiefs were considered divine beings, direct descendants of the gods, they possessed powerful *mana and* anything they touched or their shadow fell upon became *kapu*. If the shadow of a high *ali'i* fell upon a commoner, he was put to death. The shadow of a commoner could not fall upon a high-ranking chief, his house, his robe, his *malo* or any of his belongings. The highest chiefs only went out at night when they appeared godlike wrapped in feathered cloaks and helmets; they were *ali'i o Po* or *ali'i* of the night. If a commoner used a possession of a high *ali'i*, the penalty was death. If a commoner climbed over the fence surrounding his residence or went through his private doorway, the penalty was death. If a commoner entered the lands of a high *ali'i*, the penalty was death. When a commoner entered the presence of a high chief, his head could never be higher than the chief's and it was forbidden to sit on the door threshold of the residence of a chief. The head of a divine chief was *kapu* due to its concentration of *mana* and it was forbidden to pass anything over the head of a high chief. The *kapu* of *ni'aupi'o* chiefs was equal to the gods; they were characterized by inactivity and immobility.

In the Hawaiian Islands, a place or thing could be declared *kapu* or taboo to protect and preserve it. *Kapu* sticks or *pulo'ulo'u* topped with balls of white cloth were placed around a forbidden area or residence of a high chief to indicate it was taboo and *kapu* wands or *ko'o ko'o lua*, pointed sticks tipped with dog hair and feathers, would also indicate places or things that were taboo. *Kahuna* who were craft specialists had the intellectual knowledge and ability to create products considered divine, works of the gods and therefore *kapu*. In the Marquesas Islands, a warrior's spear with which he had killed a man became *tahbu* and the weapon was given the victim's name. The taboo system reached its fullest development in Polynesia and early Hawaiian Island settlers brought its basic concepts with them. The *kapu* system introduced by *ari'i* from the islands of Tahiti, such as the warrior/priest Pa'ao were more severe, many violations were punishable by death and there were *ko kanawai* who enforced the *kapu*. The word *taboo* is one of the few words from Polynesian languages incorporated into the English language. It came from the account of Captain James T. Cook during his visit to the island of Tongatabu in the Tonga Islands in 1777, when Tongan chiefs were not allowed to eat aboard Cook's ship; it was *tabu*. Another Polynesian language word included in English was tattoo from the Tahitian word *tatau*. In the Hawaiian Islands, the word for taboo is *kapu*. In the language of the Tonga Islands the word for taboo is *tabu*, in the Fiji and Samoa Islands and among the Maori of New Zealand it is *tapu*, a combination of *ta* meaning to mark, and *pu* meaning with intensity, sacred or forbidden; having a connection with the gods. Maori chiefs also traced their genealogy back to the gods, sacred chiefs were *ari'i tapu*, and their temples were *wahi tapu* or sacred places.

In the Hawaiian Islands, two kinds of fish were considered taboo or *kapu* during their spawning seasons as a conservation measure and were alternately forbidden for six months not to be eaten under penalty of death. They were the sacred *aku* or tuna and *'opelu* or mackerel because they accompanied the warrior/priest Pa'ao on his voyage to Hawai'i Island from Ra'iatea Island, Tahiti. When Pa'ao's brother, Lonopele, sent storms to sink Pa'ao's canoe, schools of fish calmed the seas. The *aku* helped propel the canoe against the storms and the *'opelu* swam in front of the canoe breaking the waves. *'Opelu* was caught during the summer and *aku* was *kapu*. During the winter *aku* was caught while *'opelu* was *kapu*. The first night of Hinaiaeleele or July was *kapu*, no fires could be lit, no sound could be heard, no canoe could be launched, or land and only *kahuna* were allowed to open the fishing season. The high priest sacrificed a pig, an *'aha* prayer was recited at *ko'a Ku'ula*, the fishing *heiau*, and a man was sent into the forest for *pala* ferns. The next morning, the head fisherman wearing a white *malo* took the sacred *pala* ferns and put out to sea. After prayers to the god *Ku*, the head fisherman cast his net and if he and his crew caught *'opelu* they returned to shore amidst shouts of joy. Some of the *'opelu* were taken to the *heiau* where the *kahuna* placed them on the *lele* or altar and the high chief offered them to the gods, then scooped out and ate the right eye of the fish. The next day, 'opelu fish became noa or free for all, but the aku became kapu, prohibited for the next six months. (Alexander 2001) In the Hawaiian Islands, fishing was accompanied by religious ceremonies to establish the correct relationship to the gods, fishermen observed many religious rites and new fishing canoes were not built or launched without prayer and sacrifice.

THE POSITION OF WOMEN IN HAWAIIAN SOCIETY

Throughout Polynesia, the social position of women was lower than men, although there were exceptions. High ali'i women might share rule with male high chiefs and nowhere else in Polynesia did women hold as much social, religious, and political power as in the Hawaiian Island. Men and women worked in different areas governed by male and female gods. Women were considered dangerous, impure and profane or noa and were forbidden from entering the sacred precincts of a heiau. Women worshipped at the Hale o Papa specifically for women and were excluded from being heiau sacrifices. The Hawaiian kapu or taboo system was oppressive to women controlling their position in society, although they could become wahine ali'i or female chiefs and were able to transmit their genealogical ranking to their children. 'Ai kapu or sacred eating was considered a communion with the gods originating when Wakea and Papa created separation of the sexes. Men and women had separate eating houses, used different utensils and their food was prepared separately. It was believed food was capable of carrying evil psychic influences into the body taking possession of men, therefore it was dangerous for men to eat with women. Only men were allowed to cook because while the earth was female most of the food that grew from the earth was male. Men and women could not eat food cooked in the same imu or oven and men were required to prepare two ovens for daily food. It was kapu for men and women to eat together except in a canoe at sea and persons with different degrees of sacredness also ate separately. Men who ate with women no longer had the right to eat with other men and men who ate with those of lower rank became inferior themselves.

'Ai kapu or sacred eating was due to the idea ali'i eating was considered a religious act, a worshipping of the gods, and women were considered "unclean and defiled by blood". (Kamakau 1992 [1961]) Women were forbidden from eating any food offered in sacrifice to the gods because these foods were forms of male gods. Foods forbidden to women in the Hawaiian Islands included pork, turtle meat, shark, ulua or red fish, most kinds of bananas, yellow coconuts and taro, although women were allowed to eat dog. During that four principal kapu periods each month, women were forbidden to ride in a canoe or have sexual intercourse. Women were isolated in a location outside the home during menstruation and childbirth when they were considered unclean or haumia, it was blood that caused the concept of female impurity. After each menstrual period women were required to take a kapu kai or ceremonial bath, purification by seawater. Volcanic eruptions were considered menstruations of the goddess Pele who "went to the sea after erupting" for purification. The gods despised all bloody things finding them ho'o pailua or disgusting. Female menstrual blood was not only polluting, it was considered both dangerous and sacred. A women's vagina represented a passageway between Po and Ao, between the dark divine spirit world of the gods and the world of humans, it was the "path of the gods", and it was believed children emerged from Po. (Shore 1989) Women were considered dangerous needing to be controlled and the female organ was associated with misfortune. The Maori of New Zealand believed in the destructive power of the female sex organ, the passage through which man entered the world was also credited with his destruction. In a society where women were excluded by kapu or taboo from religious practices, many became priestesses resorting to "mysterious activities and [were] the source of magical powers" dangerous to men. (Mauss 1971) Kapo, goddess of magic, sorcery, and fertility, was the elder sister of the goddess Pele and mother of Laka, goddess of the hula. Kapo had a detachable vagina with which she was able to entrap her victims. (Beckwith 1970 [1040]) In mythology, Kapo sent her flying vagina or kohe lele to light upon a tree as a lure to attract the pig god Kamapua'a and prevent her sister Pele from being raped. The Polynesian belief in the destructive energy of the female sex goes back to Lilith in Hebrew mythology, who was Lil in Sumerian legend and the goddess Kali in ancient Vedic India. "That which destroys man is the mana of the female organ. It turns upon man and destroys him". (Best 1904)

DEIFICATION OF POLYNESIAN ANCESTORS

The Polynesians believed themselves to have descended from a line of ancestors connecting them to the first humans and the gods of Kahiki. "The high chief was akua or god-like because he came from Kahiki". (Fornander 1916-1920) The word akua came from makua or matu'a in Proto-Polynesian and matuqa in Austronesian meaning parent or first ancestor. Polynesian high chiefs were considered divine or akua and were worshipped even before their death. "The king [high chief] was considered a manifestation of his gods and was a god to other men" (Valeri 1985), but they were not yet completely gods. No living man could become a god, it was only after passing through the portal of death could ancestors become deified and begin their spiritual immortality. To Polynesians, most humans were born with divinity, some had so much they were considered gods. "Some men and women were *akua* in this life, most became *akua* after death". (Handy 1923) The Polynesian "endowed his universe with mysterious powers . . . Once upon a time man himself was god, now he peopled the world with gods . . . he attached himself to them". (Mauss 1971) The gods of India also originated as mortal men who became divine beings after death. The idea of a divine origin of rulers and priests developed in the Near East where "Sumerians viewed kingship as divine in origin . . . [with rulers] deriving their power from the gods". Kingship in the antediluvian 'Ubaid civilization prior to the Sumerians was recorded in the *Sumerian King List* where kingship was believed to have descended from heaven; their rulers were thought of as demigods, part men and part gods.

Throughout Polynesia, deification of ancestors was universal. The major Polynesian gods were deified ancestors who commanded the early migratory voyages of the Polynesians and souls of these deified ancestors lived on in the spirit-land of Kahiki and were called upon by their descendants for assistance with life's problems. Polynesians continued to deify their deceased ancestors as *'aumakua* gods to be consulted by the living and *'aumakua* use dreams to offer solutions to the problems of the living. Polynesian gods were created in the image of man, they had once been living men, but with supernatural powers. Eventually, the priesthood created a new theology placing the gods into a family with divine parentage such as the sky-father and earth-mother. "Man created their gods and the gods created man." (Buck 1939)

THE PILLARS OF KAHIKI

The ancient Polynesian concept of the world was their island group surrounded by water extending to the horizon where the dome of the sky joined the sea. The dome of the sky contained the levels of the heavens including the sun, moon, and stars. After the gods created the world, the sky was so close to the earth mankind had to crawl until the dome of the sky was pushed up. *Kukulu* were pillars supporting the dome of the heavens and there were openings through which the sun entered in the morning and set at night. It was thought the sun traveled through a tunnel under the earth from the west, where the sun set at night, to rise again in the morning in the east. In ancient Egypt, when the sun set in the west they believed it entered the *Duat* or underworld traveling through a tunnel beneath the earth to rise again in the east.

To voyage beyond the dome of the sky where it met the horizon was to "break through the sky". In Polynesian mythology *Kukulu o* Kahiki or Pillars of Kahiki stand along the horizon supporting the dome of the heavens, separating *Ao* from *Po,* the earth from the heavens, allowing man to voyage beyond the horizon, beyond the sky into the celestial regions and become divine. These pillars were located in the direction of Kahiki indicating the route taken by ancestors of the Polynesians; a journey back to the Fiji Islands, through Melanesia, to the islands of Sumatra and Java, back to India and finally to Sumer, Mesopotamia in the Near East, the location of Kahiki, where Hawaiian demigods or *kupua* who were born from the union of a major god and human being originated. Hawaiian *ali'i* were considered divine, sacred *akua* with supernatural powers originating as *kupua* possessing divine *mana. Ali'i* were *kupua* during life and *'aumakua* after death. "After death the spirits of [*ali'i*] chiefs and commoners alike passed to this spirit-land, a mysterious region situated toward the setting sun, where the cradle of their race was to be found". (Hiroa 1945) On Ra'iatea Island, Tahiti, souls of the dead would gather at Te Mehani, a sacred mountain crater where they were sorted out, some would go below and others were sent to the mythical Kahiki, their ancestral homeland to the west. The name Kahiki goes back to the Near East, but as memory of the Polynesian ancient homeland became lost Kahiki came to signify the islands of Tahiti, location from where the conquerors of the original settlers of the Hawaiian Islands originated.

THE HAWAIIAN HUNA

Max Freedom Long (1890-1971), an American educator who moved from Los Angeles, California, to the island of Hawai'i in 1917 to work as a teacher became interested in ancient Hawaiian religious beliefs. Long described a theory of metaphysics linked to ancient Hawaiian knowledge known as *ho'omana* or *ho'omanamana*, meaning to create *mana* or life energy. He called these teachings *huna*, meaning hidden or secret, and that Hawaiian priests known as *kahuna* were "keepers of the secret". Initially, Max Freedom Long learned about Hawaiian metaphysical beliefs from William Tufts Brigham, first curator of the Bernice P. Bishop Museum, who spent forty years studying the society, culture, and religion of the Hawaiian Islands. After meeting Brigham, Long spent the next sixteen years trying to understand the meaning behind Hawaiian chants and prayers. Although ancient Hawaiian *kahuna* spiritual practices had been suppressed by western missionary influence before and during Long's stay on Hawai'i Island, their ancient traditions still existed in secret. Long left the Hawaiian Islands after the death of William Brigham in 1926, but continued his research in California publishing his first book on the Hawaiian *huna* in 1936, titled *Recovering the Ancient Magic.* Long believed Hawaiian *huna* knowledge had an origin going back to ancient Egypt, possibly back to the lost civilization of Mu. William Reginald Stewart, a retired journalist, learned of the same ancient religion from a Berber tribe located in the Atlas Mountains of North Africa, who had a secret Amazigh language for their ancient religious oral traditions using words similar to Polynesian languages, suggesting Proto-Polynesians were among the original keepers of *huna* knowledge that has been preserved throughout Polynesia. Long was able to trace evidence of the *huna* tradition to ancient India where *mana* is known as *prana*, through Island Southeast Asia, to the islands of Samoa and Tahiti, and at stopping points along the Polynesian journey to the Hawaiian Islands.

Max Freedom Long selected Hawaiian words for *huna* principles, but because their meanings actually differ from Long's usage a controversy arose as to whether his theories were authentic. Many Hawaiian natives and *kahuna* dismissed the *huna* as being developed for a western audience and merely new age mythology, explaining the word *huna* was never used in the ancient Hawaiian religion. The words Long used for man's three selves, *'unihipili*, *'uhane* and *'aumakua* do not actually mean subconscious, conscious and super-conscious respectively, although Hawaiian religion did include the Binary Soul Doctrine, the belief man has two souls or spirits that are the meanings of the Hawaiian words *'uhane* and *'unihipili*. The ancient belief of mankind possessing two souls that separate at death goes back to the dawn of civilization, to ancient Egypt and Israel, Vedic India, the Hawaiian Islands and to North America with many including a third soul, a combination of the two creating a higher being (Novak 2002) equivalent to the Hawaiian *'aumakua*.

In the Hawaiian creation legend, the gods created man using two kinds of clay, red and white, and because of this mankind was able to have two separate spirits, his conscious and subconscious minds or "selves". Belief in the Binary Soul Doctrine was so universal among the earliest known civilizations, it points to an earlier culture and a single world religion. The Binary Soul Doctrine was known to ancient Egyptians who believed man has two souls, the conscious mind or *ba,* that was aware, intelligent and could communicate, and the subconscious mind or *ka*, the soul that recorded all memories and emotions and was able to travel away from the body in dreams. At death, the *ba* and *ka* separated and souls of the dead passed through the *Duat* being united to be reborn with the sun into the *khu* or *aakhu*, a complete being corresponding to the Hawaiian *'aumakua*. There was also an equivalent to the Hawaiian *huna* in the Vedic civilization of ancient India where mankind had three separate souls, the *asu* or conscious soul, the *manas* or subconscious soul and the *parmatman* or supreme divine soul. In ancient Israel, the *ruach* or spirit was the conscious, immortal mind that returned to God after death and the *nephesh* or soul was the subconscious mind that was vulnerable and could be harmed after death. In Arabia and parallel to Israel were the *ruh* and *nafs*. The concept of man having separate souls progressed from the Near East and India, through Island Southeast Asia, into Polynesia and as far east as North America where the Lakota Sioux Indians believed man has three souls; a conscious cognitive soul or *nagi,* a subconscious physical soul or *woniya* and a higher divine spiritual soul or *nagila*. The ancient Mexican Toltec religion had a version of the Binary Soul Doctrine believing in two parallel worlds, the *tonal* or material world, and the *nagual* or spiritual world representing mankind's two separate minds and life's purpose was to integrate these together. According to Max Freedom Long, the Hawaiians believed each person is comprised of three separate independent selves and man's goal is their unification, to create a more spiritually evolved consciousness. To Hawaiian *kahuna,* man consists of two separate spirits or souls along with a third higher consciousness.

This ancient belief in the three-part nature of mankind is suggested by modern references to man's mind, body, and soul. (Novak 2002) After thousands of years, mankind is reviving the ancient knowledge of binary souls. Modern science has concluded man has both a conscious and subconscious mind located in the two hemispheres of the brain. In the early 1900s, modern psychology through the work of psychiatrists Sigmund Freud and Carl Gustav Jung reintroduced the concept of separate and distinct minds coexisting in mankind Freud described as the "id", "ego" and "superego" and Jung described as the subconscious, conscious and super-conscious minds. The *huna* is a psychological system of mind, body, and soul as advanced as modern knowledge. (King 1985) In both the *huna* and Freudian psychoanalysis, the *'unihipili* and the "id" are reservoirs for mankind's unresolved conflicts. Both have techniques for understanding and resolving these negative complexes, it is through the subconscious mind that man contacts his *'aumakua* or higher self. (King 1985) In the Hawaiian *huna*, the *'aumakua* is our highest self, our super-conscious mind and trustworthy parent created out of the union of our two binary souls, *makua* means parent and *'au* is a prefix meaning paternal group. Centered above the head, *'aumakua* energy expands to envelope the entire body, it is the location of our divine spirit or *akua;* our direct connection to God. The *'aumakua* self was also known as *kino kupaianaha*, the marvelous and extraordinary body. The *'uhane* is our conscious mind with the power of speech and reasoning, expressing our thoughts and feelings. The *'uhane,* our objective, rational, analytical mind, has free will to control our actions and choices in the human social world. It is located in our head, *'u* means I and *hane* means to give life and spirit. The *'unihipili* or *'uhinipili* is our hidden subconscious mind, it is receptive, recording all our emotions, memories, thoughts, and actions. It is our natural instinctual intelligence concerned with our basic survival, controlling our physical body and is centered in our solar plexus. *'U* means I, *hini* means weak or with caution and *pili* means to unite or join.

In the Hawaiian Islands, man's consciousness is composed of two separate minds known as the *'uhane* and the *'unihipili* and a third higher mind created out of the union of our two binary minds is our connection to the divine, the *'aumakua*. All three contain different levels of spiritual power; the energy level of the *'unihipili* is called *mana*, the higher frequency energy level of the *'uhane* is called *mana mana* and the highest energy level of the *'aumakua* is called *mana loa*, the divine energy of creation. A related Hawaiian belief is each individual has three *piko's* or navels. Their *piko po'o*, located at the crown of the head, connects a person's spirit or soul to the spiritual realm, their *piko weana* or navel, location of their umbilical cord, connects a person to his parents and the present world and their *piko ma'i*, located at the genitals, represents their future generations. The two lower centers, the *'uhane* and *'unihipili*, reside within the body unlike the higher self, the *'aumakua*, located above the head and connected to the two lower selves through a cord of *aka* substance described by Max Freedom Long as an invisible, sticky, fluid ectoplasm extending outward in a fine line or thread originating from the region of our solar plexus attaching to whatever we touch or focus our eyes upon. When these threads are interwoven they form an invisible cord of *aka* substance over which *mana* can flow, creating connections between people and objects, transmitting thoughts and feelings not limited by material obstacles or distance. In ancient Vedic India there was a belief system similar to the Hawaiian *huna*, where *prana* was the primeval energy force of the universe similar to *mana* and *akasha* was the primal matter of the universe comparable to *aka* substance, a medium filling the universe through which *mana* travels. According to modern quantum physics, the recently discovered dark matter/energy dominating the universe may be equivalent to the *mana* energy of the Polynesians and its invisible fluid substance or *aka* over which *mana* flows.

The Hawaiian *huna* has an ancient origin that has been traced back to the Caucasian Berber tribes of North Africa, the Amazigh, or Imazighen, the "free or noble people" who lived in the Sahara Desert when it was green and fertile. As the Sahara dried up, they relocated to the Nile Valley of Lower Egypt and now live mainly in the Rif and Atlas Mountains of Morocco in North Africa. The Berber tribesmen are descendants of the Kharu people believed to have originated in the Caucasus area between the Black Sea and Caspian Sea before migrating south to the mountains of Syria and the Upper Galilee Region of Israel and then into North Africa. The Berber system of religious belief is very similar to the Polynesians and Berber words used in their religion are phonetically identical to those used in Polynesian languages even though their Amazigh language is not related to Polynesian languages. Many Berber tribesmen who left Egypt and North Africa sailed down the Red Sea into the Indian Ocean migrating to the Indus River Valley of ancient India where Berber religious beliefs influenced Proto-Polynesians. Religious beliefs similar to the *huna* are known to have existed on the islands of Sumatra and Java eventually reaching the islands of the Pacific Ocean. It is likely some Berber tribesmen were included in the migrations of the Polynesian ancestors.

DUALITY IN THE HAWAIIAN RELIGION

The Hawaiian and Polynesian concepts of mankind were dualistic in nature. The Hawaiian creation chant, the *Kumulipo,* is divided into *Po* and *Ao*. Night or *Po*, the primeval, spiritual world of the gods, coexists with day or *Ao*, the material world of mankind. Male is positive, spiritual, divine and sacred, possessing knowledge, strength, and life; represented by *Po* and the right side. Female is negative, profane, passive, darkness and death; represented by *Ao* and the left side. Man's origin descended from the gods above and woman's origin was formed from the earth below. The Hawaiian pantheon of gods had a dual nature with multiple forms, positive and negative, merciful and cruel. The *kapu* system of religious law separated the superior and sacred from the inferior and profane, *kapu* from *noa*. The Hawaiian religion had a dual concept of Kalana i Hau'ola, the Hawaiian name for the "Garden of Eden". It was a land of life-giving dew known as Paliuli, the green cliff, or *Kane huna moku*, the hidden island of the god *Kane* containing the life-giving waters of *Kane,* where spirits of their righteous dead enjoy the delights of the earth without labor or death in the heavenly afterlife of Kahiki. It was also the land from where ancestors of the Polynesians had originated, their lost homeland where the first man and woman were created and lived with their ancestral gods.

LEAPING PLACES OF THE SOUL

It was universally believed throughout Polynesia that after death, souls would set out upon a westward journey to Kahiki, "Our true home is the spirit-land. This world is but the briefest resting place". In the Hawaiian Islands, migrating souls would pause at gathering or leaping places usually located on a cliff overlooking the ocean along the westward or northern edge of each island called *leina a ka 'uhane* or "leaping place of the soul", the soul's last resting place. When a sufficient number of spirits or souls assembled at a *leina a ka 'uhane* they would plunge into the sea continuing their journey downward and westward to Kahiki and the afterlife. "After death the spirit of man turns towards the setting sun to retrace the long journey to the ancient homeland in the west". (Hiroa 1945)

On the island of Hawai'i, there were jumping off places located in all districts. *Makahanaloa* is in the district of Hilo, *Kukui-o-pae* is in the district of South Kona, the sixty-nine foot cliffs of *Lae o Kumukahi* were the jumping place in the Puna District and *Leina Akua* at *Ka Lae,* the southern point of Hawai'i Island, was the jumping off point in the district of Ka'u. An entrance to *Ao o* Milu was located at the mouth of Waipi'o Valley, in the district of Hamakua, a place called Keone that sands have long ago covered up and concealed. At the extreme northwest point of the Hawaiian island of O'ahu is *Ka Lae o Ka'ena,* the jumping off point located near Ka'ena Point where a large rock on a level plain overlooks the sea and *Kaimalolo,* in the Wainene District on O'ahu, is another jumping off point. *Pu'u Keka'a,* also known as Black Rock, located at the north end of Ka'anapali Beach along the west coast of the island of Maui, is where souls of the dead leap into the underworld and another Maui Island jumping off point is Kahekili's Leap located at the 636-foot-high Kahakuloa Head. A leaping place on Kaua'i Island is located just north of Polihale State Park, an extension of Barking Sands Beach, the westernmost point of Kaua'i Island at the southwestern end of *Na Pali* or the Mana Coast, where souls plunge into the sea from cliffs known as *Ha'ele'ele* below the Polihale Heiau 500 feet up the *Na Pali* Coast dedicated to Milu, god of *Po* and the underworld. Another Kaua'i Island leaping place is on a rise overlooking Hanapepe Bay located along the south coast of the island. On the island of Moloka'i there is a jumping off place between Koolau and Kona near the Kalaupapa Peninsula along the northeastern coast of the island. There was a leaping place also known as Kahekili's Leap located at the cliffs of Kaunolu Village on the southwestern tip of the island of Lana'i, *Ka Papa Ki'iki'i* is the leaping place on Ni'ihau Island and *Mauloku* is the leaping place on the islet of Lehua. In the Hawaiian Islands, when souls arrived at their leaping place there was often a breadfruit tree of spirits known as *'ulu o lei walo* or the quietly calling breadfruit tree that was a gateway for souls. One side of the tree was dry and dead, the other side was green and alive and souls would climb the tree. If a soul climbed the dry side it would live, but if it climbed the growing side it would fall down into the underworld of Milu, unless saved by its ancestral guardian *Ao 'aumakua* restoring its spirit and welcoming it to the spirit realm. Otherwise, it was sent to *Po ia* Milu, the dark world of Milu or *Po pau 'ole,* the realm of endless night.

On the island of Tahiti, spirits of the dead also journey westward from its northwestern peninsula known as Tata'a Point. On Ra'iatea Island, Tahiti, Faaroa is the extinct volcanic crater on top of Mount Temehani where *Te Tumu*, the foundation rock, stands in the darkness. It is an entry to *Te Po*, the realm of the gods, where souls would congregate before their journey into the afterlife. Rohutu noanoa or fragrant Rohutu was the perfumed, flowering paradise of the Arioi Society floating above the volcano where souls enjoyed the delights of life without labor or death, it was ruled by *Romatane*, god of paradise. Located in the air above Mount Temehani, it was described as "a perfumed place of light and enjoyment", a land where there was no aging, pain, sickness, or sadness with an abundance of food and endless festivities, including many young and beautiful women. In the Tonga Islands, souls of the dead followed the rays of the setting sun along *hala ki* Pulotu, or the path to Pulotu that ends at a leaping place along the western coast of Tongatapu Island to join their ancestors in the afterlife on Pulotu, an island far to the northwest, home of many gods and souls of departed chiefs where souls are bathed in the healing waters of the "fountain of life" and restored to their youth. In the Samoa Islands, souls of the dead departed from the coastal village of Falealupo, located at the extreme western cape of Savai'i Island on their journey to Pulotu or Bulotu, an oceanic underworld where plants perfect in their growth, covered in the richest fruit and the most beautiful fragrant flowers, were replaced immediately upon being picked. At Falealupo, at the west end of 'Upolu Island, there are two circular openings in the rocks where souls departed under the ocean to Pulotu and there was a leaping stone where souls from Savai'i Island entered the sea, swam to 'Upolu Island, crossed overland to Falealupo and continued on to Pulotu. In the Fiji Islands, after a man's death his spirit would leave his body and ascend along the "pathway of the shades" to the summit of the Kauvanda Range, the sacred mountain, then journey to the Wainiyalo River, the river of shades or spirits, now named the Ndravo River, where the god *Themba* would ferry the shades across the water in his great canoe. The shades headed for the bluff at Nathengani, but before reaching the cliffs they had to cross a bridge that was actually a monstrous eel. If it writhed it was a sign to move on, but if the eel was still the shade or spirit was to wait for his wife who had been strangled after his death and would soon join him. The bodies of women put to death were regularly laid at the bottom of their husband's grave to serve as a cushion for their husband to lie upon and were called *thotho* or grass, being compared to the dried grass placed under floor mats in Fijian houses. On Kandavu Island, Fiji, Nainggoro Rock was the canoe that ferried the dead to the afterlife and there were jumping off places in the Lau Islands of Fiji, located on the west or northwest coast of each island. First, the souls went to Nai Thimbathimba, the jumping off place on or near each island, then the souls were ferried by canoe to Nai Thombothombo, land of souls, located along the westward facing cliffs of the Mbua Coast of Vanua Levu Island, Fiji. From there the spirits leapt into the sea from a *balawa* tree and journeyed northwestward toward the far away home of their ancestors called Nakauvandra or Qaloqalo, "island of the blessed". Near Vanua Levu Island, Fiji, is a canoe-shaped island thought to be a ship of the dead. Burotu was the location of the spirit-land afterlife of the Fiji Islands an island paradise far to the northwest also known as Mbulotu or Mbulu. The island of Burotu contained the "water of life" where it was possible to regain one's youth and vigor, it included an abundance of sea life, an idyllic landscape of fruitful gardens, courtship, and marriage; it was "like life on earth only better". A soul's journey to the afterlife was fraught with dangers, the serpent god *Degei* judged souls of the dead, the righteous went on to Burotu, land of eternal life and joy, the unsuccessful were eaten by the gods. The name Burotu, Bulotu, or Pulotu for the spirit-land of Polynesian legends originated from their ancient homeland on the island of Buru in the Moluccas Islands of Island Southeast Asia. The land of Bouru, the western island home of the dead in mythology of the Gilbert Islands, appears related to Buru Island where several place names are the same as mythological Gilbert Island paradises. In Austronesian languages, *pulo* means island and *tu* means sacred or of high rank. The name Burotu is also found in Southern Arabia with Burohotu, their name for the underworld of the dead. According to Dr. A. Carroll, the origin of the name of the spirit-land of Burotu goes further back to a location along the central part of the Euphrates River of Mesopotamia known as Buruttu or Burutu. In the Marquesas Islands, souls of the dead would leap off the west facing high cliffs of Kiukiu on the northernmost island of Hiva Oa. On Rarotonga Island, in the Cook Islands, spirits leapt from a *pua* tree into the ocean below on their way to Avaiki. In New Zealand or Aotearoa, located far to the south, the leaping place known as Te Reinga was located near Cape Reinga, at the extreme northern cape of New Zealand's North Island, where a sacred *pohutukawa* tree marked the spot where spirits dropped down into the sea on their journey to the spirit-land.

Throughout Island Southeast Asia there was belief in an afterlife. The world of the Proto-Polynesian Batak of the island of Sumatra consisted of three sections; a heaven above that was the dwelling place of the gods and ancestors, the earth in the middle that was the dwelling place for man and the spirits and the neither world below occupied by the serpent of the underworld. The houses of the Dayak of the island of Borneo, the Batak of the island of Sumatra and the Troadja of Sulawesi Island had a central post associated with a deified ancestor linking the three regions of the universe. The *tongkonan* or traditional house of the Troadja was built on stilts and represented the universe, the roof was the upper world of the gods, the floor was the human world, and the space beneath the floor was the underworld. As the Polynesians migrated eastward and their previous homeland dropped below the visible surface of the sea in the west, where the sun sets at night, they believed it was descending into *Po*, realm of the gods, which also came to mean the underworld, abode of spirits of the deceased. Throughout Polynesia there were a series of underworlds where souls of the deceased gradually descend toward extinction in the darkness and oblivion of *Po*. In the Maori afterlife, the spirit of the deceased was offered food and if it ate, it could never return to the living. Either the soul was set free and bathed in the "water of life" becoming immortal or the soul was devoured by the gods.

LEVELS OF THE HEAVENS

Hawaiian sacred mythology describes the beginning of the world where supernatural beings shape creation. The god *Kane* first dwelt alone in the darkness of *Po* and then created three levels of heaven as concentric layers above the sky; the highest level or *lewa lani* was for *Kane,* the next level *lewa nu'u* was for *Ku* and the lowest level *lewa lani lewa* was for *Lono*. There were spirit gods or *'uhane lewa* made from spittle of the god *Kane*, numberless spirits of the air without bodies created to serve the gods, along with deified males and guardians appointed by the gods. Then, the gods created the earth as a garden for mankind and *Lono*, god of fertility, covered the earth with vegetation. (Beckwith 1970 [1940]) In mythology of the Tuamotu Archipelago, the universe was also composed of three layers with each containing its own sky. The upper level was for happy souls, the living occupied the middle level, and the lower level contained wandering souls in distress. In Polynesia, the number of layers of heavenly paradise varied from three in the Hawaiian Islands, to as many as ten or twelve in New Zealand. In the creation mythology of the Tahitian Islands, the dome of the sky was lifted until there were ten layers of heaven. The Rarotongans also had ten levels of heaven and the Samoans of the Manu'a Islands had nine levels of heaven. The idea of different levels of heaven goes back to the Near East and ancient Saba or Sheba on the Arabian Peninsula where there were seven layers of heaven. Throughout Polynesia there were sky worlds where souls of those distinguished by divine descent and those with notable achievements in life such as souls of priests, warriors, and craftsman possessing superior *mana* ascended into the heavens.

THE UNDERWORLD, LAND OF THE DEAD

In the Hawaiian Islands, the land of the dead was divided into two regions; an upper region ruled by Wakea, where souls of the fortunate chosen few who observed the religious rites and ceremonies dwelt in everlasting happiness having all their desires fulfilled and a lower region, a realm of intense darkness, fire and evil, where souls of those not sufficiently religious went under control of Milu who had been a high chief of Waipi'o Valley, but because of his cruel and evil deeds had been cast down into the underworld where he became its chief. The underworld of Milu was "an abode of misery, a place of impenetrable darkness and distress, of unending fire and lost spirits, where souls must lie under *kou* trees of Milu's world drink its waters and eat lizards, butterflies, and moths for food". In ancient Arabia, there was a god named *Milu* whose realm was beneath the sea. (Fornander 1996 [1878]) The underworld of the Marquesas Islands was located in three regions below the earth. The lowest afterlife was where food was plentiful and women were lovely, above this was a region with only adequate provisions and above that, next to the earth, was an underworld of demons. There was also an underworld in the Samoa Islands, a "subterranean abode" where souls were eaten by the gods.

The night marchers or *oi'o* of the Hawaiian Islands were *huaka'i po,* processions of the night. In Waipi'o Valley on Hawai'i Island, a phantom army of ghostly apparitions of ancient *ali'i* chiefs and warriors led by the spirit of Kamehameha the Great, in a long torch-carrying fearful procession accompanied by chanting, the beating of drums and sound of shell trumpets, traveled down the valley at sunset or just before dawn, their feet not touching the ground. Most often they marched on the nights of the god *Kane* or *Po Kane* between the twenty-seventh and twenty-ninth of each lunar month and on *Po Akua*, night of the full moon on the fourteenth, on their way to the entrance of the underworld or *Lua o* Milu, located at the mouth of Waipi'o Valley. In the Hawaiian Islands, there are *Ao kuewa* or *Ao 'auwana*, realms of desolate wandering souls or *'uhane hele* without a guardian *'aumakua*. Spirits that had no place in the *'aumakua* realm were thought to wander places such as the plains of Kama'oma'o on Maui Island, the plain of Kaupe'a or Pukaua on the island of O'ahu, Uhana on Lana'i, Ma'ohelaia on Moloka'i, the plain of Mana on the west side of Kaua'i and Halali'i on the southwest coast of the island of Ni'ihau.

ANIMISM

The ancient Hawaiian religion was animistic, believing all natural phenomena were of supernatural origin, that spirits of the divine became manifest into features of the natural landscape and any natural object could represent a god. Unseen gods and spirits inhabited all forms of nature, both living beings and inanimate objects filled the sea, sky, and land, controlling nature and mankind by influencing events in the natural world through their *mana*. Animism also includes worship of spirits of deceased ancestors thought to represent the supernatural. Before the establishment of urban civilization, the largest unit of society was the extended family and spirits of family ancestors were worshipped. As tribal clans developed, ancestors of the clan chiefs were worshipped and as the clans united creating a centralized government, ancestral deities of the rulers became gods of the state religion.

The term animism originated from the word *anima*, the Latin word for breath, life, or soul introduced in 1720 by Georg Ernst Stahl (1660-1734), a German chemist and physician, when he used the word *animismus*. Stahl theorized all matter contained a vital force and animal life had an immaterial soul. Animism was re-defined to include "belief in spiritual beings" by English anthropologist Sir Edward Burnett Tylor (1832-1917) in his book *Primitive Culture*, published in 1871. Tylor thought the foundation of mankind's religion was found in the concept of an immortal soul. Attempts by early man to explain the difference between life and death and separation from the body during dreams and visions suggested man's soul was distinct from his body and belief in an existence after death. The Hawaiians believed a soul or spirit was present in humans, animals and plants including inanimate natural objects, similar to the belief of Pierre Teilhard de Chardin (1881-1955), a French philosopher, Jesuit priest, and author of *The Phenomenon of Man* written in the 1930's and published in 1955, who was also of the opinion consciousness exists not only in all forms of life, but in inanimate objects as well. English philosopher Herbert Spencer (1820-1903) suggested gods originated from the worship and offering of sacrifices to spirits of deified "heroes" and ancestors who appeared to the living as ghosts and were able to reside in animals and objects in nature and animism was an early stage of religion. Oxford University professor and Sanskrit scholar Friedrich Max Muller (1823-1900) proposed early man worshipped the elements and phenomenon of nature and early evidence of ancestor worship can be found in the text of the ancient *Rig Veda* of Vedic India, which he translated and published in 1869, where spirits of dead ancestors known as *pitris* were prayed to for earthly protection. The Hawaiian concept of life was not restricted to the physical world, it included a spiritual realm as well. Hawaiians believed spiritual forces acted upon events in their lives and therefore, their activities were accompanied by religious ceremonies and prayers to appease these forces. The Hawaiians thought man was able to move between these two worlds, that man's present material existence was preparation for a spiritual afterlife and man had a separate soul or spirit that continued to exist after his death. In the ancient Hawaiian religion, there was no distinct separation between the natural world and the spiritual world of the supernatural beyond our physical senses. All forms of nature were thought to be manifestations of the spiritual world and the natural world was both conscious and divine. According to modern quantum physics, consciousness is a fundamental property of matter and permeates all of nature; every object contains a primitive form of consciousness.

THE ARRIVAL OF HAWAIIAN GODS

In Hawaiian mythology, the major gods arrived in the Hawaiian Islands at different times. *Ku,* prototype of the male gods and *Hina*, prototype of the goddesses, together represented human reproduction and were the first to arrive from Kahiki, land of the gods. *Ku* means erect and *Hina,* the moon goddess, means lying down and represented feminine attributes such as children, seduction, beauty, and dance. They landed on the island of Lana'i at Ku-moku or "gods' landing" and became the original ancestral gods and first parents of the Hawaiian people. (Beckwith 1970 [1940]) *Ku* and *Hina* are thought to have arrived before the gods *Kane* and *Kanaloa* who landed at Ke'ei on the island of Hawai'i, also coming from the ancient homeland of Kahiki, although some believe *Kane* arrived first explaining his seniority. The god *Lono* arrived last (Pukui 1972), he landed on Hawai'i Island in a boat with square sails, has a tradition of bringing plants for cultivation and later descended from the heavens on a rainbow to Waipi'o Valley. The four major Hawaiian gods having originated as deified ancestors represent distinct eras of colonization and are associated with the plants and animals they transported with them when they arrived on the Hawaiian Islands. In Hawaiian legends, heroes and heroines are often said to have been children of *Ku* and *Hina* establishing their royal ancestry. In Waipi'o Valley, statues of *Ku* and *Hina* were probably located at the ancient Honua'ula Heiau built on Waipi'o Beach (Fig. 33). The hierarchy of Hawaiian gods reflected the societal class structure established according to blood inheritance. The ruling *ali'i* worshipped the major gods *Kane, Ku, Lono,* and *Kanaloa,* lower level deities derived from the four major deities were worshipped by the lower social classes. The lesser gods had binominal names, the first part was the name of one of the four major gods followed by a name indicating the particular function of the lesser god who was associated with family ancestral lines, individuals, and special occupational groups.

In the Hawaiian Islands, the god *Kane* as *Kanenuiakea* or *Kane* of the wide expanse was considered god of creation; of the sun, stars, sky and the heavens. He was the originator of life on earth who provided sunlight and freshwater. *Kane* represented the Supreme Creator God *'Io* and was god of male fertility and procreation, the forests and the land. *Kane* was the most revered of the four major gods and was god of the "waters of life", of rain, freshwater, sunlight, springs, irrigated agriculture, and fishponds. It was the god *Kane* who created the first woman from the soil of the earth. The god *Ku* was a father figure and god of the junior line of ruling *ali'i* chiefs and priests. *Ku* means to stand erect or to strike, he was god of judgment and warriors, the power behind war and god of human sacrifice. *Ku* represented male power and was god of the works of men, of canoe and house building, fishing and bird catching. *Ku* represented the powerful right side of man and was associated with *Hina,* the supreme female goddess. *Lono,* the most benevolent of the four major gods, was god of the senior line of *ali'i* chiefs, of non-irrigated agriculture, healing, peace, the harvest and god of the Makahiki festival. *Lono* was god of weather phenomena, of the wind, dark clouds, rain, winter storms, thunder, lightning, and rainbows. *Kanaloa,* the great octopus, was god of the ocean and its creatures, of saltwater and the negative aspects of the god *Kane,* of darkness and death; the ocean was symbolic of death. In Southern Polynesia, the god *Kanaloa* was often worshipped as the Creator God and on the islands of Samoa *Kanaloa* was the Supreme God known as *Tagaloa.* On the islands of Tonga he was *Tangaloa* and on the islands of Tahiti *Kanaloa* was known as *Ta'aroa,* but in the Hawaiian Islands the god *Kanaloa* became Prince of *Po* or the underworld after he and his spirits rebelled against the god *Kane* because they were denied kava or *'awa,* a sacrificial offering and sign of worship. *Kanaloa* was conquered by *Kane* and thrust down into the underworld where he became known as Milu, ruler of the underworld.

To ancient Hawaiians and throughout Polynesia supernatural forces filled the sea, sky and land, all elements and forces of nature were thought to be manifestations of the major gods. *Kane,* god of creation, was associated with the sky and the upper clouds, sun, light, lightning, spring water, freshwater, coral and the colors white and yellow. *Ku,* god of war, was associated with high mountains, high seas, canoe making, and the color red. *Lono,* god of agriculture and peace, was associated with the moon, rain clouds and heavy rain, thunder, rainbows, southerly Kona winds and storms during the rainy season, black rain clouds and *hiwa* or the color black. *Kanaloa,* god of the sea, was associated with ocean winds, canoes, the sea bottom, seawater, tides, the subterranean world and the colors red and black. The major gods often appeared as living beings with the attributes of each god revealed by their *kino lau* or many forms. Animals were manifestations of the gods and animals of the god *Ku* were the dog or *'ilio,* eel or *puhi, ulua* fish, *'io* or the hawk and the *'o'o* bird. Animals of the god *Lono* were the *pua'a hiwa* or black pig, a sacrifice to *Lono,* and the *'aweoweo* and *kumu* fish. Animals of the god *Kane* were the owl or *pueo,* hawk or *'io* and the *o'opu, 'ama'ama* and *aholehole* fish. Animals of the god *Kanaloa* were also the *'ama'ama* and *aholehole* fish and the octopus or *he'e,* squid or *muhe'e,* starfish or *pe'ape'a,* shark or *mano,* large fish and marine mammals, the whale or *kohola* and dolphin or *nai'a.* Plants were also manifestations of the gods. Plants associated with the god *Ku* were forest trees of *ohi'a lehua* and *koa,* coconut or *niu, noni,* breadfruit or *'ulu, 'ie'ie vines* and the stem of the *ki* or ti plant. Plants of the god *Lono* were the *kukui* tree, gourds or *ipu,* sweet potato or *'uala,* ti or *ki* plant leaf and medical plants. Plants of the god *Kane* were taro or *kalo,* banana or *mai'a,* sugarcane or *ko,* bamboo or *'ohe,* the *wauke* plant for making tapa and *popolo* or the black *'awa* plant. Plants of the god *Kanaloa* were also the banana, bamboo and black *'awa.* Hawaiians developed their own separate pantheon of goddesses from *Hina* who arrived with the god *Ku.* The goddess *Haumea* was the daughter of *Hina* and mother of *Pele,* goddess of volcanoes, whose eruptions were considered menstruations because women went into the sea for purification after their menstrual cycle. *Kapo, Hi'iaka,* and *Laka* were sisters of *Pele* and were also goddesses.

SORCERY

The majority of the Hawaiian sorcery deities were female forms of the goddess *Haumea* whose name means impure (Valeri 1985) and many women became sorceress as a result of being excluded by taboo or *kapu* from religious practices. The Polynesian use of sorcery goes back to the Fiji Islands of Western Polynesia where evil spirits were conjured up and controlled by sorcerers who could read omens, command evil spirits and pray people to death. In the Hawaiian Islands, to pray someone to death a *kahuna 'ana'ana* would recite a prayer or *pule 'ana'ana* and after the *'ana'ana* spell had been cast upon a man he would die. *'Ana'ana* ceremonies occurred at night and needed bait or *maunu,* anything from the body of the victim containing his *mana* such as his hair, a tooth, nail clipping, saliva or excrement, enabling the *kahuna* to perform the rite of *pule 'ana'ana* or praying to death. After prayers to *Uli,* god of sorcery, the bait was burned, buried or thrown into the sea. In the Hawaiian Islands, chiefs had assistants who would carry spittoons into which the chief's spittle was collected for safe disposal. A *kahuna 'ana'ana* was required to secure the services of three enslaved *'unihipili,* subconscious spirits of deceased persons, and when these enslaved spirits were given *mana* they gave the *kahuna* power. The *'unihipili* were able locate a victim, enter his body and absorb his vital force, causing numbness starting at his feet and gradually moving up to his heart causing death. Spirit catchers were *kahuna* able to see wandering souls of the living or *kahoaka*, capture them in a gourd and demand a fee for their release, to revive their owners. The spirit catchers would raise the nail of the large toe and force the spirit back into the body, it would pass through the ankle, knee and to the chest, where breathing would start again, and life would be restored. In the Fiji Islands of Western Polynesia sickness and insanity were considered the work of sorcerers.

In the Hawaiian Islands, sorcery was always suspected when an *ali'i* died, the cause of their sickness, *mai waho* or sickness caused from outside, being attributed to the fact they had been bewitched by a sorcerer causing their soul to leave their body. A counter sorcerer, a *kahuna ho'opi'opi'o*, was employed to counteract the spell or a *kahuna kuni* would avenge the death or illness caused by the *kahuna 'ana'ana* sending spirits to confront the evil spirits of the hostile sorcerer revealing who had sent them. The *kahuna kuni* was able to determine who caused the illness, saving the intended victim and sending illness or misfortune to those who had caused it or avenging their death by killing the murdering sorcerer in retaliation. In New Zealand, after sprinkling a victim with water from a taboo or *tapu* source, Maori sorcerers were able to see the perpetrator and would build a ritual fire to destroy the spirit of the enemy. In the Marquesas Islands sorcerers enlisted supernatural forces to achieve the demise of an adversary and even a rumor could cause the victim to die from anxiety. *Kuniola* ceremonies, *kuni* means "to burn or kindle", were used when a person was very ill and showed signs of having been prayed to death or *'ana'ana,* where part or all of their body had turned black. They were performed in daylight witnessed by a crowd of people, a ritual fire was lit using green *olomea* wood with leaves of *'akia* and *kukui* nuts for fuel. Bait from the victim such as nail cuttings, clothing, hair or spittle was thrown into a fireplace called a *kapuahi kuni* and after three days of prayer the ashes were scattered in the sea, then the *kahuna kuni* could see an apparition of the spirits of those who had perpetrated the illness or death. A rainbow, rain, lightning, and thunder would appear and then the ill person could be treated. Another remedy to counteract *'ana'ana* was the *imu loa* or long oven used as a sweat bath, the *imu* was covered with a thick layer of plants the patient would lay on for as long as ten days as prayers were chanted. The idea that sickness and death were afflictions caused by the gods due to a violation of *kapu* or taboo laws was common throughout Polynesia. Hawaiians believed evil spirits, such as those of children who had never reached maturity in this world due to abortion or infanticide, were getting revenge upon the living and purification was necessary to counteract evil forces. Seawater was used universally throughout Polynesia to wash away evil influences. Fire and heat were also used, it was believed evil spirits feared heat and fled from fire. Heated stones were placed on the victim to drive demons out of the body and one of the purposes of fire walking was destruction of evil forces. Ceremonies were performed where evil spirits were cast into an object that was disposed of. *Akua lele* or "flying gods" were fireballs in the night sky considered omens of impending death.

Kaula were prophets and prophetess with extraordinary powers who did not participate in state religious ceremonies, but lived isolated independent lives having an "intuitive communication with the gods". They were permanently possessed by a god or *uluhia o ke akua* (Valeri 1985) having *'ike papalua*, supernatural "double" knowledge or extrasensory perception and were sought out by chiefs for advice. They could see forces at work in the present so clearly they were able to predict the future, such as the death of rulers or overthrow of governments and spoke without fear of chiefs and men. This rare gift of "second sight" or *ha'awina 'iki* was *mana* granted by the gods, it was *'e'epa* or strange and mysterious without explanation. (Pukui 1972) On Hawai'i Island, there were sacred *Kaula o Pele* who were selected as young men and were not allowed to cut their hair unless they went to the volcano and threw it into the fire pit, most eventually became *kahuna*. There were female prophets, *kaula wahine,* who wore priestly white clothing and officiated at the *Hale o Papa,* where women worshipped. *Kaula* also means rope or string used as a tool in their rituals. It was during the reign of Kalauniohua that Waahia, a revered *kaula* of great power from Waipi'o Valley, was burned to death at the Keeku Heiau in Kailua-Kona on Hawai'i Island and it was Kapoukahi, a *kaula* prophet from Kaua'i Island, who advised Kamehameha the Great to build a *heiau* on the hill of Pu'ukohola. In 1813, after Kamehameha returned to Hawai'i Island from the island of O'ahu, he met with Kapohe, the "last prophet", a *kaula* who is said to have recited his celebrated prophecy or *wanana* that "the islands will be united, the *kapu* of the gods overthrown, those of the heavens [chiefs] will be brought low, and those of the earth [commoners] will be raised up". Like Kapihe, the prophet Ke'aulumoku predicted Hawaiian culture would be turned upside down and actually anticipated Kapihe's prophecy by several decades, "the many indeed now in high exalted places, shall go back to low and humble places". Ke'aulumoku condemned the fratricidal wars and encouraged Hawaiians to unite under one chief and is reported to have recognized the young warrior Kamehameha as a future leader who would impose order on the warring chiefs. In the chant *Haui ka Lani* or Fallen is the Chief, the prophet Ke'aulumoku predicted the death of Ka'u chief Keoua Ku'ahu'ula, unification of Hawai'i Island and Kamehameha's rise to power. The chant was composed during 1782-83, eight or nine years before Keoua's death. (Fornander 1916-1920) *Haui ka Lani* means both the chief falls and the sky falls since the chief's genealogy began with the gods in heaven. (From *Prophet of the Earth Overturned; Ke'aulumoku on Early Contact in Hawai'i* by John Charlot, 2003)

THE HAWAIIAN HEIAU

The word *heiau* or *haiau* in the Hawaiian Islands designates any sacred place devoted to worship and was the place where sacrifices to the gods were performed. The word *hei* means sacred place and *hai* means to sacrifice. *Au* means current or movement and may refer to the transfer of *mana* or spiritual power from the divine to mankind. Ritual sacrificial offerings including food and material goods were made attempting to maintain *pono;* a proper relationship between mankind, nature and the gods. First-fruits offerings of bananas, coconuts, and particularly taro were made to secure an abundant season of growing crops and the first fish caught was offered to ensure good fishing. The flesh of sacrificial animals was burned upon altars sending their essence and odorous smoke rising up to the gods as it was in the temple of Ur located in Sumer, Mesopotamia. Sacrifice established man's relationship to the gods. Food offerings brought into *heiau* and placed upon altars were not consumed by man, they were the gods' share. The spiritual essence of other food offerings were consumed by the gods, but the actual food was eaten by *kahuna* and their attendants. Throughout Polynesian there was a belief offerings of first-fruits would ensure fertility of the crops and an offering of a person slain in war would promote success in warfare.

The Hawaiian *heiau* were massive open-air temples, the largest and most elaborate stone structures in Polynesia. Hawaiian *heiau* were of simple construction with walls of stacked lava rock and platforms of waterworn stone carried from the beach as a smooth walking surface, there were grass-covered structures for *kahuna* and high chiefs and crude, grotesque images stood before altars where sacrifices and prayers were offered. *Heiau* could also be a simple object or element in the landscape where a god would manifest himself. The Hawaiian word *heiau* comes from *fare heiao*, a sacred miniature god house near a temple or *marae* containing remains of deceased family members or tribal ancestors in the Tuamotu Islands, originally part of the Tahitian or Society Islands. On Ra'iatea Island, Tahiti, the *to'o*, an image of the god *'Oro,* was kept in a *fare heiao* or house of sacred treasurers when not in use. "The Tahitian *marae* is a place set aside for religious rites and ceremonies. It is marked by upright stones and usually also a rectangular stone platform that stands at one end of the rectangular court indicated by a level pavement or by a stone-wall enclosure". (Emory 1933) There were two periods of *heiau* construction and worship in the Hawaiian Islands, early *heiau* built during the 'Ulu and Nana'ulu period and those built after the arrival of the warrior/priest Pa'ao in the eleventh century from Ra'iatea Island, Tahiti, when the original 'Ulu line was replaced by the Samoan Manu'a Island 'Ulu-Hema line of high chief Pili Ka'aiea. Early *heiau* were open platforms or courtyards where ceremonies were visible and everyone was allowed to participate. The later *heiau* type was built directly on the ground with a perimeter stonewall typically to a height of about five feet enclosing the sanctuary, they were not for public viewing. The walled *heiau* was introduced by Pa'ao, the warrior/priest who arrived from the islands of Tahiti. Pa'ao enclosed the ancient open platform *heiau* with stonewalls, a visible sign of the new separation between commoners and their gods. Pa'ao established the first *luakini heiau* on Hawai'i Island, the Waha'ula Heiau in Puna, altered the Paka'alana Heiau in Waipi'o Valley, where two white stones said to have been brought to Hawai'i Island by Pa'ao were worshipped by the inhabitants including high chief Liloa, and rebuilt the Mo'okini Heiau in Puuepa, Kohala, at the northern point of Hawai'i Island. The major gods became unapproachable to the worship of commoners only ruling chiefs, priests and high *ali'i* had access to them. The high *ali'i* became sole heirs of the ancient gods and living gods themselves. In ancient Sumer, Mesopotamia, religious temples were dwelling places of the gods where "kingship descended from the heavens"; only high chiefs and priests were allowed access into the temples.

Heiau were sacred places of worship, offering and sacrifice in the Hawaiian Islands, sites where *mana* was concentrated and transferred through religious ceremony. *Heiau* began as simple family shrines consisting of an upright stone and developed into raised stone platforms or *ahu* with paved courtyards. *Ahu* in the islands of Tahiti were identical to *afu* found in the Ellice Islands and paved rectangular courtyards with upstanding stones on raised stone platforms were common throughout Micronesia. Hawaiian *heiau* ranged in complexity from single structures surrounded by a wooden fence, to massive walled stone temple enclosures with several structures on stone platforms and carved idols of the major Hawaiian gods. The Polynesian origin of Hawaiian *heiau* goes back to Viti Levu Island of the Fiji Islands, to the *nanga* or *nangga*, sacred stone open-air enclosures of inland Melanesian tribes where during their *baki* rituals the living would worship and communicate with their ancestors, where young men were initiated into the community at the Solevu ai Vilavou or Festival of the New Year and first-fruits of the yam harvest or Vula ni sevu were held. Afterward, the Vilavou or initiates held a great feast where women of the tribe entered the *nanga* followed by an orgy of sexual license. *Nanga* were built on level ground beside a river or stream in the shape of a parallelogram about 100 feet long by 50 feet wide surrounded by irregularly shaped stones set into the ground vertically forming a perimeter stone wall eighteen inches to three feet high, gaps about every six feet in the line of stones created *katumbas* or entrances allowing access to the grounds and sacred trees were planted around the site. Two pyramidal stone mounds nine feet square at the base, five feet high with sloping sides and flat platforms four feet by six feet at the top forming altars for offerings to the gods were located at the east end and the main entrance into the sacred enclosure was a narrow passage between them. Two internal partition walls five feet high, three feet wide at their base and two feet wide across the top covered with flat stones ran north and south dividing the *nanga* into three separated enclosures with openings in the middle of the partition walls allowing passage from one compartment to another. At the east end was the little *nanga sewa*, in the center and larger than the other two enclosures was the great *nanga levu*, at the west end was the sacred *nanga*, the *nanga tambutambu* or "holy of holies" containing the sacred kava bowl along with bowls containing body paint used during ceremonies and just outside the enclosure to the west was a small sacred *bure kalou* or temple structure with a cone or bell-shaped roof called the *vale tambu.* (Fison 1885, Thomson 1908) The description of the *nanga* from *The Hill Tribes of Fiji*, 1922, by A.B. Brewster, pages 94, 96 differed slightly. He described the *nanga* as,

> "the *nanga* is a stone enclosure . . . faced east and west . . . and was . . . a parallelogram. . . . The eastern and western bases were twenty-one feet broad, and the northern and southern forty-two feet long. At each corner were pyramids of stone nine feet square at the base, five feet high, with a flat top surface six feet by four feet, which formed altars upon which were laid the offerings to the gods."

Fijian spirit houses or *bure kalou* (Figs. 53 (1&2)) were tribal halls and home of *Kalou-Vu,* ancestral gods of all Fijians, and *Kalou-Yalo,* spirits of deceased chiefs, where strings of cowry shells were hung from the roof. Inside a priest or *bete* would sit on a raised platform where the gods would descend to earth down long streamers of *masi* or white tapa cloth suspended from the high ceiling. A god would enter the *bete* who would have a seizure and become possessed speaking in a strange voice. In the Tonga and Samoa Islands, their temple form was a house on a raised platform surrounded by a fence, both the structure and grounds were taboo. Sacred structures of Polynesian tradition had their origins in ancient India and in Sumer, Mesopotamia, where stepped, pyramidal raised platforms or *ziggurats* evolved from ancient burial mounds dating back to 4000 BC, during the 'Ubaid civilization. Known as *duku* or holy mounds they were where divine judgment was rendered. These early structures had courtyards containing sacred objects and representations of their ancestral gods placed on raised platforms. The name of the chief god of the Sumerian pantheon was *Anu* and *ziggurats* were where man and the gods could interact. There were large truncated pyramids located in temples across Western Polynesia and in the Tahitian Islands, in the Hawaiian Islands large truncated pyramid forms were known as *ahu,* although these were rare. (Linton 1925) Perhaps, the *ziggurats* of Sumerian temples that existed as early as 3500 BC were the origin of the stepped Polynesian *ahu*. In front of the *ahu* was a courtyards containing stone backrests, a sacrificial altar with a refuse pit, a platform with representations of their gods, tombs of their venerated ancestors and often they included sacred trees and ceremonial water located in a stream, pool or container used during purification rites.

In the Hawaiian Islands, large important *heiau* were usually constructed on hilltops, high land overlooking a valley or village and on a peninsula of land jutting out into the sea. Most *heiau* were rectilinear in plan, although some were rounded or free form and some were sacred spaces in the landscape such as the Na Imu Kalua Ua Heiau at Na'iwa on Moloka'i Island to promote rain consisting of a series of open compartments on the ground about two feet square formed by flat stores placed on edge at right angles to each other. There were *heiau* that were sacred birthplaces in the landscape, natural rock outcroppings with no built structures, such as the Kukaniloko Heiau probably first utilized after the Kapawa migration from Rarotonga Island in the Cook Islands at AD 650, site of royal *ali'i* birthstones at Wahiawa on the island of O'ahu. The Pohaku Ho'ohanau, next to the Holoholoku Heiau, site of royal *ali'i* birthstones along the Wailua River on Kaua'i Island and there were several landscape *heiau* on sacred flat ground on Kaua'i Island such as the Kaahu Heiau and Kopahu Heiau at Waimea, Kaua'i, and the Naulili Heiau at Makaweli, Kaua'i. At Wailuku, Maui, Malumaluakua, and Olopio were landscape *heiau*. The Honomuni Heiau on Moloka'i Island was "a level stretch of grassy land" used for washing bones of deceased *ali'i* chiefs, it was called Kapukapuakea connecting it to the Taputapuatea Marae of Ra'iatea Island, Tahiti.

HAWAIIAN HEIAU OF HUMAN SACRIFICE

At the ancient city of Haran in Northern Mesopotamia, Terah, father of the biblical Abraham was believed to have said, "We must honor the gods with our lives and with our sacrifices. Our entire culture is built upon the blessings bestowed upon us by *Anu*, the Supreme God of Sumer. Being civilized is to sacrifice". Terah migrated from the city of Ur of the Chadeans to the city of Haran after the birth of his son Abraham. The night before Abraham's birth astrologers for King Nimrod, after seeing a comet cross the sky, predicted he would rule the whole world causing King Nimrod to order Terah to sell the newborn child so he could kill him. Terah hid Abraham in a cave and substituted the newborn child of a slave woman to be killed. Abraham was placed in the care of a foster mother for ten years and had been saved by the human sacrifice of another infant. A comet was said to have crossed the night sky during the birth of Kamehameha the First and he was also to be killed.

It has been theorized the practice of human sacrifice began during mankind's hunter-gatherer past to appease the gods and keep predators away. The practice of human sacrifice can be traced back to the steppes of Central Asia and Sumer, Mesopotamia, where human sacrifices were performed on the platform tops of stepped ziggurat pyramids. In mythology of Vedic India documented in the *Rig Veda,* it was through sacrifice the world was created. Purusha, a primeval giant with a thousand heads, eyes and feet, sacrificed himself to create mankind and the gods. He used his ritually dismembered body to create the sky and earth, the sun and moon, and the different castes of the ancient people of India. The Brahmin caste was created from his mouth, the Kshatriya caste from his arms, the Vaishya from his thighs and the Sudra from his feet. Purusha was sacrificed on an altar of fire to "feed the gods", his primordial act of sacrifice created the universe; creation itself was an act of sacrifice.

"Beat the drums and offer human sacrifice". ('I'i 1983 [1959]) At times when Hawaiian society was threatened, such as by war or famine, human sacrifices or *hai kanaka* were offered in an attempt to appease the god *Ku*. This was the ultimate *heiau* sacrifice and only the highest divine chief, being closest to the gods, was allowed to consecrate human sacrifice. (Valeri 1985) The human body was a burnt offering to the gods and included other fragrant things; sacrificial victims were food for the gods sustaining their existence. Women were never used as human sacrifices; even sacrificial animals were male. (Valeri 1985) In the Hawaiian Islands human sacrificial victims were generally criminals, *kapu* breakers, war captives, or enemies of a ruling chief; no infants, women, the aged or deformed were suitable. *Mu* agents of the *kahuna* brought human sacrificial victims to the *heiau* with victims often being killed by a blow from behind. Human sacrifice was a religious rite increasing the *mana* of one who sacrifices and was most often conducted for success in war or after victory to re-establish order in conquered lands. Human sacrifices were performed at a *po'okanaka heiau* or temple of the human head, another name for *luakini heiau*. Skulls of human victims were often placed on posts of the *paehumu* or fence surrounding the inner temple, the *luakina* or house of sacrifice, of the *luakini heiau* and there were as many as twenty-six *luakini heiau* on Hawai'i Island. During times of war, human sacrifices were the first killed or captured in battle and were known as "first fish". Enemy *ali'i* chiefs taken prisoner in battle were slain and placed upon the altar, their sacrificed bodies becoming part of the world of the divine.

CANNIBALISM IN THE HAWAIIAN ISLANDS

Human sacrifice was a symbolic form of cannibalism, the feeding of *Ku,* god of war, in the hope of gaining his favor. (Kikawa 2008) It occurred during Hawaiian religious rites when slain enemies were sacrificed to become "food for the gods", when eating of an eye during a religious ceremony symbolized eating the whole body. By consuming even a small piece of flesh from the body of a sacrificed enemy who had been slain or captured in battle and offered to the gods, their divine *mana* was absorbed and transferred to the conqueror who acquired the courage of the slain warrior enhancing his power. Cannibalism in Polynesia occurred for various other reasons such as for food in order to survive at sea and during famine or when the flesh of a slain enemy was consumed for revenge and to inspire terror. The death of an enemy often did not satisfy their desire for revenge and flesh of the "long pig that speaks" must be eaten. Another form of cannibalism was out of affection,

> "the Hawaiians are not cannibals . . . they never killed a man for food. It is true that in sacrifice they eat certain parts of the victim, but there it was a religious rite, not an act of cannibalism . . . when they eat the flesh of their dearest chief, it was to do honor to their memory by a mark of love: they never eat the flesh of bad chiefs."

> (From *Contributions of a Venerable Savage to the Ancient History of the Hawaiian Islands*, 1957 [1868], by M. Jules Remy in French and translated by William T. Brigham, page 13)

There are said to have been Hawaiian cannibalistic chiefs known as *lo ali'i 'ai kanaka* or chiefs who eat men. A man eating chief called Kalo 'Aikanaka migrated from the islands of Tahiti. He first arrived at Kaua'i Island, moved to Wahiawa, near Kukaniloko, location of the sacred royal *ali'i* birthstones along the North Shore of O'ahu Island, where he held cannibal feasts. Cannibalism in the Hawaiian Islands was thought to have originated from the Taputapuatea Marae on Ra'iatea Island, Tahiti.

TYPES OF HAWAIIAN HEIAU

The Stone of *Kane* or *Pohaku o Kane* was a family *pu'uhonua*, a place of refuge. (Kamakau 1992 [19961]) The word *pohaku* is a combination of the word *Po*, realm of the gods, and *haku* or lord. It was actually not a *heiau,* but a shrine to the family *'aumakua* god where offerings and sacrifices for atonement of sins were placed. The *Pohaku o Kane* was in the form of a single erect phallic conical stone monument one to eight feet in height usually waterworn, either plain or slightly carved with ti plants and greenery planted around its base; the name of the god *Kane* means male. The location for placement of these stones was determined by the gods and was revealed to a *kahuna* in a dream. During ceremonies, the Stone of *Kane* was sprinkled with holy water or *pi kai*, anointed with coconut oil and the upper part of the stone was often covered with a piece of black *kapa* or tapa, the color worn by *kahuna* on special occasions. Sacred pillars were common throughout the Near East and the origin of the Hawaiian *Pohaku o Kane* was probably the biblical Bethel Stone. Jacob, the biblical patriarch, rested his head upon a stone as a pillow and dreamt of a ladder reaching the heavens with angels ascending and descending, then God revealed Jacob's divine destiny. Upon awakening, Jacob set the stone on end as a pillar, anointed the stone by pouring oil over it as an offering, and named the place Bethel meaning "House of El" or "House of God". In the Marquesas Islands, a high chief was raised on a stone slab where he was anointed with oil at the time of his installation. (Linton 1925) Included within the *Pohaku o Kane* was an altar or *kuahu* where men of the family could speak with their family gods; it was a *puka no ka lani,* "a gate to heaven". (Kamakau 1992 [1961]) The *Pohaku o Kane* were also considered phallic symbols and the god *Kane* represented male and procreative power, this symbolism was transported from the lingam stone of the *Siva* cult of ancient Vedic India. In the evening, wood was laid in an *imu* located directly in front of the *Pohaku o Kane* and at dawn the *imu* would be lit and an offering to the gods of a red fish and a tapa cloth were buried in front of the stone monument. A pig was cooked, the *'awa* chewed and when the *imu* was opened, the pig was cut up and the *'awa* strained into cups. After praying for forgiveness of their sins, male family members drank the *'awa* and the sacred feast began with the smoke of the *imu* purifying the family. (Kamakau 1992 [1961])

The *ko'a* or *ko'a Ku'ula* were fishing shrines or *heiau* associated with fish god *Ku'ula*, patron of fishing who had once been a deified fisherman on Maui Island, and a stone fish image was found at many of these *heiau*. Most were small simple altars of coral and the word *ko'a* means coral, some were platforms with an upright stone representing *Ku'ula* surrounded by coral deposited by fisherman to promote a good catch and others had small courtyards containing a number of small houses serving as sleeping quarters for fisherman. *'Aoa* shrines were built near royal fishponds to increase the number of fish and give thanks and an *imu* was included where feast foods were prepared for dedication ceremonies. *Ko'a heiau* were usually built along the seashore and first fish caught were offered to the gods on a stone altar upon landing. *Ko'a heiau* were also built at fishponds, along river and stream banks, in forests and on sea-bird islands by bird catchers for success in taking large numbers of birds.

Ho'oulu 'ai heiau were to increase food production, (Valeri 1985) they were where first-fruits offerings were made to secure abundant harvest. *Ho'oulu ua heiau* were to ensure rain and increase food production, *ho'oulu i'a heiau* were where fish were offered to ensure successful fishing. Small temporary shrines called *loulu heiau,* made from *loulu* palms, were also to ensure good fishing and *ho'oulu kanaka heiau* were to increase population. *Ipu o Lono* were small agricultural *heiau* built during periods of drought to pray for rain and was also the name of a calabash gourd shrine located in a family men's house for offerings to the god *Lono* and their family god. A gourd called *ipu hulilau o Lono* hung from a pole in each *hale mua* or men's eating house was filled with fish and *'awa*. It represented the body of *Lono* and twice daily the head of the household would carry the *ipu hulilau o Lono* to the center of the *hale mua* praying and partaking of the offerings. The location of the *ipu* was considered a *kuahu*, an altar, or place of worship in the home, sacred to the god *Lono*. *Waihau heiau* were agricultural *heiau* for worship of the god *Lono* and *unu heiau* were a single line of stones standing on end in an oval or crescent shape with an open mouth and were also agricultural *heiau, lapa'au heiau* were medicinal *heiau* and *ho'ola heiau* were for treating the sick, there was one in each district. *Hale ma'o* were small temporary structures for use by *ali'i* to receive gifts or *ho'okupu* and were covered in tapa cloth stained a reddish color. (Valeri 1985) There were also celestial navigational *heiau* for blessing canoe travel to islands in the Hawaiian Archipelago, the islands of Tahiti and unknown lands, such as the Mahukona Heiau located in North Kohala, Hawai'i Island. *Waikaua heiau* were *luakini heiau* to ensure success in war, they were dedicated to *Kaili* or *Kuka'ilimoku,* god of war, and *waikaua* was also the name of a robe worn in battle.

On Hawai'i Island, religion was divided into two groups each with a separate hereditary order of priesthood corresponding to the two major classes of *heiau*. *Mapele heiau* were the priestly order of Kuali'i, order of the god *Lono,* (Kamakau 1964) and *luakini heiau* were the priestly order of Holoa'e that came down from Pa'ao, order of the god *Ku* or *Kunuiakea.* The priestly order of Kanalu established after repeated global catastrophes caused by a "warrior wave", an *iminami* or megatsunami, may date back to about 20,000 BC, time of *Kai a Kahinali'i,* the "flood that made the chiefs fall down". Global flooding occurred about 4800 BC, the time when Wakea, the first *ariki*, and his elder brother Lihau'ula, the first priestly ancestor, departed from the near total decimation caused by coastal flooding of their Proto-Polynesian Austronesian homeland on the island of Gilolo or Halmahera Island in the Moluccas Islands of Island Southeast Asia. Then, the function of the ruling chief or *ariki* and priest or *tufunga* became the restoration of life, to repopulate the land and increase food supplies. *Mapele heiau* were agricultural *heiau* where offerings of pigs and tapa cloth along with first-fruits were made to ensure the fertility and abundance of the crops, they were never used for human sacrifice. The houses and fences of *mapele heiau* were constructed of *lama* wood and could be constructed by an *ali'i* or *kahuna* and their ceremonies were open to all.

THE LUAKINI HEIAU

Luakini heiau, the most important and largest temples in the Hawaiian Islands, were reserved for the high *ali'i* chiefs and their delegates, they became the site of the royal rituals and were property of the ruling high chief of the district or island, the *ali'i ai moku. Luakini heiau* were often large elaborate complexes with platforms or stone walled enclosures and inside were carved images of the major gods. The sacred structures and fences of *luakini heiau* were constructed of *'ohi'a* wood with the bark peeled off and their administrators were high priests or *kahuna nui* who oversaw the major rituals and were of the order of *Ku*. Only a high chief could build or refurbish a *luakini heiau* that could be entered only by important chiefs and *kahuna* of the order of *Ku*. If a subordinate chief built or refurbished a *luakini heiau*, it was an act of rebellion. These were walled temples, *po'okanaka heiau* or temples of the human head named from placing skulls of sacrificed victims on posts of the wooden fence or *paehumu* surrounding the inner temple or *luakina* upon whose altars humans were sacrificed to the god *Ku* to ensure success in war, survival during emergencies such as famine, pestilence or upon the death of a chief. Only a high chief could undertake rituals involving human sacrifice and victims were usually captives or transgressors, the ruling chief was purifying society from the disorder brought about by their sins. *Luakini heiau* were often constructed before going to war and afterward, the defeated high chief and his followers were among the first human sacrifices. Hawaiians believed victory in battle depended upon how well a *luakini heiau* was constructed, the god *Ku* would look down upon the *heiau* prepared by opposing chiefs choosing one over the other. Defeat in battle was thought to be due to a defect in their *heiau* construction, that rituals had been neglected or something had offended the god *Ku*. (Neller 1989) When a chief conquered a rival in war, his victory was not complete until all *luakini heiau* of the defeated chief had been re-consecrated to the god of the conqueror. The family *'aumakua* gods of ruling chiefs were prayed to at these temples and they became state *heiau* where royal rituals were performed. The *luakini heiau* at the royal center became the focal point of the religious activity of the entire kingdom. Direct contact with the most important gods of society was possible only for the ruling chief and his high priest or *kahuna nui*. The major gods were *kapu*, only high chiefs, and *kahuna* who were keepers of the major gods and their attendants at the *heiau* were allowed to see them. The high chief was "the supreme mediator between men and the gods . . . the supreme sacrificer, the man closest to the divine". (Valeri 1985)

Building a *luakini heiau* was an event of major religious importance involving elaborate dedication rituals. First, the high chief would ask his *kahuna* or priest if it was necessary to construct a new temple or if it was sufficient to renovate the existing one. Most *heiau* were not always in use and after they were constructed and rituals performed, they might be abandoned until needed again. If the *kahuna* decided a renovation was adequate, the existing structure was remodeled; its old platform stones redressed and altars refurbished, it would be re-fenced and its sacred structures rethatched. Its central idol, the *haku 'ohi'a*, was replaced and its other idols refurbished. If a new *heiau* was required, a *kahuna kuhikuhi pu'uone* or architect was consulted to select a suitable site. *Kuhikuhi* means to describe and *pu'uone* means sand, the architect would create a model of the new *heiau* in wet sand for approval of the high chief. They were also geomancers knowledgeable in the art of the placement of structures on a site by reading the geographic features of the land. Most often the new site was covered in ruins of an ancient temple, it was a requirement that all new *luakini heiau* be located on the site of an ancient abandon *heiau*. (Stokes 1991) These ancient sites were sacred portals of the gods of *Po* and *kahuna kuhikuhi pu'uone* were consulted because they knew the locations of these ancient *heiau*. "It is not the *heiau* which makes the place sacred, but the place which makes the *heiau* sacred."

> First, the entire land was made free or *noa*, the trail was cleared and all fires extinguished. A tour of the kingdom took place where a *kahuna* and a man impersonating the demigod Kaho'ali'i stopped at the altar along the boundary of each *ahupua'a* to collect tribute or *ho'okupu* of pigs, food, feathers and tapa for the *heiau* construction. The inauguration rituals of a new *luakini heiau* began with the construction of the stonewall surrounding the grounds. Rites of purification enabled the *ali'i* and *kahuna* to enter the site and *kapu* restrictions were lifted allowing workers to enter the grounds so construction of the inner temple or *luakina* could begin. The workers slept on the *heiau* grounds and their tools were consecrated. Then the fence, *pa*, or *paehumu*, separating the inner temple from the outer *heiau* grounds was constructed of wooden posts with carved images and planks of *'ohi'a* wood. Often the heads of human sacrificial victims were fixed on top of the posts. "Surrounded with wooden pales [posts] above four feet high, upon which were fixed a number of human skulls, belonging to those who had at different times been sacrificed to their deities." (From *An Authentic Narrative of a Voyage Performed by Captain Cook and Captain Clerke, Volume II*, 1783, by William Ellis, page 180)

Purification rites or *huikala* began the *luakini heiau* construction process. Five temporary booths were constructed on grounds outside the site of the inner temple, the *luakina* or house of sacrifice which the *ali'i*, *kahuna* and construction workers entered in succession. They were consecrated and purified in stages, moving from one booth to another, enabling them to enter the inner temple or *luakina* site within the *luakini heiau* that had been made *noa*, suspending its divine purity. Once construction of the *paehumu* enclosing the inner temple site was completed and the platform stones were securely in place, elevated terraces paved with smooth waterworn stones were added for the various wooden structures. Entry into the sacred *luakina* or inner temple was guarded with crossed *kapu* sticks and some had *ki'i akua* statues on either side. Construction of Hawaiian *luakini heiau* had similarities to the Fijian *nanga* where temporary huts were erected outside the *nanga* grounds and it was forbidden for workers to leave until construction was completed.

ELEMENTS OF LUAKINI HEIAU

The inner temple or *luakina* of the *luakini heiau* contained several structures (Fig. 51). The most sacred and first to be built was at the far end of the enclosure, the *lananu'u mamao* or *'anu'u* oracle tower. The oracle tower was a wooden framework scaffold twenty-four to thirty feet or more in height, eighteen to twenty-four feet square at its base, it sloped slightly inward toward the top and contained three platforms or *kahua* symbolizing the sky and two levels of the heavens. The towers of the *luakini heiau* were built of strong *'ohi'a* wood timbers covered with small poles or *aho*.

The type of wood used for structures within a *heiau* indicated its function, *'ohi'a* wood is red, and *luakini heiau* were war temples. During religious ceremonies *'anu'u* towers were covered with white *'oloa kapa* cloth leaving a small entrance on one of the sides where a curtain could be pulled back allowing the high chief and high priest to enter the interior. The *kapa* or tapa covering was perishable and was replaced whenever consultation with the temple god was required. Hawaiian *'anu'u* towers were observed by Captain James T. Cook while sailing down the coast of Kaua'i Island on January 21, 1778. At every village Cook observed white obelisk-shaped objects, one as high as fifty feet and after going inland Cook found they stood in the temples or *heiau* and their parts had names similar to those in the islands of the South Pacific. Sometimes, the area where the *'anu'u* tower stood was separated from the rest of the inner temple or *luakina* with a tapa screen which was the case at the Paka'alana Heiau in Waipi'o Valley. Offerings were made on the lower floor or *lana* symbolizing the sky. The middle floor or *nu'u* was for rituals by the *kahuna* and their assistants who stood there during religious services, it symbolized the heavenly level above the sky where those who had been deified resided. The third floor or *mamao* was the most sacred platform only for the high chief and his *kahuna nui.* (Malo 1951 [1898]) It represented the highest heaven, the place where the gods who ruled the universe resided, and was the top floor of the *lananu'u mamao* or *'anu'u* tower. After being wrapped in white tapa cloth or *'oloa* shutting out the sun, the high chief and his high priest would enter and hear the voice of the temple god who took possession of the *kahuna nui* revealing his will and the future, this was why the tower was also known as the oracle tower.

"We observed at every village, as we ranged along the coast in the ships, one or more elevated white objects resembling pyramids, or obelisks; one of which supposed by Captain Cook to be at least fifty feet in height . . . another of the same kind [was] about half a mile distance. . . . As soon as they reached it, they perceived it . . . bore a striking resemblance . . . to those they had seen at Otaheite [Tahiti] and other islands in this ocean. It was an oblong space, [surrounded] by a stone wall four or five feet high. The enclosed space was loosely paved and at one end was placed the obelisk or pyramid, called by the natives henananoo [he annu], which was an exact model of the larger one. . . . It was about twenty feet in height, and [about twelve] feet square at the base. Its four sides were formed of small poles . . . hollow within from the top to the bottom. It appeared to be in a ruinous state, and had been originally covered with a thin greyish cloth."

(From *A Voyage to the Pacific Ocean for Making Discoveries in the Northern Hemisphere* 1776-1780, Vol. II, 1784, by Captain James Cook and Captain James King, Chapter XI, pages 139, 140)

In the Marquesas or Hiva Islands the oracle house, *fa'e tukau* or *fa'e tu'a*, was the most prominent ceremonial structure in their temple or *me'ae* (Fig. 52). Located on a stone platform, it was a large structure perhaps eighteen feet square in plan with a high obelisk-shaped roof as high as sixty feet. In the interior of the oracle house was a frame structure, a shrine called the *'ananu'u*. In the Hawaiian Islands, the oracle tower was known as *lananu'u* clearly the Marquesas oracle house was the forerunner of the Hawaiian oracle tower. Located along the roof ridge of the Marquesas oracle house was the figure of a mythical sacred red bird, the *manu ku'a*, and ridge ornaments known as *hukihuki* were three pieces of wood sharpened at the ends covered in red and white tapa from which long streamers of white tapa cloth were hung on either side of the roof indicating taboo. In the Fiji Islands, *bure kalou* had a similar form and function to both the Hawaiian and Marquesas oracle structures, but *bure kalou* also served as town council halls and guest residences. They were rectangular or square buildings located on high stone-faced mounds with sloping sides, a high-pitched roof and ridgepoles projecting three or four feet at each end (Figs. 53 (1&2)). (Handy 1971 [1926]) In the

Samoa and Tonga Islands "god houses" were ceremonial structures in the form of common round-ended dwellings elevated on earth mounds, some with stone facing. Both the form and use of tower shrines throughout Polynesia suggest they were derived from an ancient Vedic Dravidian temple form originating in Southern India where wooden ceremonial towers were constructed on elevated platforms. Although rare, a second tower called the *opu* tower was placed adjacent and built identically to the *'anu'u* tower. Captain Cook estimated the height of one tower at forty-five feet and the *'anu'u* tower of the Hikiau Heiau in South Kona was as high as sixty-five feet.

In front of the *'anu'u* tower and located on a low semicircular or crescent shaped *unu* paving stone platform were sacred, carved wooden *'ohi'a* god idols, *ki'i akua* of *luakini heiau*. They also stood on the right side of both the entrance to the courtyard and inner temple, guarding *heiau* entrances and watching over *heiau* altars. These carved anthropomorphic images in which the major gods resided during religious ceremonies were horrifying in appearance inspiring fear, had enormous grotesque heads, abnormally large grinning open mouths shaped in a figure eight with protruding tongues and stood with their knees flexed in the sacred *ha'a* bent leg stance. Some had rows of shark's teeth and often the images placed inside the *heiau* had human hair, eyes of mother of pearl and were known as *makaiwa* or mysterious eye images. The central *ki'i akua* was of the god *Ku*, the *haku 'ohi'a*. Directly in front of the idols was the *kipapa*, a paving of large stones at the foot of the *'anu'u* tower, and located inside the area defined by the idols was the *lele*, an elevated wooden sacrificial altar stand, a raised platform supported on legs tall enough to where burnt offerings placed on the *lele* could be seen from a distance. In front of the *lele* was the *'ili'ili*, a paving of small waterworn stone pebbles where offerings were deposited before being placed on the *lele*. Offerings remained on the altar until they rotted and were thrown into the *luapa'u* or refuse pit to make room for fresh offerings. On the legs of the *lele* were gourd guards to keep rats away from the offerings.

The *hale mana* or *mana* house (Fig. 54) was the most sacred and largest house in the inner temple or *luakina* complex, it housed the high chief and high priests during religious ceremonies and was where small mobile god images were kept wrapped in tapa that were displayed during temple ceremonies. They were *akua ka'ai* images, carved portable wooden god images on short handles placed on top of poles adorned with banners and feathers, and along with *akua hulu manu* images of the god *Ku* were carried into battle to inspire warriors and in processions during religious rites. The *akua hulu manu* were feathered god images made in the shape of a head and neck, their wicker frames were made of *'ie'ie* aerial roots like the feathered helmets. Covered with red feathers and some yellow and black feathers, their eyes were often inlaid with pearl shells and dog or shark teeth were placed in their mouth. Some were mounted on wooden bodies wrapped in tapa or placed on top of a wooden pole like the *akua ka'ai* gods and some even wore feathered cloaks. Their feathers were similar to those used in *'ahu 'ula* cloaks of the *ali'i*, usually red feathers with a border of yellow feathers and a crest including some black feathers. Red feathers were from the *i'iwi* bird and yellow were from the *'o'o* or *mamo* birds. These sacred images were housed in the *hale mana* and went everywhere with the high chief and his *ali'i*, such as the feathered war god of Hawai'i Island, *Kuka'ilimoku* or *Ku* snatcher of islands, brought to Hawai'i Island by the Ra'iatea Island warrior/priest Pa'ao as the god *Kaili* (Fig. 46). The high *ali'i* chief and *kahuna* lived in the *mana* house during temple rites, it was where *ali'i* ate their meals and contained tombs of chiefs and priests. *Mana* house construction began with the *'aha helehonua* ceremony determining the layout of the *hale mana*. The *'aha helehonua* or *'ahaku* cord was a knotted sennit measuring cord providing standardized units of length for laying out the sacred houses of *luakini heiau*. *Kahuna* aligned the corner posts of the *mana* house, they ritually stretched the cord around stakes connecting the four corners of the *mana* house symbolically binding the land to their god and the high chief, *'aha helehonua* means "cord binding the land". The Hawaiian *hale mana* was probably modeled after the *fare ia manaha* or house of sacred treasures located just outside *marae* of the islands of Tahiti. It housed the mobile ark, the *fare atua,* containing *to'o* of the god *'Oro* and was also laid out in a ceremony with a sennit fiber cord. (Johnson 2000) The *hale mana,* house of divine power, was the most important house in the *luakini heiau*, it had an open side facing the *heiau* entrance, housed the temple's most sacred divine objects such as the high chief's portable *akua hulu manu* god image and contained a *kuahu,* an altar where sacrifices were performed for atonement and cleansing (Figs. 51, 54).

The *hale pahu* or drum house, located between the *mana* house and the *lele* or altar, contained the temple's sacred *pahu heiau* or *pahu pu'ule* religious prayer drums made from hollowed out cylindrical sections of coconut palms or *niu,* breadfruit trees or *'ulu,* and were covered with a tightly stretched shark or ray skin held in place with coconut fiber cordage (Fig. 55). They possessed great *mana* signaling the gods who spoke through the drums sounded each morning at dawn and at ceremonial occasions. Human teeth were inlayed into the drums increasing their *mana.* The base of more finely made drums featured human images with flex knees and inlaid shell eyes holding an *'aha* cord above their heads. The sides and back of the *hale pahu* were enclosed, the front was open with only support posts facing the *'anu'u* tower, the idols and *lele* altar. Large temple or *pahu heiau* drums were played while standing, one located in the Bishop Museum in Honolulu is forty-six inches high and twenty-four and one-half inches in diameter and is said to have come from the Papa'ena'ena Heiau on Diamond Head, O'ahu Island. The lower section of the drums are composed of studs and a base ring, the drumhead lashings are either through holes in the upper part of the drum or tied to a lower stud and back through a hole in the shark or ray skin. *Pahu heiau* temple drums and *ha'a* bent leg dancing were first introduced to the Hawaiian Islands by La'a mai Kahiki upon his return from the island of Ra'iatea, Tahiti, and Hawaiian *pahu* drums were modeled after Tahitian *pa'u* drums. In one legend La'a mai Kahiki's drum was named Kaeke and in another legend he had two drums named Hawea and Opuku. *Kahuna* sounded the *pahu* drums to call people to the *heiau* and to consecrate human sacrifices.

The *hale imu* or *hale umu*, located next to the *hale mana*, was the earth oven house where temple fires of *luakini heiau* were lit and where burnt offerings to the gods were singed or cooked. The *hale wai ea* was the smallest house in the temple complex; it was only two Hawaiian cubits long, one cubit wide and one cubit high. The Hawaiian cubit or *ha'ilima* was the distance from the elbow to the extended middle finger. (Johnson 2000) Wooden *akua ki'i* idols stood on either side of the *hale wai ea. Wai ea* means "water of life", it was where holy water, a combination of seawater and coconut water to which sea moss and turmeric or *'olena* were added, was kept in a bowl made from a human skull. Inside the *hale wai ea* was a pit called *luakini* or *luapa'u,* the refuse or bone pit for disposal of decayed offerings. The *luapa'u* pit was sometimes located under the *'anu'u* tower or located outside the temple itself lined with stone. The *hale wai ea* was where the divine *'aha* cord, a coconut fiber cord representing the connection between the gods, land, high chief and his subjects was stored. The divine *'aha*, known as *kaha* in the Tuamotu Islands, was a sacred woven cord made from strands of braided sennit coconut fiber or inner bark fibers of the *olona* plant and a single cord was called an *aho.* The *'aha* cord included one strand of a rare red seaweed found only in the deep ocean of such importance the *'aha hulahula* rite could not be completed until it was obtained. (Handy 1971 [1927]) During the *'aha hulahula* rite the braided cord was displayed, stretched and tied, and its divine powers called upon. It was "through the manipulation of *'aha* cords during *heiau* rituals that divine power was controlled". (Kaeppler 1993) "The gods became a positive and productive power only after having been bound in the *'aha* binding rite inside the temple". (Valeri 1985)

The *'aha* cord of the Hawaiian *kapu loulu* ceremonies at *luakini heiau* has similarities to the *aka* cord of the Hawaiian *huna* and quantum mechanics of modern physics. The *'aha* cord bound the Hawaiian kingdom to the heavens connecting the high chief to the divine. In the *huna* divine *mana* energy flows through the *aka* cord, the universal medium connecting the consciousness of the universe, and in modern quantum mechanics dark matter transmits energy and conscious across the universe corresponding to the *mana* and *aka* substance of the *huna*. The origin of the sacred braided Hawaiian *'aha* cord was the sennit wrapping cords of the *to'o*, an image of god in the islands of Tahiti (Fig. 37). The *'aha* cord symbolized the divine power of the high chief to unify society, binding together all genealogies of *ali'i* and commoners, "from the heavens fell the *'aha* [cord] to the spot [kingdom] favored by [the god] *Kane*". The *'aha* cord of the high chief or *'aha kapu ali'i* symbolized the high chief's genealogical connection to the divine power of the gods, spiritually binding together the *ali'i* and community with the gods and destiny of the kingdom with the heavens. The sacred *'aha heiau* rituals attempted to control the power of the gods for the benefit of mankind. The high chief was known as *haku*, the word *haku* in the Hawaiian language means lord, master or ruler, and it also means to braid or to put in order. (Kaeppler 1993) The origin of the word *haku* was the Proto-Polynesian Austronesian word *fatu* for chief or leader also meaning rock land boundary marker and temple stone backrest. The weaving of the *'aha* cord took place at the inauguration of a high chief, the *'aha* was not inherited and each high chief had his own *'aha kapu ali'i*. The previous high chief's sacred cord was unraveled upon his death dissolving his social bonds and strands of *'aha* cords were woven into the caskets or *ka'ai* in which bones of high chiefs were entombed. (Valeri 1985) Sacred *'aha* cords were hung from the masts of the canoe of a high chief symbolizing his *mana*. The *'aha* cord was a sign designating the presence of a high chief, it was stretched between the outer taboo or *kapu* posts of his residence and when another high chief approached the *'aha* cord was said to fall off on its own accord allowing an approaching high chief to step over it. The word *'aha* also refers to the ruling council of chiefs governing early Hawaiian settlements before the Tahitian invasion and arrival of the *ari'i*. The *'aha* councils were symbolized by the woven *'aha* cord where each single cord or *aho* represented a member of the council.

The space within the walled enclosure of *luakini heiau* was known as the *kahua* or courtyard and its exterior stonewalls often had built-in benches for spectators to observe ceremonies suggesting an origin from the assembly areas or *tohua* of the Marquesas Islands that contained similar seating. (Linton 1925) Outside of the *pa* or outer wall of the *heiau* grounds was an area of level pavement called the *papahola* and this was probably where the majority of the audience stood when religious rites inside were in progress. The *Hale o Papa* or House of the goddess *Papa* was located on the *papahola* and was where religious services were held for *ali'i* women of *ni'aupi'o* ranking. (Valeri 1985) Women were not allowed to enter the sacred precinct of the *heiau* and worshipped Hawaiian goddesses outside its outer wall. The *Hale o Papa* often had stonewalls, a *lele* or altar where offerings of pig, bananas, and *kapa* or tapa were placed along with *ki'i* images of Hawaiian goddesses such as *Hina,* a female deity associated with the moon. Women of high birth performed ceremonies outside the *Hale o Papa* on the *papahola* to cleanse and purify warriors, removing the taboo or *kapu* placed upon them due to their exposure to blood. Women were separated during menstrual periods and childbirth when they were considered unclean and stayed in the *hale pe'a* or woman's house located on the *papahola.* Located beyond the outer wall some distance from the *luakini heiau* were large sacrificial *holehole* stones where sacrificial victims were killed before being brought into the *heiau*.

LUAKINI HEIAU DEDICATION RITUALS

The purpose of the *kapu loulu* dedication rituals at *luakini heiau* was "the transmission of 'mana' from the divine to the human realm", bringing freedom, prosperity, and success in war during the reign of a ruling high chief. (Valeri 1985) The people went into the mountains to collect materials for construction of *luakini heiau* structures thatched with *loulu* palm leaves. (Malo 1951 [1898]) During this time the high chief, *kahuna* and the public remained outside the *heiau* grounds seated on the *papahola*. The first ceremony beginning the *kapu loulu* rituals was the *kauila nui* ceremony that took place inside the *luakini heiau*. The high chief, *ali'i* and the public entered and were seated by rank. A *kahuna* holding an *'ie'ie* vine recited the *lupalupa* prayer; *ola, ola o Ku* or "life, life o *Ku*". Then, the divine portable images of the god *Ku*, attached to a handle or pole of *kauila* wood adorned with banners and feathers, entered the *luakini heiau;* this was known as the *kauila huluhulu* ceremony. (Valeri 1985) These divine feathered *akua hulu manu* god images were constructed on a framework made from aerial roots of the *'ie'ie* vine and were manifestations of the god *Ku*. Their featherwork was tied to a net or *nae* of *olona* fiber creating an anthropomorphic feathered head attached to a wooden body or pole of *kauila* wood. Some bodies were wrapped in tapa while others wore feathered cloaks just as high *ali'i* wore on ritual occasions or in battle. (Valeri 1985) During the *kauila huluhulu* ceremony, *akua hulu manu* images were refurbished with new feathers making them more divine and here the god *Ku* corresponds to the god *'Oro* in the *pa'iatua* ceremony on Ra'iatea Island, Tahiti. Feathers removed from images of the god *Ku* were distributed by the ruling chief to his *ali'i* adding to the divinity of their god images exactly as were feathers removed from *to'o* images of the god *'Oro*. A *kahuna* recited numerous prayers praising the gods while the feathered *akua hulu manu* gods were being refurbished. The *kauila huluhulu* ceremony in the Hawaiian Islands clearly originated from the *pa'iatua* ceremony of Ra'iatea Island, Tahiti.

A man impersonating the demigod Kaho'ali'i, the high chief's divine double and royal companion who was usually his close relative, appeared with *pala* ferns in his hand wearing a large white loincloth or *malo kea* and an ancient hairpiece. Kaho'ali'i was a dark man with white stripes on the inner side of his thighs representing the mythical ancestral deity of the walled Kawaipapa Heiau at Papa'a, Kaua'i Island, associated with the god *Ku* and human sacrifice. (Beckwith 1970 [1940]) Kaho'ali'i was accompanied by a man carrying a human skull which contained "seawater of the bleached skull" or holy water and another man carrying a *kapuo* staff announced a taboo or *kapu*. Then, the high priest or *kahuna nui* recited a long *pule* or blessing to the new feathered images of the god *Ku*.

> "Oh Kane, oh Lono of the blue sea,
> The white sea, the rough sea,
> The sea with swamping breakers,
> The sea, oh Ku, that reaches Kahiki . . .
> The sacred ocean,
> Sea of the bleached skull.
> Take the sea foam,
> That is the brine wherewithal to consecrate, . . .
> Oh Kane, here is your life-giving brine."

(From *Hawaiian Antiquites: Moolelo Hawaii*, 1951 [1898],
Bishop Museum Publication 2, by David Malo, page 239.
Courtesy of Bishop Museum Press, Honolulu)

All the people stood up along with the demigod Kaho'ali'i who unfastened his *malo* exposing himself with his penis "dangling" and ran naked in a circular route following another naked man holding an *akua hulu manu* and a *kapuo* staff. They were followed by feathered images representing the god *Ku* numbering forty or more. Kaho'ali'i ran naked before the eyes of the people in a bent leg stance with his knees pointed outward in the sacred *ha'a* dance position. "Nakedness is the garb of the gods". (Thrum 1979 [1923]) To go naked is regarded as a mark of divine birth. (Remy 1979 [1857]) The last figure in the procession was the feathered god *akua panauea*, the "slow god", and after the procession stopped the feathered god moved slowly to the front symbolizing transformation of the wild and warlike Kahoali'i whose privileged behavior allowed him to violate the rules of society, going around naked, eating with women and possessing them without restraint. Kahoali'i represented the wild, unregulated aspect of the god *Ku*.

After the *kauila huluhulu* rites were completed, the high chief ordered the *heiau* structures to be thatched and when the *kapu loulu* palm roof thatching was finished, the *haku 'ohi'a*, a carved image of the god *Ku*, was taken into the *heiau* and erected between the *'anu'u* tower and *lele* altar; dedication of a *luakini heiau* required a new image of the god *Ku* be installed. The carved *haku 'ohi'a* image was made from an *'ohi'a lehua* tree, a large, strong, straight tree of red-colored wood whose flowers nourished the forest birds providing red and yellow feathers for capes and cloaks of the *ali'i*, the *'ohi'a lehua* tree was also a manifestation of the god *Ku*. (Kirch 2010) To construct the *haku 'ohi'a*, the high *ali'i* chief, his *kahuna nui*, other *ali'i* and commoners departed for the mountains with sacrificial food offerings of pigs, bananas, coconuts, a red fish and a man who was to be the human sacrifice, one who had broken a taboo or a *kauwa* or slave. Once a flawless *'ohi'a* tree for carving the image of the god *Ku* was selected, the high chief prayed, "O thou standing *'ohi'a,* here is an offering to thee of pig and coconut. Give me life. Give life to the chiefs and all the people". Then, the high chief and the man who would cut down the *'ohi'a* tree touched it with the two sacred consecrated battle adzes of the ancient gods known as Haumapu and 'Olopu once belonging to Kaho'ali'i, the mythical ancestor said to have possessed these two famous "kingdom conquering adzes" of the gods. The *kahuna* cut a chip from the tree, then the *'ohi'a* tree was cut down using other adzes. The direction the tree fell would indicate lands the high chief and his men would conquer.

> "Ku of the forest, Ku-lono, strike gently . . .
> Cut a pathway, strike gently . . .
> Hew down the ohia Ku-makua, strike gently,
> Hew down the ohia of the forest, strike gently . . .
> Hew down the ohia of the koa forest, strike gently."

(From *Hawaiian Mythology,* 1970 [1940],
by Martha Beckwith, page 26)

The sacrificial pigs brought to the site along with the human victim were prepared. The drums of the gods were beaten, *kahuna* recited the *'aha mauha'alelea* prayer and the sacrificial *ha'alelea* victim was beheaded, *ha'alele* means abandon or forsaken. Then, the *imu* was lit and the pigs and other foods were prepared. At the end of the feast what remained of the food along with the body of the *ha'alelea* or sacrificial victim were buried by the stump of the *'ohi'a* tree. The image of the god *Ku* was carved and in a "fearful and terrifying procession" requiring absolute silence recreating *Po,* the time of the gods, it was carried down the mountain and placed on the *papahola* platform outside the grounds of the *luakini heiau.* If anyone was encountered during the procession they were killed. (Valeri 1985) The carved image of the god *Ku* was covered with ferns and *'ie'ie* vines were waved over the assembled congregation to purify them. The next day, the carved image of the god *Ku,* the *haku 'ohi'a* or lord *'ohi'a,* was taken into the *heiau* and erected between the *'anu'u* tower and *lele* altar. Another man was sacrificed before the *haku 'ohi'a* was erected; his body was thrown into the hole where the image of the god *Ku* would stand. Human sacrifices occurred at both the location in the forest where the flawless tree was cut down and in the *luakini heiau* where the carved image was erected.

The next morning, a *kahuna* placed a braided coconut cord around the belly of the *haku 'ohi'a* representing its umbilical cord and cut it with a bamboo knife, the ritual cutting of the cord and wiping it with a cloth symbolized the birth of the image of *Ku,* "sop the red blood, wear it as a wreath . . . to animate your wooden god". At first, the *haku 'ohi'a* was naked and then a red loincloth or *malo* was fitted on him "binding his loins" and all the other *ki'i* images surrounding the altar were also covered. The power of the gods needed to be controlled and by wrapping and binding the sexual organs of the *haku 'ohi'a,* power of the god *Ku* was restrained. The *haku 'ohi'a* was transformed from an *'ohi'a* tree into a "real god" and was worshipped after the ceremony was completed. (Valeri 1985) *Kaili,* the ancient feathered god of war, was presented before the *haku 'ohi'a* by the high chief, drums were beaten and the change was complete. The god *Ku* had been transformed from *Kuka'ilimoku* or *Ku,* snatcher of islands, a wild conquering warrior into *Kunuiakea* or *Ku* of the wide expanse, an immobile god representing completion. The ceremony of the *haku 'ohi'a* symbolized rebirth of the god *Ku* and transformation of the high chief who was the representative of the god *Ku* on earth, from a wild, violent personality into the divine, beneficial ruler of his people. The *kahuna* who presided over placement of the *haku 'ohi'a* fasted, eating only nectar of banana flowers used as baby food, the *kahuna* was symbolically representing himself as the god *Ku* during infancy, not yet fully developed. (Valeri 1985)

The evening before the *'aha hulahula* rites began, all the people prayed for its success; that it would not rain, there would be no wind, thunder or lightning, there would be no sound from man or beast and that the service would be perfect. (Malo 1951 [1898]) The *'aha hulahula* began with the high chief and *kahuna nui* standing in front of the *hale wai ea* where the *'aha* cord was kept conducting the *'aha* ceremony between midnight and dawn. During the *'aha hulahula* ceremony the majority of the people remained at a distance in front of the *hale mana* in silence, (Malo 1951 [1898]) those outside the inner temple or *luakina* enclosure were not allowed to enter and those inside were not permitted to leave. The high chief then killed a pig praying,

> "O Kunuiakea, O Lononuiakea, O Kanenuiakea, O Kanaloanuiakea, my gods, come ye all; here is the pig, a
> live pig; let me be saved by you, my gods. Here is your pig, your banana and your coconut; save all the chiefs
> and all the people . . . bless my land and preserve the people."

(From *Fornander Collection of Hawaiian Antiquities and Folk-lore,*
Volume VI, Part I, 1916-1920, by Abraham Fornander, page
10. Courtesy of Bishop Museum Press, Honolulu)

The high *ali'i* chief wore a feathered cloak and his high priest was naked carrying a staff of *lama* wood wrapped in *'oloa* or white tapa. Nakedness symbolized submission and in the presence of the gods, it was abandonment of self, leaving the human realm and entering the divine. The *'aha* cord was returned to the *hale wai ea* after having been stretched from one part of the *heiau* to another and while carrying the *'aha* cord *kahuna* moved with the sacred *ha'a* stance. The *'aha* cord symbolized the high chief's connection to the divine, the binding of his people together, and corresponded to the *to'o* on Ra'iatea Island. Both objects were constructed of braided sennit cord and were worshipped as representing the divine. (Valeri 1985)

Prayer chants during the *'aha hulahula* ceremony were recited accompanied by sacred formalized *heiau* dancing known as *ha'a* performed only by men, women could not take part in *heiau* ceremonies. (Kaeppler 1993) The bent leg stance *ha'a* dance was "a series of formalized movements performed with back straight and with knees thrust forward, spread apart and flexed and was performed during sacred religious rites". Sounding of the temple *pahu heiau* drum indicated the presence of a god and was accompanied by *ha'a* dancing and chanting or *oli*. The *ha'a* dance had probably been brought to Hawai'i Island from the island of Tahiti by La'a mai Kahiki, along with the *pahu hula* drum that often included carved representations of *ha'a* dancers (Fig. 55) and *ka'eke'eke* or bamboo pipe drums. The Proto-Polynesian Austronesian word for religious dancing was *saka*, in the Hawaiian and Tahitian Islands it was *ha'a,* in the Marquesas Islands, among the Maori of New Zealand and in the Tonga Islands it was *haka* and in the islands of Samoa it was *sa'a*. "Social dancing termed *hula* belongs to the people and the *ha'a* dance belongs to the gods." (Kaeppler 1993) *Hula* dancing began as *hula kahiko,* an ancient form of worship during religious ceremonies and eventually became social. *Hula* became a rain and agricultural fertility dance as well a dance for human fertility. Modern *hula 'auana* is performed without religious rituals and is accompanied by modern musical instruments. On the islands of Tahiti, *hula* is known as *hura*.

Twice the *kahuna nui* asked the high *ali'i* chief if the *'aha hulahula* service had been successful and if no sound had been heard during the *'aha* service, it was *maika'i* or acceptable. ('I'i 1983 [1959]) The *kahuna nui* then declared the high chief, his *ali'i* and all the men were saved; "Your adversary will be defeated. His land will be yours". At dawn after hearing of the chief's reply announcing the *'aha* service had been successful, the men outside the *luakina* rejoiced (Kamakau 1976), their kingdom would be prosperous in the coming years. At daylight, the *imu* was lit, the pigs and sacrificial lawbreakers were killed and a feast began. The *kuili* rites inaugurating the *mana* house began after the *kahuna nui*, high priest of the *luakini heiau*, performed the *'aha hulahula* ceremony. After the tree had been felled to make the *haku 'ohi'a,* it had been followed by cutting trees for construction of the *mana* house and other houses of the *luakini heiau.* (Valeri 1985) About the same time as the *haku 'ohi'a* was being transformed into the god *Ku,* the *mana* house was being decorated with a netting of knotted cords known as *'aha limalima* or *maku'u* hung along its ridgepole with finger-like tassels, the word *limalima* means tassels. (Malo 1951 [1898]) Thatching grass left hanging over the opening to the *hale mana* known as its *piko* or navel cord was trimmed and the *mana* house was symbolically born. After a prayer or *pule* for trimming the opening was recited, *kahuna* and their assistances entered the *mana* house and prayed in unison until daybreak. They sat in two groups on either side of the *mana* house eating *pua'a* or pigs cooked in the *heiau imu* and the next day more pigs were cooked.

It was during the *kapapaulua* ceremony or *ulua* fishing rites that the "great sacrifice", climax of the *kapu loulu* rituals, occurred. It began during the night with an *ulua* fishing expedition when the *ulua kahuna* and several fishermen went out to sea attempting to catch the elusive *ulua* fish with bait and a special sacred fishhook. The fishhook was modeled after the famous Manaiakalani fishhook of legend the demigod Maui used to catch *ulua* fish when he pulled up the islands (Fig. 56). The *ulua* fish represented an enemy of the ruling chief and *ulua* fishing was symbolic of fishing for land, conquest by the high chief over his adversaries. (Valeri 1985) The *kahuna* of the *kapapaulua* ceremony entered the *'anu'u* tower holding the red *ulua* fish and prayed, then placed the *ulua* fish on the sacrificial altar along with the human sacrifices. If an *ulua* fish was not caught a human "fish" was substituted and dragged to the *heiau* with an *ulua* fishhook in his mouth as though he were really a fish. (Malo 1951 [1898]) It was during this ceremony that captive warriors were sacrificed. If an enemy chief had been slain in battle, the victorious high chief "grasped the line from which hung the famous hook called Manaiakalani and hooked it into the mouth of the dead victim - a chief defeated in war" (Kamakau 1976), recited a prayer condemning the traitor and dragged his body to the *heiau* for sacrifice. The vanquished chief, along with two pigs were roasted over the fire and laid upon the stone pebbles or *'ili'ili* beneath the *lele* altar before being placed upon the altar where the sacrificed chief's body was placed face down with each arm over the body of a pig laid on either side along with bunches of bananas and coconuts and he was consecrated to the gods. (Kamakau 1976) After war there might be many such victims and if ten men were sacrificed they were laid upon altars with pigs on either side, the burnt offerings remaining on the altar until the flesh had fallen from their bones. (Kamakau 1964 [1870]) The *kapapaulua* ceremony on Hawai'i Island was related to human sacrifices performed at the 'Opoa Peninsula on Ra'iatea Island, Tahiti, where the god *Ku* was known as *Tu,* god of fishing, and sacrifices to the god *Tu* included red *ulua* fish. The human sacrificial victims of the *kapapaulua* ceremony were food for the gods and not for human consumption, although an exception was the rite of Kaho'ali'i during the *kapu loulu* rituals of the *luakini heiau* dedication ceremony, when a man impersonating the demigod Kaho'ali'i ate part of god's share, the eyes being a substitute for the entire body. Kaho'ali'i ate the eyes of the man offered in sacrifice as his body was being placed upon the *lele* altar. Kaho'ali'i had the privilege of scooping out the eyes of the human victim and drinking them in a cup of *'awa* on behalf of the god *Ku,* to whom the victim was offered. By this act, the royal companion acquired "divine vision" for himself and his high chief. (Valeri 1985) In the islands of Tahiti, eating of an eye was said to give a high chief powerful vision and in New Zealand, victorious Maori chiefs also ate the eyes of their slain enemy.

The *hono* service was part of the "day of great sacrifice", it began with a procession led by a man carrying an *akua ka'ai* or portable stick god accompanied by the demigod Kaho'ali'i into the forest to obtain evergreen tree branches to decorate the *luakini heiau*. Upon returning the *akua ka'ai* was set into beach sand while chiefs, priests and commoners took a purifying bath in the sea, a *kapu kai*. Each man returned from the sea carrying a piece of coral in his hand symbolizing purification and placed it outside the *luakini heiau,* then entered the *heiau* where they spent the night. The next day, *kahuna* of the *hono* service had the men sit cross-legged in eight rows in the *ne'epu* position with their left leg crossed over their right leg and the palm of their left hand placed over the palm of their right hand, sitting one behind the other as if in a canoe. Each of the eight rows began at one of the *ki'i* images converging at the *lele* altar with the burnt offerings. Their backs were toward the images of their gods only the high chief and the *hono kahuna* faced the gods. The people sat perfectly still in silence looking at the sacrifices and the *hono kahuna* consecrated them by waving *'ie'ie* vines sacred to the god *Ku,* whose woodland deity was known as *Kuka'ie'ie,* then recited the *hono* prayer calling "put up your hands" and all raised their right hands pointing to the place of the gods in heaven. They all prayed in unison careful not to move lest they be put to death. The *hono* prayer consecrating the sacrifices placed upon the *lele* altar lasted up to an hour. ('I'i 1983 [1959])

> "O Ku, O Kunuiakea,
> O Lononuiakea,
> O Kanenuiakea and Kanaloa,
> Here is a gift, a sacrifice; . . .
> A rebel to country, a land grabber.
> Curse those rebels outside and inside.
> Who, with bowed head and pointed finger,
> Plot to take the land.
> Grant life to me, the "ridgepost"
>   of the government.
> And to all the chiefs,
> To the masses, to the people,
> To the kingdom from one end to the other.
> *'Amama*, it is freed.
> The prayer has gone on its way."

(Hono Prayer from *Na Hana a ka Po'e Kahiko = The Works of the People of Old,* 1976, Bishop Museum Special Publication 61, by Samuel M. Kamakau, page 143. Courtesy of Bishop Museum Press, Honolulu)

The day of the *kapapaulua* ceremony was also known as "the day of the great transparent cloth" because after the *hono* prayer two men carrying coconut palm leaves attached them with braided coconut fibers to all four corners of the *lananu'u mamoa* or oracle tower and when all four corners were decorated, the tower was wrapped in a white transparent tapa cloth or *'oloa,* this rite was called the *'aha ho'owilimo'o.* Then, the two men danced to the sound of beating drums, the high chief and his *kahuna nui* entered the *lananu'u mamao* or oracle tower and spoke directly with the gods who took possession of the high priest revealing the future, the *hono* ceremony was now complete. The *hono* rites were the final temple ritual, when they were completed all requirements of the *kapu loulu* dedication of the *luakini heiau* had been met and *kahuna* were able to lift the *kapu*. Now all participants began a transitional process from the world of the divine back to the world of the profane, they "descend from the world of the gods to the world of men". At the beginning of the *kapu loulu luakini* ceremonies, it had been necessary for men to separate themselves from women who were impure in order to establish contact with their divine male gods, now the men re-established contact with women and returned to the secular world outside the *heiau*. All the men gathered at the *Hale o Papa,* mixing with the women where female *ki'i* images had been set up, fires started, dogs and chickens cooked, bananas laid upon the altar and a feast began. With the dedication of the *luakini heiau* completed, the men who took part could now return to their wives, although the *kahuna* of the *luakini heiau* did not associate with women and remained.

Dedication of the *luakini heiau* in the Hawaiian Islands and war rites in the Tahitian Islands closely resembled each other, sacred *'aha* sennit bindings were included in both ceremonies. In the Hawaiian Islands, the man who impersonated Kaho'ali'i ate the eye of the human victim. In the islands of Tahiti, the chief pretended to do the same and both ceremonies included bringing coral from the sea to the temples. In the Tahitian Islands, the chief was girded with a sacred loincloth and in the Hawaiian Islands, it was placed on the *haku 'ohi'a* of the god *Ku*. There are also similarities between the *kapu loulu* dedication ceremonies at the *luakini heiau* of the Hawaiian Islands and initiation ceremonies at the temples of the inland Melanesian Nanga Society on Viti Levu Island of the Fiji Islands. In their *baki* or admission ceremony a priest or *bete* led a procession to the *nanga tambutambu* where a sacred kava bowl filled with water had been placed. The priest dipped a green kava branch into the water and sprinkled each of the young initiates, a ceremony with similarities to those of the *kapu loulu*. As the *kapu loulu* ceremonies proceeded human sacrifice evolved from bloody to "bloodless". (Valeri 1985) The human sacrifice that occurred in the forest during the *haku 'ohi'a* rite was by decapitation and the victim in the *luakini heiau* was probably killed by a blow to the head or was buried alive being placed in the hole where the *haku 'ohi'a* image of *Ku* was erected. Sacrifices occurring after the *haku 'ohi'a* ceremony symbolizing the transformation of the god *Ku* arrived at the *heiau* bloodless, without any evidence of violence. After the transformation of the image of the god *Ku,* sacrificial victims were killed outside the temple grounds because blood was polluting and now must not be spilled inside the *heiau,* these bodies were purified and washed of any traces of blood before being brought inside the *heiau* to be sacrificed upon the altar. (Valeri 1985)

In the Hawaiian Islands human sacrifice or *hai kanaka* was conducted by sanctified priests, it was the consecration of a victim to the gods rather than his execution and generally human victims arrive at the *heiau* already dead. (Valeri 1985) Human sacrifice was the highest form of sacred religious ceremony and was required to be performed only in sacred consecrated locations. When a human victim was sacrificed, he was transformed from the "world of men into the world of the gods . . . establishing a means of communication between the sacred and the profane". The word sacrifice means "to make sacred" and the sacrificial victim acted as a mediator between the sacrificer and the gods. The sacrificer's state was altered when sacred power or *mana* was transferred from the victim to the sacrificer uniting him with the gods. (Hubert and Mauss 1964) For the ritual of human sacrifice to be justified its first purpose must be to affect the conditions of the collective society. (Hubert and Mauss 1964) In the Hawaiian Islands after military conquest, human sacrificial offerings transformed the chaos of war into peaceful order. When an existing vanquished high *ali'i* chief was killed his lands symbolically died with him, they were claimed by the conqueror and divided among his chiefs. When the conquered chief was sacrificed and ritually transformed into a divine being, order and peace were restored to the land and its people, destruction became order and productivity. (Valeri 1985)

Rene Girard, an anthropological philosopher, was born on December 25, 1923, in Avignon, France, and in 1947 he migrated to the United States of America. According to his theory of rivalry and imitation or "mimetic desire", conflict is fundamental to human society and through human sacrifice violent disorder is transformed into peaceful order, the sacrificial victim becomes divine through the power of the sacrifice. In the Hawaiian Islands, the sacrificial victim was seen as the cause of the conflict and became a scapegoat; his death representing a symbolic death of the violent conqueror, transforming him into the new peaceful ruler. The origin of the scapegoat goes back to ancient Israel where on the Jewish Day of Atonement, the high priest laid hands upon the head of a goat, confessed all the iniquities of the children of Israel transferring the sins of the people to the animal that was let lose to wander in the wilderness. For sacrifice to be effective the sacrificer was required to have a personal relationship with the victim and at the end of Hawaiian warfare victims of human sacrifice were often rival *ali'i* brothers. Governing in the Hawaiian Islands often began with fratricide and ended with incest, the destruction of rival brothers and incest with high-ranking sisters demonstrating the divine power and transcendence of the ruler. Incest in Hawaiian society was forbidden to all but a select few, the exception being the small minority of *ali'i* to which incest was a requirement.

> "Hawaiian society is very much based upon war as a means of conquest and internal control. A successful war makes available resources that allow the king [high chief] to maintain the support of a large number of nobles and clients and to acquire more. At the same time, as a show of force, it discourages potential rebels."

> (From *Kingship and Sacrifice, Ritual and Society in Ancient Hawaii,* 1985, by Valerio Valeri, page 348)

The *luakini heiau kapu loulu* ceremonies were symbolic of Hawaiian *ali'i* spiritual and political control, their divine right to rule. The sacrificed vanquished chief was transformed from the profane into the divine; he was consecrated with divine power that was transferred to the victor adding to his *mana* and divinity. The sacrificial rite transformed the victorious conqueror from a violent individual into a legitimate ruler and divine representative of his people restoring life back to the conquered lands. "Now the new lands could become a source of new life, the conqueror could fertilize the new land and its women". (Valeri 1985) *Kapu loulu* rituals were "the ultimate in ceremonial worship in the Hawaiian Islands and for that matter in all Polynesia". *Kapu loulu* ceremonies at the *luakini heiau* transformed participants from the ordinary world of the profane to the extraordinary realm of divine symbolism and terror. These performances with constant chanting, beating of drums and the smell of burnt offerings had an emotional and spiritual impact adding to their understanding of the sacred and *mana* or spiritual power.

Throughout Polynesia political authority and divinity had a foreign origin arriving from beyond the sky. The "stranger kings" appeared from the sea, from beyond the horizon or beyond the dome of the heavens; from Kahiki, land of the gods. The conquering "stranger kings" like the gods needed to be controlled, after seizing power through violent force they were transformed from a state of uncontrolled power into divine, benevolent leaders of society, concerned with the welfare of their people. (Valeri 1985) These new "stranger kings" were coastal sea people, not people of the soil as was the original population, the true owners of the land. Conflict existed between the "native commoners" and conquering "stranger kings", between the land and sea. The "stranger kings" violated the existing moral order committing acts of fratricide and incest. In Hawaiian mythology, the origin of the sacred ruling *ali'i* chiefs began with incest, with the union of Wakea and his daughter Ho'ohokukalani. In Western Polynesia, the origin of the "stranger kings" went back to the Fiji Islands where two population classes developed. The *iTaukei,* originally referred to the inland-dwelling people of the Fiji Islands with simple social organizations who were considered "owners of the land". The term *iTaukei* now applies to the indigenous population. *Turaga,* a Fijian word for man, refers to the chiefly ruling class who were later Proto-Polynesian settlers. The Polynesian *ariki* were coastal sea people with elaborate social organizations who became the sacred chiefs, foreign "stranger kings" arriving from the sea who were identified with the gods. Chiefly dynasties were founded through the union of a "stranger king" and daughter of an indigenous "native" ruler, the "stranger king" married the land and his descendants became gods. The Fijian word for guest is *vulagi* or heavenly god, *vu* means origin, root, or ancestral god and *lagi* means sky. Throughout Island Southeast Asia, there are many accounts of Austronesian-speaking settlers arriving as outsiders with superior knowledge becoming rulers and introducing new political and religious systems that changed society. It was commonplace for an outsider arriving from the sea to be installed as a chief, but their control over the land was limited. In mythology of the islands of Sumatra and Timor in Island Southeast Asia, strangers arriving from the sea became rulers although the indigenous natives remained in control of the land and throughout Melanesia when the more advanced Lapita settlers interacted with the Melanesian population, they became their "stranger kings".

THE MAKAHIKI FESTIVAL: SEASON
OF THE GOD LONO

On Hawai'i Island, the typical Polynesian cultural theme of the conquering "stranger kings" and subjugated "native commoners" was demonstrated in the rituals of the Makahiki festival. Historically, this festival began in the Hawaiian Islands after the Tahitian migrations and development of Hawaiian chiefdoms. For eight months of the year *luakini heiau* were dedicated to *Ku*, Hawaiian god of war, with strict *kapu* or taboo; this was a time of war and human sacrifice. *Ku* originated from *Tu*, Tahitian god of the sea, and was a deity of the conquering "stranger kings". During the four months from late November through March, *luakini heiau* rituals removed the god *Ku* installing *Lono* or *Lonomakua*, god of fertility of the land. It was the winter solstice first-fruits festival of rebirth and renewal, now the kingdom was free from warfare and sacrifices. The god *Ku* who was connected to the *ali'i* and the sea opposed the god *Lono* and the *maka'ainana* or commoners who were associated with the land.

The Polynesian and Hawaiian year was divided into two seasons; *kau*, the dry summer season, and *ho'oilo*, the wet winter season. The Makahiki festival began at the end of the dry or *kau* season. At the latitude of the Hawaiian Islands, appearance of the star cluster Pleiades, *Na Huihui o Makali'i,* "The Nets of Makali'i" or the "Seven Sisters" on the eastern horizon occurred just after sunset on November 17th marking the beginning of the Hawaiian New Year, start of the Makahiki festival and arrival of the winter rainy season or *ho'olo* with its "Kona storms" softening the land for the new planting season. The Pleiades were known throughout Polynesia as the star cluster of Mataliki or Matali'i, *mata* means eyes and *liki* or *li'i* means little. In the Tonga Islands the Pleiadas were known as Mataliki, in Samoa as Matali'i, in Tahiti as Matari'i and by the Maori of New Zealand as Mataraiki, "eyes of the chiefs". There were similar seasonal first-fruits fertility festivals throughout Polynesia that included food offerings, dancing and sporting events. An annual first-fruits festival occurred in the Tonga Islands known as 'Inasi when agricultural produce was distributed for the welfare of the nation, "to ensure the protection of the gods", and in the Samoa Islands there was a sacred first-fruits festival during the month of May dedicated to *Fe'e*, the Samoan octopus god of war brought to the Manu'a Islands by the god *Tagaloa,* when travel was restricted, work ceased and there was feasting and games. In the islands of Tahiti a first-fruits festival, the Parara'a Matahiti in honor of *Romatane*, god of paradise, had many similarities to the Hawaiian Makahiki festival, it was a time of dancing, feasting and sports competitions. In the Fiji Islands, their New Year first-fruits festival occurred in November with the rising of the sea worm or *palolo* to the ocean surface and the harvest period of early maturing yams, before the festival began labor was suspended, noise was not allowed and everyone remained in their houses.

In the Hawaiian legend of Hawai'iloa, Makali'i is the name of the mythical navigator of his canoes and demigod who brought food from Kahiki. There is even a legend where the Pleiades seven star cluster is from where the Hawaiian people first came to earth. In ancient Sumer, Mesopotamia, the Seven Sages appear in the *Epic of Gilgamesh*. In the Indus River Valley of India, the Pleiades were said to be wives of the Seven Sages and the rising of the Pleiades marked the beginning of the Vedic New Year. In the Hawaiian Islands, the rising of the Pleiades in the heavens, also known as the "rainy stars", signified the beginning of the season of growth and abundance. The Hawaiian Makahiki was a New Year and first-fruits festival similar to those found throughout Polynesia and they existed in Proto-Polynesian Austronesian societies. The first-fruits festival reached its greatest development in the Hawaiian Islands where it announced the annual return of the god *Lono* and was a time of peace, extravagant rejoicing and celebration. "The sun had scarcely set when the sound of the conch began to echo through the island increasing as the night advanced." The Makahiki festival began during the first full moon of November after the star cluster Pleiades appeared near the belt of Orion and lasted until the Pleiades star cluster was seen again on the eastern horizon before sunrise in March/April, after the wet season ended. The use of the constellation Pleiades to mark the start of the year goes back as early as 4000 BC, to ancient Sumer, Mesopotamia, in the

Near East when Sumerians held their annual harvest festival celebrating the New Year with feasting, music, singing and dancing. During the Makahiki festival war was taboo or *kapu*, labor was suspended, many religious ceremonies were cancelled and sacrifices consisted only of food offerings. It was a time of feasting, sporting events, and gift giving, when districts competed with each other to offer the most bountiful gifts to their island's main *heiau* to be distributed among the people.

The beginning of the year occurring during the spring equinox of March 20th to 22nd at the end of the winter season was typical of ancient civilizations, but the Hawaiian New Year celebration, the Makahiki festival, occurred at the end of the autumn harvest as though they were facing another frozen winter. Since the Hawaiian Islands are located in the tropics, where crops can be grown year round, this celebration probably originated during a time when ancestors of the Polynesians lived in a temperate climate further north where crops had to be stored before the frost and carried the Pleiades New Year with them into the Pacific Ocean from their ancient Near East homeland. The Dayaks of the island of Borneo also celebrated their New Year at the rising of the Pleiades, as did sea traders of the land of Saba or Sheba on the Southern Arabian Peninsula, now known as Yemen, who celebrated a New Year festival lasting for one month commencing with the rising of the Pleiades in the night sky at which time peace was observed throughout the land. (Hewitt 1907) In the Indus River Valley civilization of ancient India, rising of the Pleiades signified the New Year as it did in Sumer, Mesopotamia. The star cluster Pleiades, also known as the "Seven Sisters", was even depicted in a cave painting of a star map found in the Cave of Lascaux, France dating from 14,500 BC.

The *kapu kuapola* ritual or "rite of the god star Pola" on Hawai'i Island began the annual Makahiki festival. The high chief and his *kahuna nui* gathered at the altar of the Hikiau Heiau along the shore of Kealakekua Bay with the appearance of the star cluster Pleiades after sunset. ('I'i 1983 [1959]) The ritual lasted until sunset the next day and at its conclusion the high chief's coconuts were broken, these were green coconuts and their water symbolized renewal and life. (Kirch 2010) Then, the altar of the Hikiau Heiau was closed freeing the kingdom from warfare and sacrifices during the time of the return of the god *Lono*, appearing in the form of rain during the season of harvest and replanting. That night, everyone feasted and took a purifying bath in the sea. The next day, the image of the Makahiki god, *akua loa* or the "long god", was assembled and decorated and the festival formally began. The image of the god *Lono* was a straight round *kauila* wood pole about twelve feet high and three or four inches in diameter with a carved bird figure at its upper end. A wooden crosspiece or *ke'a* about six feet long was tied to the upper part of the pole and a piece of white tapa or *kapa* cloth, 150 to 200 square feet in size, hung from the *ke'a* representing the sail of the boat upon which the god *Lono* arrived on Hawai'i Island. It was draped with feathered *leis* and *wi,* skins of the *ka'upu* bird or albatross, hung from each end along with fronds of the *pala* fern Hawaiians resorted to in times of famine (Fig. 57).

The *akua loa* was carried in a clockwise direction around Hawai'i Island on the main coastal trail, the *alaloa*, signifying the god *Lono* overseeing the land making a complete tour of the kingdom lasting for twenty-three days. The annual procession led to the border of each *ahupua'a* where a *kahuna* would collect tribute for the god *Lono,* mainly pigs, dogs and fish along with other non-food items including tapa, rope and feathers; anything needed for daily life. The *ho'okupu* were ceremonial offerings to the gods and they were left at the altar or *ahu* symbolizing the god *Lono* upon which was placed the image of the head of a pig or *pua'a*, carved from *kukui* wood and stained red with earth containing iron oxide pigment; this altar was the origin of the word *ahupua'a*. The Makahiki procession was closely connected to the *ahupua'a* land organization that developed into a system of taxation. The *akua poko* or "short god" toured lands of the ruling high chief for four days moving in a counterclockwise direction signifying his loss of power. When the *akua loa*, image of the Makahiki god, returned to the Hikiau Heiau a similar image known as *akua pa'ani* or the "god of sports" was planted in the sand on the beach and the *hi'uwai* or water splashing celebration began (Fig. 57). Fires were lit along the shore all around the island; it was a festival of bathing and unrestrained sexual activity, a time of feasting, dancing and sporting games.

Before the biblical Flood the length of the year was an "ideal" 360 days, 12 months of thirty days as were the Sumerian and Egyptian lunar calendars. After the biblical Flood the Hawaiian lunar calendar year was 12 months of thirty days with an additional five days at the end of each year. The *pa'ani kahiko* or "ancient games" occurred during the additional five days. This was the time to celebrate the coming of the New Year when the *ali'i* and commoners alike warmed and dried themselves at fires, dressed in their best holiday garments of fine tapa and decorated themselves with ornaments, whale tooth pendants and feathered wreaths. The high chiefs who had lost their sovereignty went into seclusion and the high priest or *kahuna nui* was blindfolded during the five days so he could not see the people violating the normal taboos that had been suspended. (Alexander 1891, Makemson 1941) This was the time of the return of *Lono,* when the god of the "native commoners" reclaimed his rule beginning the Makahiki, the Hawai'i Island's New Year and annual first-fruits festival. It was "a time when men, women and chiefs rested abstaining from all work, either on the farm or elsewhere, it was a time of entire freedom from labor" and featured recreational sports, singing, dancing and feasting. (Malo 1951 [1898]) Even the monthly taboo days of the gods were suspended during the Makahiki festival.

The god *Lono i ka* Makahiki or *Lono,* god of the Makahiki, sent his two brothers to find him a wife on earth and at Waipi'o Valley on Hawai'i Island, beside the falls of Hi'ilawe, found the beautiful Kaikilani. Together they lived at Kealakekua Bay, where the god *Lono* lived as a man and high chief who became jealous because of another man's attention to his wife. *Lono* went into a jealous rage striking his wife in the head so violently with a *konane* board she fell dead and afterward, crazed with guilt, he traveled around Hawai'i Island like a madman challenging every man he met to a boxing match or wrestling match. *Lono* had a large triangular canoe built and filled with provisions that required forty men to carry it to its launching place. *Lono* then sailed away to Kahiki, promising to someday return on an "island shaded by trees, covered over by coconuts, swarming with fowl and swine". (Beckwith 1972 [1951]) The Hikiau Heiau was built later along Kealakekua Bay at the location where *Lono* was said to have left Hawai'i Island. Each year a basketwork "tribute canoe" filled with food was set adrift representing the canoe on which *Lono* had departed. The god *Lono* has parallels to *Vishnu*, god of fertility, dancing and sports in the Vedic Indian mythology of the *Rig Veda* and with the Hindu god *Krishna*, an avatar of *Vishnu*. On the last night of the Makahiki festival the crowd left the sea that now became *kapu*. A great bonfire was lit and the following morning canoes were put out to sea with the high chief and others fishing for *'ahi*. When they returned from fishing with the first catch of the year all the male *ali'i* ate fish from the catch renewing their connection to the god *Ku,* who was also a god of fishing. A *kahuna* known as Hua removed and ate an eye from a fish, this was part of the first-fruits ceremony removing the taboo on food from the sea known as the *kalahu'a* rite. (Malo 1951 [1898]) Now, the blindfold covering the eyes of the high priest was removed and the god *Ku* returned to his position of authority. (Malo 1951 [1898])

The *kali'i* ritual re-enacted the foreign origin of the ruling chiefs of Hawai'i Island symbolizing the conflict between "stranger kings" from the sea, from Kahiki beyond the horizon, and "native commoners", owners of the land. *Kali'i* means to act like a king or to strike the king. (Sahilins 1992) In the evening, after the high chief purified himself bathing in the ocean, he and his men paddled out to sea in his canoe, turned around and when they landed, the high chief was dressed in his war attire and an image of the god *Lono* stood on the shore before the Hikiau Heiau surrounded by armed warriors. As the high chief came ashore with his warriors, they were met by a large number of men armed with spears barring their way. A mock battle ensued between warriors of the high chief and those of the god *Lono* in which the high chief was symbolically killed by one of the warriors of *Lono* armed with two spears. He threw one spear at the high chief that was blocked by his champion. The armed warrior approached the high chief touching him with the point of the second spear. The high chief, the "stranger king", had been symbolically sacrificed and transformed from a violent outsider into a domesticated, legitimate ruler. The *kali'i* rite was not only performed during the Makahiki festival, but each time a high chief or high-ranking *ali'i* ceremonially disembarked from his canoe. The *kali'i* rite tested if the rule of a high chief was legitimate. (Valeri 1985) A ceremony similar to the *kali'i* ritual occurred in the Lau Islands of Fiji, where the "stranger king" was symbolically killed, domesticated and reborn as a god who descended upon the land.

The high chief now entered the Hikiau Heiau and sacrificed a pig in honor of the god *Lono*. The Makahiki god, the *akua loa,* was dismantled, wrapped, and put in storage in the *mana* house of the Hikiau Heiau until next year. This was the ritual death of the god *Lono* and the end of the Makahiki season. The Hikiau Heiau was re-consecrated to the war god *Ku* and reopened. Rituals to reactivate the *heiau* included a human sacrifice placed face down on the *lele* altar, in the same prostrate position required in the presence of the high *ali'i* chief. Kaho'ali'i, a demigod and the high chief's companion, swallowed an eye of the sacrificed human victim and one from an *'opelu* fish lifting the taboo against *'opelu* or mackerel fishing, then *aku* or bonito fish became *kapu* and could not be caught for six months. With completion of the *kali'i* rite and re-establishment of the god *Ku* in the *luakini heiau,* the short reign of *Lono*, the carnival king, ended.

The Makahiki festival rite of The Net of Maoloha or *Ke Koko a* Maoloha was a traditional re-enactment originating from the myth of a great famine in ancient times when Waia was high chief of Hawai'i Island. (Malo 1951 [1898]) A net filled with food came down from heaven scattering food over the land. The food was hung out of reach of mankind, but a beneficial rat *'aumakua* climbed up a rainbow, nibbled at the Maoloha net until it broke open and food fell out onto the earth and grew again. In the re-enactment, if any vegetables were caught and remained in the net it was believed there would be famine, but if all the food fell to the ground where it could reproduce the year would be prosperous.

> "Oh Lono, a gift from Tahiti [Kahiki],
> A prayer directed to you oh Lono,
> Oh Lono of the broad leaf,
> Let the low-hanging cloud pour out its rain,
> To make the crops flourish,
> Wring out the dark rain-clouds
> Oh Lono in the heavens.
> Oh Lono shake out a net-full of food, a net-full of rain.
> Rain to make the tapa-plant flourish,
> Gather them together for us.
> Accumulate food oh Lono!
> Collect fish oh Lono!
> Wauke shoots and the coloring matters for tapa.
> *'Amama*. It is free."

(Maoloha Prayer from *Hawaiian Antiquites: Moolelo Hawaii,*
1951 [1898], Bishop Museum Publication 2, by David Malo,
page 233. Courtesy of Bishop Museum Press, Honolulu)

A wicker basket lashed between the two crossbooms of an outrigger canoe known as *wa'a 'auhau*, the "tribute canoe", represented the triangular canoe in which *Lono i ka* Makahiki was said to have returned to Kahiki. Filled with food the *wa'a 'auhau* was towed out to sea and set adrift, symbolically re-enacting *Lono's* departure and ensuring his return the next year. *Lono's* triangular canoe may have been a reference to the stars forming a triangle in the winter sky known as the Winter Triangle. Composed of the stars Betelgeuse, Sirus or the *Lono* god star and Procyon, it was from where *Lono* in his triangular canoe would have sailed to the underworld of *Po* returning the next year. In the mythology of ancient Egypt, the stars of the Winter Triangle were Isis as Sirus, Osiris as Betelgeuse in the constellation of Orion and Horus as Procyon. This was the three-oared boat of the god *Osiris*, held up by *Nun*, god of the primeval waters and father of the Creator/Sun God *Atum* or *Ra*, who ferried the dead to the "Island of Fire" in the Egyptian afterlife, to be judged in the Hall of *Osiris*.

SOURCES OF POLYNESIAN CULTURE

Polynesians reside in some of the most remote and isolated environments on earth although they have complex societies with rich cultures indicating extensive historic interaction and cultural diffusion with ancient civilizations. Polynesian and Hawaiian religious beliefs and rituals were not local developments originating from a single location, but a combination of different cultural elements transported from mankind's ancient civilizations. After migrating out of Island Southeast Asia, through the islands of Melanesia and into Remote Oceania, Polynesians lived on isolated island groups unaffected by outside influences for over two thousand years. Religious practices such as the *huna* originating from ancient Egypt have been preserved in Polynesia. Although Polynesians had a simple material civilization, their religious, mythological beliefs and theories of the origin of the universe were intellectual and highly complex preserving many ancient customs, religious beliefs and mythologies from mankind's distant past. Many Polynesian cultural and religious beliefs, such as their creation mythology, evolutionary theories, temple traditions, images of their gods, chanting and sacrificial altars, had their origins in the ancient Proto-Polynesian homelands of Sumer, Mesopotamia, ancient Egypt and the Vedic civilization of the Indus River Valley. Polynesian mythological literature has historic legends of divine ancestors, heroes and epic tales. Their creation mythology is poetic and philosophical, with the universe coming into being out of the dark void of *Po* through the divine energy or *mana* of a Supreme Creator God. The Hawaiian Supreme Being was known as *'Io* and in Hawaiian mythology mankind was created from the union of Wakea, the sky-father and *Papa*, the goddess/earth-mother. Polynesians developed a pantheon of four major gods with numerous lesser gods as had the Sumerians and the custom of having altars to the family gods located in their homes also goes back to Sumer, Mesopotamia.

The Hawaiian god *Kane*, like the Indian Vedic sky god *Varuna*, elevated the heavens after creation allowing light to enter illuminating the universe. In both Sumerian and Hawaiian mythologies man was created when the gods breathed life into images formed from the soil of the earth. The Polynesian concepts of psychic power or *mana* and taboo originated in Vedic India, as did the Polynesian social system with its inherited aristocracy where the population was born into a specific social class determined by their genealogy. The caste system of Vedic India was first mentioned in the ancient *Rig Veda* with the creation myth of the primeval being Purusha. Polynesians temple complexes contained sacred groves of trees, a custom originating with the Vedic civilization of ancient India, as were sacred baths and temple towers. Sacrificial offerings of produce and animals to the gods took place on fire altars of Vedic India, where religion was based upon sacrifices to the gods. Polynesian temples and household shrines devoted to worship of their ancestral gods containing carved images where spirits of deified ancestors could enter originated from ancient Sumer, Mesopotamia. The spirituality of ancient *huna* tradition, whose origin goes back to ancient Egypt, has been preserved due to the isolation of the islands of Polynesia including the religious concepts of mankind's dual soul, the Binary Soul Doctrine, and psychic power or *mana*. Ancestor worship, the "root of all religions", including veneration of the physical remains of deified ancestors was transported into Polynesia from their ancient homelands going back to the origins of mankind. Polynesian cultural and religious beliefs retain elements from man's vanishing ancient cultural past representing an early age of mankind's development nearer the beginning of human history.

Temple on the Island of Hawai'i, 1816

An ink, wash and watercolor over pencil of the Ahu'ena Heiau, built upon a great stonework platform at the northern end of Kailua Bay, Kailua-Kona, Hawai'i Island, by Louis Choris artist aboard the Russian ship Rurick. Among the figures in the foreground on the beach are thought to be Queen Ka'ahumanu and her stepdaughter. The watercolor is located in the Honolulu Museum of Art, a gift of the Honolulu Art Society, 1944 (12159)

King's Temple in the Bay of Tiritatea
Published in 1822

A hand-colored lithograph by Jean Pierre Norblin de La Gourdaine after Choris from *Voyage Pittoresque Autour Monde*. Courtesy of Private Collection/Bridgeman Art Library, New York

The Ahu'ena Heiau
A painting by Herb K. Kane

The Ahu'ena Heiau dates to before 1812 when King Kamehameha the First took up residence at Kamakahonu and restored the *heiau* site maintaining it until his death in 1819. Courtesy of Herbert K. Kane, LLC

Fig. 47

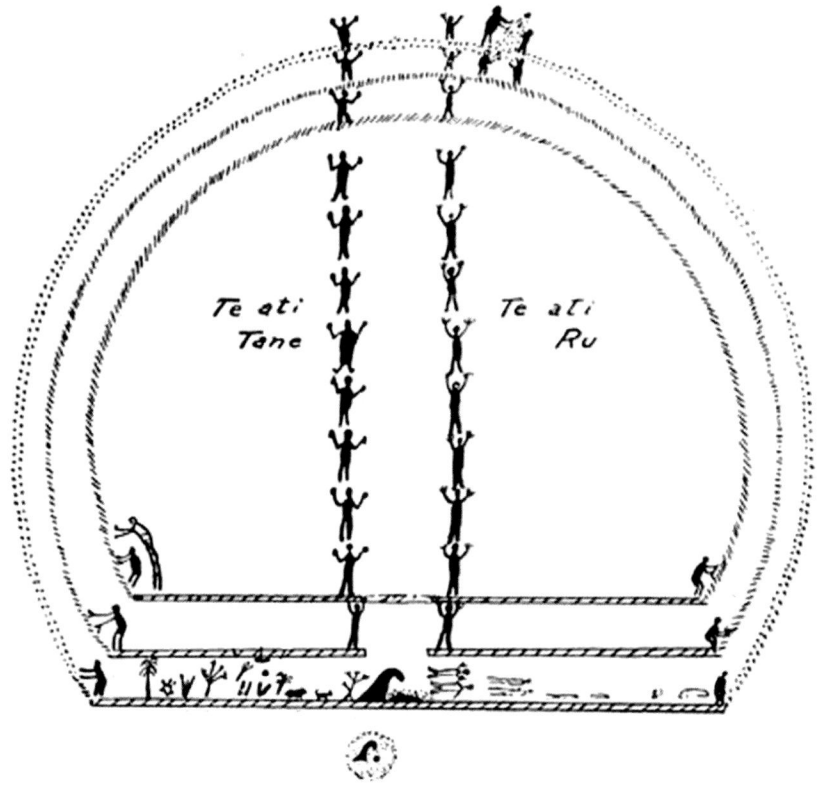

Te ati Tane

Te ati Ru

Caillet Creation Chart of the Tuamotu Islands, 1859

Xavier Caillet was a French naval officer who lived on Anaa Island and became Resident Administrator of the Tuamotu Islands. In the Caillet Creation Chart, probably made in collaboration with Paiore of Anaa Island, the world evolved from an egg shown below the first level containing the god *Te Tumu*, the source or foundation, and the goddess *Te Papa*, the stratum rock. The egg exploded creating three levels of the earth including man, animals and plants. On the first level the sky lay flat upon the earth and sea, then after people greatly multiplied the strong raised the layer above by standing upon each other's shoulders. (Emory 1939, 1940) The drawing is located in the Bishop Museum, Honolulu

Fig. 48 (1)

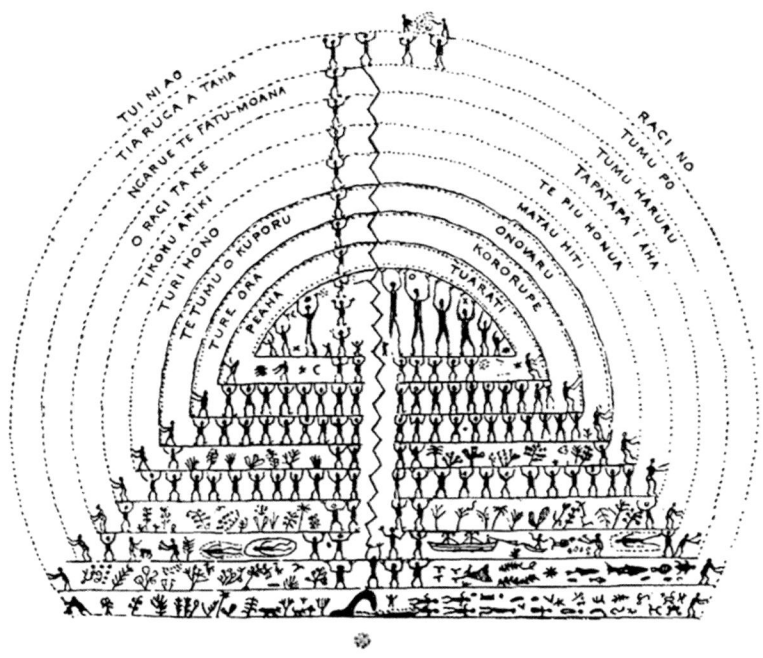

Paiore Creation Chart of the Tuamotu Islands, 1869

A drawing by Paiore, high chief and *tohunga* or priest of Anaa Island, who became Regent of the Tuamotu Islands. It has been said the drawing was first made with a stick in sand and reproduced on paper. It was photographed in 1892 and a copy is in the Bishop Museum, Honolulu. The Paiore chart elaborated on the earlier Caillet chart increasing the levels of creation from three to ten. The circle of dots below the lowest level represents the egg of the unformed universe. The lowest level represents a time when the world was inhabited by animals unknown to Tuamotu Islanders, when the sky lay low over the earth and sea. It shows the first man born without arms who died, a second man born with one arm but with no legs who also died, then a third man who was born perfectly formed. Afterward a woman came and from their union, mankind began (Emory 1939, 1940)

Fig. 48 (2)

ʻIo, the Hawaiian Hawk

An 1899 hand-colored lithograph by Frederick W. Frohawk from *Aves Hawaiienses: The Birds of the Sandwich Islands* by Scott Wilson and A.H. Evans, 1890-1899

An image of ʻIo, the Hawaiian hawk or *buteo solitarius,* from *Report of the Scientific Results of the Exploring Voyage of H.M.S. Challenger during the years 1873-76,* Plate XXI.

ʻIo, the Hawaiian hawk, was the name of the ancient Hawaiian Supreme Being and the animal *ʻaumakua* of Hawaiian *aliʻi*

Fig. 49

Photograph by Charmian Vistaunet

Photograph by Jason Wehmhoener
from *Wikipedia Commons* and in the
public domain

Photograph by Sergi Reboredo

Akua Ki'i, Sacred Images of the Gods at
Pu'uhonua o Honaunau, Hawai'i Island

Fig. 50

 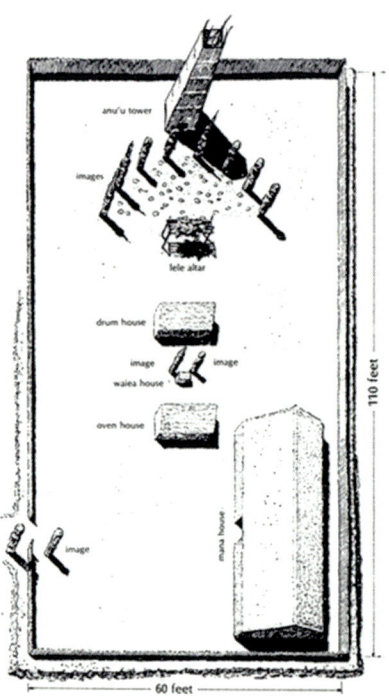

The Luakini Heiau
circa 1810

The *luakini heiau* on the right is a drawing of the Waha'ula Heiau on Hawai'i Island by Paul Rockwood depicted in *Fragments of Hawaiian History* by John Paul 'I'i and the *luakini heiau* on the left is the Papa'ena'ena Heiau from "Hawaiian Feudalism" by William H. Davenport. The plan of the Papa'ena'ena Heiau is from early descriptions, it stood at the foot of Le'ahi or Diamond Head overlooking Waikiki Beach on the island of O'ahu. The Waha'ula Heiau contained a *lananu'u mamao* tower with a row of eight large *akua ki'i* or sacred carved wooden idols located in front of the tower surrounding the *lele* or altar and *akua ki'i* also guarded the *heiau* entrances. The *hale pahu* or drum house was where drums of the gods were kept which were sounded each morning at dawn. The largest house in a *luakini heiau* was the *hale mana* with an open front facing the *heiau* entrance. The *hale imu* or oven house was located adjacent to the *hale mana*. The *hale wai ea* was a small house located between the *hale imu* and *hale pahu* with two wooden *ki'i* idols, one standing on either side, and the high chief and his *kahuna nui* conducted *'aha* ceremonies from the *hale wai ea* before dawn

Fig. 51

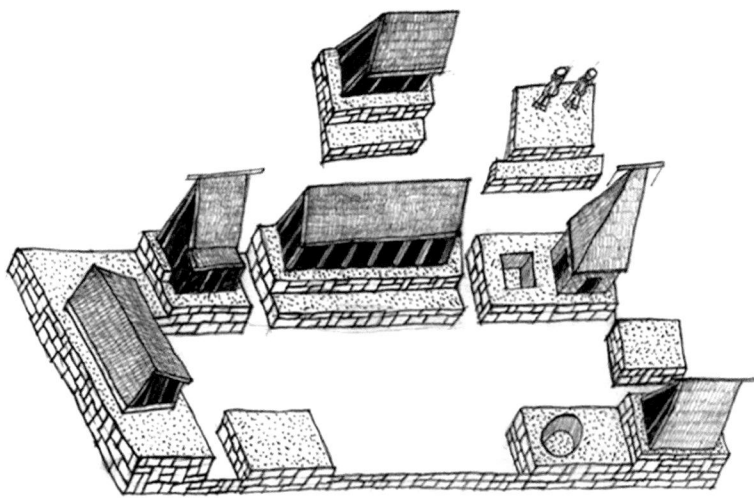

A drawing of a reconstruction of the Marquesas *tohua,* a tribal assembly area and dance floor surrounded by stone terraces with viewing sheds for chiefs, warriors, and important visitors including a sacred place containing a *me'ae* or temple with a priest's house, an oracle tower, and *tiki*

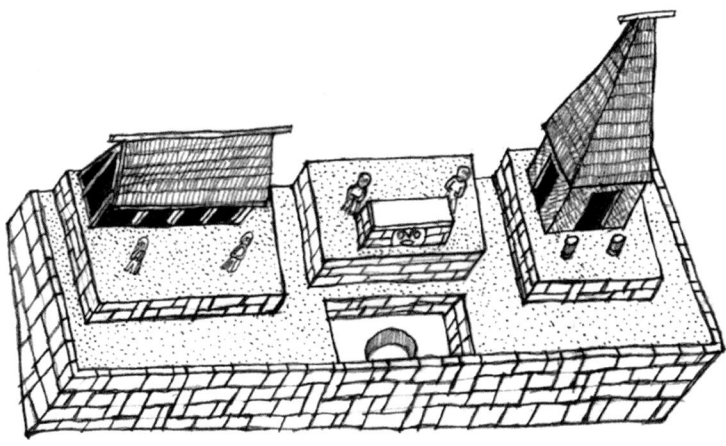

A drawing of a reconstruction of the Marquesas *me'ae* or temple with houses for priests, an oracle tower, sacrificial pit, and *tiki*

Marquesas Tohua and Me'ae

Fig. 52

**A Fijian Bure Kalou at the Polynesian Cultural
Center, O'ahu Island, Hawaiian Islands**
Photograph by Rhea Sencio

Bure Kalou Na Vata-ni-Tawake, Mbau, Fiji
Illustration from *Fiji and the Fijians, Vol. II:
Mission History* by James Calvert, 1858

Fijian *bure kalou* were traditional temples to Fijian gods, *Kalou-Vu* were root gods and *Kalou-Yalo* were deified mortals and lesser spirits, and a *bete* or priest resided at the *bure kalou*

Fig. 53 (1)

Bure Kalou Na Tavasara, Taviuni, Fiji

Bure Kalou Na Utuutu, Rotuma Island
Illustrations from *Fiji and the Fijians, Vol. I:*
The Islands and Their Inhabitants by Thomas Williams, 1858

Fijian *bure kalou*, traditional spirit houses or temples, are tall ceremonial rectangular structures sitting on stone-faced platforms. Although built for religious purposes they also functioned as armories, counsel, and reception halls

Fig. 53 (2)

The Inside of the House, in the Morai, in Atooi, 1777

A watercolor of the interior of the *hale mana* or *mana* house in the *luakini heiau* in Waimea on Kaua'i Island by John Webber, artist on James T. Cook's third voyage into the Pacific Ocean, from *Cook and King 1784, Atlas.* Courtesy of the Mitchell/Dixson Library, State Library of New South Wales, Sydney

An 1818 hand-colored version by Gallo Gallina of the 1783 engraving by Edmond Scott after the 1777 watercolor by John Webber. Courtesy of the Alexander Turnbull Library, Wellington, New Zealand

Fig. 54

© Canterbury Museum
Christchurch, New Zealand -
All rights reserved

Courtesy of the Bishop
Museum, Honolulu

Hawaiian Pahu Prayer Drums

Images of two sacred Hawaiian *pahu* prayer drums. The drum on the left features human images with flexed knees in the *ha'a* dance position holding an *'aha* cord above their head

Fig. 55

The Manaiakalani Fishhook
Photograph by David Franzen

A copy of the sacred Manaiakalani fishhook, legendary "fishhook from heaven" constructed of wood with a bone tip. Courtesy of the Bishop Museum, Honolulu

Fig. 56

The Makahiki Festival
A painting by Herb Kawainui Kane

The annual procession of the Makahiki Fesrival. The *akua loa banner,* god of the Makahiki Festival, was carried around the shoreline for 23 days each year. Courtesy of Herbert K. Kane, LLC

Boxing Match before Cook [Hawaii], circa 1779
Photograph by Christine Takata

An ink and watercolor drawing by John Webber of the Makahiki Festival when *akua pa'ani,* the god of sports, was planted in the beach sand during *pa'ani kahiko,* the ancient games. Courtesy of the Bishop Museum, Honolulu

Fig. 57

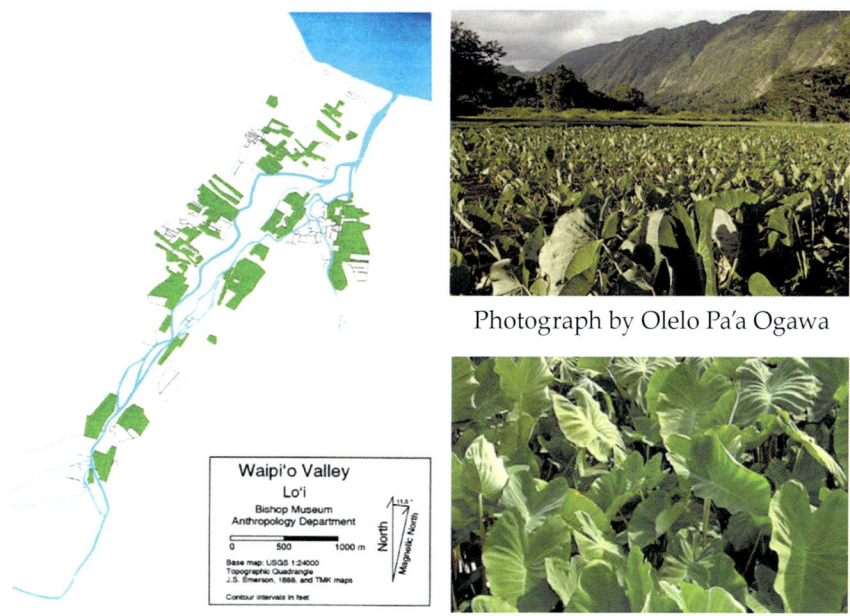

Photograph by Olelo Pa'a Ogawa

Courtesy of the Bishop Museum
Anthropology Department, Honolulu

Lo'i or Taro Pondfields in Waipi'o Valley
Photograph by Noel Morata

Chapter 7

Agriculture And Population

O my god of the maturing of the taro,
O Ku-of-joint-effort,
In the morning our taro will be pulled up,
Clustered together, carried on poles;.
The imu for the taro will be lighted, . . .
The taro baked in the imu,
The imu opened, the taro peeled;
Our taro will be pounded, placed in a calabash;
It will be mixed, this taro of ours –
And of Ku-of-joint-effort.
Firewood will be chopped, the imu lighted.
Men, women and children will eat . . .
Of the poi, of our taro,
The mighty planter's and yours,
O Ku-of-joint-effort. . . .
That life may be given to the earth.
'Amama, the kapu is freed;
The prayer has gone on its way.

(Prayer for the *taro* harvest from *Na Hana a ka Po'e Kahiko = The Works
the People of Old* by Samuel M. Kamakau, 1992 [1976], Bishop
Museum Special Publication 61, pages 36, 37. Courtesy
of Bishop Museum Press, Honolulu)

*Viewed from the great elevation at which we stood, the charming valley, spread out beneath us like a map, with
its numerous inhabitants, cottages, plantations, fish ponds, and meandering streams, (on the surface of which
the light canoe was moving to and fro) appeared in in beautiful miniature. . . . The next morning unveiled to
view the extent and beauty of the romantic valley. Its entrance from the sea, which was blocked up with
sand-hills, fifty or sixty feet high, appeared to be a mile or a mile and a half wide. The summits of the hills,
which bordered the valley, seemed 600 feet above the level of the sea. They were nearly perpendicular, yet
they were mostly clothed with grass, and low straggling shrubs were here and there seen amidst the jutting
rocks. A number of winding paths led up their steep sides, and, in several parts, limpid streams flowed, in
beautiful cascades, from the top to the bottom, forming a considerable stream, which, meandering along the
valley, found a passage through the sand-hills, and emptied itself into the sea. The bottom of the valley was
one continued garden, cultivated with taro, bananas, sugar-cane, and other productions of the islands, all
growing luxuriantly. Several large ponds were also seen in different directions, well stocked with excellent
fish. A number of small villages, containing from twenty to fifty houses each, stood along the foot of the
mountains, at unequal distances on each side, and extended up the valley till projecting cliffs obstructed the
view. . . . I proceeded about a mile and a half along the south side of the valley, to the village of [Napo'opo'o],
containing forty-three houses.*

(From the *Journal of William Ellis: A Narrative of an 1823
Tour of Hawaii, or Owyhee*, 1963 [1826], by
William Ellis, pages 266, 268)

*From the lofty precipice on the south-east of Waipio, I had an enchanting view of a Hawaiian landscape of
singular beauty and grandeur, embracing . . . the deep and charming valley below; the dwelling-place of twelve
or fifteen hundred inhabitants . . . the numerous garden-like plantations of bananas, sugar cane, potatoes, the
cloth plant, and kalo [taro], in the different stages of advancement, from recent planting to maturity, some with
narrow, and some with broad green leaves of different shades, embossed upon silvery water . . . the unruffled
fishponds; the quite hamlets near the cliffs, the small scattered thatched huts of the inhabitants, with their low
and diminutive doors, the tents of traveling chiefs, pitched near the sand banks at the sea shore.*

(From *A Residence of Twenty-One Years in the Sandwich Islands,*
2013 [1848], by Hiram Bingham describing Waipi'o Valley
as a lush agricultural area in 1830, pages 379, 380)

*We came suddenly to the verge of a pali [cliff], about 1,000 feet deep, with a narrow fertile valley below, with
a yet higher pali on the other side. The prospect below us was very charming, a fertile region perfectly level,
protected from the sea by sand hills, watered by a winding stream, and bright with fishponds, meadow lands,
[taro] patches, orange and coffee groves, figs, breadfruit, and palms.*

(From *Six Months in the Sandwich Islands*, 1998 [1873], by Isabella
Bird upon first sighting Waipi'o Valley, page 91)

THE EARLY SETTLEMENTS ON HAWAI'I ISLAND

The Hawaiian Islands include eight main populated islands; Hawai'i Island is the largest with a land area of 4038 square miles and was the most heavily populated island during pre-contact times. Early settlements on Hawai'i Island were small founding populations located along the well-watered windward or *ko'olua* coast, concentrated near the mouth of river valleys. These fertile valleys had reliable sources of water, high rainfall and perennial streams. When ocean trade winds arriving from the northeast reach the mountain ridges their moisture falls as rain, creating ravines and valleys, streams reaching the sea with waterfalls hundreds of feet high and luxurious tropical growth.

Of the valleys along the Kohala Coast of West Hamakua, Hawai'i Island, Waipi'o Valley is the largest receiving over 100 inches of rain annually and was the site of one of the initial settlements on Hawai'i Island beginning with a population of perhaps as few as 100 individuals occurring between AD 300 and AD 400, possibly as early as 50 BC to AD 125. Waipi'o Valley's original Marquesas or Hiva Island population first settled along the edge of the sea surviving on the abundant marine resources of fish, shellfish, sea turtles and seaweed. Cultural remains such as fishhooks, other fishing artifacts and shells indicate a maritime economy. Upon their arrival on Hawai'i Island, early settlers found only a limited number of native plants suitable for food, but their voyaging canoes carried the supplies necessary for their future survival. They carried food plants for replanting including roots, shoots, seeds and cuttings, as well as plant materials for housing, utensils, containers, fiber and medicine. The domesticated animals they transported including pigs, dogs and chickens were bred and multiplied. Most major economic plants and animals reaching Polynesia had their origin in Island Southeast Asia and Melanesia and were dispersed by man. They had been transported through Melanesia to the Fiji Islands, the islands of Tonga and Samoa and into Central and Eastern Polynesia.

Hawai'i Island's tropical climate and rich volcanic soil made it ideal for the transplantation of crops and its original Polynesian settlers introduced *koa,* coconut or *nui, noni* breadfruit or *'ulu, 'ie'ie* bananas or *mai'a,* sugarcane or *ko,* arrowroot or *pia,* taro or *kalo,* sweet potato or *'uala,* and paper mulberry or *wauke.* It is believed the original Polynesian settlers, including those who arrived after canoes had been sent back to their homeland and returned, brought as many as twenty-nine introduced plant species to the Hawaiian Islands. Waipi'o Valley is an ideal location for agriculture, it has a wide, flat floor of alluvial soil and being on the windward side of Hawai'i Island, a stable, constant source of water from the high annual rainfall. The windward side of Hawai'i Island always receives the most rain. Water flowing through the Wailoa River system of Waipi'o Valley is perennial, its primary water source are streams whose headwaters are located at the upper end of the valley. They are the Kawainui, Alakahi, Kiawa or Ko'iawe and Waima Streams that flow year-round and are fed by both their watershed and extensive groundwater. Behind these upper tributary valleys are dense dike formations from an ancient caldera that collects great volumes of groundwater in elevated reservoirs. (Stearns and MacDonald 1946)

THE POLYNESIANS REACH THE AMERICAS

Although most of the food plants of the Hawaiian Islands originated from Island Southeast Asia, there were exceptions such as the sweet potato, known as *'uala* in the Hawaiian Islands and *kumara* throughout Southern Polynesia. The sweet potato was probably first transported from South America to Easter Island about AD 400, as suggested by Thor Heyerdahl, carried to the Marquesas Islands by about AD 700, and from there dispersed throughout Polynesia reaching the Cook Islands by AD 1000 and the Hawaiian Islands by AD 1200, where it made possible the development of dry field agriculture. The place of origin of the sweet potato or *Ipomoea batatas* found in Polynesia was Ecuador and Northern Peru in South America, where it has been dated back to 8000 BC, its name in the Quechua language of the Andes region is *kumar* or *cumar.* First noticed in 1866 by German botanist Berthold Seemann (1825-1871), the Southern Polynesian words for the sweet potato, *kumala* and *kumara*, are almost identical to its name in South America. Other words in the native South American Quechua language of the Andes region are similar or identical to words in Eastern Polynesia such as *awki* for chief or grandparent that is *ariki* in Polynesia. In Peru *apay* means to carry, in Polynesia it is *hapai* and *kiri* means skin in both languages. The bottle gourd found in Polynesia had been domesticated in the Americas about 7900 BC, probably along coastal Peru and later in Eastern Asia about 5000 BC, although bottle gourds from Asia probably arrived in Island Southeast Asia and Melanesia after Polynesian settlers had already reached Remote Oceania. The bottle gourd or *lagenaria siceraria* was probably introduced into Eastern Polynesia about AD 1000, originating from Peru, South America. It was known throughout Polynesia by the name *kimi*, the same name used in ancient Peru. The red chili pepper, whose origin was also South America, reached Hawai'i Island by AD 1100. A celebrated red chili pepper tree that grew at the Paka'alana Heiau in Waipi'o Valley was known as *ka nioi wela o* Paka'alana or the burning *nioi* tree of Paka'alana. The origin of the papaya was Southern Mexico or Central America and the place of origin of the pineapple was Brazil in South America.

There is a legend in the Marquesas Islands, recorded by E.S. Craighill Handy in 1930, of a large double-hull canoe named Kaahua leaving the island of Hiva Oa, voyaging eastward toward the rising sun in search of new lands or *he fenua imi* and arriving at Tefiti or Jefiti, a foreign place probably along the coast of Northern Peru or Ecuador. In another legend of the Marquesas Islands, the coconut is said to have been brought from a land far to the east called Ootoopoo by a god named *Tao.* (Porter 1823) In a legend from Ra'iatea Island, Tahiti, an expedition sailing east passed Easter Island reached "a land of ridges", probably Peru and the Andes Mountains. In 1609, Garcilaso de la Vega recorded a legend where a people described as "giants" landed along the coast of Peru in a large fleet. These voyagers were either Polynesians or Caucasians originating from the city of Harappa in the Indus River Valley of India. According to their oral history, Gilbert Islanders of Micronesia discovered South America in their distant past, it was a vast land far to the east, "farther away than all the islands to the eastward", and they referred to it as Maiwa. Sighting the Andes Mountains, they called them "the wall at the side of the world . . . a land that stretches to the north without end and to the south without end . . . a wall of mountains up against the place where the sun rises". (Grimble 1972) To the Gilbert Islanders a continent was a barrier whereas the ocean was a highway.

There is evidence Polynesians had prehistoric contact with the Americas long before the arrival of Europeans. Voyages to the coast of the Americas from the Hawaiian Islands were first described by English missionary William Ellis in 1823 and the *Chant of Kuali'i,* recorded by Abraham Fornander in 1878, described a voyage to Kahiki, a foreign land far to the east where the people were not like Hawaiians and spoke a strange language; this was clearly not the islands of Tahiti and was most likely North America. The Chumash Indians located along the Southern California Coast in the area of the Santa Barbara Channel Islands and later the neighboring Gabrielino Indians, built sewn-plank canoes unique to native America indicating influence from Polynesia. The Chumash word for sewn-plank canoe, *tomolo'o, tumula'o* or *tumulaa'au*, was derived from the Hawaiian word for the wood used in their construction, *kumula'au* means tree trunk. Redwood and pine tree logs that floated from North America to the Hawaiian Islands had been used for canoe hulls. Since the nineteenth century, it has been noted the two-piece shell fishhooks used by the Chumash Indians were similar to those found in Polynesia and a ceremonial headdress of Polynesian design found with the Chumash Indians has been radiocarbon dated to AD 601. The first queen of the Chumash Nation was named Lahui and the word *lahui* in the Hawaiian language means nation. (Jones and Klar 2005)

Polynesians had contact with the indigenous Mapuche "people of the land" along the south central coast of Chile, South America. Sewn-plank canoes of Polynesian design known as *dalcas* were used by a group of Mapuches on Chiloe Island known as the Huilliche and they used the name *curanto* for an earthen oven derived from the Polynesian underground oven, the *imu,* or *umu.* Polynesian polished stone adzes found on Mocha Island, also off the coast of Chile, South America, are known by the Polynesian name *toki* and during December, 2007, several human skulls with Polynesian features were found on Mocha Island. Chicken bones have been found at El Arenal near Chile's Arauco Peninsula, containing DNA matching chickens from the islands of Tonga and American Samoa, possibly dating from as early as AD 700. On Easter Island, there is a *totora* reed plant that grows in freshwater of the three volcanic crater lakes and the origin of the *totora* reed is Peru. There is a tradition on Easter Island of the reed plant arriving with their early ancestors and being first planted within Rono Kao Crater and there are *toromiro* trees on Easter Island whose origin is Chile. (Barrau 1963)

FOOD FROM THE SEA

The original Hawaiians settlers were dependent upon the sea for subsistence. They employed intensive marine exploitation with much their dietary protein coming from seafood and gathered seaweed or *limu*. Meat from pig and dog was a more infrequent source of protein. Fishermen or *lawai'a* fished the deep offshore coastal waters. The near shore rocky coastal shallows were where women and children combed tidal pools and shallow shoreline waters. Fishing by hand or with baskets they collected fish and shellfish such as limpets or *'opihi* from the rocks, seaweed or *limu,* sea cucumbers, sea urchins and crabs. Cowry shells and conch shells were used for meat and conch shells were made into shell trumpets. Men fished shoreline pools with a spear, hook and line, and nets fishing by torch light at night, women also fished along the banks of rivers and streams catching several types of fish or *i'a*, crabs or *papa'i*, lobsters or *ula*, eels or *puhi* and shrimp or *'opae*. Baskets traps made from *'ie'ie* vines using food as bait caught fish and shrimp. Nets and fishing lines were made from the inner bark of the *olona* plant and fishhooks were made of bone or shell. At night, six-foot-long spears made from the hardwood called *kauila* were used in combination with *lama* or torches made from sections of bamboo using *kukui* nuts for fuel, fish were attracted to the light of the torches. Long, narrow community fishing nets or *hukilau*, were spread in a large circle near shore. *Huki* means to pull and *lau* means leaf, *ki* or ti leaves were attached to the top of the nets and their movement in the ocean current frightened the fish driving them toward shore and then the two ends of the net were pulled ashore trapping the fish, *hukilau* nets were possessions of the *ali'i*. Fish poison or *hola* was sometimes used, made from the poisonous *'auhuhu* plant or bark of the *'akia* tree, it was placed under stones in tidal pools fish would frequent as well as in streams. The powerful toxin would stun the fish, they would float to the surface and be collected. In the Marquesas or Hiva Islands, the fruit of the *hutu* tree was used as a toxin to shock fish. Salt or *pa'akai* was collected through evaporation, seawater was left in shallow ponds to evaporate becoming brine and was then placed in man-made saltpans.

THE SETTLEMENT OF WAIPI'O VALLEY

When early Polynesian voyaging canoes landed on an uninhabited island and permanent occupation was decided upon by a voyaging chief, he would devise a settlement plan to determine the location of their initial settlement in relation to freshwater, fertile soil and maritime resources. Polynesian societies were based upon shared resources ensuring mutual survival on remote and isolated islands. At first, Hawai'i Island was settled by a small population from only several canoes carrying food plants and domesticated animals, they inhabited the narrow windward coastal strips of land where freshwater was plentiful, such as Waipi'o Valley. The early settlements were independent chiefdoms with genealogical bonds of kinship through common ancestry. Hereditary chiefs controlled the distribution of food and wealth for the common good. Social hierarchy was minimal having a low population density with arable land and water being plentiful. The chief would divide lands among the heads of families, look after his people and intercede with the gods on their behalf. Their settlements expanded along the coastal strip, developing into semi-independent chiefdoms dependent upon the abundant marine resources for survival with their introduced food plants providing limited agriculture.

As their population increased they expanded inland into fertile agricultural areas as early as AD 600 and then the unique Hawaiian culture and language began to evolve. As permanent inland settlements were established, the first settlers survived on meat of the abundant birds easily captured, their eggs and any edible plants and berries that could be found. The large flightless *moa nalo* goose was easily captured and soon became extinct. They cleared the dense existing vegetation planting crops the original settlers had transported in the well-watered alluvial soil of Waipi'o Valley. The initial settlers were almost totally dependent upon the sea for their subsistence until their crops became plentiful and the domesticated animals they transported reproduced in sufficient numbers to allow for expansion of settlements inland from the sea into a land-based economy. An extended family *'ohana* management system evolved around the developing agricultural fields. The first settlers built *'auwai* irrigation ditches with simple tools, they modified natural stream flows devising new routes to carry a constant flow of freshwater gradually downhill to their *lo'i* or taro pondfields and housing sites. As the population expanded inland, they developed systems of land management and water control using knowledge acquired even prior to their settlement of Polynesia. After they developed an extensive irrigation system, pondfields were increased to support larger more concentrated settlements and inland expansion advanced further up the valley eventually reaching the forested upland. They created the *ahupua'a* land organization ending their coastal dependence leading to an economically self-sufficient agricultural society. The lands of an *ahupua'a* typically included a valley stream supplying freshwater and extended from the mountains to the sea and out to an offshore reef. Its boundaries were generally defined by topographic features such as hills or *pu'u*, ridges, valleys and craters or by areas of specific vegetation and were strictly enforced. Resources within the *ahupua'a* were restricted to its inhabitants and violators were often killed. Residences were able to exchange goods and services through a distribution system between *'ohana* groups, some living in the upland regions and others located along the coast. (Kirch 2010)

A period of dramatic population growth and expansion began about AD 1050, time of the Tahitian migrations. The windward valleys of the Hawaiian Islands became densely populated with inland settlements requiring more complex water management systems to support the increasing population that could provide the labor force necessary for large public works projects. Irrigated *kalo* or taro was introduced in nearly every valley containing a permanent stream. Native lowland forests of *loulu* palms were cleared and agricultural production increased. (Dye 1994) In Waipi'o Valley, an intensive large-scale irrigation system developed and the entire floor of the valley became a complex network of irrigated taro pondfields or *lo'i* watered by long irrigation channels or *'auwai;* it was one of the most extensive taro wetlands in the Hawaiian Islands. Terracing allowed for expansion of irrigated pondfields, enlargement and construction of large fishponds increased the population. "The people and the land prospered as a sophisticated civilization developed, including the largest network of wet land taro fields and hundred acre fishponds, ever found anywhere in the world." Irrigation systems were high labor investments creating a political organization of ownership and control within the Hawaiian chiefdoms. Increases in agricultural production created a highly specialized society supporting hereditary chiefs, priests, warriors and craftsmen created by the Polynesian genealogical ranking system.

WAIPI'O VALLEY EVOLVES INTO AN ARCHAIC STATE

With the combination of Tahitian *ari'i* social ranking and structure of the *ahupua'a* economic system, Hawai'i Island's initial society based on traditional kinship with a minimal distinction between chiefs and commoners, evolved from a "complex chiefdom" into a primitive "archaic state" or "stratified feudal society" with a more centralized government unique to Polynesia and due to the isolation of the Hawaiian Islands, it was not influenced by any adjacent culture. (Kirch 2010) Hawai'i Island society became organized into an *ali'i* pyramidal genealogical ranking system with status determined by one's genealogical closeness to the high chief who ruled with divine authority. Socioeconomic classes developed separating the elite ruling *ali'i* from the *maka'ainana* or commoners and a system of economic redistribution determined all goods produced throughout the *ahupua'a* were under direction of the *ali'i ai ahupua'a* who controlled economic trade, from food of the sea, inland agricultural harvest, to products of the forests. Land rights were altered, now all lands within the *ahupua'a* came under state control and were owned by high *ali'i* chiefs, the separation between chiefs and commoners widened.

The boundaries of the *ahupua'a* formed the economic and social world of the *maka'ainana,* but activities of the *ali'i* encompassed the entire Hawaiian Archipelago. (Hommon 1976) "The *maka'ainana* were the fixed residences of the land; the chiefs were the ones who moved from place to place". (Malo 1951 [1898]) As population and food production increased and *ali'i* chiefs acquired more prestige and political power, they were able to mobilize large labor forces capable of constructing and maintaining large royal residential centers, massive *heiau* structures, extensive irrigation systems and fishponds, and an *ahupua'a* taxation system capable of funding their construction. In the Hawaiian Islands productive agriculture was achieved with help from the gods and *ho'oulu 'ai heiau* were where first-fruits offerings were made to ensure a successful season of crops. Hawai'i Island developed a state religion authorizing the political and social order, along with a full-time priesthood performing human sacrifices inside walled temples where commoners were excluded. *Ali'i* control was maintained through agricultural production and military power, *ali'i* chiefs were capable of drafting a standing army with large numbers of warriors enabling wars of territorial conquest. During the "Little Climate Optimum" from AD 900 to AD 1250, Hawaiian agricultural production increased, but the "Little Ice Age" from AD 1350 to AD 1800 created climatic changes causing a reduction in food resources and then the only method available to ensure economic security was territorial expansion and war. (Hommon 1976, Nunn 1999) Chiefly control originally based on genealogical kinship bonds became based on military power and territorial expansion through conquest, frequently breaking the bonds of kinship. (Kirch 2010) The sociopolitical system that developed in the Hawaiian Islands became the most complex in all of Polynesia with an elaborate inherited genealogical ranking system and an increase in pyramidal social stratification. (Kirch 2010) *Ali'i* high chiefs ruled by divine right, controlling the land and craft specialists who produced prestige items such as magnificent feathered cloaks and helmets reinforcing the high chief's divine status. Tahitian *ari'i* conquerors, who had been the third wave of Proto-Polynesians from Island Southeast Asia and migrated through the low islands and atolls of Micronesia, became depended upon the sea for survival not upon the land and *ali'i* took control of marine resources leaving agriculture to the "native commoners". In the Hawaiian Islands, commoners or *maka'ainana* retained control of the land, but were required to provide tribute or *ho'okupu* of labor and large amounts of food, tapa, feathers for cloaks and helmets, woven mats and wooden containers to the *ali'i*. The "chiefs came from the gods, commoners merely came from the earth".

THE LO'I TARO PONDFIELDS, 'AUWAI IRRIGATION CHANNELS AND FISHPONDS OF WAIPI'O VALLEY

"Waipi'o Valley developed as a typical windward settlement but on a vastly larger scale. Fishing and the collecting of shellfish from the sea were widely practiced, but also an extensive system of aquaculture was developed. *Loko* was a general Hawaiian term for any type of enclosed body of water. In contrast to the rest of Oceania, the Hawaiian Islands claimed a sophisticated aquaculture system . . . Fishponds existed nowhere else in the Pacific in types and numbers as in prehistoric Hawai'i."

(From *Hawaiian Aquacultural Systems*, 1973, PhD dissertation,
University of Arizona, Tucson, by William K. Kikuchi)

A system of intensive wet taro production developed with irrigation channels or *'auwai* diverting stream flow into stone-lined pondfields or *lo'i, 'au* means flow or current and *wai* means water. Wet taro production requires flowing water and Hawaiians became experts at constructing terraced wet taro pondfields or *lo'i* and conducting water through irrigation channels or *'auwai*. Knowledge of irrigation control for agriculture goes back at least to 6000 BC, to the ancient 'Ubaid civilization in Mesopotamia. The Tigris and Euphrates Rivers did not overflow their banks as the Nile River in Egypt did and the 'Ubaids developed advanced systems of irrigation and canal construction. In Waipi'o Valley, *'auwai* were constructed to divert water from a stream, pool or spring into irrigation channels moving it gradually downhill causing a minimum of erosion. If the slope of an *'auwai* was steep its embankments would be lined with stone and *'auwai* were constantly maintained to prevent soil and debris from impeding water flow. Water was fed into *lo'i* pondfields through an inlet including a dam or *mano* made of loose stone, earth, and grass. Only half the volume of *'auwai* water was diverted and inlets into each *lo'i* could be shut off with stones when the *lo'i* was flooded. The construction and maintenance of irrigation systems and fishponds were supervised by a *konohiki* and approved by a *luna wai*, a specialist who controlled water distribution and channel maintenance. *Konohiki* were lower-ranking *kaukau ali'i* (Kameieleihiwa 1992) who managed lands of the *ahupua'a* on behalf of the ruling chief who they were often related to. Taro *lo'i* were communal projects and tenants of taro pondfields held water rights to the irrigation system and were required to maintain the dams and channels or lose their rights.

An *'auwai* or irrigation channel was dug from its lower end upward and on the day when it was time to divert stream water to the *'auwai*, an *'aha'aina laulima* or feast of many hands was held. The *kahuna* set the date and the *konokihi* brought a large pig and *poi* for all the workers, a red fish and *'awa* root was brought for the *kahuna* who presided over the opening ceremonies. When the building of the *'auwai* was complete a stream dam or *mano* was built. An *imu* was dug in the *'auwai* near the point where the water was to enter and the pig was cooked. Everyone feasted along the banks of the new *'auwai*, then the dam was opened and water flowed into the new *'auwai* over the *imu*. (From Ancient Hawaiian Water Rights. In the *Hawaiian Almanac and Arrival for 1894* by Thomas G. Thrum)

Man-made freshwater fishponds were *koko i'a; loko wai* were natural freshwater fishponds located inland from the shore and *loko kuapa* were fishponds constructed in shallow seawater with a rock wall or *kuapu* built in an arc from the shoreline enclosing a portion of the ocean with as many as seven sluice gates or *makaha* allowing circulation. *Loko 'ume'iki* were shore ponds with walls built in an arc upon coral reefs that were submerged at high tide allowing fish to enter with numerous open stone-lined channels leading in and out of the fishpond. Nowhere else in Polynesia was aquaculture developed to the extent as in the prehistoric Hawaiian Islands, Waipi'o Valley had a large number of fishponds including both an inland brackish water fishpond or *loko pu'uone* connected to the sea by a river and freshwater fishponds or *loko i'a* fed by streams and waterfalls. There were two major fishponds located directly behind the ancient sand dune burial mounds at the front of Waipi'o Valley. On the eastern or Hilo side of the valley was the large Lakakea fishpond that still exists today, it contained brackish water and was connected to the sea by the Wailoa River. *Lalakea* means white-fin or white-tip shark and both *pua 'ama'ama* or gray mullet and *pua awa* or milkfish thrive in brackish water. A narrow stationary *makaha* or sluice gate constructed of straight hardwood uprights tied to cross members with sennit cordage was installed between the pond and the river ensuring a constant flow of water. Brackish water fishponds had from one to four *makaha* gates, although the Lakakea fishpond had only one. Openings in the gate allowed young fish hatched at sea to enter the pond, but after growing larger they were unable to escape through the gate's narrow openings that also prevented predators from entering the pond. On the western or Kohala side of Waipi'o Valley was the large Muliwai fishpond and just inland of the Muliwai fishpond was the Waiomoa fishpond. The Mokapo pond was the royal bathing pool located between the Muliwai fishpond and the sand dunes at the front of Waipi'o Valley. There were numerous small fishponds concentrated along the Kohala side of the valley where canals led off waterfalls and side streams and there were also small fishponds in Hi'ilawe Canyon.

Typically, a *kia'i loko* or fishpond supervisor built a small thatched *hale kia'i* or guardhouse located near the *makaha* of a royal fishpond manned at night during high tide to guard against poaching. The *kia'i loko* was in charge of keeping the fishpond clean and fertilizing it with plant material. *Lo'i* or taro pondfields were also utilized as fishponds, called *loko i'a kalo* they were stocked with saltwater fish caught along the shoreline able to tolerate freshwater or with freshwater fish that found their way from streams through irrigation channels. Two species of fish, the *o'opu* and the *aholehole*, thrive in algae-rich freshwater. Fishponds were very productive with an estimated yield of between 300 and 500 pounds of fish per acre per year averaging perhaps 350 pounds. (Kikuchi 1973) Fishponds were a prized possession of every high *ali'i* chief and ownership of one or more was the ultimate symbol of status and power. Fishponds were usually under direct control of a chief or his *konohiki* and fish harvested from these ponds were often exclusively for the use of a high *ali'i* including his chiefs, priests and household. Fishponds were of no direct benefit to commoners as the ponds were *kapu,* both royal fishponds and royal taro pondfields were *ko'ele,* for the exclusive use of the *ali'i.* "Fishponds became the symbols of the chiefly right to conspicuous consumption and to ownership of the land and its resources". (Kikuchi 1973)

HAWAIIAN LAND DIVISIONS

Hawaiian land use divisions began with the *mokupuni,* an island or group of islands run by an *ali'i 'ai moku,* the "chief who eats the island" or *ali'i 'ai aupuni,* the "chief who eats the kingdom". *Moku* means cut off or detached suggesting the original homeland of the Polynesians, before they inhabited the islands of the Pacific Ocean, must have been a large continental landmass. The Hawaiian Islands are divided into large districts or *moku o loko,* covering areas from beyond the edge of the sea to the summits of interior mountains and Hawai'i Island is divided into six *moku o loko,* each was run by an *ali'i nui* or an *ali'i* whose title included the name of the district. The next land division is the *ahupua'a* that vary in size and shape. Typically, it is a long narrow strip of land averaging approximately one-half mile wide, a wedge-shaped section of land at a right angle to the shoreline running from the sea or *kai* to the forested uplands or *uka. Ahupua'a* extend beyond the shoreline to the outer edge of the reef or if no reef is present to about one half mile from the shore where fishing was most productive. Large *ahupua'a* extend further into the sea, while small ones extend only as far out as a man could stand. On Hawai'i Island, each *moku* is divided into from 70 to 100 *ahupua'a* that were controlled by an *ali'i 'ai ahupua'a.* The size of *ahupua'a* vary from a few 100 acres to as large as 10,000 acres. On geologically older lands with a topography of stream valleys, *ahupua'a* are typically distinct watersheds with boundaries being ridges or cliffs on either side, on younger lands their boundaries are more arbitrary. (Kirch 2010) Inland, *ahupua'a* become narrower as they reach the forested uplands or *uka* at the 1700-foot to 5000-foot elevation. Inland forests were also called *wao* and at higher elevations were forests of the spirits or *wao akua.* Large *ahupua'a* extend into the forested areas with only a few large *ahupua'a* reaching the summit of mountains. On the islands of Lana'i and Moloka'i there are *ahupua'a* extending from the coast across the mountains to the opposite coast. The Waipi'o *ahupua'a* includes the entire valley along with tracts of adjacent uplands along both sides.

The *ahupua'a* was the basic unit of Hawaiian political and economic organization. Each *ahupua'a* was basically economically self-sufficient containing a variety of land and water resources from different ecological zones able to supply a wide range of food and most of the raw materials needed for survival. Food was supplied from off shore fishing areas and plants grown throughout different altitudes and soils. Land was known as *'aina* or "place of food". (Malo 1951 [1898]) From the *uka* or upland forests came hardwoods, such as *koa* or *kauila* for canoes and houses, *olona* plants for cordage and bird feathers for *ali'i* cloaks and helmets. From the *kula* or open dryland plains between the mountains and the sea came *wauke* plants for making tapa or *kapa, kukui* trees whose nuts were used for lighting, *pili* grass for thatching houses, ti or *ki* leaves for food wrappings, rain capes and thatching, and bamboo. From the *kai* or sea came fish and other seafood, *limu* or seaweed and *pa'akai* or salt. Along the shoreline there were coconut trees used for making bowls, drums and fibers for cordage and their nuts provided food and drink. Other coastal trees were used, such as the *hau* tree for making canoe crossbooms or *'iako* and floats or *ama,* the *milo* tree for food bowls and the *noni* shrub for medicine. Freshwater was most plentiful along the shoreline where water flowing underground through porous basalt lava surfaced as springs and ponds near sea level. (Hommon 1976)

Within the *ahupua'a* were *'ili* or *ili 'aina* household land divisions and the Waipi'o *ahupua'a* contained from thirty to forty *'ili 'aina* including those in the forested uplands along both sides of the valley. To the west on the Kohala side, the Muliwai *'ili* extended from the rim of Waimanu Valley down to the Waipi'o Valley floor and included the Muliwai fishpond. To the east on the Hilo side, the Lalakea *'ili* included the upland area as far as the *ahupua'a* of Kukuihaele and extended down to the Lalakea fishpond. There were *'ili pa'a* that ran completely across the valley and *'ili* that extended from the valley wall to a stream only partially across the valley. *'Ili* were not necessarily continuous, *'ili lele* or jump *'ili* were land divisions with several separate sections, typically those near the sea contained terraced taro pondfields and others were located in the forested uplands. In Waipi'o Valley, one section of an *'ili lele* contained dryland for housing and cultivation along the valley walls and another section contained irrigated taro pondfields in the central valley floor. There were *'ili kupono* lands controlled by a high *ali'i* chief other than the chief in charge of the *ahupua'a* that were often *pu'uhonua* or places of refuge. Within the *'ili* lands or *'ili 'ania* were *mo'o 'aina* located along *'auwai* or irrigation channels, these were long strips of land associated with wet taro pondfield cultivation and included rights to *'auwai* water. The smallest land unit was the *kuleana,* a house site allocated by a chief to a working family of commoners where they lived and cultivated the land. In Waipi'o Valley, *'ili* were controlled by a *konohiki,* some controlled several *'ili* and other *'ili* were controlled directly by the ruling chief.

There were two categories of Hawaiian food, *i'a* was seafood and *lawai'a* were fishermen, *'ai* were agricultural products and *mahi'ai* were farmers. Agriculture became as important as the sea and eventually the floor of Waipi'o Valley became dominated by a complex taro pondfield irrigation system. In Polynesia, extensive cultivation of taro required development of water control systems and the extent of Waipi'o Valley agriculture made Waipi'o *ahupua'a* the economic center of the Hamakua Coast and one of the most intensively farmed areas in the Hawaiian Islands. (Kirch 1994 [1977]) As the population of Waipi'o Valley grew and began moving inland away from the coast, Waipi'o Valley became the largest area of extensive wet taro cultivation on Hawai'i Island and developed one of the largest irrigation systems in all of the Hawaiian Islands supporting a large population including the *ali'i* of Hawai'i Island. The increased population provided the large number of people required for construction and maintenance of the extensive network of irrigated taro pondfields and an "archaic state" with occupational specialization and class separation between the *ali'i* and commoners began to develop. (Kirch 2010)

WAIPI'O VALLEY 'AUWAI EXPANSION

In Waipi'o Valley, there was an intensive effort to increase food production and practically every body of water was a source of food, either as a fishpond or an irrigated taro pondfield. Waipi'o Valley's extensive taro pondfield system included at least fourteen *'auwai* channels leading from streams and waterfalls into the lower valley. "The taro pondfields were irrigated by six main systems of *'auwai* or ditches: two on the east side of Wailoa Stream, three on the west side of Wailoa Stream, and one associated with Hi'ilawe Stream. Fourteen *'auwai* branched off these streams to feed the six main systems."

> (From *Archaeological and Historic Research in Waipi'o Valley, District,*
> *Hawai'i Island*, 1983, by Paul Cleghorn and Elaine Rogers-Jourdane,
> Bishop Museum Manuscript. Courtesy of Bishop
> Museum Library and Archives, Honolulu)

'Auwai were excavated irrigation channels for supplying water to taro pondfields, some were lined with stone where fast moving water would erode the walls of the canal. In Waipi'o Valley, *'auwai* led off the main streams running down the valley through taro pondfields and fishponds diverting water from side streams and waterfalls. Intensive water management was required for the wet taro or *lo'i* pondfield system. It was necessary to have a continuous flow of water to taro plants. Construction of an *'auwai* system was a community effort under supervision of a *konohiki,* who were water supervisors or *luna wai,* regulating irrigation water usage and allotments. (Malo 1951 [1898]) The *'auwai* and *lo'i* had a spiritual aspect, both *Kane*, god of freshwater and sunlight, and *Lono*, god of fertility and rain, were involved. *Ku*, god of war, was included when control of freshwater resources increased political power. To early settlers, freshwater was abundant and associated with peace and prosperity. Later, freshwater would become the ultimate prize of military conquest, freshwater became the central element of Hawaiian civilization.

> "The whole [valley] was watered in a most ingenious manner by dividing the general stream into little aqueducts leading in various directions so as to supply the most distant field at pleasure, and the soil seems to repay the labor and industry of these people by the luxuriance of the production."

> (Description of a terraced *lo'i* by Dr. Menzies, surgeon aboard
> Captain Vancouver's HMS Discovery, 1794)

There were four levels of *'auwai* irrigation systems (Figs. 58 (1&2)). (Kirch 1985) The simplest was terracing across a narrow permanent stream channel with boulders blocking and diverting water. Next, a drainage channel feed directly into the upper irrigated pondfield with water flowing between pondfields through small gateways. The third type was an irrigation channel built along the upper edge of a number of pondfields supplying each independently, allowing for more control of water distribution and the most advanced *'auwai* irrigation system had two irrigation channels including a lower one for drainage.

Oral traditions found in Waipi'o Valley's chants and mythology were the earliest source of documentation of the original vegetation. Its lowland coastal forest of native trees was rapidly altered by the original settlers. Along the leeward coast of Hawai'i Island lowland forests were replaced by taro pondfields, housing and gardens with introduced tree species. Descriptions of Waipi'o Valley by early travelers indicated the extent of cultivation of the valley floor at the time of their visit. William Ellis in 1823 described the valley walls as "nearly perpendicular, yet they were mostly clothed with grass, and low straggling shrubs were here and there seen amidst the jutting rocks". Ellis described the valley floor as "one continuous garden, cultivated with taro bananas, sugar cane, and other products of the islands, all growing luxuriantly". Isabella Bird wrote upon first sighting Waipi'o Valley in 1873, "a fertile region perfectly level . . . watered by a winding stream, and bright with fishponds, meadow lands, *kalo* [taro] patches, orange and coffee groves, figs, breadfruit, and palms". After the "discovery" of the Hawaiian Islands by Captain James T. Cook, the vegetation of Waipi'o Valley experienced a major transformation. Introduced invasive species began to cover much of the valley and the coastal sand dune and burial mound area is now covered with introduced ironwood trees.

AGRICULTURE OF WAIPI'O VALLEY

The basic Hawaiian agricultural tool was the digging stick or *'o'o* made from hardwoods such as *kauila, uhiuhi, alahe'e* or *'ulei*. They were from two to as long as six feet with either a pointed end or a flat blade at one end, sometimes with a shell chisel tip. Some had a bend where a foot could force the *'o'o* into the ground. Other tools were stone adzes or *ko'i* and volcanic glass or obsidian for cutting. The principal crops in Waipi'o Valley were those originating from Island Southeast Asia; taro, yams, breadfruit, sugarcane, coconuts and mulberry plants used for making tapa were mainly scattered among dry fields and residential sites. The original settlers who arrived from the Marquesas or Hiva Islands brought most of the principal crops and livestock including pigs, dogs and chickens, items transported by canoe from Southern Polynesia to the Hawaiian Islands. Livestock was raised mainly as feast foods for religious events, the only mammal indigenous to the Hawaiian Islands was the bat. Most of the protein in the Hawaiian diet came from seafood including freshwater fish and shellfish. Wild birds were collected with hunting rights restricted to residents of the *ahupua'a*. The food of commoners was fish, yams, sweet potatoes, taro, plantains, sugarcane and breadfruit, the upper classes added the meat of pigs and dogs. Kava, known as *'awa* in the Hawaiian Islands, a beverage made from the pepper plant *Piper methysticum* contains a narcotic tranquilizing substance. Used as a mild sedative, kava was a sacred ceremonial drink throughout Polynesia causing a tranquil state of intoxication and was consumed at all important events. *'Awa* was a necessary offering to the gods and its consumption was thought to bring one into a closer connection with the gods and ancestors. Acting as a relaxant, it made people more sociable and was believed to enable communication with the dead and supernatural, although its long-term use caused scaly skin eruptions.

Taro, known as *kalo* in the Hawaiian Islands, was the major staple crop of Waipi'o Valley due to its abundance of freshwater and the ability of Hawaiians to develop extensive irrigation and water channel systems. Waipi'o Valley had one of the largest wet taro valley floors in the Hawaiian Islands; it covered an area three miles long and three quarters of a mile wide. *Lo'i* terraces extended up Hi'ilawe Canyon and there were others located at the upper end of the valley. Taro or *kalo* was the mainstay of the Hawaiian diet in ancient times, its origin goes back to Wakea, the mythological founder of the Hawaiian people, whose first child Haloa-naka was born premature, died and was buried outside the house and from his burial place the first taro plant grew. Taro was the firstborn and mankind was second, therefore genealogically taro or *kalo* was considered more sacred and taboo than man himself.

> The tuber of the taro was baked in an *imu* or underground oven, a hole lined with stones, then pounded into a paste called *pa'i'ai*. Water was added to create *poi*, the main food of the average Hawaiian adult who consumed as much as ten pounds of *poi* per day. Taro leaves or *lu'au*, the Hawaiian feast is named after the taro leaf, and taro shoots were boiled or fried and *kulolo* was a pudding made from the taro root and coconut. The sweet potato, whose origin was South America, was a major crop on Hawai'i Island grown mainly in dry fields where there was adequate rainfall. The sweet potato was successfully grown on Hawai'i Island and in a few areas of Maui Island, increasing the carrying capacity of the land. These were areas where more recent volcanic eruptions made the soil rich in phosphorus, calcium, and other minerals essential for plant growth. "The Polynesians were skilled farmers developing intensive agriculture in tropical environments that were difficult to farm." (Shwartz 2004)

Taro has been grown in Waipi'o Valley since the time of the first Polynesian settlers. The lower valley floor was covered with wet taro pondfields or *lo'i* ranging from a few hundred to a thousand square yards. Taro pondfields of ancient chiefs were located in Waipi'o Valley, such as the *lo'i ko'ele o* 'Umi or the taro pondfield of 'Umi, *ko'ele* means land set aside strictly for use by a chief. The taro pondfield of 'Umi was irrigated by the 'Auwai Pahupohaku, a royal irrigation canal that ran the full length along the back of the sand dunes at the front of Waipi'o Valley, from the Mokapu and Muliwai ponds to the Wailoa River. (From survey maps of the Valley of Waipi'o, Hawaii by Joseph S. Emerson, 1881)

Lo'i were rectangular pondfields separated by mud embankments or *kuakua*. To construct a *lo'i*, pondfields were thoroughly soaked and embankments were raised by adding soil from lowering the pondfields by three to four feet. Embankments were six or eight feet wide and level at the top with their soil compacted. Large flat rocks or wood were added to the embankments enabling pondfields to retain water. Water channels or *'auwai* would let water into the *lo'i* to a depth of twelve to eighteen inches. The tops of the *lo'i* embankments were planted with breadfruit, bananas, sugarcane and *ki* plants, getting their moisture from pondfield seepage and also served as windbreaks. It was customary to use taro pondfields as fish ponds, taro was planted in rows leaving space in between where fish could swim. As many as 300 varieties of both wetland and dryland taro were grown. Dryland taro fields with gardens of coconut trees, breadfruit and bananas were located along the narrow dry slopes on each side of Waipi'o Valley along the base of the valley walls or *pali* and in the rainy uplands. Irrigated taro was grown in the flat valley floor. Paper mulberry was grown near houses to make bark cloth or *kapa*. Legend tells of a severe drought and famine in the early thirteenth century when Waipi'o Valley was the only land where water flowed and food was plentiful. People from all over the Hawaiian Islands came to Waipi'o Valley for food and this drought was mentioned in the story of Kila. "During a spell of great drought when a great famine was experienced over all the lands from Hawaii to Kauai, . . . Waipi'o was the only land where water had not dried up and it was the only land where food was in abundance." (Fornander 1916-1920)

Taro production has been vital to Hawaiian culture and taro in Waipi'o Valley supported a large population. Housing settlements in the Hawaiian Islands were usually dispersed with the exception of royal centers such as Waipi'o Valley, which at its peak had approximately 4000 to 10,000 residents with some oral traditions placing the population as high as 40,000. It is estimated at least 800 acres of taro were cultivated in the lower valley and together with the upper valley and slopes, a total of two square miles could have been planted in taro, enough to support 30,000 people. One square mile of intensively grown taro has been estimated to be able to feed 15,000 Hawaiians for one year. (From "Ancient Times to Today, Water Has Defined Waipi'o Valley", in *Environment Hawai'i,* Vol. 6, No. 2, August 1998) Taro became so plentiful in early Waipi'o Valley the surplus created an export trade. Dry taro or *pa'i'ai* was wrapped in *ki* or ti leaf packets or bricks for transport. Great rolls were towed from shore and loaded onto waiting canoes to be shipped to Hilo and Kohala in return for fish.

THE HAWAIIAN POPULATION

In Hawaiian mythology, the people were ancestors of the children of Kahiko Lua Mea, the "very ancient and sacred one" said to have been the first male child of La'ila'i, the first female created from the soil of the earth by the god *Kane*. Kahiko Lau Mea had three sons, the first two from his first wife Kupulanakehau and the third from another wife. *Ali'i* chiefs, the royal class, were direct descendants of Wakea, the second son. *Kahuna* or priests descended from Wakea's elder brother Lihau'ula. *Maka'ainana* or commoners came from Maku'u or Makulukulu, Kahiko's third son from the other wife and Wakea's half-brother, they were the "people who attend the land". *Kauwa* or slaves, descended from Kekeu, a son from Wakea's wife *Papa's* liaison with Wakea's slave Ha'akauilana after Wakea deserted her. Hawaiian society was divided into four social classes similar to the social caste structure or *varna* of ancient Vedic India and traditional Austronesian-speaking societies. The Hawaiian caste system resembled the caste system developed on the island of Bali where there was upward social mobility that was not true in ancient India. The word caste comes from the Portuguese word *casta* meaning breed, race or kind.

Ali'i or warrior chiefs, like the *Kshatriya*, noble warrior class of India, were the royal ruling class representing the senior genealogical branch of the Polynesians. The Proto-Polynesian Austronesian name for *ali'i* was *qariki* that became *ariki,* then *ari'i* in the islands of Tahiti and *ali'i* in the Hawaiian Islands. Leadership was a hereditary classification, the first male born of the highest-ranking senior chiefly family line, the highest bloodline, was believed to have the most divine genealogy with the most *mana* or divine power of the gods. He became the high chief or *ali'i nui* who ruled over part of an island, an entire island or several islands bearing the title *haku* or lord. Originally, the word *haku* referred to stones set into the ground in ancient Proto-Polynesian temples functioning as backrests for dignitaries and the Proto-Polynesian name for chief was *fatu*. A *ku'auhau* or genealogist would recited from memory their *ko'i honua* or genealogical chant documenting a chief's ancestral claims through generations of firstborn sons and their wives leading up to the present. *Ali'i* were required to establish their descent status through ten generations at *'Aha Ali'i,* the Congregation of Chiefs. (Hommon 1976) The genealogical ranking of *ali'i* chiefs was determined by their connection to the ruling senior line and their status in society was determined by their inherited ranking. Rank was a divine expression of potency or *mana* acquired through descent from the gods, their ultimate ancestors. No chief could fall below his ranking or rise above it, although he could raise the ranking of his children to a higher rank than his own through marriage to a woman with a higher ranking than himself or by marriage to his sister.

There were four different major *ali'i* classifications and in order of rank; they were *pi'o, niau pi'o* or *naha, ho'i* and *wohi. T*hose with higher ranking had greater *mana* being closer to the gods and there were as many as eleven degrees of *ali'i* ranking. (Kamakau 1992 [1961]) As the highest direct descendent of the gods a sacred high *ali'i nui* chief acted as an intermediary between the gods and man and was worshipped by his people. He was the divine protector of the land having responsibility for its care and distribution of the material resources of the land and adjoining sea in the interest of his people; it was understood the land and sea belonged to the gods. The high chief had two principle advisors, his high priest or *kahuna nui* who conducted important religious ceremonies and advised the *haku* or lord how to remain in the favor of the gods and his highest-ranking chief administrative minister or *kalaimoku* who advised the high chief on distribution of lands to lesser chiefs, laws and taxes, management of agricultural lands, irrigation, fishponds and fishing, military strategy and advised him of his obligations to his people. Next were head chiefs of districts, the *ali'i 'ai moku,* who had many *ali'i 'ai ahupua'a* below them each ruling an *ahupua'a* land division. Each *ali'i 'ai ahupua'a* appointed a *konohiki* or land manager to oversee agricultural production and control water use for the irrigation system of the *'auwai* and *lo'i,* they were usually *ali'i* and relatives of the ruling chiefs and were assisted by *luna* who were specialists in various tasks.

Ali'i were physically larger than commoners being from six to seven feet tall and were distinguished by their unique status garments and ornamental emblems of rank. Their magnificent royal feathered cloaks and capes, *'ahuli'i* or *'ahu 'ula* (Figs. 74, 75), along with their feathered helmets or *mahi'ole* (Fig. 76), were the sacred insignia of high chiefs. Fashioned from brilliantly colored bird feathers these garments were of incredible beauty containing great *mana*. Another emblem of high rank was the *kahili* or "plumed staff of state" seen at stately events, they were royal feathered standards made from a pole of polished hardwood with feathers of forest birds of prey attached to the top with some being as high as twenty-five feet (Fig. 77). The handles of some *kahili* were long bones of sacrificed enemy chiefs inlaid with turtle shell. Other symbols of *ali'i* authority were *pulo'ulo'u* or *kapu* sticks with a tapa-covered ball on the end and sacred chiefly *lei niho palaoa* hook-shaped sperm whale-tooth neck pendants (Fig. 60). The unique Hawaiian sperm whale-tooth necklaces were insignia of chiefly aristocratic *ali'i* status and were worn by both male and female high chiefs on occasions of state and in battle. These sperm whale-tooth pendants were carved in the shape of a curved, protruding, stylized tongue of a god. To the Hawaiians, the tongue shape was symbolic of the presence of *mana*, signifying the wearer was someone who had the authority to speak. (Cox 1988) *Lei niho palaoa* were strung on a necklace made of loops of eight-strand square braids of human hair from an *ali'i* ancestor. Early *palaoa* ornaments were made of coral, shell, animal tooth and bone, later they were made of whale tooth ivory. *Ali'i* chiefs who wore the *lei niho palaoa* claimed and made *kapu* bodies of sperm whales cast ashore by the sea. (Malo 1951 [1898]) It has been suggested its fishhook form was derived from Micronesian trolling fishhooks that were objects of great value. It has also been suggested *lei niho palaoa* resemble the head of a cobra, a warrior image that may have been transported from the Indus River Valley of ancient India into Polynesia. Similar necklaces were reserved for persons of high rank in the islands of Tahiti and the Marquesas or Hiva Islands. In the Marquesas Islands, shaped whale-tooth pendants were of great value being worn only by persons of high rank and wealth. (Porter 1986) To the Maori of New Zealand, whale teeth were known as *rei niho* and whale-tooth pendants were also brought to the Hawaiian Islands by coastal Indians from the islands of Alaska and Western Canada. The use of whale teeth as a symbol of chiefly status in Polynesia goes back to the Fiji Islands where high chiefs would wear highly polished sperm whale-tooth ornaments or *tabua*, the most valuable being stained or smoked to a deep orange color. Holes were drilled at the tip with a sennit cord attached to form a necklace and some were inscribed with tribal symbols. The name *tabua* comes from *tabu ya* meaning sacred, high priests after staring at a ceremonial whale-tooth ornament would become entranced having the gods enter them. (Tylor 1920) Sacred *tabua* were the most highly prized possessions in Fijian culture, they conveyed *mana*, the highest authority. They were the price of life and death and were presented at important ceremonies such as alliances, weddings, births and funerals, and when seeking favor of the gods (Fig. 61). *Tabua* necklaces were also worn by high chiefs and expert canoe builders in the Tonga and Samoa Islands.

Ali'i chiefs were considered direct descendants of the gods and ruled by divine right with power of life and death over the *maka'ainana* or commoners. *Ali'i* were the only landowners, they owned not only the soil but what grew upon it; they owned the fish in the sea and the time and labor of commoners. Commoners were not bound to either the soil or a chief and if an *ali'i* chief was arrogant or unfairly demanding a commoner was free to relocate his household and labor to the service of another *ali'i* chief who held title to land, whose ancestors had been given an original land grant; "genealogy was the deed and land was the wealth". Rent was paid in the form of produce from cultivation, animals raised on the land, finished products manufactured on the property, labor contributed for communal projects and a portion of a fisherman's catch was delivered to the *ali'i* chief. In return for these goods and services, the chief had ritual obligations. He confirmed the commoner's right to the land, looked after their welfare providing divine supernatural protection and petitioned the gods for abundant harvests. (Kame'eleihiwa 1992)

Kahuna, like the *Brahmin* of Vedic India, were the priestly class comprised of temple priests, prophets and specialists, such as skilled craftsman, navigators, doctors and teachers. The Proto-Polynesian Austronesian term for priest, specialist or expert craftsman was *tufunga*. The high priests or *kahuna nui* were thought to be able to communicate with the gods. The *kahuna* were the professional class, the intellectual leadership of society, they had a hereditary ranking with authority just below the ruling chiefs and were frequently their siblings or drawn from other *ali'i* families. Priests of the high chief, the *kahuna nui*, were high priests who ran the large *heiau* or temples and *kahuna pule* or prayer priests also had to be of the *ali'i* class. Although of lesser ranking than ruling *ali'i, kahuna* acquired great power and prestige. Membership in the priesthood was hereditary, determined by their genealogical inheritance through the male line, a tradition originating as far back as ancient Sumer, Mesopotamia. *Kahuna* were guardians of society's secret knowledge and rituals, the mythology of the culture and keepers of sacred chants or *mele*. They recognized a chief's divine genealogy and communicated the requirements and desires of the gods through the interpretation of omens. Professional *kahuna* were the specialists of society; *kahuna lapa'au* were medical practitioners, *kahuna ho'oulu 'ai* were agricultural experts, *kahuna lawai'a* were specialists in fishing, *kahuna hana* were master fishnet makers, *kahuna ho'okele* were expert navigators and *kahuna kuhikuhi pu'uone* were architects. *Kahuna pule* were specialists in prayer, *kahuna nui* were counselors to the high chief and *kahuna kaula* were prophets influenced by spirits, they could be possessed by the gods, would speak freely, and were feared by commoners for dealing with the supernatural. *Kahuna kilo hoku* were able to read the stars*, kahuna kilo 'opua* were able to read the clouds and together foretold the future, *kahuna kalai wa'a* were canoe masters and there were professional *kahuna* who were not part of the priesthood, such as *kahuna 'ana'ana* or sorcerers of black magic. In religious ceremonies *kahuna* had the power of life and death, they were able to select victims for sacrifice and were feared by the people. Often they had large numbers of followers, *kahuna* Kaleihoku'u of Laupahoehoe had such a large number of followers he was able to have high chief Hakau put to death and have 'Umi installed in his place.

Maka'ainana or commoners, like the *vaishya* merchant and farmer class of Vedic India and the *shudra* labor class of Vedic India, comprised the majority of the population. They were from a lower genealogical line of Polynesians ruled by *ali'i* and their genealogy had been lost. Farmers made up the majority of the *maka'ainana* which means "eyes toward the land", fisherman and laborers who constructed houses were also *maka'ainana*. They were expected to give military service to ruling chiefs and their women made tapa or *kapa* mats and fishing cordage. High status *maka'ainana* lived near the royal court functioning as servants, craftsmen, or warriors for the *ali'i*. After arrival of *ari'i* from the islands of Tahiti, commoners lost their genealogical heritage and control of their lands. They continued to have the right to produce food, but were obligated to pay tribute in the form of goods and services to the ruling *ali'i* chief to be able to live on and cultivate the land. They were also required to provide labor on *ko'ele* lands set aside specifically to support the chiefs. Perhaps 95 percent of the population was made up of commoners and slaves.

> "The condition of the common people was that of subjection to the chiefs, compelled to do their heavy tasks, burdened, and oppressed, some even to death . . . The people held the chiefs in great dread and looked upon them as gods."
>
> (From *Hawaiian Antiquites: Moolelo Hawaii,* 1951 [1898],
> Bishop Museum Publication 2, by David Malo, page 87.
> Courtesy of Bishop Museum Press, Honolulu)

> "A shark going inland is my chief, a very strong shark able to devour all on land.
>
> (From *Fornander Collection of Hawaiian Antiquities and Folk-lore,*
> Volume VI, Part I, 1916-1920, by Abraham Fornander, page
> 393. Courtesy of Bishop Museum Press, Honolulu)

Kauwa or *kaua*, like the *harijan* or *dalit* untouchables and slave class of Vedic India, were a numerically small group. They were the lowest class considered despised, worthless outcasts without *mana* who commoners had to avoid so as not to become contaminated. It was improper for commoners to eat with them, sleep near them or have their shadow fall upon them. Segregated on lands of their own, they were forbidden to mix with others or intermarry. If any member of another class had a child with a *kauwa*, the child belonged to the *kauwa* class. Marked with tattoos or *kakau* on their foreheads or corners of their eyes indicating their status (Pukui 1972), they were often selected for human sacrifice such as sanctifying the posthole in which the image of the god *Ku* stood in *luakini heiau*. Paradoxically, they had a close relationship with *ali'i* chiefs who saw them as their opposite, as dark gods, and a lesser *ali'i* or servant might refer to himself a *kauwa* in order to humble himself before his superiors. Those in charge of a high chief's goods and food were often termed *kauwa*, although a true untouchable *kauwa* would probably not have been given such personal access to a high *ali'i*. Often when their master died, several *kauwa* retainers became *moepu'u* or "death companions" being buried alive with their chief. In the Marquesas or Hiva Islands, commoners or *tuapio* were often victims of human sacrifice, but in the afterlife their status was thought to increase and then they lived with the deceased chiefs. In the islands of Tahiti, the *teuteu* or *tuti* was a slave class used for human sacrifice. In the Hawaiian Islands, many *kauwa* were war captives or descendants of slaves and it has been suggested some were descendants of a group of settlers known as Nawao or "wild people" present in the Hawaiian Islands before the arrival of the Marquesas Islanders who conquered and enslaved them. (Beckwith 1970 [1940])

THE HAWAIIAN POPULATION DECLINE

The population of the Hawaiian Islands during the first few hundred years after its initial colonization was small, it grew rapidly during the "expansion period", then leveled off and may have declined significantly suggesting "the capacity of the indigenous technological productive system to support increased population had reached its limits". (Kirch and Rallu 2007) Population declines throughout Polynesia prior to western contact were caused by the effects of climate and sea level changes due to the arrival of the "Little Ice Age". (Nunn 1999) During the "Little Climate Optimum" from AD 900 to AD 1250, Hawaiian society increased in agricultural production and population, but after the start of the "Little Ice Age" from AD 1350 to AD 1800, climate cooling caused a fall in sea level with a corresponding drop in the water table and less rainfall causing a reduction in food resources. (Nunn 1999) By AD 1650, the Hawaiian Islands reached their peak population and significant reductions in population began at least 100 years before western contact. (Hommon 1976, Kay 1994) The pre-contact population of all the Hawaiian Islands in 1778-79, after the arrival of Captain James T. Cook, was estimated by Lieutenant James King to have been 500,000. Later, he reduced his estimate to 400,000 and estimated the population of Hawai'i Island at 150,000. William Bligh, Sailing Master of the HMS Resolution, estimated the population of all the Hawaiian Islands to be 242,000 with the population of Hawai'i Island at 100,000. (Schmitt 1971) Many scholars put the figure between 250,000 to 300,000, although some estimated the pre-contact population to be as low as 150,000 believing Cook's crew overestimated the population. (Dye 1994) David Stannard believed the reduction of Lieutenant King's estimate of 500,000 was unjustified, that it was actually low and there had been constant population growth prior to western contact. Stannard estimated the Hawaiian population during first contact in 1778 at 800,000 to 1,000,000. (Stannard 1989)

Waipi'o Valley had one of the highest population densities in the Hawaiian Islands with a peak pre-contact population estimated from between 4000 to 10,000 with some oral traditions estimating the population as high as 40,000. Reverend William Ellis visited Waipi'o Valley in 1823 and estimated its population at 1325 with 265 houses scattered in small villages of 20 to 50 houses, 8 *heiau,* and 14 major ponds. Ellis observed four housing clusters in Waipi'o Valley; Napo'opo'o, Keone, Na'alapa and Kouka or Koauka (Fig. 69). In the American missionary census of 1831-32, the population of all the Hawaiian Islands was only 130,313. This represented an over 80 percent decline in population in the first 50 years since western contact which was typical of the effect western diseases had on the native populations of the Americas. (Stannard 1989) The population of Hawai'i Island dropped to 45,792 (Schmitt 1971) and the population of Waipi'o Valley was thought to be 1200. The American missionary census of 1835-36 had the population of all the Hawaiian Islands at 108,579 with the population of Hawai'i Island at 39,364 and in 1845 Waipi'o Valley's population was 921. In 1850, the population of all the Hawaiian Island was 84,165, the population of Hawai'i Island was 25,864 and in Waipi'o Valley it was 700 to 800. In the Hawaiian government census of 1853, the total population of the Hawaiian Islands was 73,138, including 2,119 foreigners, the population of Hawai'i Island was only 24,450, and in Waipi'o Valley it was about 750. After western contact Hawaiians suffered rapid depopulation caused by pestilences brought in by foreign ships such as influenza and tuberculosis that devastated the population.

> "During the forty years I have resided here, I have known of thousands of defenseless human beings cruelly massacred in their extermination wars. I have seen multitudes of my fellow beings offered in sacrifice to their idol gods. I have seen this large island [Hawai'i Island], once filled with inhabitants, dwindle down to the present few in numbers through wars and disease."
>
> (From a Nov. 27, 1826 report by John Young
> in *A Residence of Twenty-one Years in the
> Sandwich Islands* by Hiram Bingham)

Dreadful epidemics caused a sever population crash killing hundreds of thousands of Hawaiians. This "fatal impact" was caused by western contact when 18th and 19th century explorers, traders and settlers brought disease, vice and alcoholism to the Hawaiian Islands. Hawaiians became accustomed to their own germs, but due to their isolation from major Pacific Rim civilizations, they had no immunity to the infectious diseases brought in by westerners, known as *ma'i malihini* or foreign sickness. Although venereal diseases were present in the Hawaiian Islands before Cook's arrival, they were reintroduced in 1778-79 causing death and sterility. In 1804, there was a great plague known as the *ma'i oku'u* or squatting sickness, probably a cholera or typhoid epidemic, killing 15,000 and preventing Kamehameha the First from invading Kaua'i Island. Earlier, a great pestilence known as *ikipuahola* or *ma'i ahulau* occurred during the reign of Waia, son of Haloa and grandson of Wakea, leaving only twenty-six people alive and is believed to have been the same as the *ma'i oku'u* disease of 1804. (Malo 1951 [1898]) The first documented case of leprosy or Hansen's disease occurred on Kaua'i Island in 1835, brought to the Hawaiian Islands by Chinese laborers, it was known as *ma'i hookaawale* or the separating disease. In 1848 and 1849, epidemics of measles and whooping cough killed 10,000, a tenth of the remaining population. In 1849, there were an estimated 17 births and 98 deaths per 1000 Hawaiians. The 300,000 Hawaiians in 1778 were reduced to 84,165 by 1850 and 51,531 by 1872. (Schmitt 1968) The flu epidemic of 1850 devastated Waipi'o Valley and in 1853 there was a smallpox epidemic with dire forecasts of total extinction, as many as 5000 Hawaiians died. "The most immediate and often devastating consequence of western contact was the introduction of a host of diseases previously unknown to the islanders to which they had no prior exposure and lacked resistance." (Kirch and Rallu 2007)

By 1878, one hundred years after Captain James T. Cook's arrival, the total native population of the Hawaiian Islands dropped to 47,508 including approximately 3500 part Hawaiians, a catastrophic drop from 250,000 to 400,000 at western contact. In 1867, according to Father Elias Bond, a local missionary, the population of Waipi'o Valley was 640 with 300 in Waimanu Valley to the northwest. By the late 1800s, Waipi'o Valley's native Hawaiian population had been reduced to 200. *The Hawaiian Kingdom Statistical and Commercial Directory and Tourist's Guide, 1880-1881,* stated during the Mahele Period Land Commission Awards thirty to forty houses were observed in Waipi'o Valley with an estimated population of only 150. Disasters of this magnitude after first contact between Europeans and indigenous people throughout the Pacific were commonplace, indigenous people died in staggering numbers from epidemic diseases to which they had little or no resistance due to their geographic isolation. Houses were deserted, gardens overgrown and temples lay in ruins; Hawaiians faced the possibility of their extinction.

By 1785, the Hawaiian Islands were part of the fur trade route between America, Europe, and China and by 1810 they were part of the sandalwood trade. With the establishment of European and American trading centers near anchorages and harbors, the process of urbanization began. Hawaiians left their rural *kuleana* lands heading for ports such as Kailua-Kona on Hawai'i Island. Many productive traditional agricultural lands were abandoned including Waipi'o Valley. Villages previously densely populated were abandoned and reduced to ruins. Waipi'o Valley is now silent and everywhere the remains of stone platforms and walls where thatched houses once stood cover the landscape, the population of Waipi'o Valley was decimated by diseases that swept across the Hawaiian Islands. The valley floor, once a network of irrigated and terraced taro pondfields, is now abandoned and overgrown, testimony to a culture that no longer exists; their traditional way of life has vanished. "This is my culture and no matter how remote the past is, it does not make my culture extinct." (George Helm, Native Hawaiian activist and a founder of the Protect Kaho'olawe 'Ohana, from his personal notes)

Nature added to the destruction of Waipi'o Valley in 1819, 1837, 1877, 1946 and 1960 when tidal waves or tsunamis hit the valley. From 1880 to 1910, a major new crop was introduced into Waipi'o Valley, rice. Chinese and Japanese immigrants came to Waipi'o Valley and rice cultivation soon became more prevalent than taro extending over most of the valley. By the 1880s, 580 acres were in cultivation of mainly rice, although taro never completely vanished from the valley. In the 1940s an exodus from Waipi'o Valley occurred, there was a serious flood in 1941 and on April 1, 1946, an earthquake of magnitude 7.5 occurred in the Aleutian Islands, Alaska, generating a tsunami hitting Waipi'o Valley with a series of waves as high as forty to fifty-five feet sweeping inland for more than half a mile destroying what remained of the ancient Honua'ula Heiau located along the beach and remains of the Paka'alana Heiau were greatly damaged. Most of the houses and crops were swept away and afterward only thirty to forty people remained. The last severe flooding occurred in 1979 and covered the valley floor with four feet of water.

"Now Waipio is unkempt, a wild jungle of mutated abundance. The valley is a neglected maiden with a dirty face and disheveled, windblown hair. Only love and nurturing can refresh her lingering beauty."

(Bisignani 1994)

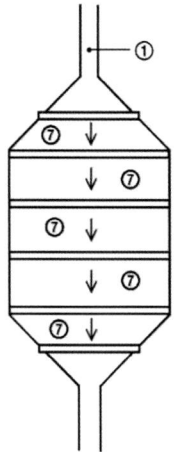

1.   Terraced taro pondfield or *lo'i*

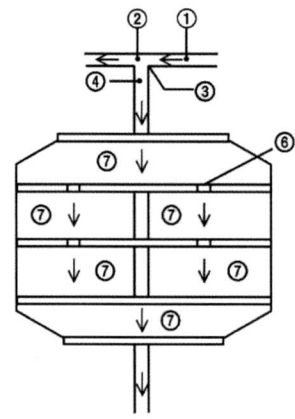

2.   Taro pondfields or *lo'i* with a single irrigation channel or *'auwai* flowing into the upper pondfield

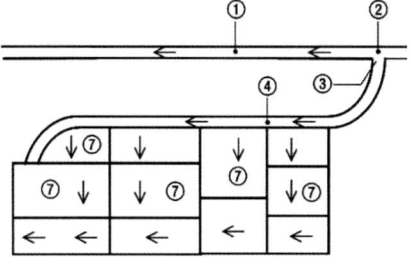

3.   An irrigation channel or *'auwai* with multiple inflows into taro pondfields or *lo'i*

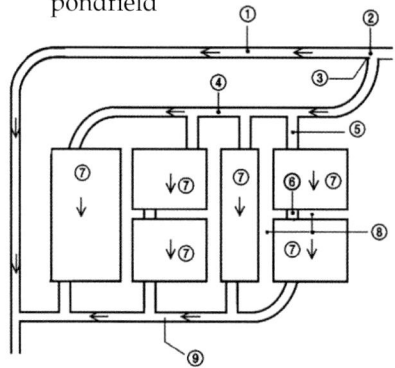

4.   An irrigation channel or *'auwai* with a return overflow into the stream below

Fig. 58 (1)

Taro Pondfield Irrigation Systems

1. Stream or *kahawai*
2. Dam to redirect water flow or *mahowai*
3. Headwater of irrigation *'auwai* system
4. Irrigation channel or *'auwai*
5. Inflow channel into taro pondfield or *lo'i*
6. Water gateway to lower taro pondfield.
7. Taro pondfield or *lo'i*
8. Earthen embankments or *kuakua*
9. Irrigation channel for outflow returning to the stream

Fig. 58 (2)

Council of Chiefs
A painting by Herb Kawainui Kane

A high *ali'i* chief in the foreground wearing a feathered cloak or *'ahu 'ula* and a feathered helmet or *mahi'ole* addressing his *ali'i* warrior chiefs before battle. The warrior on the right holds a shark tooth weapon, a *lei o mano*. Others hold a stone headed club, a *newa* or *la'au palau,* and a wooden dagger, or *pahoa* with many holding spears or *pololu*. Courtesy of Herbert K. Kane, LLC

Fig. 59

Image is from *Wikimedia Commons* and in the public domain

Courtesy of Minneapolis Institute of Arts/Bridgeman Art Library, New York

Lei Niho Palaoa

Lei niho palaoa or hooked sperm whale tooth pendants were important symbols of rank among high *ali'i* who alone were allowed to own them. They were strung on over a thousand strands of eight-ply braided human hair

Fig. 60

© Museum of New Zealand Te Papa
Tongarawa, Wellington, 0L002214

Courtesy of National Museums
Liverpool – World Museum

Fijian Tabua or Sperm Whale Tooth

The *tabua* was a sacred object, the most valuable Fijian cultural artifact. A braided sennit fiber cord *tabua* pendants were gifts of the highest value in ceremonial exchanges

© Museum of New Zealand Te Papa
Tongarewa, Wellington, 0L000598/5

© Museum of New Zealand Te Papa
Tongarawa, Wellington, 0L002067

Fijian Waseisei and Sisi Sperm Whale Tooth Necklaces

Waseisei and *sisi* sperm whale tooth necklaces could only be worn by chiefs and men of influence. They were emblems of wealth and power

Fig. 61

A Canoe of the Sandwich Islands, the Rowers Masked, 1778

An unfinished graphite, ink, wash and watercolor of a double-hull canoe with a "crab claw" sail, twelve rowers wearing gourd helmets with foliage attached and a *kahuna* of the god *Lono* carrying a small feathered *akua ki'i* god image. The watercolor is by John Webber, artist on Captain James T. Cook's third voyage into the Pacific Ocean. Courtesy of the Bishop Museum, Honolulu

A 1779 finished watercolor by John Webber of a *kahuna* traveling across Kealakekua Bay for first contact rituals. The double-hull canoe is carrying only ten rowers and the shoreline in the background represents cliffs of Kealakekua Bay, Hawai'i Island. The image is from *Cook and King 1784, Atlas*. Courtesy of the Mitchell/Dixson Library, State Library of New South Wales, Sydney

Wa'a Kaulua or Double-Hull Voyaging Canoes
of the Hawaiian Islands

Paintings by Herb Kawainui Kane
Courtesy of Herbert K. Kane, LLC

A Coastal Scene of Hawai'i Island [Probably Napo'opo'o]
circa 1836

A pen and ink wash over pencil illustration by French Admiral Theodore Auguste Fisquet from *Unless haste is made: A French skeptic's account of the Sandwich Islands in 1836* by Theodore Adolphe Barrot. Courtesy of the Bishop Museum, Honolulu

View of Houses at Kealakekua, circa 1779

An engraving by William Walker after a drawing by William Ellis, surgeon's second mate aboard the HMS Discovery and later aboard the HMS Resolution during James T. Cook's third voyage into the Pacific Ocean, from *The Ancient Hawaiian House,* 1908, by William Tufts Brigham, Fig. 90, page 106. Courtesy of Bishop Museum Press, Honolulu

A View in O'whyhee, with one of the Priest's Houses

A hand-colored version of a 1782 engraving by William Walker published in *A New Royal Authentic and Complete System of Universal Geography Antient and Modern,* 1793, by Thomas Bankes, from the circa 1779 drawing by William Ellis. Located in the Christchurch Art Gallery Te Puna o Waiwhetu, Christchurch, New Zealand

Kuka'ilimoku
Photograph by Claudia Obrocki

A feathered *akua hulu manu* image of Kuka'ilimoku, war god of Hawai'i Island, probably brought to Europe in 1779 following Captain James T. Cook's third and final voyage into the Pacific Ocean. Copyright; Ethnologisches Museum, Staatliche Museen, Berlin, Germany/Art Resources, New York

CHAPTER 8

HAWAIIAN ARTS AND SCIENCES

THE HAWAIIAN CANOE

Grant a canoe that shall be swift as a fish! To sail in stormy seas, when the storm tosses on all sides!

(A Hawaiian *kahuna's* prayer at the first blow upon felling
a tree for a canoe hull, Westervelt 1989 [1915])

To Polynesian navigators the sea was not featureless or hostile . . . Ocean spaces can inhibit contact just as mountain ranges can on land but they become highways rather than barriers when marine technology, especially navigation, becomes effective.

(Lewis 1994 [1972])

The world of our ancestors was a large sea full of places to explore, to make their home in . . . At home with the sea . . . they developed great skills for navigating their waters . . . theirs was a large world in which peoples and cultures moved and mingled.

(Hau'ofa 2008)

He wa'a he moku, he moku he wa'a.
The canoe is an island, the island is a canoe.

(Hui o Wa'a Kaulua, Lahaina, Maui)

The canoe or *wa'a* was essential to the ancient Hawaiian Islands, design and construction of the canoe was their highest technological achievement and the canoe was their most important cultural artifact. The identity of Hawaiian Islanders was tied to the construction, launching and voyaging of their canoes. They were the principal method of Hawaiian transportation for people and cargo over long distances only footpaths along the shore connected villages and their canoes allowed Hawaiians to harvest the abundance of the sea and were their vehicles for warfare. The ancient Hawaiians constructed canoes from the supply of available materials using Stone Age technology, creating truly sea-worthy, rough-water crafts that were flexible and able to bend against the force of the sea. In 1778, Captain James T. Cook described Hawaiian canoes with their one-piece hulls as technically "the finest in the Pacific". Hawaiian canoes evolved from the design of Marquesas Islands canoes also constructed with one-piece hulls, whereas Tahitian double-hull voyaging canoes were built on a dugout V-shaped keel with plank sides fitted together. The joints of the Hawaiian canoes were lashed with coconut fiber sennit cord, caulked with the resin of the breadfruit tree and were not likely to break apart at sea being both strong and flexible. Koa wood one-piece hulls hewn to within one or one and a half inch thickness made canoes of exceptional strength. With their shallow-draft hulls Hawaiians could clear coral reefs in places around islands and their lightweight canoes could be carried above high tide or into canoe sheds.

The vast forests of large *koa* hardwood trees native to the Hawaiian Islands made the Hawaiian one-piece canoe hull possible. *Koa* trees in rainforests at an elevation of between 4000 to 6000 feet matured with straight trunks and no branches up to 50 to 70 feet above ground. They were up to 20 feet in circumference and found nowhere else in the world but the Hawaiian Islands. A unique form of the Acacia tree, the nearest relative of the Hawaiian *koa* tree is found in Australia, the *koa* tree became established in the Hawaiian Islands before human settlement. The *koa* tree was a "gift beyond words" enabling the Hawaiians to build canoes that were the finest in Polynesia. (Holmes 1993) Although *koa* was the preferred wood for canoe construction other native woods were used, large *kukui* tree trunks were hollowed out into hulls, and the *wiliwili* tree was also used. Logs of redwood, fir or pine of great size sometimes drifted from the Northwest Coast of America to the shores of the Hawaiian Islands, particularly along the islands of Ni'ihau and Kaua'i. (Holmes 1993)

There were two classes of Hawaiian canoes, single-hull canoes or *wa'a kaukahi* accounting for the vast majority of canoes and double-hull canoes or *wa'a kaulua*. There were no differences between hulls of single or double-hull canoes, they were interchangeable. Single-hull canoes employed an outrigger for stability while the double-hull canoes had two similar parallel hulls connected with crossbooms or *'iako* with spreaders or *wae* and comb cleats or *pepeiao* for support. The length of the double-hull canoes varied from thirty to sixty feet and they could carry as many as thirty to forty people including provisions for voyages lasting a month or more. The largest double-hull canoe found on Hawai'i Island was seventy feet long, twelve feet wide and three and a half feet deep and there are records of an old wrecked canoe found along the coast of Hawai'i Island reported to have been 108 feet long, able to carry 120 to 140 men. (From Canoes of the Hawaiian Islands in *The Maori Canoe*, 1976, by Elson Best) Single-hull canoes varied from twelve to fifty feet long. The number of canoes on Hawai'i Island was enormous, Captain James T. Cook estimated the number of canoes when he entered Kealakekua Bay on January 17, 1779 at 3000. Cook who had previously observed Hawaiian canoe construction while on Kaua'i Island in January 1778 stated, "The hull was of one piece hollowed out and pointed at stem and stern. The sides were built up with lashed boards one inch thick. Single-hull canoes have outriggers, some have a single triangular sail with a mast and boom." In the early 1800s, at the coastal village of Kawaihae on Hawai'i Island, the beach was lined with canoes for miles.

DEVELOPMENT OF THE POLYNESIAN CANOE

There are various names for Polynesian canoes, *va'a* in Tahiti, *vaka* in the Marquesas Islands, *waka* in New Zealand, *waqa* in Fiji and *wa'a* in the Hawaiian Islands. *Wangka* was the name for outrigger canoes in the Proto-Polynesian Austronesian language. The root word for canoe in the Sanskrit language of Vedic India was *vah* or *vak* meaning to carry and *vahana* meaning boat or raft. It was technological maritime innovations that made Polynesian oceanic travel possible. Pacific Ocean travel began as far back as before 50,000 BC, during the last Ice Age, with rafts made of logs, tightly bound reeds or bamboo. Rafts made of three to nine logs with the center log being the longest creating a wedge shaped front, adjustable center boards for steering and a square plaited mat sail were capable of carrying a viable founder population group across the Lombok Strait between the islands of Bali and Lombok, the Wallace Line in Island Southeast Asia marking the eastern limit of continental Asia. The Lydekker Line marks the western limit of the Australian region and in between separating them was Wallacea, a sea barrier to plants and animals (Fig. 13). Remains of *Homo erectus* have been found on the island of Java and in September 2003 remains of *Homo erectus* were found on Flores Island, it appears *Homo erectus* may have crossed the Wallace Line even before modern humans appeared on earth. *Homo erectus* developed small fishing rafts and it is possible after observing a herd of elephants swimming to an offshore island, *Homo erectus* lashed logs together and oversea migration began. Their watercrafts were probably log or bamboo rafts with an early form of sail large enough to transport a founder population. These rafts could only travel downwind, but there were annually wind direction reversals across Wallacea. From November to April the wind blew toward the east and from May to October it blew to the west making return trips possible. On the island of Java, the ancient word for the village chief was *panggaitik* or raft commander. (Haddon and Hornell 1975 [1938]) Later, early modern man would cross the Vitiaz Strait between the islands of Papua New Guinea and the Bismarck Archipelago of Melanesia.

The maritime innovation of round bottom dugout canoe hulls required tools capable of hollowing out logs and shell adzes appeared in the Moluccas Islands of Wallacea and in the Bismarck Archipelago as early as 11,000 BC. Early dugout canoes had raised sides made of sewn planks with two log stabilizing outriggers, one on each side of the hull and a lateen sail. It has been proposed the double-outrigger canoe may have been derived from a three log raft when the central log, larger in size than the other two, was hollowed out forming a canoe and the spacing between the center and outer logs was increased. (Haddon and Hornell 1975 [1938]) Double-outrigger canoes still in widespread use throughout Island Southeast Asia are effective only in calm waters. Winds on voyages across the open ocean would cause the leeward outrigger to be driven underwater causing drag. The main transportation vessels of the Lapita people and Austronesian-speaking Proto-Polynesians were large, swift single-hull canoes with a single-outrigger enabling them to migrate eastward into the islands of Remote Oceania. Previously, migrations through Island Southeast Asia and along the outer islands of Melanesia had generally been along the coast, always remaining in sight of land. The Lapita people were ocean going blue water sailors who traveled through the islands of Melanesia and into Remote Oceania. Their single-outrigger canoes were constructed from dugout canoe hulls with extensions, outrigger floats and sails. The single-outrigger was placed on the windward side of the canoe, if placed on the leeward side when the canoe was under sail the wind would force the outrigger underwater. To enable changes of direction, the sail was movable reversing the bow and stern and a steering oar was often located at each end of the canoe. The most advanced single-outrigger canoes were developed in Micronesia, they had deep V-shaped hulls reducing lateral drift and to compensate for drag caused by the single-outrigger, canoe hulls were constructed asymmetrically curving away from the outrigger equalizing drag and enabling the canoe to travel in a straight line. They had a triangular lateen sail on a central mast that could be rotated and attached at either end for changing direction and there was a large storage platform on the outrigger side. The large single-hull, single-outrigger canoe could actually sail best across the prevailing winds with its triangular sail pivoting like the sail of a windsurfer.

The last major Polynesian maritime innovation was development of the double-hull voyaging canoe. Early development of this new maritime technology took place in Western Polynesia in the Fiji, Tonga and Samoa Island region. The Fijian *wanga drua* canoe was an adaptation of outrigger canoes of Micronesia, it had hulls of unequal lengths with the secondary hull reduced in size and pointed at either end functioning as an outrigger float. The canoe could sail with either end forward, the mast was located midway along the larger hull and an oceanic lateen sail similar to those of the Micronesians was attached to the mast. (Haddon and Hornell 1975 [1938]) Later, in the Tuamotu and Tahitian Islands, Polynesians would develop the *pahi* double-hull voyaging canoe thirty to sixty feet long with a V-shaped keel, built-up plank sides with seams sewn together supported by internal ribs. These hulls were of equal length with symmetrical cross-sections and were attached with crossbooms creating a large stable platform between the hulls. Double-hull canoes were able to cover far greater distances in the open ocean having a greater carrying capacity then outrigger canoes and were actually more stable when fully loaded than when empty. Some were over 100 feet long and eight feet deep, able to carry large groups of men and women with shelters protecting supplies of planting material and domesticated animals over great distances, they could travel 120 miles or more per day. Their hulls were pointed at each end serving as either the bow or stern and their masts were movable being fastened with strong ropes to each hull. Tacking into the wind was done by shifting the position of the mast and sail or by shunting. The lateen sail was replaced with the V-shaped inverted sail without a main boom positioned apex down and a curved edge along the top of the sail allowed the wind to spill over reducing stress. This type of sail was developed further in sails of the Marquesas Islands and was perfected in the "half claw" sails of the islands of Tahiti and the "crab claw" sails of the Hawaiian Islands. Double-hull voyaging canoes were able to sail within 75 degrees of the true wind direction and sat high in the water making them capable of great speed. Paddles used for propulsion were adapted for steering under sail and some steering paddles were as long as thirty-three feet with a blade fourteen feet long and twenty-one inches wide. There were even two-story double-hull canoes in the Tonga and Fiji Islands (Fig. 62).

THE POLYNESIAN SYSTEM OF NAVIGATION

The ancient Polynesians who set sail on one of mankind's greatest adventures had a remarkable tradition of advancing their navigational knowledge that had been passed on verbally for countless generations. They sailed under the command of chiefs and navigator priests using the stars of the night sky as their guide.

> "[They] made the greatest voyages of discovery against the greatest odds that men have ever faced. In boats which, for grace and speed and pure sophistication of design were a thousand years or more ahead of their times."

> (From *Migrations, Myths and Magic from the Gilbert Islands,* 1972, by Arthur F. Grimble, page 154)

Polynesians voyagers used celestial navigation, zenith stars and the rising and setting of stars along the horizon as their compass during ocean voyages turning the trackless ocean into a network of sea routes, an *ala moana* or "pathway of the sea". Hawaiians identified as many as 200 to 300 stars and the rising and setting positions on the horizon of more than 150 stars, such as the three stars forming the belt of the Constellation of Orion or *Na Kao* that rose due east and set due west. Using "star pits" along the horizon and zenith stars Polynesians were able to determine latitude and longitude. Polynesians developed the fore and aft navigational star path system known in the islands of Tahiti as *'avei'a* and elsewhere in the South Pacific as *kavenga* or *kaveinga*. Positions along the horizon where stars rise and set in succession remain the same throughout the year giving navigators a directional point of reference. (Lewis 1994 [1972])

Successful colonization required the ability to discover unknown islands and return. Later, settlement voyages would follow with groups of canoes and supplies. Voyages of discovery were made by departing after the wind direction had shifted or tacking into the wind on the outward leg of their journey, if no new landfall was located and supplies were running low a rapid return trip downwind was possible. Sailing direction was determined by alignment with a set of stars moving one after another above a point on the horizon known as a "star pit". In the Hawaiian language these horizon points are known as *lua*, in Tahitian they are known as *rua*. A star rising in the eastern sky from a "star pit" on the horizon travels across the sky setting in a corresponding "star pit" on the western horizon. This was the navigator's "star compass", he would remember their star pattern and adjust course throughout the night. For their return voyage, the navigator who had previously been looking astern during the outward trip seeing the setting star chain, would set the return course. Once an island had been located navigators would be able to repeat the voyage.

At any given latitude certain zenith stars would pass directly overhead and if a navigator knew which star passed directly over his destination island, he would be able to determine when he was approaching its latitude. To reach the Hawaiian Islands navigators from the islands of the South Pacific would sail north knowing the prevailing winds would move the canoe to the west. They would make as much progress to the east of their target as possible and when reaching the correct latitude would turn west and sail downwind to make landfall. (Holmes 1993) The zenith star for the Hawaiian Islands was *Hokule'a*, the "star of gladness", now known as Arcturus, for the islands of Tahiti the zenith star was *'A'a* or *Hokuho'okelewa*, "the canoe guiding star" currently known as Sirius or the Dog Star, and for the islands of Samoa it was the star *Hikianalia*, now known as Spica. The Hawaiians were aware of Polaris, the North Star they called *Hoku pa'a*, "the fixed star", and knew five of the planets they called *Hoku hele*, "the traveling stars", or *Hoku 'ae'a*, "the wandering stars", and meteors were called *Hoku lele*, "the flying stars". Sailing south from the Hawaiian Islands to the islands of Tahiti, they crossed the equator and then *Newe* or *Newenewe* became their "guiding star".

> "If you sail for the Kahiki groups [the Islands of Tahiti], you will discover new constellations and strange stars over the deep ocean . . . When you arrive at *Piko o Wakea* [the equator], you will lose sight of *Hoku pa'a* [the north star] and then *Newe* [the Southern Cross] will be your southern guiding star."

> (Instructions in ancient Hawaiian astronomy as taught by
> Kaneakaho'owaha, a counselor to Kamehameha the
> First, in *Pacific Marine Review*, Vol.
> 17, no. 2, July, 1920)

Polynesian long distance voyaging was "an enterprise that properly should rank among the great achievements of human history". (Emory 1963) The Polynesians, "confident in their skill and courage regularly covered thousands of miles of open sea" (Fig. 63). Polynesian navigators would wait for favorable weather conditions before departing on long distance voyages beginning at dusk, aligning their departure when island landmarks were still visible known as "back sighting". Upon reaching the open ocean they navigated by stars of the night sky. The period of the most extensive Polynesian voyaging occurred during the "Little Climatic Optimum", a time of warm gentle trade winds, calm seas with few storms and frequent westerly winds. (Holmes 1993) Most sailing was done at night, daytime was for rest and sleep. During the day their canoes were guided by the direction of seasonal winds, currents, wave patterns and by the sun. They were able to stay on relative course during daylight hours and course corrections were made as soon as the stars came out at night. If drift caused by current, wind or a storm carried the canoe off course during the day realignment using the fore and aft star path system at night would put the canoe back on course. Polynesians were able to make long distance voyages across thousands of miles of open-ocean navigating by the stars, winds and seas.

> "When the night was a clear one they steer by the stars; and this is the easiest navigation for them because those being so many, not only do they note by them the bearings on which several islands with which they are in touch lie, but also the harbours in them, so that they make straight for the entrance by following the rhumb [path] of the particular star that rises or sets over it."

> (From an account of traditional Tahitian navigation in the
> Journal of Spanish Captain Jose de Andia y
> Varela after visiting Tahiti in 1774)

Polynesian navigators had an acute awareness of nature and were able to adjust course using large amounts of information from the natural environment; from the surface of the ocean, clouds in the sky and from below the water's surface. Individual island destinations were not just tiny dots, there were many signs that could be detected far beyond the sighting of land and islands could be located from far out at sea. Small islands such as low atolls could be easily missed if only visual sighting was relied upon. Ocean swells generated by trade winds could be felt through the pitch and roll of the canoe and wave patterns were distorted by the presence of land. Waves would bounce back and curve around islands indicating land well before it was visible enlarging the landfall target area and sea life seen close to the ocean's surface was an indication land was near. Even a small island had a target area of perhaps a fifty-mile diameter making landfall on a specific island possible and because most islands are part of a larger group or archipelago the amount of information revealing their location was greatly enlarged, for example the landfall target area of the Hawaiian Islands stretches for 416 miles. Certain cloud formations would indicate land from as far away as fifty miles; the lagoon of an atoll would leave a greenish reflection on the underside of clouds, a reef would leave a pinkish color, bright areas on clouds would indicate an extensive area of sand or surf and clouds above wooded areas were darker in color. Cloud formations above mountains can be seen at great distances; clouds piling up on the horizon indicate a high island is disrupting the flow of trade winds. On a cloudless day, land would "loom" above the horizon as a shimmering column of reflected light shooting into the sky. Sea birds sleep on land, head out to their ocean feeding grounds at dawn and return to land at dusk, their flight forms huge clouds of birds indicating the direction of landfall. Changes in the color of water from blue to light green indicate a submerged reef and submarine phosphorescence far below the ocean surface appearing as underwater streaks of light indicate the direction of land.

Polynesians developed several tools to aid navigation. Their star compass divided the horizon into twelve, sixteen, twenty-four or thirty-two equal distant points to help align a canoe to "star pits", the rising and setting points of stars along the horizon. A star compass with thirty-two star points was used across the Indian Ocean suggesting the Proto-Polynesian/Micronesian "star compass" system probably originated from Asia. On islands throughout Polynesia sighting stones and even stone canoes were set up so future navigators could sight along them learning the required star path. Proto-Polynesian navigational stick charts (Fig. 64) originating in the Marshall Islands of Micronesia mapped changes of wave patterns, currents and ocean swells as they passed islands or chains of islands. Waves hitting an island's windward shore are reflected back and diverted around the island, stick charts mapped the refraction of wave swells as they bent around islands and chains of islands. Navigators would feel the wave swell patterns from the motion of the canoe. Stick charts were made from a lattice of curved strips of split bamboo or coconut frond midribs bound together with coconut sennit and would indicate the altered directions of ocean swells when deflected by the presence of islands represented by white cowry shells or coral pebbles. Although not constructed to scale, these stick sea charts were used as navigational teaching tools. There were three types of stick charts used in the Marshall Islands, the *Mattang* chart showed the abstract general concept of swell patterns around a single island or atoll and was for instructional purposes only. The *Meddo* chart specifically illustrated four or five islands in the Marshall Island group with their wave patterns and the *Rebbelib* chart mapped the entire Marshall Island Archipelago. Stick charts are significant in the history of cartography, they were the first mapping of ocean features in history.

Hawaiian canoe building was a religious activity; so many things could possibly go wrong only a supportive god could ensure success. Each step of a canoe's construction was steeped in religious rituals to appease the gods and acquire their protection against accidents and difficulties. Religious ceremonies occurred when a tree was felled for a canoe hull, during all phases of canoe construction and at the canoe's launching. It was believed only supportive deities could ensure against a felled tree being rotten, a log rolling out of control while it was being hauled to shore or a hull developing a crack as it neared completion. Forests were considered the realm of the gods and wood was considered a sacred manifestation of the major gods, no tree could be cut without first petitioning both the gods and appropriate *ali'i* chief. Ceremonial rites were performed by a master canoe builder or *kahuna kalai wa'a* whose expertise, skill, and craftsmanship in canoe design increased his *mana*. Religious ceremonies were held upon completion of canoe construction, the finished canoe was consecrated with accompanying feasts and giving thanks to the gods. Prayers for launching canoes were made to *Kane*, god of the forest and *Kanaloa*, god of the sea.

In selecting trees for canoe construction the *'elepaio*, a small Hawaiian bird known as a form of *Kupulupulu*, god of the *koa* forest, was closely observed. It would follow canoe builders through the forest as they searched for suitable trees and its behavior could identify defects in the trees. Religious ceremonies were conducted during construction addressing the god *Ku* and several of his forms. The goddess *Lea,* deity of canoe building, was the wife of one of these forms of *Ku* and her animal manifestation was the *'elepaio* bird. After a fine *koa* tree was located, the *kahuna kalai wa'a* would sleep at a sacred *hale mua* before a shrine of his deity to obtain a revelation in a dream as to whether the tree was sound. If he dreamt someone was standing naked before him, a sign of misfortune, he knew the *koa* tree was rotten and would not go up into the woods to cut the tree, but if his dream was of a handsome well-dressed man or woman, he knew the tree would make a good canoe. After a prayer at the *heiau,* adzes for cutting the *koa* tree were "put to sleep" under the *kuahu* altar in the *mana* house and awakened by dipping them in the sea. The *kahuna kalai wa'a* brought offerings of pig, red fish, coconuts and *'awa* to the site of the selected tree and after prayers to *Ku*, god of the forest, the *kahuna* and his assistants would sleep at the foot of the *koa* tree. When a royal canoe was to be constructed, a human sacrifice was sometimes buried at the base of the tree. They would build an *imu* and in the morning cook the pig and red fish and burn a chip from the *koa* tree. They ate the food within the vicinity of the tree and what remained was buried along with the *malo* of the *kahuna* as an offering to the gods. After a final prayer the tree could be cut.

> "O Lea, woman who builds canoes,
> Goddess of canoe making,
> I have come up to cut a tree for a canoe,
> Here if my gift, a free will offering,

A sacrifice to you, O Lea,
Here is the red fish, a red loin cloth.
Grant me much skill, strength and wise thinking,
Grant me patience.
All hindrances and obstacles, . . .
Make them be trifles, . . .
Make the strokes of my adze strike well,
Let the chips fly at each stroke
Until the work is finished.
'Amama ua noa, the prayer is freed."

(Prayer by Kalokuokamaile, canoe builder, astronomer, advisor to the court and half-brother of Kamekameha the First, recited before felling a tree for a canoe from the article Canoe Making and Descriptions in *Ka Nupepa Kuokoa*, December 7, 1922, Hawaiian Ethnographic Notes, Bernice Pauahi Bishop Museum. Courtesy of the Bishop Museum, Honolulu)

The *kahuna kalai wa'a* would begin felling the tree by making two horizontal cuts into the trunk about three feet apart, then splitting the wood off in between. Once it was cut down the *kahuna kalai wa'a* would begin trimming off tree limbs and tie an *'ie'ie* vine around the top of the tree. The tree was topped off, the taboo or *kapu* removed and all could proceed to work on the canoe hull. After the tree had been felled *Lea,* goddess of canoe building in the form of the *'elepaio* bird, would advise on the soundness of the tree. The bird would walk the entire length of the tree, if it walked without stopping the tree was sound, if it stopped and pecked at the bark it was a sign the tree was rotten and filled with insects and if the *'elepaio* bird avoided the tree altogether it was healthy and strong. Where the bird traversed the tree was to be the top opening of the canoe and if the bird flew above the tree and circled it meant the *kahuna* should rotate the tree. If the canoe opening should be on the side, the bird would fly in that direction. If the bird stood in one spot on the trunk of the tree and remained there, it indicated there was a defect at that point; the *'elepaio* bird was considered a reliable predictor of a tree's condition.

HAWAIIAN ADZES

Hawaiian tools were made of wood, stone, bone and shell, metal was not originally available to the islanders. The most important Hawaiian construction tool was the stone adze or *ko'i*, its head was made from dense, fine-grained basaltic lava rock or *'ala* and the adze handle or half was made from hard *olopua* wood. Adzes ranged from over two feet long including the half to finger size chisels (Fig. 65). Adze makers, known as *po'e ka ko'i,* were specialized stone craftsman who supplied canoe builders with a tool kit of many types of *ko'i* or stone adzes of different sizes, shapes and weights, hafted at different angles for use in canoe construction such as the *ko'i 'awili* and *ko'i kupa* used for hollowing out the canoe hull. Where the hollowed out hull was too narrow for ordinary adzes such as the bow and stern, the *ko'i kupa 'ai ke'e,* a socketed, swivel-headed adze was used. The edge of the adze could be turned to any angle and it was named for *Kupa'aike'e,* the mythological god who was said to have invented it. (Holmes 1993) The *ko'i pahoa,* a chisel adze, and the *ko'i pa'ahana* were used for canoe hull shaping, the *ko'i kukulu* was used to shave the sides of the canoe hull and the *ko'i hulu* and *ko'i oma* were used for smoothing and finishing the canoe hull.

Metal adzes were utilized after western contact, before Captain James T. Cook's arrival in the Hawaiian Islands only small amounts of metal had been found washed up on beaches attached to pieces of wood or arrived with the few foreigners shipwrecked on Hawaiian shores and there was a Hawaiian saying, "all above, all below the sea, the land, and iron cast upon the shore, all belong to the king [high chief]". (Remy 1979 [1857]) Once freed from the wood, metal could be pointed or given an edge through abrasion just as stone tools. When Cook first arrived on Kaua'i Island, he traded iron nails that could be fashioned into fishhooks for fresh water fish, pigs and sweet potatoes, introducing a supply of iron. The demand for nails became so great, "a moderate size nail will supply my ship's company very plentifully with excellent pork for the day, and as to potatoes and taro, they are attained upon still easier terms". (Captain Charles Clerke 1778) While trading in Alaska, Cook so diminished his supply of iron before wintering in the Hawaiian Islands, he prepared his ship's forges to melt down a damaged anchor to make thin iron sheets that could be cut into blanks for adzes and chisels.

The working edge of the stone adze was wedge-shaped whereas the metal adze was more knife-like. Penetrations from each impact of the metal adze were deeper, but the stone adze was more durable requiring less frequent sharpening and for shaping and finishing touches many Hawaiian craftsman still preferred the stone adze that was more easily controlled than the metal adze and more precise, it could remove a finer shaving.

"In watching the shaping of a canoe I have seen the old canoe-maker use for the rough shaping and excavating an ordinary foreign steel adze, but for the finishing touches he dropped the foreign tool and returned to the adze of his ancestors, and the blunt looking stone cut off a delicate shaving from the very hard *koa* wood and never seemed to take too much wood as the foreign adze was apt to do."

(From *Ancient Hawaiian Stone Implements,* 1974 [1902], in
the Memoirs of the Bernice Pauahi Bishop Museum,
Vol. 1, no. 4, by William T. Brigham, pages 409, 410.
Courtesy of Bishop Museum Press, Honolulu)

The most important adze quarry on Hawai'i Island was the Keanakako'i Adze Quarry located on the upper slopes of Mauna Kea between the 11,000-foot and 12,400-foot elevations, it covered seven and a half square miles where an especially hard fine-grained, blue-black basaltic stone known as *hawaiite* was formed when the later stage of an ancient lava flow quickly cooled as it flowed beneath a 400-foot thick glacial ice cap covering about 26 square miles of the summit of Mauna Kea during the last Ice Age. The process of adze making began by selecting a suitable stone and using a hammer stone to reduce it to the desired shape and size of the finish adze. Soaking the rough stones in a bowl containing liquor made from vegetable juices, sap from *palai* ferns and green *kukui* nuts was believed to soften the stones making them more workable.

"After splitting the rock and obtaining a long fragment, they [the adze makers] placed it in a liquor made from vegetable juices (wai la'au), . . . After keeping keeping the stone in the liquor a few days it was thought to become softer and more easy to work."

(From *Hawaiian Antiquities: Moolelo Hawaii*, 1951 [1898],
Bishop Museum Special Publication 2, by David Malo,
pages 77, 78. Courtesy of Bishop
Museum Press, Honolulu)

Adze makers would take the crudely formed adzes home for finishing, they would grind and polish the rough edges until finally producing smooth sides and a fine edge. The completed adze was then lashed to an 'L' shaped handle or haft made of *olopua* or *hau* wood cut with a heel and the stone was attached with cords of *olona* or coconut sennit with a piece of dry leaf from the *hala* or pandanus tree or from the banana tree laid between the wood and stone. *Hau* wood is light and strong with branches that are naturally curved. Adzes made from conch shells and extremely hard *alahe'e* wood was useful for making softwood canoes. Other canoe tools were chisels, hammer stones, clamps, drills and caulking tools. Small chisels were usually made from the same stone as adzes, some had wooden handles and were used to make narrow rectangular lashing holes along the rim of canoe hulls.

CANOE CONSTRUCTION

Canoe hauling was a laborious and dangerous task, first the hull or *kino* was rough-hewed removing existing branches, and bark then the log was roughly shaped lightening it for hauling to a canoe shed located near the beach.

"O Lea, women who builds canoes,
Goddess of canoe making,
And Mokuhali'i and Kura'aike'e,
Male gods of canoe making,
Here is pork,
A pork gift, a sacrifice, an offering
From Kalokuokamaile
Grant him much skill,
Skill and *mana*, unlimited *mana*,
So therefore you are obliged to Kalokuokamaile for his pork,
'Amana ua noa, the prayer is freed."

(Prayer by Kalokuokamaile from the article Canoe
Making and Descriptions in *Ka Nupepa Kuokoa,*
December 7, 1922, Hawaiian Ethnographic
Notes, Bernice Pauahi Bishop Museum

Courtesy of the Bishop
Museum, Honolulu)

Fire was sometimes used to assist in hollowing out canoe hulls, red-hot rocks placed along the log to be formed into a hull would slowly burn out areas to be removed. The stern end had a neck or *maku'u* providing an attachment point for hauling ropes; a small canoe hull required three ropes, a larger canoe hull four or five. As the log was hollowed out, it was kept wet to prevent drying and checking between work sessions. The hollowed out section of the hull that held water was covered with coconut fronds. Some canoe hulls were left to cure at the spot where they had been cut, others were hauled to shore and cured after being exposed to the sun for three months or more ensuring they were completely dry before construction began. A religious ceremony and festival was conducted to protect the canoe hull from being damaged until it was safely housed in a canoe shed.

> "O Ku-pulupulu,
> O Ku-alana-wao,
> O Ku-moku-hali'i,
> Care for this canoe;
> Care for its bow;
> Care for its stern;
> Until it reaches the shore;
> Care for it until it is placed in the *halau* [canoe shed]."

(Prayer by Peleioholani, a Hawaiian ruling high chief of O'ahu, recorded by N.B. Emerson from *Na Pule Kahiko, Ancient Hawaiian Prayers*, 1983, by June Gutmanis, page 77. Copyright; Bess Press, Honolulu)

The route was cleared, hauling ropes were attached to the neck of the hull, and often the whole village would haul the canoe hull. A canoe guide would ride on the rough canoe hull or *ka'ele* and a *kahuna kalai wa'a* would walk alone about sixty feet to the rear of the canoe hull because space behind the hull was reserved for the gods whose presence was there in spirit. Once in the canoe shed or *halau wa'a*, the canoe hull was mounted on wooden canoe supports or *lona* curved to fit the bottom of the canoe. Hulls were first positioned bottom up and the outer hull was shaped, it was tapered at both ends for the pointed bow and stern, the sides were trimmed and the bottom rounded. Then the hull was rotated, the top flattened and the hull further hollowed out leaving brackets for the seats.

Finished canoes were not left in the water or sun when not in use. Saltwater, sun and rain were hard on hulls, lashings and joints, and to reduce these problems canoes were placed in sheds for protection. There were two types of canoe sheds, permanent stonewall structures with an open end facing the sea and temporary post structures without sides; both had thatched roofing. Some sheds large enough to accommodate a sizable double-hull canoe could also function as a living, dining or assembly structure. When hull finishing work was about to begin a sacred *'aha* cord was stretched across the opening of the canoe shed indicating only craftsmen could enter; it was *kapu*. A distinctive feature of Hawaiian canoes was a small flat horizontal projection of 1" or 1½" extending just beyond the stern of the hull. It was left after the neck at the stern where hauling ropes had been attached was removed, this was known as the *momoa* or *moamoa*. When the warrior/priest Pa'ao departed from Ra'iatea Island, Tahiti, heading for Hawai'i Island, a prophet named Makuak'aumana wished to join the voyage, but the canoe was full so he leaped off a cliff in spirit form landing on the *momoa* and was able to sail to Hawai'i Island, where it became traditional the *momoa* was where the canoe *akua* or spirit rode protecting the canoe at sea. Smoothing was done using rubbing stones or *'o'io* of graduated coarseness made from *pahoehoe* lava, fine coral and pumice or *ana*. (Holmes 1993) Dried breadfruit leaves functioned as sandpaper and polishing stones or *pohaku 'anai wa'a*, bamboo leaves and dried sharkskin were used for polishing. The outside of the hull was painted first, paint was made of juice from the inner bark and roots of the *kukui* tree and buds of the banana tree which were mixed, pounded into a liquid in mortars with stone pestles and mixed with charcoal made from burned pandanus leaves. The black paint was called *pa'ele* and *kukui* nut oil was applied as a lacquer. Paintbrushes were made from the aerial roots of the pandanus tree, one end was beaten so the fibers were frayed. Two or three coats of *pa'ele* were applied to the hull. Paint for the canoes of high chiefs had ochre added making it red in color. (Holmes 1993)

With the hull or *kino* completed, accessories such as plank wash strakes, end covers, braces and seats were added. The sides of the dugout hull were raised with the addition of side and end pieces. Plank wash strakes or *mo'o* six to eight inches high and one inch or less thick were made of *'ahakea*, a light colored, yellowish wood or from wood of the breadfruit or *'ulu* tree, usually there were two or more lengths on each side left in their original light color or stained yellow. During construction side strakes were suspended from the canoe shed rafters for trimming and shaping. Wooden clamps or *puki'i wa'a* held the strake sections in place while they were being lashed to the canoe hull. The strake sections were fitted to the canoe body with a double scarf joint and three-ply coconut sennit lashing called a *kaholo* (Fig. 66). Hawaiian cordage or *'aha* was mostly made of coconut fibers, although some was made from *hau* tree bark and fibers of the *olona* plant, the fibers were braided into cords with round or rectangular cross sections of different sizes from thread to rope. The seam between the strake and dugout hull was an overlapping joint and any additional strakes were fitted to the one below in the same manner. Lashing holes were narrow horizontal openings about eight to nine inches apart through which rectangular woven sennit lashings were passed; tightly filling the holes keeping out water. Holes were bored with rotary bow drills having shell or sea urchin drill points and small stone and shell chisels were used for making the slits. Lashings were countersunk, barely visible on the exterior being protected from damage caused by wear and abrasion; protruding sennit lashings would impede the speed of the canoe through the water. "They are built of several pieces sewn together . . . in so neat a manner that on the outside it is difficult to see the joints . . . of boards closely fitted together and well secured to the body of the vessel." It was the coconut sennit lashings and caulking made from the resin of the breadfruit tree that held the Hawaiian canoe together.

"What have I, O Tane [Kane],
O Tane [Kane], god of beauty!
'Tis sennit!
'Tis sennit of the host of heaven,
'Tis sennit for thee, O Tane [Kane]!
Thread it from inside, it comes outside,
Thread if fully, tie it fast.
This is the fashion of thy sennit,
O Tane [Kane],
To hold thy canoe,
That she may go over long waves,
And over short waves;
To the near horizon,
Even to the far-off horizon.
This sennit of thine, O Tane [Kane],
Let it hold, let it hold!"

(From The Song of Hiro, the great navigator and explorer from
Ra'iatea Island, Tahiti, in *Ancient Tahiti*, 1971 [1928], Bishop
Museum Bulletin 48, by Teuira Henry, page 550.
Courtesy of Bishop Museum Press, Honolulu)

End pieces were specially designed to cover each side of the bow and stern sections of the hull not covered by strakes and cover the open ends of the hull. Vertical elliptical extensions at the bow and stern or *manu* were originally carved abstract symbols of birds or spirit images as ornamentation, the bow *manu ihu* kept the canoe from driving into the back of a swell and the stern *manu hope* would break the face of a following wave that would otherwise wash over the canoe. A median canoe bow cover or *kaupo'i* provided extra protection from water washing over the bow. Canoe seats or *nohona wa'a* were boards of *'ohi'a lehua* wood fitted to the sidewalls of the hull resting on support blocks, comb cleats or *pepeiao*, left along the inside of the hull wall. Canoe spreaders or *wae wa'a* were curved U-shaped supports inserted within the hull, lashed to two horizontal support comb cleats or *pepeiao* one on each inner side of the hull into which holes were drilled and crossbooms or *'iako* were lashed to the spreaders and comb cleats. Spreaders also functioned as a frame supporting the sides of the canoe hull. (Haddon and Hornell 1975 [1938])

Double-hull canoes had two parallel hulls connected and kept 2½ to 4 feet apart with two to as many as six connecting crossbooms or *'iako* made of *'ohi'a lehua* wood. The distance between hulls was limited by the strength of sennit lashings connecting the crossbooms to the each hull, in rough weather the hulls would move separately putting great stress on the lashings. In the Hawaiian Islands crossbooms were originally straight, later the curved crossbeam was developed that had straight ends over the hulls and was curved upward in the middle raising the height of the platform or *pola* between the hulls helping to keep passengers and cargo dry. Wood for these arched booms was from the *hau* tree whose twisted growth patterns provided the necessary curvature. For long voyages, a movable thatched structure or *hale lanalana* made of light poles and beams was built on the platform or *pola* for keeping plant materials dry so they could be replanted. Outrigger canoes were more common than double-hull canoes because of their ease of handling and their multiple uses, they had two outrigger crossbooms projecting outward on the port side lashed to a float or *ama* on the water line through holes in the float. The inboard section of each outrigger crossboom was straight and outboard it curved downward to the upper surface of the float, crossbooms were made from the lightweight curved branches of the *hau* tree. The float or *ama* was usually made of *wiliwili* wood due to its buoyancy and was curved upward at its front end so as not to dig into the water. Canoe lashings binding the *'iako* to the hull or *'aha hoa wa'a* were both flexible and incredibly strong, able to withstand forces of thousands of pounds per square inch. Lashings were usually made of *'aha* or coconut sennit fibers braided or twisted into twine that would tighten when wet. The most elaborate lashing known as *pa'u o Lu'ukia* was considered sacred and reserved for canoes of *ali'i*. The name comes from the story of Lu'ukia who defended herself against advances of her lover Mo'ikeha by wearing a chastity belt of such intricate weaving Mo'ikeha was unable to undo it.

The Hawaiian "crab claw" sprit sail is thought to have evolved from the oceanic sprit "half claw" sails of the Marquesan and Tahitian Islands that were triangular in shape with the apex of the triangle at the foot of a mast, the Hawaiian mast or *kia* was made of *'ohi'a lehua* wood. The inverted triangular "crab claw" sail had a distinctive adjustable upper curve, its name being derived from its shape. The triangular sails, *la* or *pe'a*, were mounted apex down with the lower end of the flexible boom sprit tied near the foot of the mast, the upper end of the boom sprit curved inward toward the mast head. A rope extending from the upper end of the sprit to the top of the mast continued down to the deck from where the sail could be adjusted reducing wind pressure. In single-hull canoes, the mast was set through holes in the seats and rested in a socket or shoe. In double-hull canoes, masts were set in a socket on the *pola* or had a notch cut in their lower end and were placed on a crossboom or *'iako* and lashed in place. Voyaging double-hull canoes having two sails were easier to handle than canoes with one large sail. The sails were made of long narrow horizontally woven matting panels of saltwater resistant *hala* leaves made from the pandanus tree, pleated into strips, and sewn together. Feathers or tapa streamers called *lei hulu manu* were attached to the top of the boom sprit or mast to indicate wind direction. The sails of the canoes of Hawaiian high *ali'i* chiefs were painted red and had a red-feathered pennant hanging from their masthead. Canoe sails for high chiefs and war canoes had an emblem woven into the center of the sail, a white circle with twelve red rays probably a representation of the sun.

In the Hawaiian Islands, after the beginning of the "Little Ice Age", long distance voyaging declined and canoe travel became limited to coastal and inter-island voyages. The design of the large canoes changed, they were now chiefly for warfare and local transportation, paddling replaced sailing as the main form of propulsion. Paddling was the most common means of propulsion over short distances, but long voyages required sails. Hawaiian paddles or *hoe* were made from a single piece of hardwood usually *koa*. They had a long, straight, thick, rounded shaft four to five feet in length with short wide oval shaped blades. Flat on the back surface and slightly convex on the forward surface, many ancient paddles had a short thickened rib known as *io* or *ude* located at the tip of the blade to prevent cracking, a detail also found on canoe paddles in the Central Caroline Islands of Micronesia. Steering paddles, some as long as eighteen feet, were made in the same general shape as other paddles, but were proportionately larger. They functioned as both a steering rudder and keel acting to prevent sideways drift. A rope safety cord that passed through a hole near the top of the steering paddle shaft was attached to the canoe to prevent the paddle from being swept away and lost in rough seas. (Holmes 1993) Canoes carried stone anchors or *heleuma* with drilled holes for rope attachment. A mat cover or *pa'u* made of pandanus leaves or *lau hala* was used to prevent swamping during heavy weather, the mat usually covered from the top of the strakes on each side in the mid-section of the hull where baggage and freight was stored and a larger woven *pa'u* with large holes for paddlers could be fitted over the entire hull opening. Small holes or *holo* were located along the upper edge of the strakes so mat covers could be held in place using a cord that crisscrossed across the mat known as an *alihi pa'u*. (Haddon and Hornell 1975 [1938])

Canoe ladders or *paepae wa'a* allowed canoe launching and landing along rocky, cliff bound coasts, a development unique to the Hawaiian Islands (Fig. 67). The *'ohi'a* wood canoe ladders were made of several ramp sections 10 to 30 feet long and 8 to 12 feet wide, they reached from a flat area at the top of a cliff and extended into the water, the last section floated with the ocean swells and was removable. The canoe ladder was attached by tying it through holes drilled in the rocks.

> "In one place, where there were a few low rocks about thirty feet from the shore, they erected a kind of ladder. Two long poles, one tied to the end of the other, reached from these rocks to the top of the cliffs. Two other poles, tied together in the same manner, were fixed parallel to the first two, and about four to five feet distant from them. Strong sticks, eight to ten feet long, were laid across these at right angles, and about two or three inches apart, which being fastened to the long poles with *ie*, the tough fibrous roots of a climbing sort of plant, found in the woods, and thus formed the steps of this ingenious and useful ladder."

> (From the *Journal of William Ellis: A Narrative of an 1823 Tour of Hawaii, or Owhyee,* 1963 [1826], by William Ellis, page 219)

A canoe would be paddled into position, ride a wave surge toward the rocks and onto the canoe ladder ramp where men standing in position at the water's edge would grab the canoe keeping it from sliding backward and together with the paddlers would carry the canoe up the ladder to level ground where it was stored in a nearby canoe shed. (Holmes 1993)

CANOE DEDICATION CEREMONY

When assembly of a canoe was complete, the final dedication ceremony named *lolowa'a* or "imparting brains to the canoe" was held. Before launching an *'aha* prayer was recited by the *kahuna kalai wa'a* or canoe maker standing with the owner at the bow of the canoe. The owner placed a small pig, named Lono or "brains", in the stern of the canoe. If the pig walked from the stern to the bow and sat down without jumping out, it was a favorable omen and the *kahuna kalai wa'a* would declare the canoe was strong and would have no accidents. He said to the owner, "this is a canoe to sail in; it will not meet with misfortune in the foamy sea, nor in the deep sea".

> O Mokuhali'i, Kura'aike'e, Lea
> Here is pork,
> A reward, a gift, an offering,
> A sacrifice to you.
> The canoe is finished,
> Ready to be launched in the sea,
> That is the place for it to seek profit and wealth;
> Watch thou carefully.
> Be on guard for coral beds and stones of the reefs,
> For the waves and billows of the ocean,
> Steer the canoe over the depths of the sea,
> Let the canoe go over the waves of the sea,
> Till it becomes worn, moss grown and aged.
> *'Amama ua noa*, the *kapu* is lifted, it is removed."

> ('*Aha* prayer to the gods of canoe making for the launching of a
> Hawaiian canoe by Kalokuokamaile from the article Canoe
> Making and Descriptions in *Ka Hupepa Kuokoa*, February
> 8, 1923, Hawaiian Ethrographic Notes, Bernice
> Pauahi Bishop Museum. Courtesy of the
> Bishop Museum, Honolulu)

The canoe dedication took place on the beach near the *halau,* an *imu* was built, and food prepared while the canoe was being decorated with forest ferns. After a feast of pig, coconuts, *'awa* and bananas, the canoe was taken out on a practice run and if the owner caught a red fish it was a good omen. The entire population of a district would take part in the launching ceremonies for a large canoe holding a consecration feast or *aha'aina ho'ola'a* containing prayers to *Kane,* god of the forest, from where the canoe trees were cut and *Kanaloa,* god of the sea, over which the canoe would travel. During the launching ceremony for a new canoe, it was "made to drink seawater" by being rocked up and down until waves poured over its bow and stern and when enough seawater filled the hull, it was removed with new canoe bailers or *ka*. By drinking seawater the new canoe was blessed by the god *Kane*. Launching ceremonies where canoes were given a spirit life was a Proto-Polynesian Austronesian tradition going back to Island Southeast Asia. In preparation for a lengthy voyage a canoe would be well stocked with provisions, a bed of sand and stones on the *pola* provided a place for cooking and an image of their god was housed in the thatched structure on the *pola*. Each voyage however short or long began with a prayer,

> "O Ku of the mountains, of the uplands, of the forest;
> O Ku, the ancestor of the canoe,
> O Ku, the benefactor of canoe builders,
> O Ku who has given the gift,
> O Ku who has guided the adzes,
> O Ku . . . who has formed out of nothing this mighty vessel . . .
> Guide this vessel . . .
> O Kane of the universe,
> Prepare the stars in the heavens,
> O Lono of the clouds,
> Clear the heavens,
> Make clear the guiding stars,
> O Kanaloa of the sea . . .
> Accept this consecrated canoe . . .
> *'Amama*, it is free."

(Prayer before a canoe voyage from *Na Pule Kahiko*,
Ancient Hawaiian Prayers, 1983, by June Gutmanis,
page 78. Copyright; Bess Press, Honolulu)

Throughout Polynesia and in the Hawaiian Islands, it was commonplace for deceased *ari'i* or *ali'i* to be buried in canoes facing westward suggesting the belief spirits of the dead were about to take a long journey to the land of their origin. The Great Caves of Niah in northwest Borneo, best known for their Neolithic human remains dating back to 38,000 BC, also contains a group of beached Austronesian dugout canoes or "death ships" allowing souls of the deceased to reach the afterlife. There were canoe coffins in the Lau Islands of Fiji, in the Samoa Islands bodies were set adrift in a canoe to reach the afterlife and in the Marquesas Islands there were canoe shaped coffins. American author Herman Melville described a wooden image of a deceased warrior chief in the Taipival Valley of Nuku Hiva Island in the Marquesas Islands, "seated in the stern of a canoe . . . holding his paddle with both hands in the act of rowing, leaning forward . . . as if eager to hurry on his voyage." In the Hawaiian Islands, canoes in caves symbolized death and old canoes often served as coffins in caves and lava tubes. The canoes were cut in half with the cut end either left open or closed with a wooden plank. The body was wrapped in *kapa* with a moss pillow added and cordage was tied around the outside of the canoe. The deceased was either laid straight, face up or seated as if voyaging into the afterlife.

HOUSING

The house was an important and good thing for a man's residence and health with his wife and children, his friends and those who enjoyed his hospitality.

A good thing was the house for warmth and a shelter from rain and cold, daylight and heat.

(From *The Ancient Hawaiian House*, 1908, in Memoirs
of the Bernice Pauahi Bishop Museum, Vol. II. no. 3,
by William Tufts Brigham, page 76. Courtesy
of Bishop Museum Press, Honolulu)

EARLY HOUSING

When the first settlers arrived in the Hawaiian Islands, they brought with them knowledge about housing construction and many of the Hawaiian terms for housing components were the same as in other places throughout Southern Polynesia. *Hale* is the Hawaiian word for house, it is *fare* in Tahitian, *fale* in Samoan and *bale* on the island of Sumatra. The earliest Hawaiian housing was of light construction due to the mild climate and was dispersed along the windward coasts that had an abundance of fresh water and fertile alluvial soil. Houses were located along freshwater streams adjacent to large tracts of productive arable land, near fishing grounds and across from openings through barrier reefs allowing canoe access to the open sea. Caves were sometimes used as dwellings, modifications included clearing, leveling, building platforms paved with smooth stones on the cave floor and stone walls were used to block entrances and create separate chambers. Early Hawaiian houses were small thatched huts arranged in clusters with rounded ends built directly on the ground or on low rock platforms with stone lined fire hearths in their interiors. Later, although rounded end houses continued in limited numbers, rectangular end houses became predominant. In the islands of Tahiti, rectangular housing represented an earlier form and rounded end housing was a later *ari'i* form. The residential complexes of commoners were small, they included a few sleeping houses, a cooking house with an earthen oven, perhaps a men's house with a shrine and storehouse with each structure consisting of only one room. The residential compounds of ruling chiefs and prominent people were much larger being composed of at least six separate houses for themselves and family members with facilities scattered over a large area (Fig. 68), ruling chiefs and others of high rank maintained several such housing complexes. Residences of high chiefs or *hale ali'i* were always built on raised platforms indicating their high social ranking and *kahili* or feathered standards were placed outside signifying their royal status. Originally, the term *lanai* meant a structure located near a house providing a covered sitting area, a roof with no sidewalls allowing for maximum ventilation. Later, the *lanai* became directly attached to the house.

ELEMENTS OF HOUSING COMPOUNDS

The *hale mua* or men's house was the main house and first to be constructed, it was where men ate their meals, offered sacrifices to their gods and where business was transacted; women and children were strictly forbidden. The *hale mua* contained a sacred *'aumakua* shrine, an altar or *kuahu* to the family god and an *ipu hulilau*, a gourd in which food and kava or *'awa* were placed for prayers to the god *Lono*. When a male child was about four or five years old, he was moved from the women's eating house, *hale 'aina,* to the *hale mua*, eating and resting house of the men, where he would eat food from the *ipu o Lono* and be dedicated to the god. Some *hale mua* of important *ali'i* included an outside extension, generally in the shape of a semi-circle or oval of stones, a shrine or *heiau* containing an altar and images of the gods. House lots or *pa hale* were fenced areas containing from one to four structures grouped closely together. Housing compounds contained a number of communal sleeping houses or *hale moe,* with their interiors partitioned into different spaces reserved for different groups of people. There were also *hale noa,* sleeping houses without *kapu* or restrictions for family members, relatives and retainers. Principal structures contained built-in cupboards and a fireplace for heat and light. The *hale kua* was for making tapa or *kapa* and *kua* was the name of the wooden anvil upon which tapa bark was beaten, sometimes a *hale ho'olu'u* was constructed to hold dye-making materials. The *hale kua* were surrounded by a stonewall creating a drying yard where *kapa* was dried and bleached. The *hale pe'a* were the women's menstrual houses and the *hale papa'a* or *hale ho'ahu* was a storage shed for crops and tools. There were several *hale imu* or *hale umu* cooking sheds containing below ground *imu,* stone lined oven pits, one for men and one for women who ate separately and from different foods. When chiefly housing compounds were located along the coast, there were canoe sheds or *halau wa'a,* a fishing house or *hale lawai'i* built as a shelter for nets and lines and perhaps even a fishpond. There were housing compounds for extended families or *'ohana* known as a *kauhale* located throughout the *'ahupua'a,* a fisherman's compound was located near the coast, a farmer's near his fields.

HOUSING IN WAIPI'O VALLEY

Housing settlements in fertile valleys such as Waipi'o Valley developed along the dry side slopes at the base of the valley walls and in the upper areas of the valley, the main valley floor was reserved for agriculture and was subject to flooding. Waipi'o Valley's housing was concentrated in five areas; Keone, Na'alapa, Koauka, Napo'opo'o and Lalakea (Fig. 69). Housing developed in a dense linear pattern along the back of the sand dune area in the front of the valley, an area known as Keone. The area along slopes at the base of the cliff on the Kohala side, between the Neneuwu and Naalapa waterfalls, was known as Naalapa and further up the valley on the Kohala side was the smaller Koauka housing area. There were a large number of houses at the mouth of Hi'ilawe Valley known as Napo'opo'o and a small number of houses were located in Lalakea along the base of the cliffs further up the valley on the Hilo side. No housing was located in the forested uplands outside of the valley; these were lands controlled by the ruling chief. There were major foot trails or *alanui* in Waipi'o Valley running up each side of the valley along the base of the cliffs and above the valley rim on the Hilo side. The Opailolo Trail ran up the valley and continued to Waimea and the Kealai Trail exited at the rear of the valley. The Muliwai or 'Z' Trail is a zigzag path that climbs up the cliff near the beach on the Kohala side leading to the adjacent Waimanu Valley.

There were several types of residential construction. Some houses had sidewalls of wood or stone and some had no sidewalls with their roof rafters connected directly into the ground. Rafters were either straight or curved; roofs either gable or hip. The gable roof is thought to have been the original pre-contact Hawaiian housing form and the hip roof became a later form more popular after western contact. (Brigham 1908) Houses were grouped together with meandering paths between them without any geometrical pattern. In Waipi'o Valley, settlements expanded inland along the lower slopes of the valley walls, the valley floor was reserved for cultivation of wet taro. Houses built on the sandy flood plain near a stream had their floor raised above ground level allowing floodwaters to pass under the house, their flooring poles would span between side walls, wall plates became sills and wall post became piers. (Brigham 1908)

The oldest and simplest house form was a roof with no sidewalls where the roof rafters were attached directly into the ground, these required less materials, labor and skill, and were often houses of commoners. Their framework was made of vertical ridge posts or *pou hana* supporting a main ridgepole or *kauhuhu*. The roof rafters or *o'a* were either straight or curved and were embedded directly into the ground (Fig. 70). As the housing form the original settlers brought with them evolved, rounded ends became square and rectangular houses became larger, but the structures remained a single room. They were set on elevated stone-faced rectangular platforms similar to those constructed in the Marquesas or Hiva Islands, some containing a raised sleeping area across the full length of the interior of the house. These were windowless structures usually with only one low entry door about three feet high. Crossed *kapu* sticks were sometimes placed across doorways indicating entry was forbidden. The Hawaiian house door could not be locked to protect against intruders, but a door stone could be suspended on the inside of the house above the entry door with a trip cord causing the stone to fall disabling or killing an intruder. (Brigham 1908)

The low entry was often the only source of ventilation although some houses had a small air hole located high up in the gable wall. Because an enemy could thrust a spear through the house walls people slept with their head toward the center of the house.

Hawaiian homes provided storage, shelter and security. (Apple 1971) Storage space was required to protect possessions, food and clothing from the elements and from the eyes of thieves and legal confiscators since all property ultimately belonged to the high chief. (Apple 1971) Houses were needed for shelter against heat, cold and rain. Houses at higher elevations had a fireplace or *kapuahi* built with flat stones set on edge in the center of the room for warmth. Security and privacy were necessary during periods of taboo or *kapu*. These windowless, completely enclosed structures provided seclusion when silence was required, if a person was even seen outside during a *kapu* period the penalty could be death. During these periods when commoners and lesser chiefs were hidden inside, high chiefs and priests were free to hold their religious activities in vacant villages, along empty trails, seacoasts and offshore fishing grounds. (Apple 1971)

Temporary shelters were commonplace in farmlands and forests, at stone quarries, canoe construction and salt making sites. At fishing sites along sunny coastal areas fishermen needed permanent shelters, inland sites were generally seasonal and temporary shelter was needed to provide sleeping quarters at higher elevations where crops were grown, birds hunted and timber cut. These shelters typically had low stone windbreaks 'C' or 'U' shaped with a limited floor area, roof hatching of ti leaves and interior stone lined hearths for heat. High chiefs were mobile, they traveled between islands and along the coasts by canoe, temporary compounds constructed for high chiefs were for business, holding court and pleasure with as many as 100 people accompanied each high chief. When Hawaiians were working away from home they still needed structures for storage, shelter from weather and security during *kapu* periods and housing areas contained both permanent and temporary structures.

Often commoners could not even stand upright in their dwellings and lived mainly outdoors. These small houses served only as an occasional shelter from weather, for storage and security. Commoner's houses often accommodated only two sleeping adults with a small storage area, some were only eight feet long and four to five feet wide with a ridge height of only four to five feet. (Apple 1971) Both dwellings of chiefs and commoners had low entry doors and to enter one had to crawl on all fours rather than walk-in. Most houses had only one entry door, the *hale mua* or men's house had two doors, one in the front and one on the side. A chief's house had two or three doors and the door to the chiefs sleeping area was low and extremely taboo. Structures inside major *heiau* and houses of high chiefs were similar in construction.

The residences of high chiefs were elaborate compounds or *kauhale* containing several additional structures having specific functions. One large executive house served as an office and conference room for high chiefs who held court within their compounds. The women of high chiefs had separate living quarters along with a secluded menstruation house and there was also a house or shed for women's work (Fig. 68). Some high *ali'i* were so sacred they only went out at night, remaining in large thatched houses during daylight hours to prevent their shadow from falling upon commoners. When a chief was in the presence of a chief of higher rank, he was required to keep his head below the level of the head of the higher ranking chief, lower chiefs were either seated on the floor, kneeling or squatting. High chiefs slept on raised platforms so their heads would remain at a high level. The houses of high chiefs had high sidewalls creating a high ridge height and lower chiefs were required to have their house ridges below the high chief's, the chiefly class had different degrees of sacredness and their house ridge heights reflected their status. Large chiefly houses had sidewalls twelve to fourteen feet high with ridge heights up to twenty-three feet above their stone platforms. The upper size limit of their floor area was determined by the availability of long timber lengths for wall plates and ridgepoles, generally houses were about twenty-four feet long and twelve feet wide, (Brigham 1908) although some of the largest houses were as long as forty to seventy feet and twenty feet wide. Both high chief's housing complexes and major *heiau* were sacred as were the people who occupied them, rock walls and wooden fences surrounding these complexes created a permanent *kapu* or taboo. A sacred *'aha* cord was stretched across the entrance to a chief's residence and if it was approached by another high *ali'i*, it was said to fall to the ground of its own accord, allowing him passage. Not all barriers between the sacred and the commonplace were physical, some were invisible lines created by perimeter stakes with white tapa bark cloth flags or a coconut wrapped in white tapa. (Apple 1971)

CEREMONY AT THE COMPLETION OF A HOUSE

Upon completion of the construction of a new dwelling, a consecration ceremony known as *moku ka piko* was held when thatch overhanging the entry doorway to the house was trimmed by a *kahuna pule* or praying priest. Holding a block of wood behind the thatch, he cut to the rhythm of his prayer. (Malo 1951 [1898]) A *kuwa* prayer signifying the birth of a new dwelling was symbolized by "cutting of the 'piko' or the umbilical cord of the house followed by the placing of greenery around the house and feasting". It was believed a new house should not be occupied until it had been blessed and at the time when the owner was ready to move in the house had already been furnished.

"Then they called in the priest to make a prayer at the cutting of the bunch of grass left hanging over the doorway of the house, . . . and when the prayer was ended the owner of the house entered and settled with comfort."

(From *The Ancient Hawaiian House*, 1908, in Memoirs of the
Bernice Pauahi Bishop Museum, Vol. II. no. 3, by William
Tufts Brigham, page 78. Courtesy of Bishop
Museum Press, Honolulu)

"The priest stood at the door with all the friends and neighbors of the owner around in readiness for the feast that was to follow, and holding in one hand the stone adze, and in the other a block of wood . . . [the priest] chopped the grass when he came to the proper place in the prayer . . . the tuft [of grass] was called the "piko" [umbilical cord] of the house."

(From *The Ancient Hawaiian House*, 1908, in Memoirs of the
Bernice Pauahi Bishop Museum, Vol. II. no. 3, by William
Tufts Brigham, page 103. Courtesy of
Bishop Museum Press, Honolulu)

When a death occurred within a house no loud wailing was permitted before the body was cleaned and dressed so as not to startle its spirit that could be lingering in the house. (Green 1926) *Kahu* or caretakers would take the body out through a hole cut in the gable end of the house and then the opening would be closed. The body was not taken out through the doorway so as not to contaminate the entry door or allow the ghost of the dead to find its way back into the house. The dead being removed through a hole in the house wall and not through the doorway was also a custom of the Tlingit and Haida Indian tribes of Alaska. Corpses were considered defiling and any tools, mats or clothing that came in contact with dead bodies were either placed in the burial cave beside the body or burned. People who came in contact with a dead body were required to purify themselves by bathing in the sea, a *kapu kai,* then the house and all of its contents were sprinkled with saltwater mixed with coconut water, sea moss and turmeric or *'olena* by a *kahuna* in a ceremony of purification, a *pi kai*. In the islands of Tahiti, if a man died in his house it was burnt to the ground with all his belongings.

HOUSING CONSTRUCTION

Advice from a *kahuna kilokilo,* reader of the sky and predictor of the future, was sometimes employed to select the most desirable location for the house. Unfavorable site locations included the edge of a cliff or *pali* with the door facing the cliff where spirits could leap up and enter the dwelling, on top of a mound that could cause loneliness, on a hill or *pu'u* where the house could slip down the hill unless the entry were built facing the hill, on a burial ground or site of a *heiau*. When houses were built in rows, it was thought the owner of the highest house would become rich while neighbors with houses facing each other would fight.

House foundations or *kahua* were either natural soil or dry-masonry platforms generally rectangular, outlined with large stones. The space between foundation walls was filled with stone rubble, the upper surface leveled. Flooring was smooth lava or sand finished with small water-worn pebbles or *'ili 'ili* of basalt rock or coral covered in dried grass and mats of *lau hala*. (Apple 1971) For a house with sidewalls, soil had to allow for embedment of posts. For a house with roof rafters reaching the ground, soil had to allow for embedment of rafter ends stabilized with roof length log sleepers held in position with pegs and weighted down with rocks for additional support. Roof rafter ends could easily be attached to low masonry sidewalls. Masonry sidewalls also had a social advantage, height of the sidewalls increased the height of the roof ridge from the ground and height of the roof ridge indicated the social ranking of the occupants. A high platform also increased the ridge height and a deeper embedment of the posts allowed for higher sidewalls and therefore a higher roof. Posts embedded into soil were subject to rotting quickly and a raised stone platform minimized this problem. Raised platforms would sometimes extend out in front of the house where its outer vertical edges were sloped or battered and covered with stone facing.

The foundations of structures built on *heiau* platforms had floors raised slightly above the platform level with their post embedded into the *heiau* platform. Timber selection for structures built at a *heiau* and for one or a few structures of a high chief's housing complex had specific rules. All embedded posts were required to be of the same wood including all horizontal structural members, wall plates and ridge polls. All rafters were required to be the same wood, although it could differ from the wood posts and horizontal members. All house framing members were preferred to be of hardwood due to its ability to withstand wind. Timbers selected for *heiau* and houses of high chiefs were to be of the highest quality and were considered sacred, their timbers could have no holes or bends, the bark was peeled off after the tree was felled and they were submerged in water to keep the wood workable. (Apple 1971) Many hardwoods were used for housing construction, the best woods were *naio, uliuli, mamane, olopua* and *kamani* for posts and beams, *lama* and *ha'a* for rafters, although *'ohi'a lehua* was considered inferior. *'A'ali'i, mamane* and *naio* were used for purlins and *koa* was used more for canoes than for house timbers. (Brigham 1908)

The first step in the construction of a Hawaiian house was to level and clear the site and locate the four corners of its rectangular floor area. Corner posts or *pou kihi* would determine the house width and length. An architect or *kahuna kuhikuhi pu'uone* would decide the height of the sidewalls that were usually from five to six feet and the number of sidewall posts about six to eight inches in diameter were spaced three to four feet apart. Post were stripped of bark and made as straight as possible. The length of each post or *pou* included both the exposed section above the platform and the buried section, an embedment of at least three or four feet was required. Posts were adjusted by the use of a base rock firmly positioned in the hole that was filled and compacted around the post. When wall posts were in position the wall plates or *lohelau,* poles of a little more than two inches in diameter, were placed in notches cut into the two rows of wall posts and lashed together. Ridgeposts or *pou hana* were then positioned in the gable end walls, midway between the corner posts. Height of the ridgeposts would determine the height of the house and social status of the owner; *pou hana* was also a term referring to a person of importance. Ridgeposts were cut with a concave end to receive the ridgepole. A deeper post embedment was required for ridgeposts that were never attached to the other gable end wall posts but "stood alone", they had a sacred quality and in ancient times beneath one of these posts a sacrificial victim was offered to the gods. After the wall plates and ridgepole or *kauhuhu* were in position and the ridgepole securely lashed to the ridgeposts, rafters or *o'a* could be added. The lower ends of the rafters were shaped into a fork or *kohe* with the underside cut back in the form of a chin or *auwae* and notches were cut on the outer surface of the rafter about six inches above the fork and on the post for lashing. The upper ends of the rafters crossed each other resting on the ridgepole. A second ridgepole or *kaupaku* was added, it was the same length as the main ridgepole only smaller, about one inch in diameter and sat in forks formed by the crossed rafters, then the secondary and main ridgepoles were lashed together. Diagonal bracing was required on the large houses to provide stability and diagonal poles or *holo* were attached to the inner side of the roof framework. (Apple 1971) A temporary scaffold or *oloke'a* was constructed in the interior of the house allowing workers to position the ridgepole and rafters, the scaffolding was cut in pieces after the house was completed and removed out the entry door.

A temporary mid-span ridgepost was added before placement of the ridgepole. This center post or *halake'a* was slightly taller than the ridgeposts, it prevented the ridgepole from deflecting before installation of the rafters and created an upward arch in the ridge at mid-span. The height of the temporary center post was the distance from the platform to the top of the ridgeposts plus a *kiko'o*, the distance between the thumb and tip of the index finger. Sitting directly on the platform, the temporary center post was kept in place by the bow of the ridgepole and weight of the rafters. This eliminated the need to open existing platforms so if burials or sacrifices were located under the platform they would remain undisturbed. Burials directly beneath house floors were an ancient practice in Polynesia and also occurred in the Hawaiian Islands. Human victims were sometimes buried alive under the supporting posts of sacred structures in the islands of Tahiti, a human sacrifice was made when a temple or *marae* structure was erected and the body of a human sacrifice was placed in the foundation of the central post supporting the roof. In the Fiji Islands, bodies of human sacrifices were also buried beneath house posts. The soul of the sacrificed victim would become a protective spirit for the structure, later a fish was substituted. Infanticide was a common practiced throughout Polynesia, it controlled population growth on islands with limited resources and was widely practiced in the Hawaiian Islands where a large percentage, perhaps as many as two-thirds of children were killed soon after birth. The practice of infanticide arrived with settlers from the islands of Tahiti and was a custom of the Arioi Society whose priests were celibate and its members were not allowed to have children, when they did the infants were killed either by the mother or by a relative and buried beneath the house floor.

The traditional low entry door or *ni'o* was only about two and a half feet high forcing a person to enter and exit on their hands and knees. Even the entry door of a high chief was only three and a half feet high. Entry door openings were framed with wood posts called *lapauila* or *kunakuna*, preferably made of *'ahakea* wood that had a reddish yellow color similar to chiefly red. The arched lintel was called a *hoaka* because it resembled the crescent shaped moon. Vertical doorways were installed in houses having no vertical sidewalls because their roof extended to the ground, a small projection was built with sidewalls and a small sloping roof section filled the remaining opening (Fig. 70). Doorways were either sliding or hinged requiring more carpentry than the rest of the house. Installation of a sliding door assembly was a rare and complex construction, the doorframe had a grooved piece above and below with a sliding door panel. A pump drill was used to bore holes to attach the doorframe with wooden pins. (Brigham 1908)

Wall purlins were slender horizontal poles from one-half inch to one inch in diameter made from trees with long straight branches. *'A'ali'i, mamane* or *naio* wood was preferred and all purlins were made from the same wood, they extended the full length of the house although they were not one piece, but would be lashed together maintaining a consistent diameter. There were main purlins or *'aho pueo* and thatch purlins or *'aho* lashed to posts and rafters. Main purlins were one inch in diameter spaced between eighteen inches and fifteen inches apart, thatch purlins were smaller than main purlins and were three-quarters to one-half inch in diameter as were the vertical rods. Thatch purlins were fastened to each other and to the posts, rafters and vertical rods and were the horizontal member to which the thatch was tied. Usually, there were three thatch purlins between the main purlins spaced five to six inches apart with vertical rods placed midway between the posts and rafters. (Apple 1971) Purlins were never lashed to the ridgeposts; they "stood alone".

The art of thatching a house was called *lolelau*. Thatch or *ako* was attached to the horizontal purlins on both the walls and roof. The preferred thatching material was sweet smelling *pili* grass, it was a higher quality thatch then pandanus leaves or *hala*. (Brigham 1908) Thatch was tied to the purlins with braided *'uki'uki* grass. Thatching started at the lowest horizontal row and moved up so the rows would overlap and shed rain. When thatching on each side of the roof reached the ridge the space was covered using an additional ridgepole as a thatch purlin, grass was tied to it covering the openings on either side. Long poles or *lolo* were added above the second ridgepole to act as thatch purlins so even more thatching could be applied, this would raise the ridge height as much as two or three feet and was reserved for chiefs. Sometimes extra thatching extended down the corners of the house providing additional protection against leaks. Large heavy fishing nets were placed over the grass thatching as it dried to prevent it from curling up and to keep it in place during windy weather. (Brigham 1908) Some houses had no interior lining, their interior surface was the back of the thatch, others added a thin layer of grass behind the thatch next to the purlins so it could be seen from the inside, the lining was stitched to the thatch purlins before the exterior thatching was applied creating a smooth interior finish. There were techniques that covered the purlins, but left the house post and rafters visible and linings were sometimes made of crossed ti or *ki* leaves. Hawaiian cordage or *'aha* was of the highest quality and strength, coconut sennit cord was typical although cords of *olona* were stronger, but were not commonly used. Europeans noted Hawaiian cordage was "perfectly well made . . . and much stronger than our lines of twice the size." Fibers used to attach house parts were made of coconut, bark, vines and grasses braided into cords either round or rectangular in cross section and made in sizes from threads to ropes. (Apple 1971)

In cold mountainous regions a fireplace was necessary for heat in the sleeping area. Located in a shallow pit in the center of the dwelling and aligned with the door, it was surrounded with flat stones set on edge. The fireplace was not used for cooking which was done outdoors in an *imu*. House furnishings were minimal, household items were often stored in containers and hung from the rafters in nets. Floors were covered with several layers of matting made of plaited pandanus leaves or *lauhala*. Mats were piled up in the sleeping area or *moena* creating a raised area usually extending across one end of the house (Fig. 71), bed mats were finely pleated *makaloa* mats made mainly on Ni'ihau Island and were often rolled into a corner. The bed or *hikie'e* had sheets and blankets or *kapa moe* made from the paper mulberry plant. Five or six of these sheets were attached forming a blanket that was quite warm. There were woven pillows stuffed with leaves, carved wooden headrests used as pillows (Fig. 72) and even a stone pillow shaped like the wooden ones. There were wooden stools and stone lamps for light. Household food equipment was only a small bench that held a few utensils or *'umeke,* wooden and stone bowls or *pola* and plates or *pa*. Gourds cleaned and dried in the sun were used as calabashes for holding water, they could reach diameters of twenty inches and were hung with netting or *koko* made from *olona* cord and some were decorated with geometric designs. Bowls, plates and platters were made from soft grain wood that was easy to cut, other household equipment was made from stone such as the mortar and pestle and *poi* pounders. Cups were either made from wood, stone, gourds or coconut shells and finger bowls were used during meals. Wooden boards or *papa ku'i 'ai* were where taro was pounded into *pa'i*, the thick paste for making *poi*. Hawaiian houses were dark having no windows, stone lamps with oil from *kukui* nuts and wicks made from *kapa* were used for lighting. Torches made from bamboo stuffed with *kukui* nuts were called *lama*. The *kukui* nuts were baked, their shells removed and threaded onto the stalk of a coconut palm leaf or bamboo to make a large torch called a *lamaku*. Approximately ten to twelve kernels were strung and each kernel would burn for approximately five minutes. The torch would burn with a bright light, but the charred kernels had to be removed or the torch would go out or give a poor light, they also produced too much smoke for use indoors. Stone mirrors or *kilo pohaku* were an ingenious Hawaiian development, dark colored circular stone disks of highly polished basalt rock about three to four inches in diameter and less than one half inch thick were covered with a shallow layer of water, the dark stone background gave off a clear reflection.

FEATHERWORK

O *'aumakuas* of the night,
O 'aumakuas of the day,
To Kane in the night,
To Kanaloa in the night,
To all my ancestors in the night,
Brush aside the darkness, come forth into the light,
This is I – the one who has mana,
Grant me wisdom,
Grant me a good catch,
Go up to the mountains, to the mountain tops,

Drive down all the birds,
Put them on the gums where they will stick fast.
'Amama, it is freed.

(Bird-Catching Prayer from the article Ka Moolelo o na manu o
Hawaii Nei in *Ka Nupepa Kuokoa,* May 2, 1863, Hawaiian
Ethnographic Notes: HEN I: 481 (HI. L. 1.3 #1), page 2,
Bernice Pauahi Bishop Museum. Courtesy of
the Bishop Museum, Honolulu)

FEATHERED CAPES AND CLOAKS

Feathered capes and cloaks, *'ahuli'i* or *'ahu 'ula* and crested feathered helmets or *mahi'ola* are probably the best known and most distinctive artifacts of early Hawaiian culture, these sacred insignia and symbols signified rank and were worn by high Hawaiian *ali'i* chiefs. Royal robes and helmets were worn during affairs of state and in combat, although their foundation of finely woven netting offered only minimal protection. The capes, cloaks and helmets contained great *mana* and were symbolic of authority instilling fear in their enemies during battle and inspiring their troops. Feathered capes and helmets were "battle apparel". The cape was pulled across the left side of the body and held forward with the left hand to help stop the thrust of a dagger or the point of a throwing spear, the right hand being free to wield a weapon. The woven foundation of helmets offered protection against a shower of sling stones. (Pukui 1972) Their protective quality was thought to be supernatural, wrapping of the sacred to protect its *mana* was a custom found throughout Polynesia, and in the Hawaiian Island *ali'i* chiefs were wrapped in feathers to protect their divinity and contain their sacredness. Feathered cloaks and capes were the physical representation of divine *mana*, the most beautiful art form of native Hawaiian craftsmanship and the most prized items of the *ali'i.* They were observed by Captain James T. Cook in January 1778 on the island of Kaua'i.

"The ground of them is a network, upon which the most beautiful red and yellow feathers are so closely fixed, that the surface might be compared to the thickest and riches velvet, which they resemble, both as to the feel and the glossy appearance. The manner of varying the mixture is very different, some having triangular spaces of red and yellow alternately; others a kind of crescent, and some that were entirely red, had a yellow border . . . we found that they were in high estimation with their owners."

(From *Captain Cook's Third and Last Voyage to the
Pacific Ocean in the years 1776 to 1780, 1778,*
by James Cook, Book III, page 161)

Feathers have always been part of human self-adornment. There were feathered headdresses among Proto-Polynesian Austronesians of Island Southeast Asia and throughout Melanesia chiefs wore feathered war headdresses. The use of bird feathers for personal ornamentation was widespread throughout Polynesia, although cloaks and capes covered in feathers were most highly developed in the Hawaiian Islands. There had been some tradition of featherwork in locations from where settlers of the Hawaiian Islands originated, such as feathered helmets and breast gorgets worn by Tahitian chiefs, feather cloaks were part of the chief mourner's costume of the islands of Tahiti and on Ra'iatea Island, Tahiti, a red feather cloak was presented at the consecration of a new high chief. Elaborate Marquesan headdresses were adorned with red and green feathers. Polynesian featherwork or *haku hulu* attained its highest level of achievement in the Hawaiian Islands, "nowhere was the featherwork more beautifully and skillfully done than it was by the feather craftsmen of old Hawai'i . . . featherwork was the most prestigious artistic medium for Hawaiians." (Kappler 1978) Techniques for making Hawaiian feathered capes, cloaks and helmets were exclusively a Hawaiian invention. The Hawaiian name for feathered capes and cloaks was *'ahu 'ula* meaning red shoulder garment. Throughout Polynesia red was the royal color of high chiefs and the gods, red feathers were believed to create a layer of divine protection symbolizing authority and the right to rule. The color and shape of the *'ahuli'i* or *'ahu 'ula* would indicate the rank of the wearer, the color of these items began to change in the Hawaiian Islands due to the scarcity of yellow feathers, but their name remained the same. Yellow became the royal color reserved for feathered capes and cloaks of high chiefs, those of lesser chiefs were yellow mixed with red and the color for priests and the gods remained red. In the Hawaiian Islands, the two most abundant forest birds had red feathers, while rare yellow feathers came from several black birds having only a few yellow feathers.

   The origin of the feathered capes in the Hawaiian Islands was the early *ki* or ti leaf rain cape, *kui la'i* or *ahu la'i*, used for protection against rain and cold by fisherman who had no shelter from the rain while fishing in outrigger canoes (Fig. 73). The foundation of the cape was a coarse mesh of ordinary fishing net to which ti leaves were attached creating rain capes. The first

Hawaiian feathered capes were made of large black feathers from hawks, brown feathers from roosters and white feathers from the white-tailed tropic *koa'e kea* bird. Rectangular feather capes with a trapezoidal shape were an intermediate stage between ti leaf capes and fine circular capes. Rectangular capes used a smaller fishnet mesh than ti leaf capes. Some rectangular capes had smaller feathers fastened to a strip of more finely woven material and then attached to the cape. Later, a much finer net backing for capes or *naepuni* was developed made from the *olona* plant native to the Hawaiian Islands and not found elsewhere in Polynesia. The bark was stripped, soaked, scrapped and twisted into threads called *nae*, then the threads were tied with fishing knots into a netting, small bunches of feathers were attached to the netting with much finer threads making elegant feathered capes possible.

Birds that supplied the colorful feathers of yellow, red and green inhabited the mountains and Hawaiians generally lived near shore considering mountains to be an adobe of evil spirits. Due to the value of feathers men became bird hunters or *po'e hahai manu*, people who hunted birds or *po'e lawai'a manu*, people who "fished for birds". They lived in the cold of higher elevations studying the habits and roosting places of the forest birds. During the molting season bird catchers or *kia manu* removed most of the flowers from an *'ohi'a* tree and put *kepau* or bird-lime made from bark of the breadfruit tree or *pilali* made from *kukui* tree gum along branches containing the remaining flowers, although sticky fruit from the *papala kepau* or "bird catcher plant" and glue from seeds of the *'oha wai* tree were preferred. When birds landed to feed on nectar of the remaining *'ohi'a lehua* blossoms they became stuck and were snared using fine *olona* cordage. Many were released after the desired feathers had been removed and *kukui* oil was used to clean off the birdlime. Sometimes unusual trees planted in forest clearings would get the attention of curious birds who could be caught on long, slender poles or *kia manu* covered with flowers and smeared with the sticky bird-lime. Birds providing yellow feathers were limited in number, they were caught during molting season and it is believed these birds were not killed, a few colored feathers were plucked and they were released to renew their plumage. There were two seasons for bird hunting corresponding with the two flowering seasons of the *'ohi'a lehua* tree. In lower elevations, the season was during March, April and into May and the later upland season was during August, September, October and into early November.

Bird feathers were used to some extent as currency. The most highly valued were pale yellow feathers called *'e'e* coming from the *'o'o* bird, a black bird with small bright yellow tufts under each wing joint and near its tail found only on Hawai'i Island and the *mamo* bird, a black bird with a few deep yellow almost orange feathers also only found on Hawai'i Island. Being rare *mamo* feathers were the most highly coveted for the capes and cloaks of high chiefs and the amount of yellow in a feathered cape or cloak was an indication of social ranking. King Kamehameha the Great's full length golden cloak contains 450,000 yellow feathers from an estimated 80,000 rare *mamo* birds and is said to have occupied nine generations of high chiefs or about 200 years in its construction (Fig. 74). (Alexander 1891) The *i'iwi* bird had all bright red feathers and was found throughout the Hawaiian Islands and the *'apapane* bird had dark crimson feathers not often used in featherwork. Black feathers were from the *'o'o*, *mamo*, *'i'iwi*, and *apapane* birds. Rare olive green feathers were from the *'o'u* bird along with greenish yellow feathers from the *'akialoa* bird, white feathers came from the tropic *koa'e kea* bird with brilliant green feathers coming from its head. Early capes had the neck and front edges covered with fine red and yellow feathers; the remainder of the cape was covered with more coarse feathers from domestic fowl and hawks. With further development, the shape of capes became more curved and new geometric patterns were added, fine netting made from two-ply *olona* cord tied with fishing knots and cut to the required shape evolved, feathers were arranged in bundles of six to eight per bundle according to their size and tied together before being attached to the netting. These circular capes became highly developed in shape and design, they were curved at the neck having two straight sides (Fig. 75). Most capes had a lower border of yellow feathers and a red background with crescent patterns in yellow and black with green feathers used primarily along borders. The usual method of fastening was a firmly braided cord of *olona* fiber from the upper corners of the cape or cloak long enough to tie securely. The size of the capes later expanded into larger feathered cloaks having the greatest social prestige, they were only for the highest *ali'i* chiefs. These cloaks, capes and helmets protected high *ali'i* chiefs wrapping them in feathers and were a mark of their social ranking; capes became the sign of chiefs, cloaks the royal robes of kings. The sacred geometric design motifs of the garments consisted of crescents, triangles, small circles and horizontal stripes, rectangles were rare. Crescent design symbols appeared in almost all cloaks and capes indicating specific chiefly family genealogy and ranking, geometric design patterns were inherited. The construction of cloaks and capes was prohibited to commoners, although women from chiefly households manufactured many high value items including cloaks and capes. It was not forbidden for women to handle feathers and bird catchers were accompanied by their wives who often plucked and sorted feathers.

> "The principle ornaments of the men are the feathered caps and cloaks; some of the later reached down to their heels, and have the most magnificent appearance. They are made for the most part of red and yellow feathers, which are tied upon fine network."
>
> (From *An Authentic Narrative of a Voyage Performed by Captain Cook and Captain Clerke, Vol. II, 1783,* by William Ellis, page 155)

FEATHERED HELMETS

Hawaiian feathered helmets or *mahi'ole* were made in different styles reflecting the social position and ranking of the wearer and feathered helmets like their cloaks were a unique Hawaiian development, "crested helmets covered with colored feathers were the natural complement of the feathered cloaks" (Fig. 76). Chiefs wore feathered helmets into battle mainly for ornamentation making the head look larger and more formidable although the woven wicker *'ie'ie* root foundation offered some physical protection. The crescent ridge of the helmet came from a traditional hair style with the hair closely cut on the sides and a ridge of hair on top called *'oki mahi'ole,* the same name given to the helmet. This ridge decoration was a mark of rank and the helmet ridge evolved into an imposing crest.

> "[Helmets] are composed of the same kind of feathers [as the cloaks] which are sometimes intermixed with black; they are secured upon a kind of basket work made in the form of a helmet . . . both caps and cloaks, however, are only to be seen in the possession of the principle people."
>
> (From *An Authentic Narrative of a Voyage Performed by Captain Cook and Captain Clerke, Vol. II,* 1783, by William Ellis, page 155)

Over the woven wicker *'ie'ie* vine aerial root helmet structure, a more delicate netting made from the *olona* plant was cut and fitted to the shape of the helmet. Feathers in bunches were attached to the netting, usually red with a crest of yellow and lines of black and green. Lesser chiefs wore helmets without feathers and helmets with mushroom shaped ornaments were worn by warriors and were probably not feathered (Fig. 76).

There were rare *ka'ei* feathered girdles or sashes worn only by high chiefs in the Hawaiian Islands and only two are known to have existed. The feathered *Ka'ei Kapu o* Liloa, the Sacred Sash of Liloa, was kept at his home in Waipi'o Valley. It was a long featherwork band constructed of *olona* netting with rows of human teeth along one end. The origin of the Hawaiian feathered girdle was the royal *maro 'ura* or red-feathered girdle, insignia of a high chief and the gods of Ra'iatea Island, Tahiti. Both Tahitian and Hawaiian royal feathered girdles were about ten feet long and were the most sacred royal symbols of rank and power.

KAHILI STANDARDS

Also having feather decorations were *kahili* standards. Grand *kahili* were ceremonial insignia of royalty used on state occasions by both men and women and a *kahili* pole could be ten to twenty five feet tall with a cylindrically shaped feather cluster or *hulumanu* as large as two feet in diameter and more than six feet in height attached at its upper end, each line of royalty had its own feather combination displayed outside of their royal residences. Tall *kahili* could be seen at a distance announcing the arrival of a ruling high chief. The poles were made of rounded *koa* wood and some were actually spears. Large bird feathers were used for ceremonial *kahili* standards such as from the white-tailed tropicbird or *koa'e kea* and red-tailed tropicbird or *koa'e 'ula*, along with feathers from the *pueo, mamo, 'o'o* and *'i'iwi* birds. The grand *kahilis* were used for solemn ceremonies of state such as funeral processions (Fig. 77). Wooden handles of smaller hand *kahili*, three to four feet long, were often inlaid with bone, highly polished tortoise shell or whale tooth ivory. When human bone was used as an inlay it was considered a great honor. The origin for the *kahili* was the *ki* or ti plant.

> "Made of a bunch of feathers fixed to the end of the thin piece of smooth and polished wood: they were generally made of the tail feathers of the cock, but the better sort of people have them of the tropical bird's feathers, or those belonging to a black and yellow bird called mo-ho ['o'o]. The handle is very frequently made of one of the bones of the arm or leg of those whom they have killed in battle, curiously inlaid with tortoise shell."
>
> (From *An Authentic Narrative of a Voyage Performed by Captain Cook and Captain Clerke, Vol. II,* 1783, by William Ellis, page 156)

Smaller hand *kahili lele* were waved over the heads of *ali'i* to ward off bad *mana*.

FEATHERED GOD IMAGES

Feathered *akua hulu manu* were anthropomorphic god images, symbols of divine power and the most sacred *heiau* images. (Valeri 1985) *Akua hulu manu* were important in Hawaiian burials being filled with *mana* of the gods, they guided souls of the deceased through the afterlife returning their spirit to the realm of the living as an *'aumakua. Akua hulu manu* were kept in the *hale mana* of *luakini heiau* and during the *kauila huluhulu* ceremony they were refurbished with new feathers making them more divine, they were able to transmit divine *mana* to the human realm. In warfare they provided spiritual protection to those who possessed them. Some of the feathered *akua hulu manu* gods, particularly images of the war god *Kaili,* have survived. *Kuka'ilimoku* (Fig. 46) was the most famous of the *Ku* battle gods, it was a small wicker figure covered with red feathers and a headdress of yellow feathers carried into battle on a *kauila* or *kauwila* wood pole and was said to cry out so loudly during battle it could be heard above sounds of the fighting. *Akua hulu manu* feathered gods were also built of wickerwork from aerial roots of the *'ie'ie* vine and covered with a net of *olona* fibers to which feathers were attached. The feathers were mostly red from the *'i'iwi* bird with yellow and black feathers from the *'o'o* bird and some had human hair, eyes of pearl shell and dog's teeth. The origin of these feathered war gods can be found with *Kaili* or *Tairi,* feathered war god of the god *Ta'aroa* from the islands of Tahiti, before the god *'Oro* existed. It was a stone or gourd wrapped in sennit with sacred feathers. Later, there were divine wooden *to'o* images of the god *'Oro,* an abstract human male figure covered in tapa, woven sennit fiber and covered with red and yellow feathers from the district of 'Opoa on Ra'iatea Island, Tahiti.

FEATHER LEI

Lei hulu manu or feather *lei* were worn by *ali'i* women in the hair as a wreath, *lei po'o,* or as a necklace, *lei 'a'i* (Fig. 78). The feather *lei* were made of yellow, red and black feathers tied to a cord, usually several strands of *olona* fiber. Hair combs decorated with feathers or *huli kua* were also worn by female *ali'i.* (Malo 1951 [1898], Pukui 1972)

> "The women too have their share in the ornamental way: that which they value most is the erai [lei]. This is a kind of ruff or necklace made of red, green, black, and yellow feathers, curiously put together, and in most elegant patterns."
>
> (From *An Authentic Narrative of a Voyage Performed by Captain Cook and Captain Clerke, Vol. II*, 1783, by William Ellis, page 156)

Two Story, Double-Hull Kalia Canoe, Tonga Islands

A 1795 engraving by Jacques Louis Copia from a 1791-92 drawing by Piron of a *kalia* canoe with a two level platform and triangular sail. Courtesy of the Alexander Turnbull Library, Wellington, New Zealand

An 1845 hand-colored version of a lithograph by J. Honegger from *Naturgeschichte und Abblidungen der Menschen* by Heinrich Rudolf Schinz, Zurich

Fig. 62

A Polynesian Voyaging Canoe

A Polynesian double-hull voyaging canoe crossing the vast expanse of the Pacific Ocean guided by stars of the night sky, perhaps heading for the Hawaiian Islands. These were truly astronauts of the past

Fig. 63

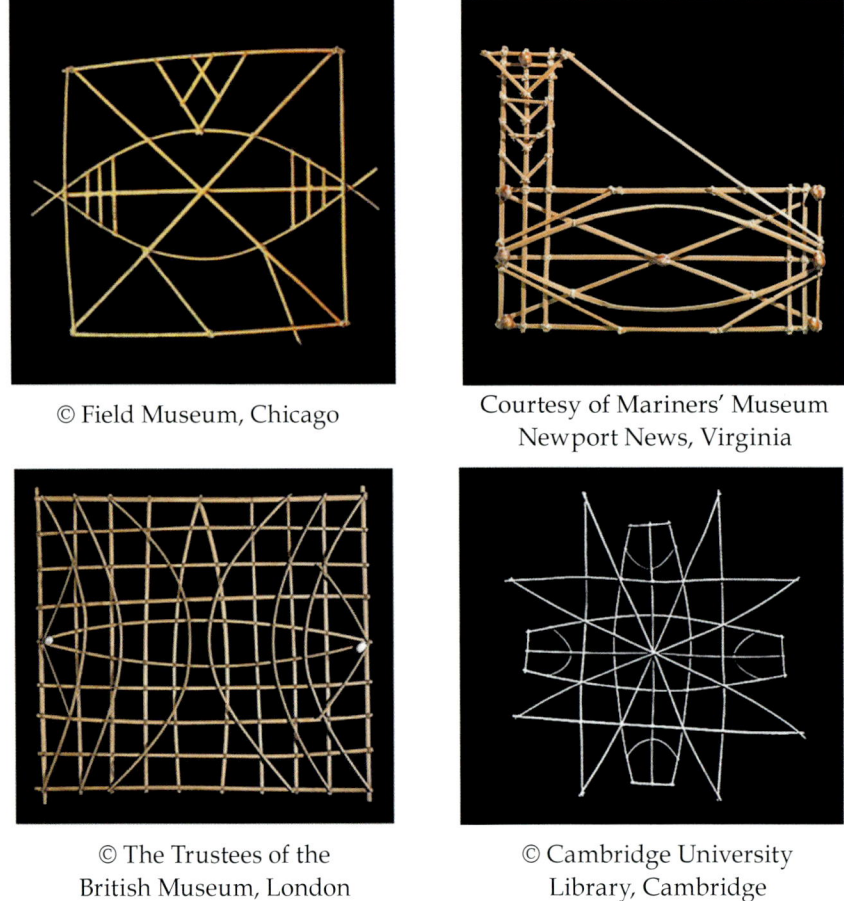

© Field Museum, Chicago

Courtesy of Mariners' Museum
Newport News, Virginia

© The Trustees of the
British Museum, London

© Cambridge University
Library, Cambridge

Navigational Stick Charts

Marshall Island's navigational stick charts represented ocean mapping of refraction and bending of ocean currents and wave swell patterns as they passed by chains of islands. Constructed by Proto-Polynesian *ariki* voyagers, they were the first mapping of ocean features in history

Fig. 64

© The Hunterian,
University of Glasgow

Hawaiian Adzes

A collection of Hawaiian hafted adzes and a petroglyph of a man with an adze or *ki'i pohaku ko'i* located at Puako, Hawai'i Island, from *The Hawaiian Canoe* by Tommy Holmes, 1993. Copyright; Bess Press, Honolulu

Fig. 65

Hawaiian Canoe Wash Strakes

Canoe wash strake sections or *mo'o* attached to the hull of a Hawaiian canoe with sennit fiber lashings or *kaholo* and lashing of a two-piece *manu*, from *The Hawaiian Canoe* by Tommy Holmes, 1993. Copyright; Bess Press, Honolulu

Fig. 66

Hawaiian Canoe Ladder
Photographs by Kenneth Emory, Bishop Museum, Honolulu

An abandoned canoe ladder located at Kahaual'e in the Puna District of Hawai'i Island, 1931. From *The Hawaiian Canoe* by Tommy Holmes, 1993. Copyright; Bess Press, Honolulu

Fig. 67

**Sandwich Islands: Houses of Kraimokou,
Prime Minister of the King**
circa 1819

A hand-colored version of an engraving houses of an *ali'i* chief in Honolulu, Hawai'i by Alphonse Pellion, an artist who accompanied French explorer Louis de Freycinet aboard the ship Uranie. It shows the chief wearing a ceremonial cape and helmet and his wife, Likelike, beating tapa or *kapa* cloth. Surfboards or *papa he'e nalu* were prize possessions of *ali'i* and in the foreground is an *alaia* surfboard. The colored engraving appeared in Freycinet's *A Voyage Around the World,* published in 1825. Image is from *Wikimedia Commons* and in the public domain

Fig. 68

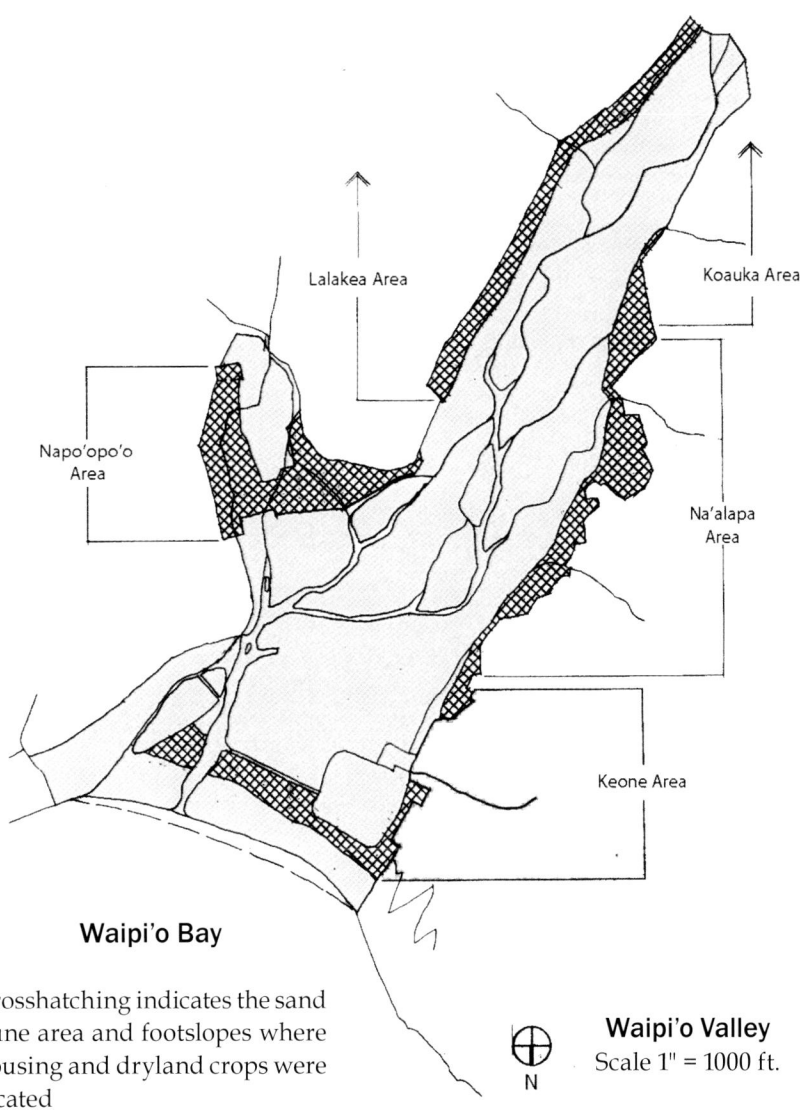

Lalakea Area

Koauka Area

Napo'opo'o
Area

Na'alapa
Area

Keone Area

Waipi'o Bay

Crosshatching indicates the sand
dune area and footslopes where
housing and dryland crops were
located

Waipi'o Valley
Scale 1" = 1000 ft.

N

Waipi'o Valley Housing Area

Fig. 69

A View of the Huts and a Boat House, at O'whyhee
1785

An engraving by William Walker after a circa 1779 drawing by William Ellis showing 'A' frame housing construction with thatched roofing extending to the ground and a small canoe house or *halau wa'a* is shown on the right. Published in *Lady's Magazine,* May 1, 1785, by G. Robinson. Courtesy of the National Library of Ireland, Dublin

Fig. 70

The Interior of a Hawaiian Grass House

Published in *The Spell of the Hawaiian Islands
and the Philippines* by Isabel Anderson, 1916

Fig. 71

Hawaiian Woven Pillows or Uluna

Made of *lauhala* matting stuffed with leaves. The image is from *The Ancient Hawaiian House,* 1908, Fig. 101, page 125, by William Tufts Brigham. Courtesy of Bishop Museum Press, Honolulu

Tahitian Carved Wooden Headrest or Tuarua

Photograph by Harry Haase,
© Institut und Sammiung fuer Ethnologie
der George August-Universitaet
Goettingen, Goettingen, Germany

Tongan Carved Toa Wood Headrest or Kali Hahapo

Cut from one piece of wood
© Auckland Museum, New Zealand

Fig. 72

A Fisherman Wearing an Early Ti Leaf Rain Cape
circa 1900

Photograph of an example of an early ti or *ki* leaf rain cape, *kui la'i* or *'ahu la'i,* worn for protection against cold and rain. Made from feathers attached to large mesh fishing nets, the rain capes evolved into the elegant feathered capes and cloaks worn by high *ali'i* chiefs. Courtesy of the Bishop Museum, Honolulu

Fig. 73

Yellow Feathered Cloak

The Mamo Cloak of Kamehameha the First made from rare golden-yellow feathers of the *mano* bird. Courtesy of the Bishop Museum, Honolulu

Hawaiian Feathered Cloaks or 'Ahu 'ula
Courtesy of the Bishop Museum, Honolulu

Photographs by Ben Patnoi

Fig. 74

Located in the University
of Cambridge Museum of
Archaeology & Anthropology.
Image is from *Wikimedia Commons*
and in the public domain

A digitally enhanced photograph
published by the Bishop Museum
Press, Honolulu. The cape is
located in the Honolulu Museum
of Art. Image is from *Wikimedia
Commons* and in the public domain

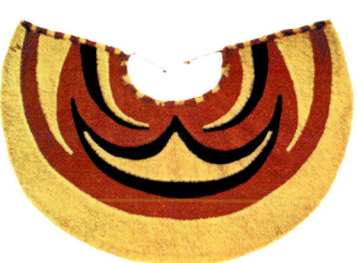

Located in the Bishop Museum,
Honolulu. Image is from *Wikimedia
Commons* and in the public domain

Located in the Australian Museum,
Sydney. Image is from *Wikimedia
Commons* and in the public domain

Hawaiian Feathered Capes, 'Ahuli'i or 'Ahu 'ula

Fig. 75

Photograph by Harry Haase,
© Institut und Sammiung fuer
Ethnologie der Georg-August-
Universitaet Goettingen,
Goettingen, Germany

© The Trustees of the
British Museum, London -
All rights reserved

Courtesy of Umi Kai and the
PA'I Foundation, Honolulu

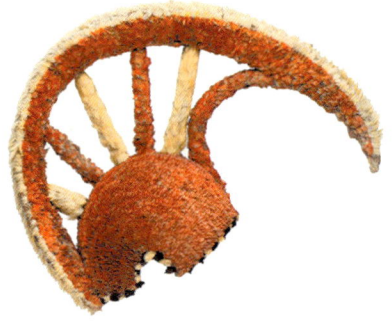

Located in the Peabody Museum
Harvard University, Cambridge,
Massachusetts. Gift of Heirs of
David Kimbell (c) President and
Fellows Of Harvard College,
Peabody Museum of Archaeology
and Ethnology, PM# 99-12-70/53559
(digital file# 99170068)PM# 99-
12-70/53559 (digital file# 99170)

Hawaiian Feathered Helmets or Mahi'ole

Fig. 76

Kahili bearers at the funeral procession of Queen Liliuokalani in November 1917. Photograph is in the Archives of the Kamehameha Schools. Image is from *Wikipedia Commons* and in the public domain

Photograph by Toby Hoogs
© Island Breeze Productions, Inc., Kailua-Kona, Hawaii - All rights reserved

Nahi'ena'ena (Sister of Kamehameha III)

An oil on canvas painting of Princess Nahi'ena'ena, daughter of King Kamehameha I, at ten years old wearing an *'ahu 'ula* or feathered cape and holding a *kahili*, a royal feathered standard, symbol of her rank and status, by British artist Robert Dampier. The painting is located in the Honolulu Museum of Art, a gift of Eliza Lefferts Cooke III, and Carolene Alexander Cooke Wrenn in memory of Dr. Montague Cooke, Jr., 1951 (1067.1)

Hawaiian Feathered Standards or Kahili

Fig. 77

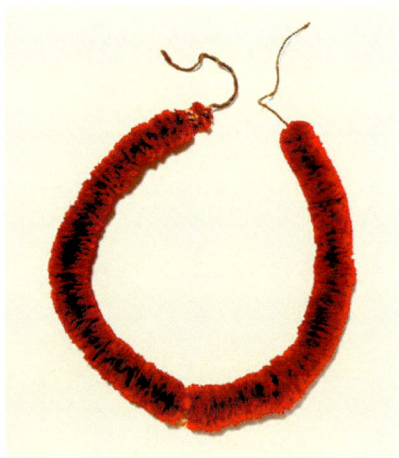

Located in the Australian Museum.
Image is from *Wikimedia Commons*
and in the public domain

Photograph by Harry Haase,
© Institut und Sammiung fuer
Ethnologie der Georg-August
Universitaet Goettingen,
Goettingen, Germany

Photograph by Ben Patnoi.
Courtesy of the Bishop
Museum, Honolulu

Eight strand *Ni'ihau Shell Lei*
located in the Bishop Museum,
Honolulu. Image is from *Wikimedia
Commons* and in the public domain

Hawaiian Feather Necklaces or Lei Hulu Manu

Fig. 78

Kaluahine Waterfall at the Mouth of Waipi'o Valley
Image is from Wikimedia Commons and in the public domain

Wailoa River, Waipi'o Valley
Photograph by Bryn Berg

CHAPTER 9

THE ARCHAEOLOGICAL SITES OF WAIPI'O VALLEY: THE LAST POLYNESIAN "GARDEN OF EDEN"

Waipio Valley, the beautiful
cliffs surround it
the sea on one side
the cliffs are hard to climb
not to be climbed
are the sea cliffs

(Old Hawaiian *mele* or chant)

WAIPI'O: THE HAWAI'I ISLAND VALLEY OF THE GODS

Waipi'o Valley is a lush valley with abundant natural beauty and resources bordered by towering two thousand foot cliffs and numerous cascading waterfalls. It is known as Waipi'o *mano wai*, Waipi'o the source of water and life, and the Valley of the Kings. Waipi'o Valley was probably named by its original settlers after the 1148 foot high Vaipo Waterfall located in Hakaui Valley, nine miles from the town of Taiohae on the island of Nuku Hiva, in the Marquesas Islands. Waipi'o Valley is the most famous and probably the earliest royal center in the Hawaiian Islands and is recognized as a traditional place of great cultural and spiritual importance, a *wahi pana* or celebrated and legendary place, a *wahi kapu* or sacred place and a *wao akua* or region of the gods.

The abundant waters of Waipi'o or Waipiko Valley provided for life, *wai* means freshwater and *piko* is the name of a variety of common *kalo* or taro plant. The valley with its plentiful taro possessed great *mana*, "there is special *mana* [the spiritual essence and divine power of the gods] in Waipi'o Valley, *mana* from long ago; *mana* still there; *mana* still alive". Waipi'o may also be a reference to the divine *p'io*, the chiefly *ali'i* class who made Waipi'o Valley home. (Kirch 2010) Waipi'o Valley is of great archaeological significance to Hawaiian culture and was of great political importance as the residence and seat of power of *ali'i nui*, the high chiefs of Hawai'i Island. It first became a royal center when Pili Ka'aiea was brought to Hawai'i Island by the high *ari'i* warrior/priest Pa'ao. It became a major religious center containing a total of eight temple or *heiau* sites, three of which were located in the front of the valley near the sand dune area and were national *heiau* of the Hawai'i Island Kingdom, along with the royal residence and royal mausoleum (Figs. 79 (1&2)).

Waipi'o Valley evolved from a simple early settlement into a complex, sophisticated *ahupua'a* reflecting development of the political organization and cultural history of early Hawaiian society. Archaeological evidence exists on its black sand beach and sand dune area, an ancient burial site for hundreds of years, of one of the earliest permanent Hawai'i Island settlements. Burial mounds of the original settlers of Waipi'o Valley were sacred, located between the beach and coastal fishponds, they were the gravesite of important chiefs and priests. Burial mounds were of simple construction composed of ocean-smoothed boulders and earth with small god houses or shrines on top. A burial in the sand dunes was typically under a pile of stones covered with sand and soil excavated from adjacent inland taro pondfields. "Burial remains have eroded from the sand dunes behind the beach on the west side of the Wailoa River". Recently, during an archaeological survey conducted by the Bishop Museum in 1983, human remains were found eroding from the sand dune area. (Cleghorn and Rogers-Jourdane 1983) The dunes had been much higher in the past, as high as fifty feet, but have eroded due to storms and tsunamis. Identical sand dune burial mounds located behind beaches have been found in the Marquesas or Hiva Islands. (Suggs 1960) In the Tonga and Samoa Islands monumental sand covered earthen burial mounds, often containing burial vaults of chiefs with a god house on top, were the focus of ceremonial and religious activity. Waipi'o Valley also contains ancient burial caves located in the steep cliffs or *pali* along either side of the valley.

There was an ancient Hawaiian burial practice of interring the bones of deceased high-ranking *ali'i* and *kahuna* inside the tops of cinder cones or *'akeke pu'u* near the summit of Mauna Kea, such as *Pu'u o Kukahau'ula*, one of a group of three cinder cones located near the peak (Fig. 80) or *Pu'u o Makanaka*, the hill of many standing people. "In olden times, it was common practice of the natives in the surrounding region to carry up the bones of their deceased relatives to the summit plateau for burial." (McCoy 1999, Alexander 1892) The summit of Mauna Kea had been a burial site for the highest born ancestors of the Hawaiians for generations, it was *Ka Mauna o Akea,* or The Mountain of Wakea. Hawai'i Island was considered the firstborn son or *hiapo* of Wakea, son of Kahiko Lua Mea, the "very ancient and sacred one", and his wife the goddess *Papa*. Mauna Kea, their son's *piko* or navel, was a depository for infant umbilical cords and a symbolic *piko* connecting Hawai'i Island to the heavens.

THE ROYAL COMPLEX OF WAIPI'O VALLEY

Several royal archeological sites exist in the front of Waipi'o Valley such as site of the royal residence that included a *heiau*, fishponds, irrigation channels, taro pondfields and a sports field (Figs. 79 (1&2)). The royal residence or Ka Haunokama'ahala was located just behind the sand dune area along the Wailoa River and also located behind the sand dune area was the Paka'alana Heiau (Fig. 81), the most revered national *heiau* on Hawai'i Island that contained the sacred royal mausoleum, *Hale o* Liloa. The Paka'alana Heiau was located in what is now a forested area called Kukuinui due to the abundance of *kukui* trees that once grew in the area. The Paka'alana Heiau was both a *luakini heiau* and *pu'uhonua* or place of refuge. Inland from the royal residence was Kahikimai, the royal taro pondfield or *lo'i*, and the sacred paving stones of Liloa were built between the bank of the *lo'i*, side entrance to the royal residence and entrance to the Paka'alana Heiau.

THE HAWAIIAN HEIAU

Hawaiian *heiau* were sacred places of worship, offering and sacrifice; the most significant architectural elements in the pre-contact Hawaiian Islands. They were where religious ceremonies were held, where *mana*, power of the gods, was concentrated and transferred to empower mankind. *Luakini heiau* could be built only by high chiefs, lesser chiefs were not permitted to construct them. They were *heiau* of human sacrifice dedicated to *Ku*, god of war. The order of *Ku* was the most severe religious order and when any public threat occurred rituals of *luakini heaiu* were attended by *ali'i* of the whole community. During times of war or on important occasions of state, human and animal sacrifices were made to gain favor and *mana* from the god *Ku*. The name *luakini* comes from *lua*, meaning pit and *kini*, meaning many or 40,000 and may have originated from the thousands of sacrificial tree pits at the Waha'ula Heiau, the first *luakini heiau* in the Hawaiian Islands. It was into these pits the decaying remains of sacrificial offerings were thrown. Sacrificial victims were generally prisoners of war or men who violated a *kapu* or taboo; women, children and the elderly were exempt. Persons employed to procure victims were known as *mu* and were the cause of great terror.

Luakini heiau could not be built on sites randomly selected, but only on sites where ancient temples built by the original Marquesas or Hiva Island settlers once stood and special priests were the only people who knew where these ancient sites were. (Stokes 1991) These priests were architects known as *kahuna kuhikuhi pu'uone* because they showed their plans or *kuhikuhi* to the chief by drawing and molding them in sand or *pu'uone*. The custom of constructing temples only on the site of a previous temple goes back as far as ancient Egypt where no temple was considered sacred unless it had been built upon the foundations of an earlier sacred temple, particularly those connected to *Zep Tepi* or the "First Time". The *Edfu Building Texts* indicate the current Temple of Horus at Edfu had been a copy of a much earlier temple built on the site. The outer walls of the temple date back to 2575 BC, and the foundations are likely far older, the original temple may date back to 10,500 BC. The Edfu Building Text identifies the temple with the "First Time" or *Zep Tepi*, "the remote epoch after 10,500 BC when temples were built by the gods".

Heiau service rituals were basically two types; *luakini heiau* dedicated to *Ku*, god of war, and *mapele heiau, Hale o Lono* or the House of *Lono*, god of peace. *Heiau* form did not determine the type of service performed, *luakini heiau* were required to be built on sites of previous temples, and they were often placed on platforms of the original structures combining later temple forms with earlier forms. *Luakini heiau* were temples of human sacrifice, no human sacrifices were performed in *mapele heiau,* they were for fertility prayers, and blessing of the crops, any chief, or *ali'i* could build a *mapele heiau*. Some *heiau* were built to sanctify distant canoe voyaging to other islands in the Hawaiian Islands or islands of the South Pacific. The *heiau* fence, *hale* or houses and other structures of *luakini heiau* were built of *'ohi'a* wood and their thatching was of *loulu* palms. The fence, houses, and other structures of *mapele heiau* were built of *lama* wood and their thatching was of *pili* grass.

Hawaiian *heiau* design fell into two major categories corresponding with two periods of temple layout and worship, the early Nana'ulu and 'Ulu period and later when the Samoan Manu'a Island 'Ulu-Hema line of Pili Ka'aiea replaced the original 'Ulu line. The two design arrangements were the platform *heiau* and the walled enclosure *heiau*, although many variations and combinations existed. Hawaiian open platform *heiau* originated with the early Marquesas Island settlers and according to Abraham Fornander, *heiau* from the early Nana'ulu and 'Ulu period were open courtyards, some containing truncated pyramidal *ahu*. The Tahitian *marae* form with stepped truncated *ahu* preceded the Tahitian *marae* form with walled enclosures. The later Hawaiian *heiau* design originated from *marae* of the islands of Tahiti with rectangular courtyards enclosed by low stonewalls containing a single or multilevel *ahu* and outer buildings. A few *heiau* of the earlier Tahitian form with truncated pyramids were found on Hawai'i Island. No two *heiau* had identical floor plans; most were rectangular in plan, some were square, some were in the shape of a trapezoid and others were oval, round or free form, although these were rare. (Linton 1925) The early temple sites in Micronesia contain ceremonial courts with god houses, stepped platform tombs and early Tahitian stepped *ahu* were identical to *ahu* of the Ellice Islands or the nation of Tuvalu.

A third type, the terraced *heiau,* were level platforms built on sloping ground, some having as many as four terraces. The smallest platform was located at the top and the height between terraces reached about three feet. All *heiau* were open-air structures, they were never roofed over. The location and orientation of the *heiau* platforms were dictated by the topography and contours of the site. (Stokes 1991) Usually *heiau* sites overlooked the sea from a prominent point of land, along the edge of a cliff or from a high sand dune, others were located on the brow of a hill or ridge of a slope overlooking a valley or village. The open platform was the early *heiau* type, these were simple stone platforms with large assembly areas and an *ahu* at one end that was sometimes expanded into a stepped truncated pyramid such as the ten-stepped *ahu* of the Mahaiatea Marae on the island of Tahiti that was 259 feet x 85 feet at its base. Polynesian *marae* evolved from temples of the secret Nanga Society of Vitu Levu, Fiji. *Nanga* temples were roughly rectangular enclosures of stones from eighteen inches to three feet high, with interior upright stones and two truncated pyramids located at one end.

The Makaoku Heiau on the mainland of Hawai'i Island, adjacent to the *pu'uhonua* or place of refuge located on the islet of Mokuola or Coconut Island in Hilo Bay, had a stepped stone pyramid said to have been thirty feet high and another was located in Puna also on Hawai'i Island. (Fornander 1969 [1878]) Polynesian stepped pyramidal *ahu* with stone facing were ancient temple/tomb burial mounds on the islands of Samoa and Tonga, tombs of venerated ancestors and deified chiefs in the form of low elongated truncated pyramids; these were taboo holy places of worship. The stepped pyramidal *ahu* of Polynesia were similar to *ziggurats* of ancient Sumer, Mesopotamia, that were sacred spirit mountains. In the Sumerian language, *zi* meant spirit or soul and *gur* or *kur* meant mountain. *Ziggurats* were three to seven levels high with a flat top upon which a shrine was located for religious ceremonies and where astronomer/priests observed the night sky. The Supreme God of heaven in the Sumerian pantheon was known as *Anu,* similar to the Polynesian word *ahu*, and their sacred raised platforms or *ziggurats*, known as "mountains of god" or "hills of heaven", date back to 3500 BC. It was common throughout the ancient Near East for a pile of stones to mark a sacred place or burial site and this was the origin of the Polynesian *ahu*. The Proto-Polynesian Austronesian word for *ahu* is *qafu,* in the Ellice Islands of Micronesia it is *afu* and in Central Polynesia the word *ahu* means to pile up earth. *Ahu* evolved from simple individual stone uprights on small stone mounds into a row of upright stones slabs on a raised stone platform marking the position of ancestral deities. In early temple construction *ahu* were located at one end of an open space containing other upright stone backrests indicating the position of participants in religious ceremonies (Fig. 84). Stones were worshipped in Vedic India with standing stones representing their deities and in the Fiji Islands the gods were thought to reside in black smooth stones (Fig. 82). Later, on the islands of Tahiti, upright stones were replaced with wooden *unu* boards carved with symbolic figurers and geometrical designs. They were six to ten feet high decorated with feathers and *unu* boards were placed along the face of existing *ahu* stones (Fig. 35 (1)). Like the stones, they would house spirits of their deified ancestors.

Early Hawaiian *heiau* constructed by the original Marquesas Island settlers of the Hawaiian Islands have either been altered or destroyed by later arrivals from Rarotonga in the Cook Islands and from the islands of Tahiti, only a few remain today. Examples of these earlier temples exist on the islands of Necker and Nihoa, now uninhabited islands in the Northwest Hawaiian Islands that are part of the Papahanaumokuakea Marine National Monument named after the goddess/earth-mother *Papa* (Fig. 83). The name means *Papa* who *hanau* or gave birth to a *moku* or island district of *akea* or a wide expanse. The practice of preserving open space in or near a village as a tribal assembly area was practically universal throughout Polynesia. The word *marae* originated from the Proto-Polynesian Austronesian word *malaqe*. In Tonga it was *mala'e* and in Samoa it was *malae*, meaning a village open space serving as a public ceremonial meeting place with religious associations, both the Hawaiian *heiau* and Polynesian *marae* were ritual spaces. These early Hawaiian Island temples or *heiau* were similar in design to temples or *me'ae* located in the Marquesas or Hiva Islands, the simple form of inland *marae* of the *manahune* located in the islands of Tahiti and to *marae* in the Tuamotu Islands. These were simple open rectangular courts with long, narrow, stepped platforms or *ahu* along one side containing a row of five upright stones indicating where spirits of their deified ancestral gods would descend to earth. (Emory 1934) These platforms were taboo and only for the gods, the main courtyard was a ceremonial assembly area on level ground where tribal dances, social functions as well as public religious rites were held and they had stone slabs functioning as sacred backrests marking the position of honored chiefs, a practice going back to ancient India. (Handy 1971 [1930]) Throughout Polynesia groves of sacred trees where divine spirits resided were planted in and around temple grounds, sacred fruit-bearing trees whose produce was offered to the gods. In the Hawaiian Islands, sacred *kukui*, breadfruit and coconut trees were planted in the outer courtyards of *heiau*. In the Tonga Islands, there were sacred temple trees inhabited by spirits. In the Marquesas Islands, there were sacred groves of banyan trees and sacred trees were planted around the *nanga* temples of Viti Levu Island, Fiji. From Sumer, Mesopotamia, to the Indus River Valley of India and ancient Egypt, sacred trees or "trees of life" have been worshipped on temple grounds.

Although alignment of most Hawaiian *heiau* was *mauka-makai* or mountain-sea, some were observatories with orientations of astronomical significance and some were navigational *heiau* containing stone canoes. On Hawai'i Island along the Kohala Coast, the Maka o Hule Heiau or Eyes of Hule Point was a navigational *heiau* with standing stones indicating the routes to the Tahitian and Marquesan Islands. On the island of O'ahu, the Ku'ilioloa Heiau at Kaneilio Point, Pokai Bay, was a navigational *heiau* built by voyagers who arrived from the Taputapuatea Marae on Ra'iatea Island, Tahiti, in the eleventh century. After building the Kapukapuaka Heiau at Laniakea on O'ahu Island, they transported foundation stones originally from the Taputapuatea Marae to build the Ku'ilioloa Heiau, also on O'ahu Island. There were Hawaiian *heiau* whose layout aligned with the movements of the sun built on an east-west axis with one side aligned with the summer solstice, the opposite side with the winter solstice and the *lananu'u mamao* tower aligned with the rising sun during the equinoxes.

HERMAN MELVILLE IN POLYNESIA

Herman Melville, a famous American author born in New York City on August 1, 1819, shipped out on the whaler Acushnet on July 9, 1842, accompanied by his shipmate Richard Tobias Greene or Toby. They deserted ship on Nuku Hiva Island in the Northern Marquesas or Hiva Islands attempting to live on a lush tropical *Eden* among gentle, unspoiled natives. The deserters traveled inland, eventually reaching a valley they thought was inhabited by the friendly Happars, but upon descending into the valley they were captured by the fierce man-eating Taipi. In 1846 Melville wrote his first novel *Typee*, an account of his stay with the cannibalistic natives of Taipval Valley.

> Melville described a first-fruits celebration taking place on a level paved area containing stone seats for chanters, dignitaries and chiefs. On festival days, their holiday costumes were tapa robes decorated with colorful flowers, feathers and other ornaments. Groups of females dressed in cheerful costumes danced and chanted on an immense plaza contrasting with the gloomy forest background. From viewing sheds located on stone platforms opening toward the interior of the plaza, chiefs and warriors looked upon groups of dancing females on the *hoolah-hoolah* grounds. Upon the terraced altars or *ahu* were deposited vast amounts of fruit, rolls of tapa, baked hogs decorated with freshly cut leaves and implements of war piled before the row of hideous idols. Fruit hung suspended in leaf baskets from poles embedded into the stone altar and along the altar was a row of tall drums made from the hollowed out trunks of large trees, their heads covered with shark skins and their barrels decorated with elaborately carved figures. Behind these instruments, young men stood beating violently with the palms of their hands upon the drumheads. (From *Typee, A Peep at Polynesian Life*, 1996 [1876], by Herman Melville)

> "The hula usually took place at the mouth of the valley, where level ground near the beach gave an opportunity for a greater number of participants, . . . their musical instruments were hollowed logs over which shark or pig-skin had been tightly stretched. These were beaten with the palms of their hands, filling the air with a pandemonium of sound."

> (From A Vanishing People of the South Seas, 1919,
> in *National Geographic Magazine*, Volume 36,
> no. 4, by John Church, pages 295, 296)

In the Marquesas or Hiva Islands, the focal point of the community was a ceremonial dance floor called the *tohua* (Fig. 52), a large rectangular area of level ground usually created by terracing surrounded by raised stone platforms. The highest stone platform or *paepae* in the *tohua* was the location of the residence of the chief and was also a guesthouse where visiting chiefs could view ceremonies held on the *tohua* below. Ceremonies were basically secular in nature, holding council meetings of chiefs and warriors, tribal village dances, feasts and other social functions. The *tohua* contained a carved stone altar, upright stones spaced along its *ahu* and stone backrest designating where priests and chiefs were seated during ceremonies held on the grounds. The name for assembly areas in the Marquesas Islands was *tohua* and on Ra'iatea Island, Tahiti, assembly areas were known as *tahua*. The *meʻae* of the Marquesas Islands contained skulls of deceased ancestors and other sacred objects and had a high roof indicating its importance. A *meʻae* located on a stone platform along Taiohae Bay on Nuku Hiva Island of the Marquesas Islands was described by Father Le P. Mathias Garcia of Paris, France, in *Letters sur lies Marquises*, 1843.

> "They came finally to two little thatched houses, one of ordinary form, the other pyramidal, and falling into decay. Rampant vegetation covered both. In the interior they saw a thousand statues of all sizes strewn about . . . on a corner, with a certain effect of decoration, were four heads of victims who had been killed and eaten. Cannibal feasts had been held here only a short time before with the religious rites which accompanied them, by the priests of the idols, the warriors, and the chiefs, who alone had the right to participate."

> "In the midst of the wood was the hallowed "hoolah hoolah" ground - set apart for the celebration of the fantastical religious rituals of these people, comprising an extensive oblong "pi-pi", terminating at either end in a lofty terraced altar, guarded by ranks of hideous wooded idols, and with the two remaining sides flanked by . . . sheds, opening toward the interior of the quadrangle thus formed."

> (From *Typee, A Peep at Polynesian Life,* 1996 [1876], by Herman
> Melville. A description of a *tohua* and *meʻae;* open spaces
> for dances, feasts and religious rituals in the Marquesas
> Islands, Chapter 12, pages 114, 115)

> "Here, beneath the deep shade of the sacred banyan trees, was erected a series of terraces and platforms . . . some 15 feet from the level of the stone-paved grove. This great "paepae" [stone platform], often 100 feet in length, was large enough to seat comfortably . . . king, his chiefs, and several hundred warriors . . . In the center stood the "tiki", a crude, grotesque image, sometimes of wood, but more often rudely carved from soft stone with tools of flint. A large stone oven stood at one end of the "paepae", and here the priest with his assistants attended to the preparation of the feast."

> (From A Vanishing People of the South Seas, 1919, in
> *National Geographic Magazine,* Volume 36,
> no. 4, by John Church, page 286)

> "This, in the old days, was the "paepae [stone platform] tapu" or Forbidden Height, the abode of dark and terrible spirits. Upon it once stood the temple and about it in the depths of night were enacted the rites of mystery, when the priests and elders fed on the "long pig that speaks", when the drums beat till dawn and wild dances maddened the blood."

> (From *White Shadow's in the South Seas,* 2006
> [1919], by Frederick O'Brien, page 180)

THE EARLY HEIAU OF HAWAIʻI ISLAND

The early settlers of Waipiʻo Valley would have followed customs of their ancestral society in the Marquesas Islands whose assembly areas or *tohua* were mostly level and rectangular, often created by terracing. Their essential feature was its level dance floor, *tohua* were secular in nature and accessible to all classes of society. *Tohua* were as large as 300 feet along an open long side sometimes defined with stone edging and a raised stone platform or *ahu* located at the rear opposite the long open side. Located on its *ahu* platform were upright stones and carved wooden figures representing ancestral deities overlooking the assembly area, on the sides of the rectangular area were low stone platforms covered with smooth waterworn stones and pebbles with viewing sheds where chiefs and warriors were able to observe the proceedings and this design would have been followed in Waipiʻo Valley. Small houses were erected on the assembly area serving as temporary residences for the gods during religious rituals. Marquesan religious temples or *meʻae* were often included in a *tohua* and contained refuge pits below their stone platforms where remains of sacrifices were disposed of just as in the Hawaiian *heiau*. (Linton 1925)

The Honuaʻula Heiau located along the beach was probably the original *heiau* in Waipiʻo Valley constructed by its first settlers from the Marquesas Islands (Fig. 33). A flat open space for village events, it was similar to Marquesas *tohua* and all that remains are stones from its stepped *ahu* located against the sand dune burial mounds. A residence of the high chief/priest was located on the earthen mound behind the *ahu* or raised platform of the Honuaʻula Heiau. It was a small rectangular structure overlooking the assembly area with an open side and a high obelisk shaped roof similar to the oracle towers of Marquesan *meʻae*

(Fig. 52). Important places of ruling families were usually connected to public open spaces and visiting chiefs were able to view the proceedings from a platform located in front of the high chief's residence. These sand dune mounds contained burial sites of honored chiefs and priests with some mounds having a small god house on top. The Polynesian tradition of earthen burial mounds can be found in Fijian "grave mounds" and Tongan *langi*. Ancient Hawaiian burial sites were in sand dunes, lava tubes, caves and holes in sheer cliffs where bones containing *mana* and considered *kapu* could be concealed and several burial caves were located in cliffs facing the ocean along the Kohala side of Waipi'o Valley. Some bodies were laid out flat, while others were buried with their knees drawn up to their chest and a rope wrapped around the legs and neck. These burial position variations reflected cultural differences between different migratory waves throughout Polynesia. Sometimes bones of *ali'i* dead were placed in a canoe meant to carry their soul to the next world. The final burial place for bones of a high chief was encased in a *ka'ai* or sennit casket. At the base of Hi'ilawe waterfall in Waipi'o Valley, there is a hidden cave where bones of famous chiefs were hidden before being placed in sennit caskets and interred on grounds of the Paka'alana Heiau in *Hale o* Liloa, the royal mausoleum, included were bones of Kauhola, Kiha, Liloa, Lonoikama, and Lole.

The Honua'ula Heiau is one of a number of early Marquesas Island sites on Hawai'i Island. Others are located along the slopes of Mauna Kea and Mauna Loa. Mauna Kea or White Mountain is the highest point in Polynesia and the most sacred earthly location in the Hawaiian Islands, closest to Wakea, the sky-father. Encircling the summit of Mauna Kea, a name shortened from Mauna a Wakea meaning Mountain of Wakea, are a total of ninety-three ancient archaeological sites, seventy-six of which were shrines dedicated to unknown deities resembling inland *marae* of the Tahitian and Tuamotu Islands. By 2009, the number of archeological sites increased to 223. Shrines around Mauna Kea are located along an ancient snow line marking the transition to the mountain's sacred summit. Perhaps they were worshipping *Poliahu,* snow goddess of Mauna Kea, *Lilinoe,* goddess of the mist or *Waiau,* the ice goddess. The summit itself was a sacred area under *kapu* or taboo, a place connecting the earth to the heavens. The home of the sky-father Wakea was considered sacred and was only accessible to the highest chiefs and *kahuna.* (McCoy 1999)

Mauna Kea in the ancient Hawaiian culture and religion was a representation of creation itself, a celestial portal into the universe. Its upper regions or *ke kualono* were thought to be located in *wao akua,* the sacred "abode of the gods". Lands from the shore to the 6000-foot elevation were originally densely forested but, as you move above the tree line from the 7000-foot elevation to the summit you enter a snow-covered mountain landscape with over one hundred cinder cones, sacred burial sites reserved for the highest chiefs and *kahuna.* An area thought to be inhabited by the gods was not only sacred in the past, but is considered a sacred location of the Hawaiian Islands today. Mauna Kea is *'aha ho'owili mo'o,* the genealogical *'aha* cord tying the earth to the heavens and the Hawaiian people to their divine origin. Mauna Kea is also an altar equivalent to the *lananu'u mamao,* sacred Hawaiian *heiau* towers constructed in three levels. The first level of the mountain was the *lana* located from the 11,000-foot to the 12,000-foot elevation, it was the least restrictive and is where most of the ancient shrines are located. Most shrines encircling the summit have one to three upright god stones or *'eho,* although some have as many as twenty-four or twenty-five. These stone slabs are generally only two or three feet high, tapered from bottom to top and set on edge. Shrines with a single upright stone are the most common. Those with pairs of upright stones may have symbolized the god *Ku* and goddess *Hina.* A small number of shrines have courtyards containing a row of upright stones. The second level or *nu'u,* from the 12,000-foot to the 13,000-foot elevation, was more sacred with less evidence of man-made features and the third level or *mamao,* above 13,000 feet, held the highest level of sacredness, it was the "realm of the gods" where only the high chiefs and high *kahuna* were allowed entry. During religious rituals the *lananu'u mamao* tower was where the high chief and *kahuna nui* communicated with the gods when it was covered with *'oloa,* a fine white *kapa* making it appear as the upper slopes of Manua Kea covered with snow. (Kanaka'ole 2009)

There is a legend that the builders of Necker Island *heiau* left one of the inhabited Hawaiian Islands after the Tahitian invasion and arrival of Pa'ao, the warrior/priest from Ra'iatea Island. The legend states after the Tahitian arrival the original Hawaiian settlers, the *menehune* people, were pushed northward to the island of Kaua'i where their high chief, alarmed his people were intermarrying with the newcomers, ordered them to sail away in search of a new home. Northwest of Kaua'i Island are the small barren Nihoa Island, Bird Island or Mokumanu, 167 miles from the islands of Kaua'i and Ni'ihau, and Necker Island or Mokumanumanu another 155 miles to the west, the only islands of the Northwest Hawaiian Islands known to have ever been inhabited. Necker and Nihoa Island ruins of early *heiau* platforms contain raised terraces at one end with a single row of upright stones. The *heiau* most similar to these on the major Hawaiian Islands was located at Waimea on Kaua'i Island and was the first *heiau* described by Captain James T. Cook in 1778 (Fig. 85). A wooden perimeter fence surrounding the Waimea Heiau had skulls mounted on its posts, skulls of deceased chiefs were considered sacred. The wooden and stone carved figures at the Waimea Heiau on Kaua'i Island wore cylindrical headdresses identical to those of the Marquesas Islands (Fig. 54). The isolation of Kaua'i Island preserved the culture and artifacts of the original Marquesas Island settlers, such as the stirrup type stone pounder used in the Northern Marquesas Islands found on Kaua'i Island. Differences in speech between Kaua'i Island and other Hawaiian Islands is due to preservation of their original Marquesas Island language.

Necker Island or Mokumanamana Island, 276 feet high and barely forty-six acres, and Nihoa Island, Bird Island or Mokumanu Island, 910 feet high and 170 acres, are part of the Papahanaumokuakea Marine National Monument. Nihoa Island was named for its jagged profile, the word *nihoa* means serrated, and there is clear evidence of its early habitation with a total of eighty-nine archaeological sites containing twenty-five to thirty-five house sites, fifteen ceremonial *heiau*, several *ko'a* or fishing shrines, burial caves, twelve acres containing twenty-five agricultural terraces indicating intensive cultivation capable of supporting an estimated maximum of 100 to 125 people, along with small stone images of their gods. Necker Island also has evidence of early habitation, although it was probably never permanent. It has a total of 52 archaeological sites, including 34 *heiau* sites with upright basalt stone slabs located on raised platforms similar to inland *marae* of the *manahune* in the islands of Tahiti and *marae* of the Tuamotu Archipelago, indicating Necker Island was probably a religious center. An explanation for the presence of so many *heiau* sites on tiny Necker Island, many almost parallel to each other and astronomically aligned with the summer and winter solstices, is about 1000 years ago the Tropic of Cancer was located directly over Necker Island (Liller 2000) and on June 21, the summer solstice or zenith of Kaula, the sun passed directly overhead casting no shadow. It was *kau ka la i ka lolo* or when "the sun rests on the brains", when the *mana* of the sun enters the worshippers. Ancient Hawaiians believed a person's shadow was a physical manifestation of their spirit and a person had the most *mana* when they cast no shadow, when their spirit was united with their body. Stone *ki'i* statues found at Necker Island sites are examples of early Hawaiian culture, a total of 13 male basalt stone figures (some only fragments) were discovered on Necker Island *heiau* platforms during the Kingdom of Hawaii Annexation Expeditions of 1894. Ranging in height from 8 to 18 inches, they have open mouths with their tongues protruding, a motif identical to one from the Marquesas Islands and tool marks on the figurines indicate the carving technique used was similar to Marquesas workmanship (Fig. 86). According to legend some of the *menehune* left one of the major islands, probably the island of Kaua'i, lived on Nihoa Island and realizing they would be unable to survive on this desolate island sailed away in search of a new home.

THE PU'UHONUA OR PLACE
OF REFUGE OF WAIPI'O VALLEY

There were four known *luakini heiau* located in Waipi'o Valley; Pa, Moa'ula, Honua'ula and the Paka'alana Heiau that was also the *pu'uhonua* or place of refuge for the valley. The Pa Heiau was located in the Napo'opo'o housing area where one parcel is referred to as Pa Luakini. This parcel was awarded to the Hawaiian Evangelical Association as a church site and all that remains of the *heiau* is an underground stone chamber, probably its *luapa'u* or bone pit where decayed offerings and victim's bones were thrown. The Moa'ula Heiau was located 2500 feet from the ocean along the Kohala side of the valley at the base of the cliff or *pali* and was built by Hakau who was possibly its human dedication sacrifice after being killed by 'Umi. (Stokes 1991) The last royal event held in Waipi'o Valley was a meeting of the Grand Council of Chiefs held at the Moa'ula Heiau where Kiwala'o, eldest son of Kalani'opu'u, was designated as Kalani'opu'u's successor and the Moa'ula Heiau was where *Kaili*, war god of Kalani'opu'u, was kept and given to Kamehameha the First. The only remaining feature of the Moa'ula Heiau is a small underground compartment three feet long, one foot wide, and one foot deep. The Honua'ula Heiau, located on Waipi'o Beach, was probably the original Waipi'o Valley *heiau*. The Paka'alana Heiau was an ancient *heiau* that existed before the time of Kila, son of Mo'ikeha, although it was reconstructed by the *ari'i* warrior/priest Pa'ao whose name means pharaoh. It had many similarities to the Israelite Tabernacle at the base of Mount Sinai during the biblical Exodus, the Paka'alana Heiau was the most sacred site on Hawai'i Island (Figs. 81, 90). Its courtyard contained a mausoleum and only a few stones from its perimeter wall remain today. The Paka'alana Heiau was also the *pu'uhonua* for Waipi'o Valley and one of the three major *pu'uhonua* sites on Hawai'i Island.

> "Here was the *Puuhonua* [*Pu'uhonua*], or place of refuge for all this part of the Island. This [was] the Hawaiian "City of Refuge". [This sanctuary was] absolutely inviolable. The gates stood perpetually open, and though the fugitive was liable to be pursued to their very threshold, he had no sooner crossed it than he was safe from the king, chief, or avenger. These gates were wide, and some faced the sea, and others the mountains, hither the murderer, the manslayer, the tabu-breaker fled, repaired to the presence of the idol, and thanked it for aiding him to reach the place of security. After a certain time the fugitives were allowed to return to their families, and none dared to injure those whom the high gods had granted their protection."

(From *Six Months in the Sandwich Islands*, 1998 [1873], by
Isabell Bird describing the Paka'alana Heiau, page 100)

Pu'uhonua were dedicated to the god *Lono* and were places of refuge, sanctuaries where fugitives could find protection from pursuit and forgiveness, where they could escape from being taken captive or being put to death. Access to a *pu'uhonua* site was difficult, often they were located on a point of land jutting out into the sea or adjacent to royal residences. They had several wide entrances, some faced the sea while others faced the mountains and their gates were perpetually open. Within larger *pu'uhonua* such as Honaunau in South Kona on Hawai'i Island there were areas containing houses surrounded by walled enclosures protecting those seeking refuge with *kahuna* performing elaborate purification rituals on those claiming sanctuary. After staying for a period of only two or three days, the offender could either enter the service of the *kahuna* or return to his home and family in safety. "No one ventured to injure those who, when they fled to the gods had been by them protected". (Ellis 1969 [1829])

During times of war, *pu'uhonua* boundaries were marked with poles and white tapa flags, they were where vanquished warriors, the elderly, crippled and children were protected. It is believed there was at least one place of refuge in every *moku* or island district, with many having more than one. Originally, places of refuge included lands of the highest chiefs, their residences and ancestral burial places. Only *ni'aupi'o* ruling chiefs with their sacred *kanawai kapu ali'i* could call for *pu'uhonua ho'ola*, *ho'ola* means life, overriding a violation of the taboos of the gods. *'Aina pu'uhonua* were sacred lands based on the inherited power of the ruling high chief, his sacred *mana* made him and his lands *pu'uhonua* or places of refuge. *'Aina pu'uhonua* could be a large section of an *ahupua'a* in size and on the island of Tahiti an entire large valley, property of the high chief Teta, was a place of refuge. In the inland Melanesian region of Viti Levu Island, Fiji, a large stone was placed in the center of the village as a place of refuge. If a man who had committed a crime was able to reach the top of the stone he was safe from his pursuers who said, "your life is now spared, not because you are innocent, but because you are on the Rock of Refuge". (Brewster 1922) In Samoa, on Upolu Island, a large *o'a* tree was considered a place of refuge due to the fact that long ago a high chief lived on the spot. (Kelly 1957) In the Marquesas Islands there were hilltop fortifications guarding approaches to the valley below serving as places of refuge. (Linton 1925) The idea of a place of refuge or *pu'uhonua*, an inviolable land where no bloodshed could occur has an ancient origin going back to the legend of creation in Hawaiian mythology. When the first man Kumuhonua was exiled from Kalana i Hau'ola or the "Garden of Eden", he wandered as a refugee dwelling on a hill called Pu'u o honua. "All of the elements of Hawaiian *pu'uhonua* are to be found in other Polynesian areas. These had to be transported to Hawaii as part of the general cultural knowledge of a Polynesian background. They were elaborated upon, and adapted to local needs and conditions." (Kelly 1957)

> *Pu'uhonua* literally means *pu'u* or hill and *honua* or earth and hilltop fortresses were common throughout Polynesia. The origin of the *pu'uhonua* in Polynesia occurred in the Manu'a Islands of Samoa where there were ridge top defensive inland fortifications against Melanesian invasions. The mound tombs of Samoan chiefs also became places of refuge. In the islands of Tonga, all god houses were on grounds enclosed by a fence and consisted of a house for the presiding deity and houses for priests offering asylum. They were places of refuge protected by the *mana* of a high chief or by the burial site of a high chief on the spot. In the islands of Tahiti, grounds of some *marae* were places of refuge along with walled hilltop defensive positions known as *fare hua* or houses of the helpless. "The fortress at Maeva on Huahine Island, Tahiti, was a *pu'uhonua*, it was a square walled enclosure one half mile on each side containing freshwater springs, houses, breadfruit trees, and bones of deceased deified chiefs were kept on the grounds adding to the site's *mana*." (Kelly 1957)

> "Much more important than physical protection was the supernatural protection and sanctity of the surrounding area. Thus each *pu'uhonua* site was closely associated with a heiau [temple] . . . not merely a place of physical refuge, but more specifically a sanctuary. In a thatched house on one of the heiau platforms were kept the bones of the deceased high chiefs, now deified. This was not a burial, but rather a deification. The powerful *mana* of these deified chiefs continued after life to surround the area and to afford protection to anyone entering the enclosure."

> (From Report 11: The Concept of Asylum, 1957, by Marion A. Kelly,
> pages 138, 139. In *The Natural and Cultural History of Honunau,*
> *Kona, Hawai'i,* October 1986, by Edwin H. Bryan and Kenneth
> Kenneth P. Emory, part 2, *The Cultural History of Honaunau.*
> Courtesy of the Department of Anthropology, Bernice
> Pauahi Bishop Museum, Honolulu)

> "It was a large enclosure, under a wide-spreading pandanus [tree] . . . a small house, called "*ke Hale o* Riroa" (the House of Riroa [Liloa]), from the circumstance of its containing the bones of a king of that name . . . directed us to a rudely carved a stone image, about six feet high, standing at one corner of the wall, which they said was a tii, [ki'i] or image of Riroa [Liloa]."

(From the *Journal of William Ellis; A Narrative of an 1823 Tour of
Hawaii, or Owhyhee*, 1963 [1826], by William Ellis
upon visiting the Paka'alana Heiau, page 273)

"The ruin made a massive figure, rising from the flat lava in ramparts twelve to fifteen feet high, of an equal thickness, and enclosing an area of several acres . . . The enclosure was divided in unequal parts; the greater, the City of Refuge; the smaller, the heiau or temple, the so-called House of Keawe, or reliquary [mausoleum] of his royal bones. Not his alone, but those of many monarchs of Hawai'i were treasured here . . . Its gate once passed, an appearance made before the priest on duty, a hasty prayer addressed to the chief idol, and the guilty man was free to go again, relieved from all consequences of his crime or misfortune."

(From *Travels in Hawaii,* 1991 [1973], by Robert Louis Stevenson
describing the City of Refuge at Honaunau,
Hawai'i Island in 1889, pages 26, 28)

If anyone seeking refuge entered the *pu'uhonua* sanctuary and was molested within its grounds, the priest of the *heiau* was obligated to have their pursuer slain, if a pursuer was able to kill within the *pu'uhonua,* the priest would then be killed by the high chief. (Ellis 1969 [1829])

THE PU'UHONUA SITES OF HAWAI'I ISLAND

There were twelve *heiau* sites designated as *pu'uhonua* or places of refuge on Hawai'i Island. Four were located in the Kona District: Havlelani or Pakiha in Holualoa, North Kona; Kapuanoni in Kahalu'u, North Kona; Ke'eku in Kahalu'u, North Kona and Honaunau in South Kona, site of the *Hale o Keawe.* Two were located in the Ka'u District; the *Hale o Lono* in Na'alehu and at Malulani in Kiolaka'a, location of the *Hale o* Keola or House of Life. There were two located in the Hamakua District: Hauola in Hamakua and Paka'alana in Waipi'o Valley. The Paka'alana Heiau that was restored by Liloa existed before the time of Kiha, grandfather of 'Umi, and is mentioned in the legend of Mo'ikeha whose son Kila sought refuge in the Paka'alana Heiau. *Lono* was god of the Paka'alana Heiau that functioned as both a *pu'uhonua* and *luakini heiau.* The *Hale o* Riroa or House of Riroa [Liloa] was a royal mausoleum whose origin was the *hale poki,* a small *heiau,* or "house of enshirement" built to house a *ka'ai* containing bones of a high *ali'i.* Located inside the outer wall of the Pala'alana Heiau, under a spreading pandanus or *hala* tree, the *Hale o* Riroa [Liloa] contained royal bones worshipped as gods. (Malo 1951 [1898]) A statue of the god *Lono* was located at the entry to the inner temple or *luakina* and a six-foot high carved stone image of Liloa stood in one corner of the *heiau* near the *Hale o* Liloa. The Paka'alana Heiau was the most sacred religious site on Hawai'i Island.

"The tabus of its great *heiau* were the most sacred on Hawaii [Island], and remained so until the destruction of the *heiau* and the spoliation of all the royal associations in the valley of Waipi'o."

(From *Heiau of the Island of Hawai'i: A Historic Survey of Native
Hawaiian Temple Sites (Bishop Museum Bulletins in
Anthropology)*, 1991, by John F.G. Stokes, page 161.
Courtesy of Bishop Museum Press, Honolulu)

One *pu'uhonua* was located in the Puna District, it was the Waha'ula Heiau in Pulama, built in the eleventh century by the Tahitian warrior/priest Pa'ao. It is said to have been the first walled *luakini heiau* to be built on Hawai'i Island. Pa'ao brought a sacrificial altar or foundation stone from the Taputapuatea Marae on Ra'iatea Island, Tahiti, and placed it at the Waha'ula Heiau. (Kikawa 2008) Its altar stone represented *mana* and power of the gods *Ta'aroa* and *'Oro* of the islands of Tahiti. Located below an active volcano, molten lava flowing from an eruption of Pu'u O'o Crater at Kilauea Volcano destroyed the Waha'ula Heiau burying Pa'ao's foundation stone. The original enclosure of this *heiau* is said to have contained a sacred grove with specimens of every type of tree found on Hawai'i Island and Pa'ao had soil brought down from the hills because the *heiau* had been built on a lava field. The Waha'ula Heiau was considered so sacred if smoke from one of its temple fires were to drift over a commoner, he would be brought to its altar to be sacrificed. Originally called 'Aha'ula or "red assembly" because its priests wore red-feathered cloaks, the *heiau* name was changed to Waha'ula or "red mouth" because it devoured men. There was one *pu'uhonua* known as *Kaula'i na iwi,* meaning where the bones of chiefs were dried, in the Hilo District on the islet of Mokuola, meaning "life island" or Coconut Island, in Hilo Bay. Located on the northwest part of the islet, *Kaula'i na iwi* was part of the adjacent *luakini heiau* located on Hawai'i Island known as the Makaoku Heiau said to have had a stone truncated pyramidal *ahu* over thirty feet high. There were two *pu'uhonua* located in the district of Kohala, making a total of twelve. The land of Kauhola Point at Hala'ula located along the northern Kohala Coast of Hawai'i Island is open space extending to the ocean with steep cliffs surrounding the point, it was an open space *'aina pu'uhonua* and a favorite retreat of Kamehameha the Great. Located about a mile east of Hala'ula at Hapu'u and associated with Kauhola Point was the *pu'uhonua, Hale o Kaili.* It was a stone pavement eighty feet by sixty feet located forty feet from the edge of the sea cliff along the east side of a small bay and part of it was located along the base of the cliff. The second *pu'uhonua* in the district of Kohala was the *Pu'uhonua o* Waiapuka adjacent to Pololu Valley.

Three of these Hawai'i Island *pu'uhonua* were considered major and were the most important. These were Honaunau in South Kona, Paka'alana in Waipi'o Valley and *Kaula'i na iwi* on the islet of Mokuola or Coconut Island in Hilo Bay, locations that were also the island's most important population and political centers. The other *pu'uhonua* offered only temporary shelter.

"There is another in which I feel much interest . . . I mean the acquisition and control of the *heiau* and *pu'uhonua* of Paka'alana in Waipi'o, of Honaunau in Kona, and perhaps the one on the islet of Mokuola in Hilo Bay . . . once in the control of the Museum they could be protected perpetually."

(In a letter from Charles Reed Bishop to a Bishop Museum
Trustee dated February 22, 1897)

THE TAPUTAPUATEA MAREA ON RA'IATEA ISLAND, TAHITI

The 'Opoa Peninsula on Ra'iatea Island, Tahiti, is the location of the Taputapuatea Marea, the national *marae* and holiest place in the islands of Tahiti and birthplace of the god *'Oro.* Inside the Taputapuatea Marae is the *ava'a* or altar, a small sacred platform twelve feet by six feet and two feet high located midway between the ends of the *ahu* facing the *marae* courtyard upon which was placed the *marea's* most sacred item its holy ark, receptacle of the *to'o,* the image of god (Figs. 35 (1&2)). This platform, the *ava'a* or "bed of the gods", was the holiest place in the Taputapuatea Marae where its holy ark, the *fare atua* or "house of god", was placed. Inside the *fare atua* was the divine object, the *to'o.* "It was the receptacle for the god *'Oro,* principle deity and "state" god of the islands of Tahiti and the *fare atua* represented the god *Ta'aroa's* empty body, a container for his son the god *'Oro,* and the *fare atua* together with the *to'o* appear to represent male and female fertility . . . an important feature of Polynesian Gods" (Fig. 87). (Kaeppler 2007) Their holy ark was described by Sir Joseph Banks as a "chest whose lid was nicely sewed on and very neatly thatched over with date-nut leaves; the whole was fixed on two poles by little arches of very neatly carved wood. These poles seemed to be used in carrying it from place to place".

The network of Taputapuatea Marae extending across Polynesia was created using founding stones from the Taputapuatea Marae on Ra'iatea Island, Tahiti. The location of the Taputapuatea Marea in the Western Tuamotu Archipelago was on Fakarava Atoll or Havaiki te Araro, its ancient capital. Known as Havaiki i Taputapuatea, it was the only *marae* in the Tuamotu Islands where human sacrifices were performed, skulls and bones of human victims were displayed and where there were ceremonies during which sacred stones were unwrapped and redressed similar to the *pa'iatea* ceremony on Ra'iatea Island. The Katipa Marae, also located on Fakahina Atoll in the Western Tuamotu Archipelago, had five low stone platforms three feet wide and seven feet long with an upright stone slab two feet high immediately in front of the *ahu* and during religious ceremonies holy arks or *fare tini atua* were placed upon these platforms. One *fare tini atua* was described as being two and one half feet high, six to eight inches wide and three feet long with poles lashed to each side enabling it to be carried on men's shoulders in religious processions. The Ragthoa Marae located on Napuka Atoll in the northeastern part of the Tuamotu Islands, had ten or twelve *fare tini atua* or holy arks containing important divine human ancestral remains such as hair, teeth, bones and rare feathers. They sat on raised forked sticks during ceremonies and were stored in the *fare ia manaha* or "house of sacred treasures" located in front of the *marae* when not in use. These holy arks must have been a remembrance of the Israelite Ark of the Covenant. A model for the origin of the Israelite Ark is found in the sacred Egyptian bark chests. Built to resemble a boat they were not set in water but, like the Ark of the Covenant, they were carried on poles by priests. During burial processions they symbolically transported a god's presence and a divine image of the deity was contained in a gold-plated shrine box.

THE TO'O OF 'ORO

Tahitian gods manifest themselves in two ways, through natural objects or *ata,* meaning shadow, and through a man-made object such as the feathered girdle or *maro* and the *to'o.* Tahitian gods did not reside permanently in these objects, but would descend into the images during religious events such as the *pa'iatua* ceremony. Tahitian *to'o* had almost no anthropomorphic features; they represented the connection between the human world of *Ao* and divine world of *Po,* between the high chief and the divine. The origin of the word *to'o* was the Proto-Polynesian Austronesian word *toko* meaning pole or staff, prop or support and also referred to shafts of light such as when the god *Tane* or *Kane* separated the heavens from the earth at the dawn of creation. (Handy 1971 [1930]) The *to'o* is in the form of a pole whose function was propping up and supporting the heavens and separating them from the earth, a theme found throughout the ancient mythology of Polynesia. The mythical *Kukulu o* Kahiki or Pillars of Kahiki were located along the horizon to hold up the dome of the heavens separating *Ao,* the world of light and human life, from *Po,* the world of darkness and the divine. These pillars kept heaven and earth separated but also connected them and it was the opening between the sky and sea created by *Kukulu o* Kahiki that allowed Polynesians voyagers to "break through" the wall of the horizon into the celestial regions beyond the sky and become divine.

> Set up the pillar to stand by, the pillar to sit by,
> the pillar to speak by, the pillar to recite by;
> Build the foundation, build the rock-strata,
> Set out the horizon.
> Let the great heavens extend.
> Prop
> The ridge-pole of the sky, the inner post of the sky; . . .
> The ridge thatching of the sky, the roof of the sky.
> The sky is entirely finished.
> The sky remained expanded in ancient times."

(Chant of the Propping of the Sky of Havai'i from the Genealogical
Book of the Pomare Dynasty [Tahiti] by Mare, before 1843.
Translation from *The Tahitian Account of Creation by*
Mare, 1849, in *The Journal of the Polynesian*
Society, Volume 47, no. 186, 1938, by
Kenneth P. Emory, pages 59, 60)

The Tahitian *fare atua* containers and *to'o* images were stored in a small house at the front of the *marae* known as *fare ia manaha* or *fare heiao,* the "house of sacred treasures", when not being used in rituals and *heiao* was the origin of the Hawaiian word *heiau.* Each chief owned his own *to'o* and the size of a family's *to'o* was an indication of their genealogical ranking. The largest belonged to high chiefs and were generally about four feet long, *to'o* of lesser chiefs were rarely longer than two feet. William Ellis described some *to'o* as "six to eight feet long, others not more than as many inches". *To'o* were "feathered gods" constructed from long cylindrical pieces of ironwood or *'aito* shaped like a staff or club covered with layers of tapa wrappings and sennit cord and consecrated with an attachment of red feathers representing the essence of divinity, they contained divine *mana. To'o* were covered mainly with red feathers from a native parakeet along with some yellow and black feathers and wore the red-feathered girdle or *maro 'ura.* Braided coconut fiber sennit cord bindings were wrapped around the *to'o* known as *'aha atua* and were placed with chanting and prayers making the *'Oro* images sacred and divine. *'Aha* was also the name of the Hawaiian sacred cord that symbolically bound the high chief to his subjects and each new high chief possessed his own sacred cord or *'aha kapu ali'i.* Most *to'o* were entirely covered with tapa wrappings and sennit cords, others had a small section of their wooden core extending at the lower end and some *to'o's* had both ends of their wooden core exposed. One end of the *to'o* was generally larger than the other and some had minimal anthropomorphic features defined by additional sennit cords suggesting a human face, arms, hands, and a navel (Fig. 37).

THE HOLY ARK OF RA'IATEA ISLAND, TAHITI

It was at the Taputapuatea Marae where the holy ark, the *fare atua* or "house of god" containing the *to'o* of the god *'Oro,* required every chief on Ra'iatea Island and those who were subjects on other islands to offer sacrifices, they "think it is the only residence of the Deity on earth". (Morrison 1935) Shaped like a miniature dwelling, the *fare atua* was an oblong chest with a roof covering of palm leaves, one end was closed, the other had an opening for the *to'o* deity covered with a sacred cloth and was described in Teuira Henry's book *Ancient Tahiti*.

> "It was a neat little ark made of sacred polished wood, with an arched roof covered with "fara" thatch, square at each end and having a level floor. Its dimensions were about four feet long, two and a half feet wide, and three feet high, varying in size according to the form of the god that was placed in it. One end was closed. The other end had a circular entrance for the god, with a close-fitting stopper of sacred cloth. To this ark were attached cords of sacred sennit forming a loop at each corner, through which polished poles of *miro* wood were passed that extended far enough for two men at each end to bear upon their shoulders. The ark containing the god rested between in the same manner that the Israelites carried their Ark of the Covenant."

(From *Ancient Tahiti,* 1971 [1928], Bishop Museum Bulletin 48, by Teuira Henry, page 136. Courtesy of Bishop Museum Press, Honolulu)

> "The general resemblance between this depository and the Ark of the Lord among the Jews is remarkable . . . it was called *Ewharre no Eatua,* the House of God."

(From *An Account of the Voyages . . . in the Southern Hemisphere, Vols. II and III,* July 17-18, 1769, by John Hawkesworth, LL.D, page 257)

And it shall come to pass in that day, that the Lord shall set his hand again the second time to recover the remnant of his people, which shall be left . . . from the islands of the sea.

And he shall . . . assemble the outcasts of Israel, and gather together the dispersed of Judah from the four corners of the earth.

(Isaiah 11:11, 12)

O Naphtali, satisfied with favour and full with the blessing of the Lord: possess thou the west [the sea] and the south [the islands of the South Pacific].

(Deuteronomy 33:23)

It appears some ancestors of the Polynesian people, particularly the *ari'i*, had been exposed to Israelite/Egyptian religious customs and culture, even traveling with Israelites on their Exodus from Egypt. Some believe Polynesians were part of the Israelite tribe of Naphtali or Dan and according to Abraham Fornander they were included in the Israelite tribe of Benjamin. On April 28, 1792, William Bligh, as Captain of the HMS Providence, visited the Taputapuatea Marae complex located on Utuhaihai or Marae Point at Papaoa in the district of Pare Arue at the southwest end of Matavai Bay on Tahiti Island, where he observed the installation of the *Ephare no t'Etuah [e-fare no te atua]* or "house of god" containing a *to'o* of the god 'Oro. It was about 6 feet long, 4 feet wide, and 5½ feet high covered in feathers with two representations of birds on top. James Morrison was the Boatswain's Mate aboard the ill-fated voyage of the HMS Bounty from 1787 to 1789 and during the mutiny on April 28, 1789. After the mutiny Morrison and fifteen others chose to remain on Tahiti Island, Morrison lived on the islands of Tahiti for nearly six months and states the ancient Tahitian religion was in many respects comparable to that of the biblical Israelite tribes. In his journal, published in 1935, Morrison described witnessing "something similar to the Ark of the Jews" at the Taputapuatea Marae located in the Pare [Oparre] District on Tahiti Island. It was a movable ark, a box three feet long, two feet wide and one foot high known as the *fare atua* or "house of god" containing images of three of their deities. The ark was covered with tapa and placed upon a stand at the most sacred place in the *marae.* On top of the box were several crudely carved raised images of birds with their wings extended and decorated with bunches of red and yellow feathers, clearly intending it to be a replica of the Israelite Ark of the Covenant.

THE PA'IATUA CEREMONY

The most important ritual in the Taputapuatea Marea was the sacred rite known as *pa'iatua,* renewing the divinity of the *to'o.* The 'Opoa Peninsula was transformed into a realm of *Po* offering a temporary home to the gods who arrived throughout the "night of silence". Fire and noise were forbidden, only the *marae* drums could break the silence. At dawn, birds announced arrival of the gods from their distant homes and as the sun arose over the mountains, the ceremony began. *Pa'iatua* means "wrappings of the gods" and all the *to'o* images of *'Oro* were assembled for renewal of their sacred outer wrappings. Described by Alain Babadzan in 1993 and published in *Clothing the Pacific* by Chloe Colchester in 2003, the *pa'iatua* ceremony revitalized the sacred *to'o*. The *pa'iatua* ceremony at the Taputapuatea Marae began with a procession of high chiefs entering the *marae* stripped to the waist. The high priest entered first followed by four priests called *hi'i atua* or "nurses of the god" carrying the *fare atua*, the wooden ark containing the *to'o* of *'Oro,* on their shoulders. They supported it on their shoulders with two nine foot long carrying poles of polished *miro* wood, one on each side of the ark, just as the Israelites carried the Ark of the Covenant being careful not to touch the ark with their bodies because of its extreme holiness. If an ark bearer stumbled and the ark fell to the ground the procession was stopped, a human sacrifice was offered to appease the anger of the gods and the procession would start again from the beginning. Following behind their holy ark were *ari'i* who carried images of their lesser gods wrapped with tapa coverings, next were professionals and craftsman with their covered gods. When the procession reached the *ahu,* the *hi'i atua* placed the ark with its god inside upon the low altar platform built against the front of the *ahu,* the *ava'a* (Fig. 35 (2)). The high chiefs and priests wore special clothing belonging to the sacred *marae* as they stood before the ark. A similar holy ark, the *ewharra no eatua* also meaning "house of god", was located on the island of Huahine in the leeward islands of Tahiti (Fig. 88). Similar holy arks or *fare tini atua* have been found in the Western Tuamotu Archipelago, a group of low lying coral atolls once part of the islands of Tahiti, those holy arks were relic boxes containing sacred objects, bones and hair of deified ancestors, wooden idols and sacred feathers were placed on the flat stone altar platforms.

Throughout Polynesia, wrapping represents man's control of the divine, wrapping a sacred object or person on ceremonial occasions was thought to control and contain their *mana* making them taboo and the origin of sacred wrapping was the sacredness of the loincloth. (Handy 1971 [1927]) At the *pa'iatua* ritual *to'o* were disassembled, their tapa and sennit cord coverings and feathers removed, their inner core pieces of *'aito* wood symbolically purified with water, rubbed with scented coconut oil and laid in the sun. The sennit cord covering of the *to'o* represented the boundary between *Po* and *Ao* and through the unwrapping and rewrapping of the *to'o* divine *mana* was transferred from *Po*, land of the gods, to mankind. The inner god figures of the *to'o* were merely uncarved wooden sticks representing the divine formlessness of *Po* before creation. Only the most important chiefs and priests could view unwrapped *to'o,* if seen by persons of lesser status it was believed *mana* of the *to'o* would cause their death. Discarded feathers from *to'o* of *'Oro* were distributed among lesser chiefs making their *to'o* more divine and the discarded sacred wrappings were placed carefully beneath a stone of the *ava'a* platform. Then, the *to'o* were refurbished with new tapa wrappings, sennit cords, and feathers renewing their *mana* and allowing them to again be possessed by the divine. A ceremony brought to the Hawaiian Islands by Pa'ao and Pili Ka'aiea at the time of the Tahitian migrations was similar to the *pa'iatua* ceremony. It was conducted during *kapu loulu luakini heiau* dedication ceremonies and was known as *kauila huluhulu* meaning *kauila* wood covered with feathers. In the Hawaiian ceremony, as in the Tahitian *pa'iatua* ceremony, sacred feathered images were redressed and in both feathers removed from god images of the ruling chief were distributed among other *ari'i* or *ali'i* adding to the divinity of their god images. The *kauila huluhulu* ceremony restored *pono*, the relationship between the gods, the universe and mankind.

Miniature god houses were common throughout Polynesia and in the islands of Tahiti, *fare atua* representing the body of the god *Ta'aroa* were in the form of tiny dwellings. Similar miniature god houses in the Cook Islands were called *'are ei 'au* or the "house of peace", they were six feet long, covered with pandanus thatching with a small doorway covered with tapa cloth and it was believed the gods resided in these houses. In the Fiji Islands, small models of *bure kalou* were constructed of sennit and in the Hawaiian Islands miniature models of *lananu'u mamao* oracle towers were made of wickerwork covered with feathers (Fig. 89). Miniature god houses mounted on tall poles found in the islands of Tahiti and the Cook Islands and Maori *pataka* were elaborately carved wooden god houses in New Zealand containing precious bird feathers erected on poles in sacred places. (Handy 1926)

CONNECTIONS BETWEEN THE HAWAIIANS
AND THE ISRAELITES

Connections exist between the Hawaiian Islands and the place of origin of the Polynesian, the Near East. Polynesian *ahu* originated from the use of a pile of stones to mark sacred places throughout the Near East and there are many similarities between biblical Israelite religious worship, customs and taboos, and those of the ancient Polynesians and Hawaiians. (Malo 1951 [1898]) Sacred pillars were common throughout the Near East and in the deserts of the Sinai and the Negev in ancient Israel sacred standing stones or *massebah* marked sacred spaces where man had come in contact with the divine. The origin of the Hawaiian *Pohaku o Kane* was probably the biblical Bethel Stone. The location of a *Pohaku o Kane* was revealed in a dream, it was anointed with oil just as the Bethel Stone was when the biblical Jacob rested his head to sleep, dreamt of heaven and later poured oil on the stone as a sacrifice to God. The laws of the Hawaiian god *Kane* were similar to both the laws of ancient Egypt and the biblical commandments. Hawaiian *kapu* laws originated from the *ture,* a code of laws of the islands of Tahiti, orally transmitted principles of social order and rules of conduct established by the *ari'i.* These unwritten laws found in many Polynesian islands originated from the early history of the *ari'i* when they resided in the Near East and the word *ture* for laws was derived from the Hebrew word *torah* meaning laws and pronounced *toura* throughout Polynesia. *Ture* laws indicate a level of cultural development more advanced than the primitive tribal cultures of earlier Polynesian migrations and were followed on the islands of Tahiti and Samoa, the Cook Islands and by the Maori of New Zealand. It has been suggested the word *ture* meaning laws was introduced by western missionaries, but since the word occurs on different islands thousands of miles apart, the idea they agreed to a recent adoption of a Hebrew word into their indigenous dialects is unlikely. The word *ture* was not a modern introduction, but an ancient Polynesian word and concept. In the Samoa Islands, the word for law is *tulafono, fono* means council, and the word *tula* probably came from the word *torah.* In the Malayo-Polynesian Arosi language of Northwest Makira Island, formerly San Cristobal Island in the Solomon Islands of Melanesia, *ha'a toraha* means law or command.

Hawaiian *kapu* or taboo resembled those of the Israelites, observation of their sacred ritual *kapu* days were *kanawai akua,* a law of the gods. The Israelites could not work, light fires, cook or travel, "leave your place", on the Sabbath. The ancient Hawaiians had four strict *kapu* or taboo periods every lunar month corresponding with phases of the moon and their observation had similarities to the Israelite Sabbath when they required absolute silence, no fires were allowed and everyone was required to remain indoors. Both the Hawaiians and Israelites had purification ceremonies for warriors returning from battle due to their contact with blood and death endangering themselves and others, blood was life and spirits of the slain could return and seek revenge. In the Hawaiian Islands, seclusion and purification of warriors returning from battle was partly due to fear of vengeful spirits of slain enemies. (Handy 1971 [1927]) In New Zealand, Maori warriors returning from battle were immersed in a body of taboo or *tapu* water as a rite of purification. In the Marquesas Islands, warriors who had slain an enemy were isolated for ten days allowing dangerous influences to wear off. Most Polynesians had a cleansing ritual for those who handled and buried the dead. In the Hawaiian Islands, after defilement due to contact with a corpse a person was sprinkled with seawater, *wai huikala* or the water of purification and forgiveness, then after a required bath in the ocean the defilement was removed. In both ancient Israel and the Hawaiian Islands, a purifying bath was required after contact with the dead, in ancient Israel it was called a *mikveh.* In the islands of Tahiti, if a person touched a dead body except those killed in war or sacrificed, he was considered unclean and could not touch any food with his hands for one month, during this time he was feed by others.

In the temples of Sumer, Mesopotamia, there were bodies of sacred holy water or *abzu* used for ceremonies of purification and holy water was used in ancient Israel. Throughout Polynesia holy water was used and in the Hawaiian Islands, it was utilized during ceremonies of cleansing and purification. In the Hawaiian Islands, seawater with red earth, *'alaea* or hematite, *limu kala* moss and *pala* ferns was holy water sprinkled on people and places for purification. *Pi kai* was the ceremony of purification with freshwater, *pi kai kea* was purification with saltwater and *pi kai 'olena* was seawater with turmeric added to remove a *kapu.* The Maori of New Zealand also used freshwater in their purification rituals, priests or *tohunga* would immerse themselves in a stream or pond during cleansing ceremonies to remove sickness and *tapu.* During ceremonies in the Melanesian *nanga* temples of the Fiji Islands, the chief priest dipped his hands into a sacred bowl of water as an act of purification, just as Israelite priests washed their hands in water from the Levar before entering the desert sanctuary of the Tabernacle. The firstborn male *ali'i* child, *hiapo* in the Hawaiian Islands and *matahiapo* in the islands of Tahiti, was consecrated to the gods. The first-born male *aho ariki* child in New Zealand was dedicated to *Io,* the Supreme Being, and all first-born male children in ancient Israel were dedicated to *Yahweh,* the Israelite God. The meat for high-ranking Hawaiian *ali'i* must be "pure" and was required to be blessed by a *kahuna,* "pork must be first consecrated in the temples before it is touched by the *ali'i,* just as "kosher" food was blessed in ancient Israel". (Valeri 1985) During the Makahiki festival fresh pork was not eaten by the *ali'i* because it could not be blessed in *heiau* that had been closed. (Malo 1951 [1898])

There were similarities between ancient Israelite customs and those of the Proto-Polynesians of Island Southeast Asia. The Batak, a Proto-Polynesian tribe located on the island of Borneo, had a seven-day week and were forbidden to work on their seventh day or *hari samisara,* just as the Israelites were forbidden to work on the Sabbath. (Kimball 1989-1993) The name of the Supreme God of the Dayaks of the island of Borneo, *Iaouah* or *Yavuah,* connected them back to the ancient Egyptian Supreme God *Iao* and the Israelite God *Yahweh.* Both the ancient Hawaiians and Israelites considered the day to begin with the setting sun and had lunar calendars. During each month Hawaiians had four taboo or *kapu* periods, one for each of their four major gods and these sacred and holy days began at sunset and were lifted after several days at dawn. There were Hawaiian holy days or *kapu hoano* from the third night through the sixth night of each month known as four nights of the god *Ku,* these were days of silence and devotion when all work was forbidden and *kahuna* remained in the *heiau* to pray. The four *Ku* nights were observed as a remembrance of the deliverance of Polynesian ancestors from oppression in Egypt, the biblical Exodus. The night of the twelfth was sacred to the god *Kane* and was "*Po o ke Akua*", Night of the Gods. The nights of the twenty-fourth through the twenty-sixth were sacred to the god *Kanaloa* and the nights of the twenty-seventh through the twenty-ninth were sacred to the gods *Kane* and *Lono.* Practices during Hawaiian *kapu* days had similarities to the Israelite Sabbath, no food could be cooked, meals had to be prepared in advance, no work was allowed, and fishing, farming and travel were taboo; these were days of silence and devotion. On these nights high priests and high chiefs remained in the *heiau* praying and performing sacrifices. Both the Hawaiians and Israelites performed animal sacrifices where only the finest animals without blemish were acceptable, "the gods would not eat an offering of poor quality". (Kamakau 1976)

Human sacrifice was a very ancient custom and the origin of Polynesian human sacrifice goes back to Vedic India and the ancient Near East. In the Hawaiian Islands, human sacrificial victims were adult males, no women, infants, the aged or deformed were suitable. The first-born or *hiapo* of Hawaiian *ali'i* were consecrated to the gods at birth. They were not actually sacrificed, a "substitute offering" was provided instead. The Northern Kingdom of Israel followed practices of the surrounding tribes including human sacrifice, such as *Kemosh*, deity of the Moabites, who demanded human sacrifice. Children were sacrificed to *Molech*, fire-god of the Ammonites, by worshipers of the fertility god *Ba'al* as burnt offerings who required the sacrifice of first-fruits including firstborn children, although this was condemned by the Israelite God *Yahweh*. The name of the Israelite Supreme Being *Yahweh* was considered so holy it was not to be spoken, as was the name of the Polynesian Supreme Being *Io* or *'Io*. Both Israelites and Hawaiians separated women during periods of menstruation and while they were giving birth when they were unclean because blood was considered contaminating to the Hawaiian god *Kane,* just as it was to the Israelite God *Yahweh*. There were similarities between Hawaiian *pu'uhonua* or place of refuge and biblical cities of refuge. In ancient Israel as government authority became centralized in Jerusalem, the population outside the city needed places of sanctuary in their own districts and on Hawai'i Island at least one *pu'uhonua* or place of refuge was located in each district.

The Hebrew's trace their origin back to Abraham and the Polynesians trace their origin back to Lua-nu'u, the Polynesian name for the biblical Abraham. The Hawaiian practice of *kahi omaka*, an ancient form of circumcision where the foreskin of the penis was slit but not removed, was introduced by Lua-nu'u or the biblical Abraham to all his descendants as a sign of their ancestry commanded by God. Although attributed to Abraham, circumcision was a more ancient rite performed with flint knives. In the Hawaiian Islands, *kahi omaka* was performed with a bamboo or *'ohe* knife from the small leafed bamboo of *Kane*. The *kahi omaka* circumcision of the sons of chiefs in the Hawaiian Islands was done in the same manner as in ancient Israel and throughout the Near East. It was an ancient *ari'i* or *ali'i* custom almost universal among Polynesians and was practiced in the Fijian, Samoan and Tahitian Islands. (Fornander 1996 [1878]) Circumcision rites practiced in interior districts of Viti Levu Island, Fiji, were associated with the sacred stone *nanga* enclosures and were performed at the *vale tambu* or "house of god". (Fison 1885) If a chief was seriously ill his son or the son of his brother along with other male children were presented to be circumcised as a *soro* or offering to their ancestral gods for the sick man's recovery. Although circumcision throughout Polynesia was generally considered a necessary physical operation rather than being religious, in both the Hawaiian Islands and the islands of Tahiti, circumcisions were performed by priests on sons of chiefs as a ceremonial rite. When a male *ali'i* child was born in the Hawaiian Islands his umbilical cord was cut in a *heiau* in a religious ceremony and again at his circumcision a religious *heiau* ceremony was held.

The name of the Tahitian warrior/priest who altered Hawaiian society and reconstructed the Paka'alana Heiau in Waipi'o Valley was Pa'ao or Parao, a name meaning pharaoh in the Hawaiian language and was Pakao or Pahao in Southern Polynesia. The layout and functions of the Paka'alana Heiau in Waipi'o Valley had numerous similarities to the Israelite Tabernacle, the "tent of meeting", constructed at the base of Mount Sinai during the biblical Exodus (Figs. 81, 90) whose form and function were modeled after an Egyptian mobile military command tent. There are also parallels to Canaanite traditions of the god *El* and the divine assembly of the "tent of *El*". "So closely allied were the ceremonies of the Hawaiian priests to those of the Jews . . . even to the manner of constructing their temples". (Taylor 1922) The portable Egyptian military command tent, the Israelite Tabernacle at the base of Mount Sinai and Hawaiian *luakini heiau* were each divided into three areas, a large rectangular courtyard twice as long as it was wide with its entrance at the middle of one of the short walls and an inner structure divided into two rooms with its entry located at the center of the courtyard. The Egyptian military command tent had a reception chamber whose length was twice its height and width and a smaller inner room that was a cube containing the golden throne of the pharaoh, the living sun god, flanked by images of the winged falcon god Horus. (From *The Divine Warrior in His Tent,* by Michael M. Holman, 2000) Access to both the Hawaiian *luakini heiau* inner sanctuary, the *luakina*, and that of the ancient Israelites was limited to a select few chiefs and priests and at the rear of the inner temple both had their "Holy of Holies". This three area division was reflected in Mount Sinai itself. The Israelite encampment was located in a level area at the base of the "holy precinct" of Mount Sinai. A large, flat plateau locate along the route up the mountain was where Aaron and 70 elders waited as Moses, who was the only one allowed to climb to the blackened summit, and speak with God.

The outer courtyards and inner temples of both the Israelite Tabernacle and the Paka'alana Heiau in Waipi'o Valley had similar layouts and proportions, both had altars for burnt offerings and containers of holy water. In the Israelite Tabernacle, holy water was kept in the *laver*, a basin or large bowl, and in the Hawaiian *luakini heiau* holy water was kept in a skull in the *hale wai ea*. In the inner temple of the desert Tabernacle at Mount Sinai sacred objects were located behind a veil or curtain. It was the "traveling tent throne" of *Yahweh,* divine warrior God of the Israelites where the "Holy of Holies", the Ark of the Covenant with two winged cherubim, was kept that only Moses and the high priest who was the representative of the Lord could enter and speak or listen to God. In the Paka'alana Heiau in Waipi'o Valley, a screened off area at the rear of the inner temple or *luakina* contained the *lananu'u mamao* tower where only the high chief and his priest could enter and speak directly to the gods, it was the most holy place in the Paka'alana Heiau, its "sanctum sanctorum". (Kalakaua 1970 [1888]) The courtyards of the *marae* of the islands of Tahiti were also divided into three zones, only priests and high *ari'i* chiefs could approach the *ahu* located at one end of the *marae;* it was occupied by the gods. The middle area was for the *ari'i* and the area near the entrance was for the remainder of the participants, such as the *ra'atira.* Outside the courtyard were *marae* for the *manahune* or commoners and women. The *nanga* of Viti Levu, Fiji were also divided into three sections; the little *nanga*, the great *nanga* and the sacred *nanga tambutambu.* Both the layout and function of elements of ancient Sumerian temples had similarities to those of Hawaiian *luakini heiau.* The Sumerian *E-Abzu* temple in Eridu, the most ancient city in Sumer, Mesopotamia, had a courtyard with a rectangular central shrine or *cella* located inside the courtyard, in a niche in one of the walls of the *cella* was a statue of the temple deity, an offering table in front of the image was for sacrifices to their god and along both long sides of the *cella* were rectangular rooms for housing priests (Kramer 1963) similar to the "apartments of the gods", houses for priests and refuges, in the courtyard of the Paka'alana Heiau (Fig. 81).

THE MAJOR HISTORICAL SITES OF WAIPI'O VALLEY

Many of the cultural and historic sites on Hawai'i Island are located on the floor of Waipi'o Valley (Figs. 79 (1&2)). The Paka'alana Heiau was located behind the beach and sand dunes about one hundred yards from the Kohala side of the Wailoa River, about 300 yards southeast of the Honua'ula Heiau and adjacent to the Muliwai fishpond. Mentioned in the legend of Kila, son of Moi'keha, the Paka'alana Heiau was restored by Pa'ao and dates to before AD 1050. (Fornander 1916-1920) It was the most sacred site on Hawai'i Island and remained so until its destruction in 1791 in war against Kamehameha the First. The Paka'alana Heiau had been a *luakini heiau* before the arrival of the *ari'i* warrior/priest Pa'ao from Ra'iatea Island, Tahiti. Pa'ao renovated the Paka'alana Heiau and afterward a descendant of Pa'ao was always appointed as the *heiau* high priest.

> "The taboo of its great heiau were the most sacred in Hawaii, and remained so until the destruction of the heiau and the spoilage of all the royal associations in the valley of Waipi'o . . . in 1791"

> (From *Fornander's Ancient History of the Hawaiian People,*
> 1996 [1878], by Abraham Fornander, page 73. Courtesy
> of Bishop Museum Press, Honolulu)

It was at the Paka'alana Heiau that Ika, chief of a bandit clan and his companions mentioned in the myth of the Kiha-pu were slain by Kila and sacrificed upon its altar. In 1919, a large stone was found covering the entrance to a tunnel connecting the Paka'alana Heiau and Honua'ula Heiau. When Alfred Hudson visited the site in 1931 he found,

> "Nothing at all remains . . . of the *heiau* or *pu'uhonua* of Paka'alana. . . . The spot now known to the people of Waipi'o as Paka'alana is located in a grove of coconut palms . . . adjoining the fish pond. Here is found an artificial cave with a large upright stone in front of the entrance. The cave is formed by three walls of sea-worn rocks covered by large flat slabs of stone. . . . The interior dimensions are: length 15 feet, width 4 feet, and height 3 feet, . . . [The site] is well known to the people of the valley, but seldom visited. . . . a *tabu* tradition pervades the spot."

> (From *Archaeology of East Hawaii*, 1930-1932, Bishop Museum
> Manuscript by Alfred Hudson, pages 153, 154. Courtesy
> of Bishop Museum Library and Archives, Honolulu)

The Paka'alana Heiau covered a large area enclosed by a perimeter stonewall some of which was visible along the inland side of the sand dunes, the stone wall remained partially intact until the tsunami of 1946 that destroyed what remained. The Paka'alana Heiau contained an inner temple or *luakina* enclosed with walls of *'ohi'a* wood and inside its inner temple were several structures and a sacrificial altar. Behind the altar was a tapa or *kapa* screen and inside the screened off area was the inner sanctum of the *heiau* where the *lananu'u mamao* or oracle tower was located, the most sacred place in the *heiau*. *Ki'i* or idols of the gods *Kane, Ku, Lono* and lesser deities stood on either side of the opening in the tapa or *kapa* screen. The tower was eighteen to twenty-four feet square at its base sloping slightly inward toward the top. It was covered in *'oloa,* a white *kapa* cloth and inside was where the gods descended from the heavens to the earth, where the high chief and his high priest would speak directly to the gods. Located along the outer stonewall inside the *heiau* enclosure were houses for priests and refuges known as the "apartments of the gods" and *Hale o Riroa* or the House of Riroa [Liloa] was a royal mausoleum located inside the outer wall of the Paka'alana Heiau under a spreading pandanus or *hala* tree. A statue of the god *Lono* was located at the entry to the inner temple or *luakina* and a six-foot high stone image of Liloa stood by the *Hale o* Liloa (Fig. 81). Located outside the *heiau* enclosure was *Hale o Papa* or the women's *heiau*, it was a small *heiau* with its own walled enclosure, altar and *ki'i* images of their goddesses.

Ka Haunokama'ahala, the royal residence, existed before Kiha's time and was built by Liloa's grandfather Kahoukapu along with Kahikimai, the sacred royal taro pondfield or *lo'i* with its *nioi* wood embankments. The sacred pavement of Liloa extended from the bank of the royal pondfield to the side of the royal residence and the Paka'alana Heiau. The pavement was originally constructed before the reign of Liloa, but he was so associated with the paving it became known as *Ka Paepae Kapu o* Liloa or The Sacred Paving of Liloa. (Malo 1951 [1898]) Between the royal residence and royal taro pondfield was the royal irrigation channel 'Auwai Pahupohaku, also associated with the royal residence was the Mokapu Pond, a sacred bathing pool created by Liloa. (Kamakau 1992 [1961]) Palm trees were located in front of the royal residence along with houses for guests designated by feathered *kahili* standards indicating royalty and tents were set up along the beach, "the tents of the traveling chiefs [were] pitched near the sand banks, at the shore". (Bingham 2013 [1848])

The Honua'ula Heiau (Fig. 33) was located at the middle of Waipi'o Beach, 300 feet from the Paka'alana Heiau and also functioned as a *luakini heiau.* There are several references to the Honua'ula Heiau being where Hakau and his chiefs were killed by 'Umi, although according to other accounts it took place at the Paka'alana Heiau. An open level ceremonial ground for community events similar to those of the Marquesas Islands, the Honua'ula Heiau was built up of waterworn stones and sand surrounded on three sides with stone platforms. Much older than the Paka'alana Heiau, it was 210 feet long running parallel to the sea and more than 90 feet wide. (Stokes 1991) Erosion has washed away the front of the site, but against the seaward side of the sand dune mounds are remains of the four to six foot high stone retaining wall where its stepped altar or *ahu* was located. The Honua'ula Heiau was an early design associated with the first Hawaiian settlers from the Marquesas Islands. It was a flat rectangular open area that held social events, religious ceremonies and festivals typical of early Polynesian settlements. The Honua'ula Heiau contained a stone platform or *ahu* with a row of upright stone and carved wooden *ki'i* on the inland side of the *heiau* representing ancestral deities and marking their positions. Upright stones along the *ahu* were probably large flat slabs set on end similar to those at the Necker Island *heiau* (Fig. 83) and the *luakini heiau* along the Wailua River on the island of Kaua'i described by Captain Cook in 1778 (Fig. 85). A movable god house containing sacred objects and a stone altar with a carved image on its side may have been located on the assembly area and other upright stones located on the flat grounds would have marked the sitting places for chiefs and officials during ceremonies. On each side of the assembly area there would have been low stone platforms with shed like structures where spectators could view tribal ceremonial events, the sheds would have been occupied by chiefs and priests observing "painted and plumed young naked dancing girls singing and chanting to the sound of the *heiau* drums". At the corners where the stone viewing platforms and the stepped *ahu* platform with its row of upright stones intersected were raised stone platforms on each side with large wooden images of their tribal ancestral gods *Ku* and *Hina* (Fig. 91). These statues stood over five feet high without feet and below their legs was a flange resting on the stone platform with a one to two foot insert extending into the stonework stabilizing the statue, a design detail originating from the Marquesas Islands. Large elevated earthen burial mounds overlooked the ceremonial plaza, the highest mound may have had the rectangular house of the chief/priest with one side open to the plaza below for viewing the ceremonies with a steep obelisk shaped roof as high as thirty feet, similar to the Marquesas *me'ae* tower, it was probably the first Hawaiian *lananu'u mamao* tower. In the Marquesas Islands, the interior of their ceremonial temple structures contained a frame shrine called the *'ananu'u* and this was certainly from where the Hawaiian *lananu'u mamao* or *'anu'u* tower originated. On either side of the chief's house would have been lower burial mounds with small thatched god houses on top. A sports field and wrestling ground was located on the Hilo side of the Wailoa River. It was a large uneven platform of sand and grass surrounded by a 660 foot long wall extending parallel to the beach, then curving as it continued up the valley. The wall made a 90 degree arc on the circumference of an 850 foot radius circle, varying from 4 to 10 feet in height and in some places it was demolished, the remains of two platforms about 16 feet square were located in the middle of the paved area. (Hudson 1932) The most popular sports were boxing and wrestling and bouts were held for public entertainment, these were violent events and a burial site for those vanquished in athletic contests was possibly located just southeast of the sports field along with a small *heiau*.

Several fishponds were located behind the sand dune burial mounds. The Lalakea fishpond, named after a Hawaiian deep-water shark, still exists and is located on the Hilo side of Wailoa River. It was a brackish water pond that existed in Liloa's time because 'Umi "walked along the Lakakea fishpond" on his way to see his father Liloa at his royal residence. The Muliwai and Waiomoa were freshwater fishponds fed by the streams and waterfalls on the Kohala side of Waipi'o Valley. The Waiomoa fishpond was fed by Waiomoa Falls and the Muliwai Pond was connected to the Wailoa River through 'Auwai Pahupohaku, the royal irrigation channel. The Hokuwelowelo Heiau was located at the edge of the cliff on the Hilo side, overlooking the mouth of Waipi'o Valley at an elevation of 900 feet. It was approximately 150 feet from both the cliff overlooking Waipi'o Valley and the cliff overlooking the sea. Associated with the Kiha-pu legend, it was supposedly where the Kiha-pu was kept before being stolen by the thief-dog Puapualenalena and was believed to have been "built by the gods". The Moa'ula Heiau was a *luakini heiau* at the foot of the cliff or *pali,* located on the Kohala side of the valley 2500 feet from the sea and was built by Hakau, who ironically may have been its first sacrificial offerings. Some report 'Umi laid the corpses of Hakau and his slain chiefs on the sacrificial altar of the Moa'ula Heiau and this was where the tongue of the god *Ku* came down from the heavens out of a black cloud on a rainbow and licked up the bodies of the offenders. The Moa'ula Heiau was altered and reconstructed in 1780 when it was site of the Grand Council of Chiefs where Kiwalao, son of Kalani'opu'u, was confirmed as successor and next *haku* or lord of Hawai'i Island. Kamehameha the First was given authority over this *heiau* where the war god *Kaili* or *Kuka'ilimoku* of Kalani'opu'u was kept. All that remained in 1932 when the site of the Moa'ula Heiau was visited by Alfred Hudson was a small underground compartment, possibly its *luapa'u* or *luakini* pit. The Kuwahailo Heiau was located on the Kohala side of Waipi'o Valley in the Ka'au 'ili land division about 1.3 miles inland near Neneuwe Falls and was said to have been built by the ancient god *Kuwahailo* or *Kuahailo* who is believed to have resided in a small cave near the top of the cliff or *pali.* In 1932, Alfred Hudson described the site as 230 feet by 100 feet with a series of terraces due to the slope of the ground, walls in good preservation three to six feet high with well-defined entrances and an underground stone chamber about four feet square beneath paving of the platform. The Pa Heiau was a *luakini heiau* located in the Napo'opo'o housing area and all that remains is an underground chamber probably also its *luapa'u* pit. The Palaka Heiau was an unknown type with a terraced three level platform located about one-half mile inland from the sea on the Kohala side of the valley near the Moa'ula Heiau and Waiomoa Falls. The Kahalekapapa Heiau was located along the shore of the Wailoa River on the Hilo side of the valley on a large earthen mound between the Lalakea fishpond and the sea, the mound was probably enlarged when the fishpond was deepened.

A fishing shrine or *ko'a heiau* was located on Waipi'o Beach on the Kohala side just above high tide level and 500 feet west of Honua'ula Heiau, it was a stone platform about twenty-two feet by fifty feet and on the ocean side it stood five feet high. Fishermen often spent the night at the shrine before fishing expeditions bringing with them the nets, clothing and food they would use. They were blessed by a *kahuna* who prayed and performed a rite of purification with seawater containing sea moss and turmeric. They slept at the shrine, but not with their wives who were required to fast and refrain from any casual sexual intercourse with their secondary husbands. Fishing shrines were often located at the end of a long beach with an upright, waterworn stone mounted on a stone platform upon which fish offerings to *Ku'ula,* god of fisherman, once a fisherman from the village of Hana on Maui Island, who would direct fishermen to abundant fishing grounds. The base of the upright stone was surrounded with coral and fishing shrines always had a good ocean view. Fishermen would place a piece of coral at the base of the upright stone to promote a good catch and upon their return would place the first catch of the day on the shrine as a sacrifice to *Ku'ula.* The site of the Waipi'o Valley *ko'a heiau* was also recorded in the Cleghorn and Rogers-Jourdane survey of 1983. Each village had a sacred place for fishermen at the edge of the sea consisting of a stone platform around which a number of small houses served as sleeping quarters and *kahuna* who directed fishing lived at the site. (Linton 1925) The Maori of New Zealand would hang their first catch from a tree as an offering to the gods and in the Marquesas Islands fishing was a communal effort accompanied by religious rites and taboos. Shrines were the most common *heiau* and anyone was able to build one, a priest was not required.

A canoe shed or *halau wa'a* was located on the beach near the fishing shrine. It was a rectangular roofed enclosure, thirty-four by forty feet, partly walled and open to the sea. A *loa* stone located two miles up the valley on the bank of Wailoa River is a naturally occurring rock outcropping, roughly pyramidal in shape, six feet long and standing four feet above the ground. The Hakalau Heiau was supposedly located in the vicinity of the *loa* stone, but no remains have been found. The bathing pool in the myth of Nanaue, son of the shark god, is located near the Neneuwe Waterfall. A spirit shrine, named Hakalaoa, was located at the base of the cliff on the Hilo side in Hi'ilawe Valley between Hi'ilawe Falls and the entry road at the mouth of the valley and at least one spirit shrine was located along the Kohala side. A stone *papamu* board for playing the game *konane* located three miles up the valley was cut into a flat-topped rock having twelve rows across and nine rows down. The number of rows and holes varied for this game, waterworn pebbles of black lava and white coral were used for the pieces and the game resemble the English game of draughts or Japanese game of go. Major foot trails or *alanui* were located along each side of the valley at the base of the cliffs and extended *makai-mauka,* from the ocean to the upper valley, the flat valley floor being reserved for taro pondfields. The Koaekea foot trail ran down from the valley rim on the Hilo side, it was enlarged for horse and rider, then into a road. The Kealai Trail exited the rear of the valley toward Waimea and the Muliwai or 'Z' Trail zigzagges up the 1200 foot *pali,* located near the mouth of the valley on the Kohala side to Waimanu Valley. The Mahiki Trail from Waipi'o Valley to Waimea was famous as the site where Hi'iaka defeated a fierce group of *mo'o* and the trail upon which *huaka'i po,* the ghostly procession of the night or the night marchers, enter *Lua o* Milu at the mouth of Waipi'o Valley and into the underworld.

THE PRESERVATION OF WAIPI'O VALLEY

Among the valleys of the Kohala Coast of West Hamakua, Waipi'o Valley was the pride of the *ali'i* of Hawai'i Island, the sacred home of many high chiefs and *kahuna* and a source of abundant supplies of food. Waipi'o Valley represents the traditional rural pre-contact Hawaiian culture and was important as a cultural and political center. Its sites preserve Hawaiian cultural heritage and although elements of nature and man have destroyed many of these locations, some existing only in oral tradition, a number of important *heiau* and other sites have excellent archaeological research potential. (Cleghorn and Rogers-Jourdane 1983) Buried remains in Waipi'o Valley have yet to be studied, only limited surface archaeological surveys have been done and almost no excavations. Its extensive traditional taro pondfields and irrigation canal systems have yet to be mapped and dated. Agricultural practices that involve making permanent changes to the landscape leave physical evidence such as stone-faced taro pondfields or *lo'i* and irrigation channels or *'auwai* embankments. The ancient sand dune area along Waipi'o Beach was a sacred burial ground and contains important buried archaeological remains. Waipi'o Valley was one of Hawai'i Island's earliest settlement sites and excavations would uncover valuable information concerning the Honua'ula Heiau on Waipi'o Beach, the original *heiau* of Waipi'o Valley, the Paka'alana Heiau, once the most revered *pu'uhonua* on Hawai'i Island, and Ka Haunokama'ahala, the royal residence. Archaeological excavations of the irrigated taro pondfields and fishponds on the flat alluvial valley floor present an opportunity to study the development of Waipi'o Valley's historic growth, its extensive agricultural and aquaculture systems and their relationship to the complex social and political *ali'i* authority. Information obtained could establish the location of the valley's housing settlements, their size and population density, order of occupation and arrangement of housing units. (Cleghorn and Rogers-Jourdane 1983) Waipi'o Valley's past represents important Hawaiian cultural heritage and its historic sites deserve protection, the site of its royal complex continues to be considered sacred. Waipi'o Valley contains numerous archaeological remains from one of the Hawaiian Island's earliest settlements to its royal residence of the 1700s, it is the only undisturbed ancient royal center site in the Hawaiian Islands. A recommendation of the Waipi'o Valley Master Plan is to "promote and encourage identification, preservation, and restoration of its examples of early Hawaiian culture and history" and the entire valley has been designated by the State of Hawai'i as archaeological site #7168 and the "Waipi'o Sand Dune Complex" as site #2115. In October 1987, a recommendation was issued by the State Department of Land and Natural Resources that the State of Hawaii should acquire lands of "historical, and cultural significance to the people of Hawai'i" to preserve archeological sites.

> "The valley is still full of sites . . . They await detailed mapping and examination to yield the important information on the past which they contain."
>
> (From *Exalted Sits the Chief*, 2000, by Ross Cordy, Branch
> Chief of Archaeology in the State Department of
> Historic Preservation, page 203.

A *kipuka* in the Hawaiian Islands is an oasis of rainforest vegetation completely surrounded by a volcanic lava flow. These "islands of life" are the source of new landscapes, eventually seeds and spores from native plants surviving in the *kipuka* regenerate the barren lava. Hawaiians believe these natural areas possess *mana*, spiritual power of the gods. *Kipuka* represent the epic mythological struggle between *Pele,* goddess of fire and volcanoes, and her younger sister or daughter *Hi'iaka*, goddess of healing and plant growth. After volcanic eruptions destroy all life in their path, the *kipuka* becomes the seedbed for the *'ohi'a* tree, the first tree species to appear on newly formed lava flows, "after *Pele* erupts *Hi'iaka* returns life". Like natural *kipuka,* cultural *kipuka* such as Waipi'o Valley are isolated areas with difficult access where traditional Hawaiian cultural customs and spiritual beliefs of native populations have persisted into modern times with the potential to regenerate Hawaiian culture. (McGregor 2007) Currently, the Hawaiian Islands are enjoying a renaissance of its ancient culture that includes relearning the Hawaiian language, dance, arts and the building and sailing of replicas of its ancient voyaging canoes in support of *Ka Lahui Hawai'i,* The Hawaiian Nation.

Cultural *kipuka* sites are *wahi pana* or celebrated places and Waipi'o Valley is of historic importance as a political, religious and royal center and is still considered sacred to native Hawaiians. It represents a cultural *kipuna*, an island of traditional Hawaiian rural lifestyle helping to preserve the cultural identity of the unique *kanaka maoli*, the indigenous Hawaiian people, and perpetuate their native Hawaiian way of life. (McGregor 2007) In the Hawaiian language, the past is *ka wa mamua* or "the time in front", whereas the future is *ka wa mahope* or "the time in back". "It is as if the Hawaiian stands firmly in the present, with his back to the future and his eyes fixed upon the past". (Kame'eleihiwa 1992) To the native Hawaiians the future lies in their rich past, in the strength, knowledge, glory and achievements found "in the ways of their ancestors".

> For thousands of years despite developing maritime technologies and navigational skills enabling discovery and colonization of islands scattered across the Pacific Ocean, Polynesians lived in some of the most isolated communities in the world. Remote Oceania was known as a "sea of islands". Their primitive societies, although lacking metal and possessing only Stone Age technology, had a great deal of interaction with other cultures and developed monumental temples and elaborate cultural traditions. The Hawaiian pre-contact society had no written language; their traditions, history and religious beliefs were transmitted only through the spoken Hawaiian language. Modern archaeology and linguistics support the validity of early Hawaiian

oral traditions that represent a record of their indigenous society. They developed intellectually complex social organizations based on a genealogical hereditary ranking system and highly spiritual religious beliefs. Ancestors of the Polynesians migrated from the Near East, the Indus River Valley of ancient India and Island Southeast Asia, each time being forced out by more technologically advanced cultures, but were able to escape by sea preserving their identity rather than being defeated and absorbed. They were able to construct sea-going canoes of the highest quality shaped with simple Neolithic or Stone Age tools. The Polynesians journeyed across the vast Pacific Ocean guided by the stars of the night sky, "Polynesians were the only deep water sailors in the world for at least two thousand years". (Herb Kawainui Kane) Polynesian history is considered sacred, they are devoted to their oral records and recent genetic evidence has been confirming their oral histories are factual. Polynesian oral literature of creation of the universe and mankind was extraordinary and their oral traditions preserved mythological stories of their gods and goddesses, records of the truly incredible voyages of their amazing ancestors and their genealogical records extend back to Kahiki, where in legend "mankind was created by the gods". "The old world created by our Polynesian ancestors has passed away . . . the stone temples have been destroyed and the temple drums and shell trumpets have long been silent. . . . The great voyaging canoes have crumbled to dust, and the sea captains and the expert craftsmen have passed away to the Spirit-land." (From *Vikings of the Pacific*, first published as *Vikings of the Sunrise*, 1985 [1938], by Te Rangi Hiroa or Peter H. Buck, page 325)

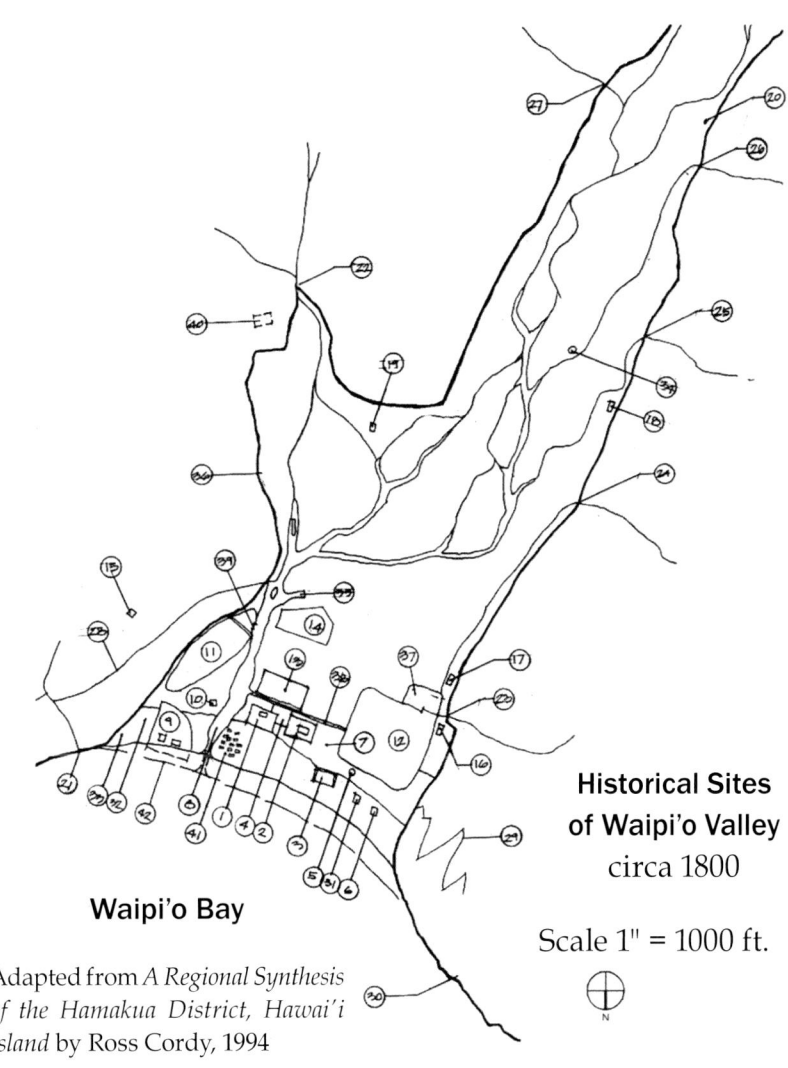

Waipi'o Bay

**Historical Sites
of Waipi'o Valley**
circa 1800

Scale 1" = 1000 ft.

Adapted from *A Regional Synthesis
of the Hamakua District, Hawai'i
Island* by Ross Cordy, 1994

Fig. 79 (1)

1. Ka Haunokama, the Royal Residence
2. Paka'alana Heiau with the *Hale o* Liloa
3. Honua'ula Heiau
4. Sacred Paving of Liloa
5. Mokapu Bathing Pond
6. Fishing Shrine
7. Sand Dune Area
8. Wailoa River
9. Wrestling Ground
10. Kahalekopapa Heiau
11. Lalakea Fishpond
12. Muliwai Fishpond
13. Kahikimai, the Royal Taro Pondfield
14. *Lo'i o* 'Umi, 'Umi's Taro Pondfield
15. Hokuwelowelo Heiau
16. Palaka Heiau
17. Moa'ula Heiau
18. Kuahailo Heiau
19. Pa Heiau
20. Waipi'o Loa Stone
21. Kaluahine Falls
22. Hi'ilawe Falls
23. Waiamoa Falls
24. Naalapa Falls
25. Neneuwe Falls
26. Kumupapala Falls
27. Kakeha Falls
28. Opailolo Foot Trail, Expanded into an Access Road
29. Waimanu Foot Trail
30. Burial Cave in Cliff
31. Canoe Shed
32. Burial Place for Vanquished Athletic Contestant
33. Unknown Heiau
34. Nanaue Pool
35. King's Landing
36. Shrine
37. Waiomoa Fishpond
38. 'Auwai Pahupohaku Irrigation Channel
39. Sluice Gate or *Makaha*
40. Cemetery
41. Guest Houses and Tents on the Beach
42. Original Edge of the Beach Before Erosion

Fig. 79 (2)

Cinder Cones near the Summit of Mauna Kea
Photograph by Amy J. Charles

Cinder Cones Covered in Snow
Photograph by *Na Maka o ka 'Aina*

Fig. 80

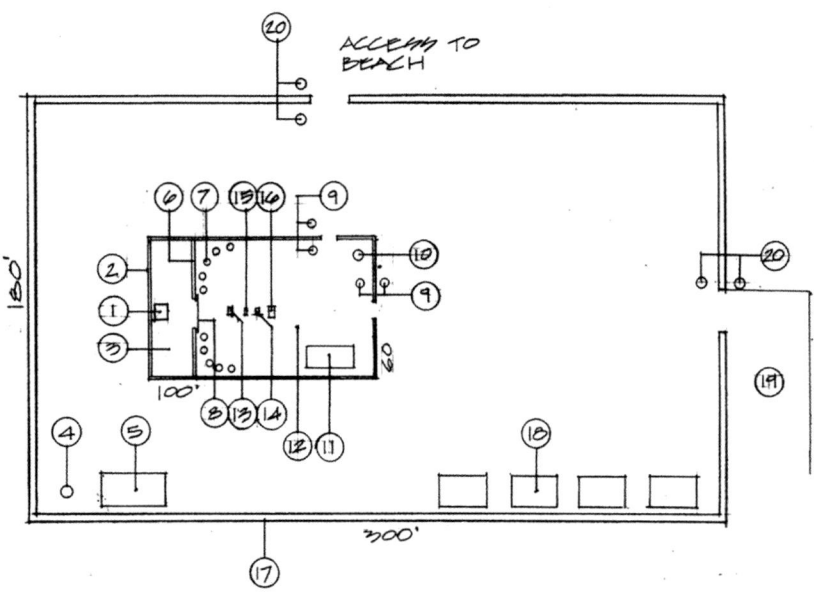

The Paka'alana Heiau in Waipi'o Valley

1. *Anu'u,* Three Story Oracle
2. *Pa* or Inner Fence of *'Ohi'a* Wood
3. Inner Sanctum
4. Stone Statue of Liloa
5. *Hale o* Liloa, a Royal Mausoleum
6. Wooden Wall with Tapa Screen
7. *Ki'i* Images of the Gods
8. Tapa Screen
9. *Ki'i* at Inner Temple Entry
10. *Ki'i* of the God *Lono*
11. *Hale Mana,* Chief/Priest House
12. *Luakina* or Inner Temple
13. *Lele* or Altar
14. *Hale Pahu* or Drum House
15. *Hale Wai Ea,* House of Sacred
16. *Hale Imu* or Oven House
17. *Heiau* Perimeter Stonewall
18. Houses for Priests and Refuges
19. Sacred Paving of Liloa
20. *Ki'i* at *Heiau* Entry

Fig. 81

Phallic Stones of the Fiji Islands

Large erect phallic stones in the Fiji Islands are fertility shrines. Worship of phallic stones extends at least back to lingam stones of the Harappan civilization of ancient Vedic India. Illustration is from *Fiji and the Fijians, Vol. 1: The Islands and Their Inhabitants* by Thomas Williams, 1858

Fig. 82

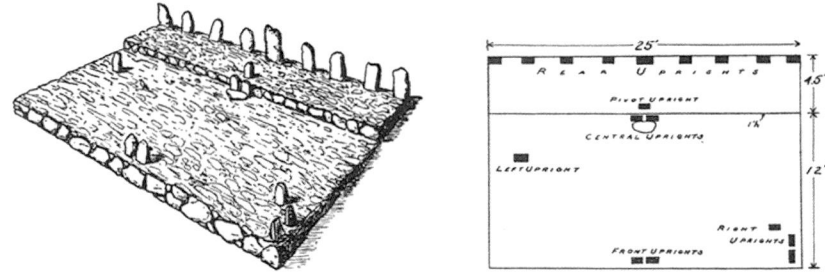

Necker Island Heiau

A composite Necker Island *heiau* with an *ahu* and upright stones resembling early *marae* of the Marquesas Islands. Images are from *Archaeology of Nihoa and Necker Islands, Bishop Museum Bulletin 53,* by Kenneth P. Emory, 1928, page 60. Courtesy of Bishop Museum Press, Honolulu

Central Heiau Site, Necker Island

Heiau where basalt stone *ki'i* figures were collected during the Hawaiian Annexation Expedition of 1894. Photograph is from *Archaeology of Nihoa and Necker Islands, Bishop Museum Bulletin 53,* by Kenneth P. Emory, 1928, Plate XIIA. Courtesy of Bishop Museum Press, Honolulu

Fig. 83

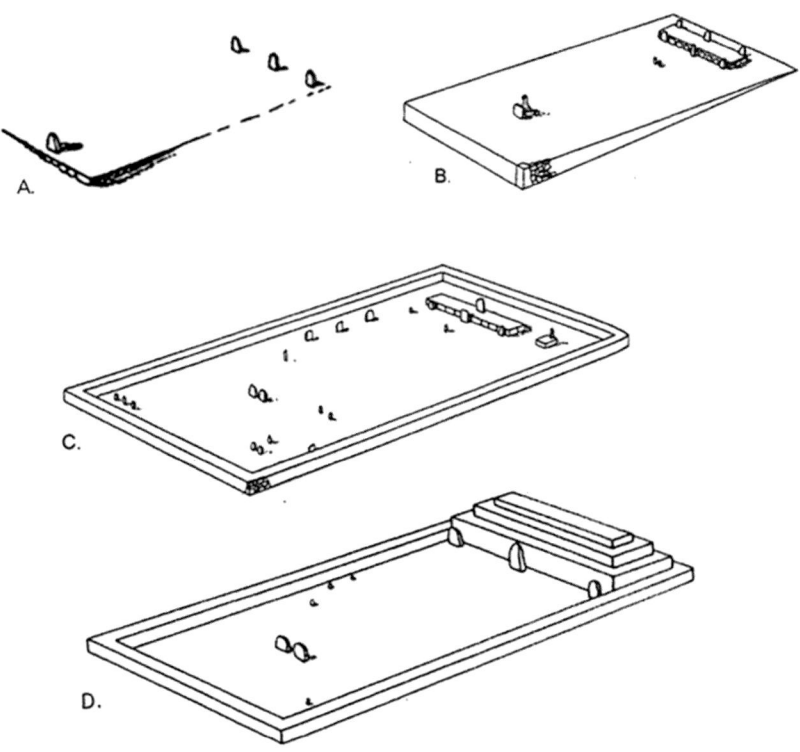

Types of Tahitian Marae

A.   A simple shrine without an *ahu*
B.   An *ahu* with three upright stones and a courtyard
C.   An *ahu* with one upright stone on the platform, three along its face and a courtyard enclosed with a low wall
D.   An *ahu* enlarged into a stepped pyramid with a flat top, three upright stones along its face and a courtyard with a low wall

   A, B and C are early inland *marae* types, D is a later coastal *marae* type

Adapted from *Bishop Museum Bulletin 116,* 1933, by Kenneth P. Emory, pages 24, 29. Courtesy of Bishop Museum Press, Honolulu

Fig. 84

A Morai, in Atooi
1778

A watercolor of the interior of the *luakini heiau* at Waimea, Kaua'i Island by John Webber, artist on Captain James T. Cook's third voyage into the Pacific Ocean. In the left foreground is the *hale mana* or *mana* house and in center is its oracle tower or *lananu'u mamao.* Courtesy of the Mitchell/Dixson Library, State Library of New South Wales, Sydney

Fig. 85

Necker Island Stone Images
Courtesy of the Bishop Museum, Honolulu

© Metropolitan Museum of Art,
New York, Source: Art
Resources, NY

Photograph by David Franzen
Courtesy of the Bishop
Museum, Honolulu

Basalt Stone Ki'i Figures from Necker Island

Necker Island has the highest concentration of *heiau* sites in the Hawaiian Archipelago with 33 ceremonial *heiau* containing platforms and basalt uprights located on the small basalt island. A total of 13 stone *ki'i* figures ranging from 8 to 18 inches in height were recovered from the Central *Heiau* Site on Necker Island probably representing deified ancestors or gods used in religious ceremonies. They are similar in design to stone statues found in the Marquesas or Hiva Islands and to images on two sculpted basalt bowls found on the main Hawaiian Islands

Fig. 86

A Tahitian Fare Atua Containing a To'o

A portable wooden Tahitian *fare atua* or house of god representing the god *Ta'aroa* with a *to'o* of the god *'Oro* placed in its opening by Adrienne L. Kaeppler of the Smithsonian Institute, Washington D.C., located in the British Museum, London. Copyright; The Trustees of the British Museum - All rights reserved

A Toopapaoo of a Chief, with a Priest making his offering to the Morai, in Huoheine [Huaheine - The Society Islands], 1789

A colorized version of an etching made from an original 1777 sepia and grey wash drawing by John Webber, artist on the third voyage of Captain James T. Cook into the Pacific Ocean. Published in *Views in the South Seas* by Boydell & Co., 1809. Copyright; National Maritime Museum, Greenwich, London

Fig. 87

**View in the Island of Huaheine [Huahine] with an Ewharra
and a small altar with an offering on it,** July 1769

An ink and wash drawing by Sydney Parkinson, artist on James T. Cook's first voyage into the Pacific Ocean on
the HM Bark Endeavor, of a house of god on Huaheine Island, one of the leeward Tahitian Islands. Copyright; The
British Library Board, London

**An Ewharra no Eatua or House of God with an altar and a tree
called Owharra with which houses were thatched,** 1773

A hand-colored engraving by William Woolett after a 1772 wash and watercolor by John James Barralet in *Account of the
Voyages . . . for Making Discoveries in the Southern Hemisphere, Vol. II.* Courtesy of the Mitchell/Dixson Library, State Library
of New South Wales, Sydney

Fig. 88

Hawaiian Feathered Oracle Tower

A miniature god house adorned with feathers modeled after the *lananu'u mamao* or oracle tower. The model was acquired on the third voyage of Captain James T. Cook into the Pacific Ocean. Copyright; the Weltmuseum Wein, Vienna

Fig. 89

The Tabernacle

A hand-colored print of the Tabernacle at the base of Mount Sinai built by Israelites on the biblical Exodus, from an engraving almost certainly by Jan Luyken of Amsterdam, 1683-85. Image is from *Wikimedia Commons* and in the public domain

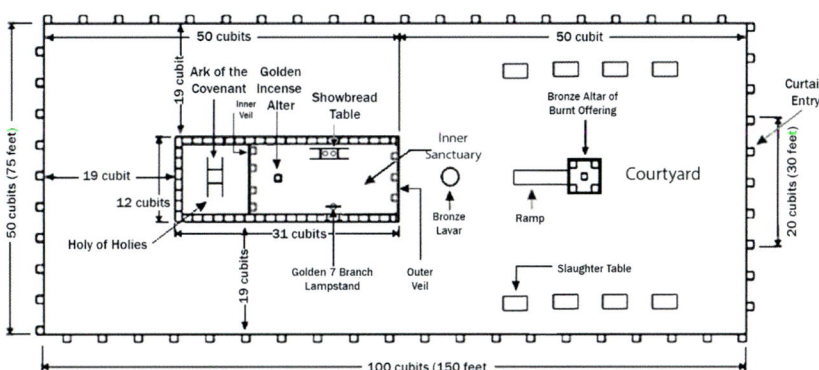

Plan of the Biblical Tabernacle

The plan layout, articles and functions of the biblical Tabernacle and the Paka'alana Heiau (Fig. 81) in Waipi'o Valley, Hawai'i Island, were almost identical. A cubit is the distance from the elbow to extended finger

Fig. 90

Wooden Statues of the Gods *Ku* and *Hina*
November 1936
Photograph by Pan-Pacific Press Bureau

Two *heiau* statues recovered from Waipi'o Valley were probably originally from the Honua'ula Heiau (Fig. 33), the early *heiau* of the first settlers from the Marquesas Islands. The statues are 5 feet 4 inches high excluding a support section below the legs, a structural technique from the Marquesas Islands for mounting statues on stone platforms. Courtesy of the Bishop Museum, Honolulu

Fig. 91

REFERENCES

AhChing, Peter Leiataua. 2004. *Polynesian Interconnections: Dwayne Johnson and King Kamehameha in Culture and Science.* Lulu Press Inc. Morrisville.

Alexander, W. D. 1892. The "Hale o Keawe" at Honaunau Hawaii. In *The Journal of the Polynesian Society*, Vol. 3, no. 3.

Alexander, W. D. 2001 [1891]. *A Brief History of the Hawaiian People.* University Press of the Pacific, Honolulu, Hawaii.

Andersen, Johannes C. 1995 [1928]. *Myths and Legends of the Polynesians.* Dover Publications Inc. New York.

Apple, Russel A. 1971. *The Hawaiian Thatched House, City of Refuge National Historical Park.* Office of History and Historical Architecture, Western Service Center, San Francisco.

Baez-Camargo, Gonzalo. 1984 [1979]. *Archaeological Commentary on the Bible.* Doubleday & Company Inc. Garden City, New York.

Barrau, Jacques. (Ed.). 1963. *Plants and the Migrations of Pacific Peoples, A Symposium.* Tenth Pacific Science Congress, Honolulu, Hawaii, 1961. Bishop Museum Press. Honolulu.

Barrera, William. 1977. *Waipi'o Valley Archaeological Survey, Ms.* On file State Historic Preservation Division Library. Kapolei.

Barrere, Dorothy B. 1969. *The Kumuhonua Legends.* Pacific Anthropological Records No. 3. Department of Anthropology. Bernice P. Bishop Museum, Honolulu.

Barrere, Dorothy M. 1975. *Kamehameha in Kona: Two Documentary Studies.* Pacific Anthropology Records No. 23. Dept. of Anthropology, Bernice Pauahi Bishop Museum, Honolulu.

Bates, G. Washington. 1854. *Sandwich Island Notes by a Haole.* Harper and Brothers, New York.

Bausch, Christia. 1978. Po and Ao, Analysis of an Ideological Conflict in Polynesia. In the *Journal de la Societe des Oceanistes*, vol. 34, issue 61, pp. 169-185.

Beckwith, Martha W. (Ed.). 1932. *Kepelino's Traditions of Hawaii.* Bernice P. Bishop Museum, Bulletin 95. Bishop Museum Press. Honolulu.

Beckwith, Martha W. 1972 [1951]. *The Kumulipo: A Hawaiian Creation Chant.* University of Hawai'i Press. Honolulu.

Beckwith, Martha. 1970 [1940]. *Hawaiian Mythology.* Yale University Press, New Haven.

Beckwith. Martha W. 1918. The Hawaiian Romance of Laiekawai. In the *Thirty-third Annual Report of the Bureau of American Ethnology.* Washington DC.

Bedford, Stuart; Matthew Springgs, Ralph Regenvanu, Colin Macgregor, Takaronga Kuautonga and Michael Sietz. 2007. The excavation, conservation and reconstruction of Lapita burial pots from the Teouma site, Efate, Central Vanuatu. In S. Bedford, C. Sand and S. Connaughton. (Eds.). *Oceanic Explorations: Lapita and Western Pacific Settlement*, pp. 223-40. Terra Australis 26, ANU E Press, Canberra.

Bellwood, Peter S. 1978. *The Polynesians: Prehistory of an Island People.* Thames and Hudson Ltd. London.

Bellwood, Peter. 1975. Archeological Research in Minahasa and the Talaud Islands, Northwest Indonesia. In *Asian Perspective*, vol. 19, no. 2, pp. 240-288.

Bellwood, Peter. 1979. *Man's Conquest of the Pacific.* Oxford University Press. New York.

Best, Elsdon. 1892. The Pre-Historic Civilization in the Philippines, the Tagalo-Bisaya Tribes. In the *Journal of the Polynesian Society*, vol. 1, no. 4.

Best, Elsdon. 1904. Maori Medical Lore. In the *Journal of the Polynesian Society,* vol. 13, no. 4.

Best, Elsdon. 1923. The Origin of the Maori, The Hidden Homeland of the Maori, and Its Probable Location. In the *Journal of the Polynesian Society*, vol. 32, no. 125.

Best, Elsdon. 1927. The Homeland of the Polynesians. In the *Journal of the Polynesian Society*, vol. 36, no. 144.

Best, Elsdon. 2005 [1924]. *Maori Religion and Mythology.* Dominion Museum Bulletin No. 10-11. Te Papa Press. Wellington.

Bingham, Hiram. 2013 [1848]. *A Residence of Twenty-one Years in the Sandwich Islands.* Sherman Converse, New York.

Bird, Isabella. 1998 [1873]. *Six Months in the Sandwich Islands.* Mutual Publishing. Honolulu.

Bishop, Marcia Brown. 1940. *Hawaiian Life of the Pre-European Period.* Southworth-Anthoensen Press. Portland, Maine.

Bisignani, J. D. 1994. *Big Island of Hawaii Handbook.* Moon Publications Inc. Chico.

Bottero, Jean. 2001. *Everyday Life in Ancient Mesopotamia.* The Johns Hopkins University Press. Baltimore.

Bovis, Edmond de. 1980. *Tahitian society before the arrival of the Europeans.* The Institute for Polynesian Studies, Monograph Series, No. 1. Brigham Young University - Hawaii Campus. Laie, Hawaii.

Brewster, A.B. 1922. *The Hill Tribes of Fiji.* Seely, Service & Co. Limited. London.

Brigham, William T. 1899. *Hawaiian Featherwork.* Bishop Museum Press. Honolulu.

Brigham, William T. 1974 [1902]. *Stone Implements and Stonework of the Ancient Hawaiians.* Bishop Museum Press. Honolulu.

Brigham, William T. 1908. *The Ancient Hawaiian House.* Bishop Museum Press. Honolulu.

Bryan, Edwin H. 1938. *Ancient Hawaiian Life.* Bishop Museum Press. Honolulu.

Buck, Peter Henry (Te Rangi Hiroa). 1939. *The Terry Lectures: Anthropology and Religion.* Yale University Press. New Haven.

Buck, Peter Henry (Te Rangi Hiroa). 1944. The Local Evolution of Hawaiian Feather Capes and Cloaks. In the *Journal of the Polynesian Society*, vol. 53, no. 1.

Buck, Peter Henry (Te Rangi Hiroa). 1959 [1938]. *Vikings of the Pacific* first published under the title *Vikings of the Sunrise.* University of Chicago Press, Chicago.

Burley, David V. and William R. Dickerson. 2001. Origin and Significance of a Founding Settlement in Polynesia. In the *Proceedings of the National Academy of Science of the United States of America,* vol. 98, no. 20.

Brewster, A.B. 1922. *The Hill Tribes of Fiji.* Seely, Service & Co. Limited. London.

Carroll, A. 1892. The Easter Island inscriptions, and the way in which they are translated, or deciphered, and read. In the *Journal of the Polynesian Society*, vol. 1, no. 4.

Cartwright, Bruce. 1929. The Legend of Hawaii-loa. In the *Journal of the Polynesian Society*, vol. 38, no. 150.

Charlot, John. 1983. *Chanting the Universe: Hawaiian Religious Culture.* Emphasis International. Honolulu.

Charlot, John. 2010. Two Early Hawaiian-Christian Chants. In *Anthrodos,* vol. 105, pp. 29-46.

Childress, David Hatcher. 1988. *Lost Cities of Ancient Lemuria & the Pacific.* Adventures Unlimited Press. Stelle, Illinois

Church, John W. Oct. 1919. A Vanishing People of the South Seas. In *National Geographic Magazine*, Volume 36, no. 4. Washington D.C.

Churchward, James. 1987 [1959]. *The Lost Continent of Mu.* BE Books. Albuquerque.

Clark, Jeffrey T. 1993. Radiocarbon Dates From American Samoa. In *Radiocarbon*, vol. 35, no. 2, 1993, pp. 323-330, Journals—UaiR, University of Arizona, Tucson.

Cleghorn, Paul L. and Elains Rogers-Jourdane. 1983. *Archaeological and Historic Research in Waipi'o Valley, Hamakua District, Hawai'i Island.* Bernice P. Bishop Museum Manuscript. Bishop Museum Library and Archives. Honolulu.

Colchester, Chloe. 2003. *Clothing the Pacific.* Berg Publishers. New York.

Cordy, Ross. 1994. *A Regional Synthesis of the Hamakua District, Hawai'i Island.* Historic Preservation Division, Department of Land & Natural Resources, State of Hawaii.

Cordy, Ross. 2000. *Exalted Sits the Chief.* Mutual Publishing Co. Honolulu.

Coulter, John Wesley. 1931. *Population of Land and Utilization of Land and Sea in Hawaii,* 1853. Bernice P. Bishop Museum, Bulletin 88. Bishop Museum Press. Honolulu.

Cox, J. Halley with William H. Davenport. 1988. *Hawaiian Sculpture.* University of Hawai'i Press. Honolulu.

Cox, Murray P., A.J. Reed, T.M. Karafet, et al. October 2007. A Polynesian motif on the Y chromosome: population structure in remote Oceania. In *Human Biology:* vol. 79, no. 5.

Cremo, Michael A. and Richard L. Thompson. 1996 [1993]. *Forbidden Archaeology: The Hidden History of the Human Race.* Bhaktivedanta Book Publishing Inc. Los Angeles.

Crowe, Ellie and William Crowe. 2001. *Exploring Lost Hawai'i: Places of Power, History & Magic.* Island Heritage Publishing. 'Aiea, Hawai'i.

Cunningham, Scott. 2001. *Hawaiian Magic and Spirituality.* Lewellyn Publications, Saint Paul, Minnesota.

Dahlgren, E. W. 1916. *Were the Hawaiian Islands visited by the Spaniards before their discovery by Captain Cook in 1778.* Almqvist & Wiksells Boktryckeri-A.-B. Stockholm.

Daniel, Hawthorne. 1943. *Islands of the Pacific.* G.P. Putnam's Sons. New York.

Daniel, Hawthorne. 1944. *Islands of the East Indies.* G.P. Putnam's Sons. New York.

Daws, Gavan. 1968. *Shoal of Time: A History of the Hawaiian Islands.* University of Hawai'i Press. Honolulu.

Day, A. Grove. 1966. *Explorers of the Pacific.* Duell, Sloan and Pearle. New York.

Decker, Robert W., Thomas L. Wright, Peter H. Stauffer. 1987. *Volcanism in Hawaii, vol. 1.* U.S. Geological Survey Professional Paper 1350, United States Government Printing Office, Washington DC.

Dening, Greg. 2004. *Beach Crossings*, University of Pennsylvania Press, Philadelphia.

Dening, Greg. 1980. *Islands and Beaches.* University of Hawai'i Press. Honolulu.

Denny, Michal and Lisa Matisoo-Smith. 2010. Rethinking Polynesian Origins: Human Settlement in the Pacific. In *LENScience Senior Biology Seminar Series,* Liggins Institute. University of Auckland.

Denoon, Donald. 1997. *The Cambridge History of the Pacific Islanders*, Cambridge University Press. Cambridge. United Kingdom.

Diamond, Jared M. 1997. *Guns, Germs, and Steel: The Fates of Human Societies.* W.W. Norton and Company. New York.

Dibble, Sheldon. 1909. [1843]. *A History of the Sandwich Islands.* T.G. Thrum, Honolulu.

Dodd, Edward H. 1967. *Polynesian Art.* Dodd, Mead and Company. New York.

Dodd, Edward H. 1972. *Polynesian Seafaring.* Dodd, Mead and Company. New York.

Dodd, Edward H. 1976. *Polynesia's Sacred Isle.* Dodd, Mead and Company. New York.

Dodd, Edward H. 1990. *The Island World of Polynesia.* The Windmill Hill Press. Putney, Vermont.

Dougherty, Michael. 1992. *To Steal a Kingdom.* Island Style Press. Waimanalo, Hawaii.

Dow, Gregory K. and Clyde G. Reed. November 2008. Stagnation and Innovation before Agriculture. In the *Journal of Economic Behavior & Organization,* vol. 77, issue 3, pp. 339-350. Department of Economics. Simon Fraser University. Burnaby, Canada.

Dudley, Michael Kioni. 1990. *Man, God, and Nature.* Na Kane O Ka Malo Press. Honolulu.

Dye, Thomas Stuart. 1987. *Social and Cultural Change in the Prehistory of the Ancestral Polynesian Homeland.* Ph.D dissertation, Yale University. U.M.I. Dissertation Services, Ann Arbor.

Dye, Tom. 1994. Population Trends in Hawai'i before 1778. In the *Hawaiian Journal of History,* vol. 28.

Ellis, William. 1783. *An Authentic Narrative of a Voyage performed by Captain Cook and Captain Clerke in his Majesty's ships Resolution and Discovery, vol. II.* Published by G. Robinson, J. Sewell and J. Debrett. London.

Ellis, William. 1963 [1826]. *Journal of William Ellis: A Narrative of an 1823 Tour through Hawaii, or Owhyhee in 1823.* Advertiser Publishing, Honolulu.

Ellis, William. 1969 [1829]. *Polynesian Researches-Hawaii.* Fisher, Son and Jackson. London.

Emerson, Nathaniel B. 1915. *Pele and Hiiaka: A Myth from Hawaii.* Honolulu Star—Bulletin Limited. Honolulu.

Emerson, Nathaniel B. 1965 [1909]. *Unwritten Literature of Hawaii; Sacred Songs of the Hula.* Charles E. Tuttle Co. Rutland, Vermont.

Emory, Kenneth P. 1933. *Stone Remains in the Society Islands.* Bernice P. Bishop Museum. Bulletin 116. Kraus Reprint Co. 1971. New York.

Emory, Kenneth P. 1934. *Tuamotuan Stone Structures.* Bishop Museum Press. Honolulu.

Emory, Kenneth P. 1938. The Tahitian Account of Creation by Mare. In the *Journal of the Polynesian Society,* vol. 47, no. 186.

Emory, Kenneth P. 1939. The Tuamotuan Creation Charts by Paiore. In the *Journal of the Polynesian Society,* vol. 48, no. 189.

Emory, Kenneth P. 1940. A Newly Discovered Illustration of Tuamotuan Creation. In the *Journal of the Polynesian Society,* vol. 49, no. 196.

Emory, Kenneth P., 1928. *Archaeology of Nihoa and Necker Islands.* Bernice P. Bishop Museum, Bulletin 53. Bishop Museum Press. Honolulu.

Emory, Kenneth P. 1959. Origins of the Hawaiians. In the *Journal of the Polynesian Society,* vol. 68, no. 1.

Emory, Kenneth P. 1963. East Polynesian Relationships. In the *Journey of the Polynesian Society,* vol. 72, no. 2.

Emory, Kenneth P., Edwin H. Bryan. 1986. *The Natural and Cultural History of Honaunau, Kona, Hawaii.* Department of Anthropology, Bishop Museum, Honolulu, Hawaii.

Eyre, David L. 2000. *By Wind, By Wave.* Bess Press. Honolulu.

Ferdon, Edwin N. 1981. *Early Tahiti as the Explorers Saw It.* The University of Arizona Press. Tucson.

Finney, Ben R. 1994. *Voyage of Rediscovery.* University of California Press. Berkeley.

Finney, Ben R. 2003. *Sailing in the Wake of the Ancestors.* Bishop Museum Press. Honolulu.

Finney, Ben R., 1979, *Hokule'a, The Way to Tahiti*, Dodd, Mead and Company, New York.

Finney, Ben R. 1999. The Sin at Awarua. In *The Contemporary Pacific,* vol. 11, no. 1, Spring 1999. University of Hawai'i Press. Honolulu.

Fisher, John L., Saul H. Riesenberg and Marjorie G. Whiting, translators and editors. 1997. The Book of Luelen / Luelen Bernart. In the *Pacific History Series No. 8.* University of Hawai'i Press. Honolulu.

Fison, Corimer. 1885. The Nanga, or Sacred Stone Enclosures of Wainimala, Fiji. In the *Journal of the Anthropological Institute of Great Britain and Ireland,* vol. 14. London.

Fornander, Abraham. 1916-1920. *Fornander Collection of Hawaiian Antiquities and Folk-lore,* vols. 4,5,6. Memories of the Bernice Pauahi Bishop Museum, Bishop Museum Press. Honolulu.

Fornander, Abraham. 1996 [1878]. *Fornander's Ancient History of the Hawaiian People* or *An Account of the Polynesian Race, Vol. II.* Mutual Publishing. Honolulu.

Friedlaender, Jonathan S. 2007. Mitochondrial DNA Variations in Northern Island Melanesia. In *Genes, Language, & Culture in the Southwest Pacific.* Oxford University Press, Inc. New York.

Furnas, J.C. 1948. *Anatomy of Paradise; Hawaii and the Islands of the South Seas.* William Slone Associates Inc. New York.

Garanger, Jose. 1979. *Sacred Stones and Rites of Ancient Tahiti.* Societe des Oceanistes. Paris.

Gifford, Edward Winslow. 1971 [1924]. *Tongan Myths and Tales.* Bernice P. Bishop Museum, Bulletin 8. Bishop Museum Press. Honolulu.

Gill, Rev. William Wyatt. 1977 [1876]. *Myths and Songs from the South Pacific.* Arno Press. New York.

Goldman, Irving. 1970. *Ancient Polynesian Society.* The University of Chicago Press. Chicago.

Gravelle, Kim. 2000. *Fiji's Heritage: A History of Fiji.* Tiara Enterprises, Nadi.

Green, Laura C. and Martha Warren Beckwith. 1926. Hawaiian Customs and Beliefs Relating to Sickness and Death. In the *American Anthropologist,* vol. 28, issue 1.

Grigg, Richard W. 1982. Darwin Point: A Threshold for Atoll Formation. In *Coral Reefs,* vol. 1, issue 1, 29-34.

Grimble, Arthur F. 1989. *Tungaru Traditions: Writings on the Atoll Culture of the Gilbert Islands.* University of Hawai'i Press. Honolulu.

Grimble, Arthur F. 1972. *Migrations, Myth and Magic from the Gilbert Islands.* Routledge & Kegan Paul. London.

Gutmanis, June. 1983. *Na Pule Kahiko, Ancient Hawaiian Prayers.* Bess Press. Honolulu.

Haddon, A.C. and James Hornell. 1975 [1938]. Definition of Terms, General Survey, and Conclusions. Bernice P. Bishop Museum Special Publication 29. In *Canoes of Oceania, vol. 3.* Bishop Museum Press, Honolulu.

Hancock, Graham and Santa Faiia. 1998. *Heaven's Mirror.* Crown Publishers, Inc. New York.

Hancock, Graham. 2002. *Underworld: The Mysterious Origins of Civilization.* Three Rivers Press. New York.

Handy, E.S. Craighill and Elizabeth G. Handy. 1972. *Native Planters in Old Hawaii.* Bernice P. Bishop Museum, Bulletin 233. Bishop Museum Press. Honolulu.

Handy, E.S. Craighill. 1923. *The Native Culture in the Marquesas.* Bernice P. Bishop, Bulletin 9. Bishop Museum Press. Honolulu.

Handy, E.S. Craighill. 1926. The Oracle-House in Polynesia. In the *Journal of the Polynesian Society*, vol. 35, no. 137.

Handy, E.S. Craighill. 1971 [1927]. *Polynesian Religion.* Bernice P. Bishop Museum. Bulletin 34. Kraus Reprint Co. Honolulu.

Handy, E.S. Craighill. 1930. *The Problem of Polynesian Origins.* Bernice P. Bishop Museum Press Occasional Papers, vol. 4, no. 8. Bishop Museum Press. Honolulu.

Handy, E.S. Craighill. 1940. Perspectives in Polynesian Religion. In the *Journal of the Polynesian Society*, vol. 49, no. 195.

Handy, E.S. Craighill. 1941. The Hawaiian Cult of Io. In the *Journal of the Polynesian Society*, vol. 50, no. 199.

Handy, E.S. Craighill. 1971 [1930]. *History and Culture in the Society Islands.* Bernice P. Bishop Museum. Bulletin 79. Bishop Museum Press. Honolulu.

Handy, E.S. Craighill. 1999. *Ancient Hawaiian Civilization.* Mutual Publishing. Honolulu.

Hanlon, David. 1988. *Upon a Stone Altar: A History of the Island of Pohnpei to 1890.* Center for Pacific Islands Studies. University of Hawai'i Press. Honolulu.

Hapgood, Charles H. 1979. *Maps of the Ancient Sea Kings.* Dutton Publishing Company. New York.

Harfst, Richard H. 1972. Cause or Condition. Explanations of the Hawaiian Cultural Revolution. In the *Journal of the Polynesian Society,* vol. 81, no. 4.

Hau'ofa, Epeli. 2008. *We Are the Ocean.* University of Hawai'i Press. Honolulu.

Henry, Teuira. 1971 [1928]. *Ancient Tahiti.* Bernice P. Bishop Museum, Bulletin 48. Bishop Museum Press. Honolulu.

Henry, Teuira, et. al. 1995. *Voyaging Chiefs of Havai'i.* Kalamaro Press. Honolulu.

Hewitt, James F.K. 1907. *Primitive Traditional History,* vol. 1. James Parker and Co. London.

Heyedahl, Thor. 1979. *Early Man and the Ocean.* Doubleday & Company Inc. New York.

Heyerdahl, Thor. 1989. *Easter Island; The Mystery Solved.* Random House Inc. New York.

Highland, Genevieve A. (Ed.). 1967. *Polynesian Cultural History.* Bernice P. Bishop Museum Special Publications 56. Bishop Museum Press. Honolulu.

Hill, S.S. Esq. 1856. *Travels in the Sandwich and Society Islands.* Chapman and Hall, London.

Hiroa, Te Rangi (Peter H. Buck). 1945. *An Introduction to Polynesian Anthropology.* Bernice P. Bishop Museum, Bulletin 187. Bishop Museum Press. Honolulu.

Hiroa, Te Rangi (Peter H. Buck). 1964. *Arts and Crafts of Hawaii.* Bernice P. Bishop Museum Special Publication 45, Bishop Museum Press, Honolulu, Hawaii.

Hoffman, Enid. 1981. *Huna: A Beginner's Guide.* Whitford Press, Atglem, Pennsylvania.

Hogbin, H. Ian. 1961 [1934]. *Law and Order in Polynesia.* The Shoe String Press Inc. Hamden, Connecticut.

Holmes, Tommy. 1993. [1981]. *The Hawaiian Canoe.* Bess Press. Honolulu.

Holt, John Dominis. 1985. *The Art of Featherwork in Old Hawaii.* Topgallant Publishing Co, Ltd. Honolulu.

Hommon, Robert John. 1976. *The Formation of Primitive States in Pre-Contact Hawai'i.* A Dissertation submitted to the Faculty of the Department of Anthropology. University of Arizona. Xerox University Micro Films. Ann Arbor.

Hooper, Steven. 2006. *Pacific Encounters: Art and Divinity in Polynesia 1760-1860.* University of Hawai'i Press. Honolulu.

Hornell, James. 1975. [1936]. The Canoes of Polynesia, Fiji, and Micronesia. Bernice P. Bishop Museum Special Publication 27. In *Canoes of Oceania,* vol. no. 1. Bernice P. Bishop Museum Special Publications 27, 28, and 29. Bishop Museum Press. Honolulu.

Horridge, Adrian. 1987. *Outrigger Canoea of Bali and Madura, Indonesia.* Bishop Museum Special Publication 77. Bishop Museum Press. Honolulu.

Hostetter, Clyde. 1991. *Star Trek to Hawa-i'i: Mesopotamia to Polynesia.* The Diamond Press. San Luis Obispo, Ca.

Hough, Richard A. 1979. *The Last Voyage of Captain James Cook.* William Morrow and Company Inc. New York.

Howard, Alan and Robert Borofsky, (Eds.). 1989. *Development in Polynesian Ethnology.* University of Hawai'i Press. Honolulu.

Howe, K. R. 1984. *Where the Waves Fall: A New South Sea Islands History from First Settlement to Colonial Rule.* University of Hawai'i Press. Honolulu.

Howe, K. R. 2007. *Vaka Moana: Voyages of the Ancestors.* University of Hawai'i Press. Honolulu.

Howe, Kerry R. 2003. *The Quest for Origins.* University of Hawai'i Press. Honolulu.

Howell, William W. 1973. *The Pacific Islanders.* Charles Scribner's Sons. New York.

Hoyes, Martha H. 2003. *Then There Were None.* Bess Press. Honolulu.

Hudson, Alfred. 1932. *Archaeology of East Hawaii.* Bishop Museum Press. Honolulu.

Hurles, Matthew E. et al. 2002. Y Chromosomal Evidence for the Origin of Oceanic-Speaking Peoples. In *Genetics,* vol. 160: 289-303, January 2002.

'I'i, John Papa. 1983 [1959]. *Fragments of Hawaiian History.* Bishop Museum Special Publication 70. Bishop Museum Press. Honolulu.

Intoh, Michiko. 1999. Cultural Contacts between Micronesia and Melanesia. In Galipaud, J-C and I. Liley (Eds.). *Le Pacifique de 5000 a 2000 avant le Presenti Supplements a l'histoire d'une Colonisation.* Paris.

Irwin, Geoffrey. 1992. *The Prehistoric Exploration and Colonisation of the Pacific.* Cambridge University Press. Cambridge. United Kingdom.

Iyengar, T.R. Sesha. 1995. [1925]. *Dravidian India.* Asian Educational Services. New Delhi.

Jennings, Jesse D. (Ed.). 1979. *The Prehistory of Polynesia.* Harvard University Press. Cambridge. Massachusetts.

Joesting, Edward. 1972. *Hawaii: An Uncommon History.* W.W. Norton and Company Inc., New York.

Johnson, Rubelite Kawena Kinney. 2000. *The Kumulipo Mind: A Global Heritage.* Honolulu.

Johnson, Rubellite K. 1993. *Mo'olelo Hawaii (World of the Hawaiians).* Department of Indo-Pacific Languages. University of Hawaii-Manoa. Honolulu.

Joseph, Frank. 2006. *The Lost Civilization of Lemuria.* Bear & Company. Rochester, Vermont.

Juvik, Sonia P. and James O. Juvik, (Eds.). 1998. *Atlas of Hawai'i/ Department of Geography.* University of Hawai'i at Hilo.

Kaeppler, Adrienne L. 1993. *Hula Pahu: Hawaiian Drum Dances, Volume 1: Ha'a and Hula Pahu: Sacred Movements.* Bishop Museum Bulletin in Anthropology 3. Bishop Museum Press. Honolulu.

Kaeppler, Adrienne L. 2007. Containers of Divinity. In the *Journal of the Polynesian Society,* vol. 116, no. 2.

Kaeppler, Adrienne L. 2008. *The Pacific Arts of Polynesia and Micronesia.* Oxford University Press Inc. New York.

Kalakaua, David. 1990. [1888]. *The Legends and Myths of Hawaii.* Mutual Publishing. Honolulu.

Kamakau, Samuel M. 1992 [1961]. *Ruling Chiefs of Hawaii.* Kamehameha Schools Press, Honolulu.

Kamakau, Samuel M. 1988. *I Ka Wa o Kamehameha [In the Time of Kamehameha].* The Folk Press. Kapiolani Community College. Honolulu.

Kamakau, Samuel M. 1992 [1976]. *Na Hana a ka Po'e Kahiko = The Works of the People of Old.* Bishop Museum Special Publication 61. Bishop Museum Press. Honolulu.

Kamakau, Samuel M. 1992 [1964]. *Ka Po'e Kahiko = The People of Old.* Bernice P. Bishop Museum Special Publication 51, Bishop Museum Press, Honolulu.

Kame'eleihiwa, Lilikala. 1992. *Native Land and Foreign Desire.* Bishop Museum Press. Honolulu.

Kanahele, George. 1986. *Ku Kanaka, Stand Tall: A Search for Hawaiian Values.* University of Hawai'i Press. Honolulu.

Kanaka'ole, Edith. April 2009. *Cultural Anchor in the Mauna Kea Comprensive Management Plan.* University of Hawai'i Press. Honolulu.

Kane, Herb Kawainui. 1991. *Voyages.* Kawainui Press.

Kane, Herb Kawainui. 1994. *Letters from My Father.* Unpublished Manuscript.

Kane, Herb Kawainui. 1997. *Ancient Hawaii.* Kawainui Press.

Kay, E. Alison. (Ed.). 1994. *A Natural History of the Hawaiian Island.* University of Hawai'i Press. Honolulu.

Kayser, Manfred, et. al. 2006. Melanesian and Asian Origins of Polynesians: mtDNA and Y Chromosome Gradients across the Pacific. In *Molecular Biology and Evolution 23 (11): 2234-2244,* 2006.

Kelly, Kevin M. 1999. *Research Report, Malaria and Immunoglobulins in Pacific Prehistory.* Department of Anthropology and Department of Environmental and Occupational Health. College of Public Health. University of Iowa. Iowa City.

Kelly, Marion A. 1957. Report 11: The Concept of Asylum. In *The Natural and Cultural History of Honaunau, Kona, Hawaii. Part II, The Cultural History of Honaunau*, October 1986, by Edwin H. Bryan and Kenneth P. Emory. Department of Anthropology, Bernice P. Bishop Museum, Honolulu.

Kikawa, Daniel I. 1994. *Perpetuated in Righteousness.* Aloha Ke Akua Publishing. Kane'ohe, Hawai'i.

Kikawa, Daniel I. 2008. *God of Light, God of Darkness.* Aloha Ke Akua Publishing. Kea'au, Hawaii.

Kikuchi, William Kenji. 1973. *Hawaiian Aquacultural Systems.* Ph.D Dissertation submitted to the University of Arizona, Department of Anthropology. University Microfilms. Ann Arbor.

Kimball, Linda Amy. 1993. The Batak Porhalaan Traditional Calendar of Sumatra. In *Archaeoastronomy: The Journal of the Center for Archaeoastronomy*, vol. xi, 1989-1993. College Park. Maryland.

King, Serge Kahili. 1985. *Mastering Your Hidden Self: A Guide to the Huna Way.* Theosophical Publishing House. Wheaton, Ill.

Kirch, Patrick V. 1998 [1985]. *Feathered Gods and Fishhooks: An Introduction to Hawaiian Archaeology and Prehistory.* University of Hawai'i Press. Honolulu.

Kirch, Patrick V. 2002 [2000]. *On the Road of the Winds.* University of California Press, Berkeley.

Kirch, Patrick V. 2001. *Hawaiki, Ancestral Polynesia: An Essay in Historical Anthropology.* Cambridge University Press, Cambridge, United Kingdom.

Kirch, Patrick V. and Jean-Louis Rallu, (Eds.). 2007. *The Growth and Collapse of Pacific Island Societies.* University of Hawai'i Press. Honolulu.

Kirch, Patrick V. and Marshall Sahlins. 1994 [1977]. *Anahulu: The Anthropology of History in the Kingdom of Hawaii.* University of Chicago Press. Chicago.

Kirch, Patrick V. and Terry L. Hunt, (Ed.). 1988. *Archaeology of the Lapita Cultural Complex: A Critical Review.* Thomas Burke Memorial Washington State Museum. Research Report No. 5. Seattle.

Kirch, Patrick V. 1984. *The evolution of the Polynesian chiefdoms.* Cambridge University Press. New York.

Kirch, Patrick V. 1996. *Legacy of the Landscape.* University of Hawai'i Press. Honolulu.

Kirch, Patrick V. 2010. *Peopling of the Pacific: A Holistic Anthropological Perspective.* Annual Review of Anthropology, vol. 39.

Kirch, Patrick V. 1997. *The Lapita Peoples: Ancestors of the Oceanic World.* Blackwell Publishers Ltd. Malden, Massachusetts.

Kirch, Patrick V. 2010. *How Chiefs Became Kings.* University of California Press. Berkeley and Los Angeles.

Kramer, Samuel Noah. 1963. *The Sumerians: Their History, Culture and Character.* University of Chicago Press. Chicago.

Kramer, Samuel Noah. 1981. *History Begins at Sumer.* University of Pennsylvania Press. Philadelphia.

Kyselka, Will and George Bunton. 1969. *Polynesian Stars and Men.* Bishop Museum Science Center. Honolulu.

Lang, John Dunmore. 1834. *View of the Origin and Migrations of the Polynesian Nation.* Cochrane and M'Crone. London.

Langdon, Robert. 1975. *The Lost Caravel.* Pacific Publications. Sydney

Lebo, Susan A. 1975. A Master Plan Proposal for Waipi'o Valley, Hawaii, *Waipi'o Valley Master Plan,* Hamakua District Development Council Inc., Honokaa, Hawaii.

Lebo, Susan A. 1999. *Life in Waipi'o Valley, Hawaii 1880 to 1942.* Bishop Museum, Honolulu.

Levin, Stephenie S. 1968. The Overthrow of the Kapu System in Hawaii. In the *Journal of the Polynesian Society.* vol. 77, no. 4.

Lewis, David. 1994 [1972]. *We, The Navigators: The Ancient Art of Landfinding in the Pacific.* University of Hawai'i Press. Honolulu.

Liller, William. 2000. Necker Island, Hawai'i: Astronomical Implications of an Island Located on the Tropic of Cancer. In *Rapa Nui Journal*, vol. 14 (4), December 2000.

Linnekin, Jocelyn S. 1983. Defining Tradition: Variations on the Hawaiian Identity. In *American Ethnologist,* vol. 10, no. 2, May, 1983, pp. 241-252.

Linton, Ralph. 1925. *Archaeology of the Marquesas Islands.* Bernice P. Bishop Museum. Bulletin 23. Bishop Museum Press. Honolulu.

Linton, Ralph. 1923. Material Culture of the Marquesas Islands. In *Memoirs of the Bernice P. Bishop Museum*, vol. 8, no. 5. Bishop Museum Press, Honolulu.

Long, Max Freedom. 1965. *The Huna Code in Religions.* De Vorss & Company. Santa Monica.

Long, Max Freedom. 1997 [1948]. *The Secret Science Behind Miracles.* De Vorss & Company. Santa Monica.

Luomala, Katharine. 1951. *The Menehune of Polynesia and Other Mythical Little People of Oceania.* Bernice P. Bishop Museum Bulletin 203. Bishop Museum Press. Honolulu.

Luomala, Katharine. 1986 [1955]. *Voices on the Wind: Polynesian Myths and Chants.* Bishop Museum Special Publication 75. Bishop Museum Press. Honolulu.

Macdonald, Gordon A. and Agatin Abott. 1970. *Volcanoes in the Sea: The Geology of Hawaii.* University of Hawai'i Press. Honolulu.

Makemson, Maud Worcester. 1941. *The Morning Star Rises, An Account of Polynesian Astronomy.* Yale University Press. New Haven.

Malo, David. 1951 [1898]. *Hawaiian Antiquities: Moolelo Hawaii.* Bernice P. Bishop Museum Special Publication 2. Bishop Museum Press. Honolulu.

Marsh, Peter. 2005. "Genetics Rewrites Pacific Prehistory". In *Polynesian Pathways*, 2002.

Marsh, Peter. 2008. "Lapita Pottery & Polynesians". In *Polynesian Pathways*, 2002.

Matisoo-Smith, E. and J. H. Robbins. 2004. Origin and Dispersals of Pacific Peoples: Evidence from mtDNA Paylogenies of the Pacific Rat. In the *Proceedings of the National Academy of Science of the United States of America.*

Mauss, Marcel. 1972. *A General Theory of Magic.* Routledge & Kegan Raul Ltd. London and Boston.

McCall, Grant. 1994. Little Ice Age: Some Proposals for Polynesia and Rapanui (Easter Island). In the *Journal De La Societe Des Oceanistes*, vol. 89.

McCoy, Patrick C. 1999. *Appendix K.* Mauna Kea Science Reserve Master Plan Final Environmental Impact Statement. Group 70 International Inc. Honolulu.

McGregor, Davianna Pomaika'i. 2007. *Na Kua'aina: Living Hawaiian Culture.* University of Hawai'i Press. Honolulu.

McLean, Mervyn. 2008. Were Lapita Potters Ancestral to Polynesians? A View from Ethnomusicology. Occasional Papers in *Pacific Ethnomusicology,* No. 7. Archive of Maori and Pacific Music. Center for Pacific Studies. The University of Auckland. New Zealand.

Melville, Herman. 1996 [1876]. *Typee, A Peep of Polynesian Life.* Oxford University Press. Oxford.

Melville, Leinani. 1990. *Children of the Rainbow.* The Theosophical Society in America, The Theosophical Publishing House, Wheaton, Illinois.

Merriwether, D.A. et al. 1999. Mitochondrial DNA Variation is an Indicator of Austronesian Influence in Island Melanesia. In the *American Journal of Physical Anthropology*, vol. 110.

Metraux, Alfred. 1971 [1940]. *Ethnology of Easter Island.* Bernice P. Bishop Museum Bulletin 160. Bishop Museum Press. Honolulu.

Michener, James A. 1959. *Hawaii.* Random House. New York.

Moffat, Riley M. 1947. *Mapping the Lands and Waters of Hawaii: The Hawaiian Government Survey*, vol. 3. Editions Limited. Honolulu.

Morrill, Sibley S. Ed. 1968. *The Kahunas.* Branden Press Publishers. Boston.

Morrison, James. Account of the Islands of Tahiti & the Customs of the Island. Published in the Owen Rutter edition of the *Journal of James Morrison, Boatswain's Mate of the Bounty.* Golden Cockerel Press. London.

Namakaokeahi, Benjamin K., transcriber and Malcolm Naea Chun, translator. 2004. *The History of Kanalu Mo'oku'auhau 'Elua: A genealogical history of the priesthood of Kanalu.* First People's Productions. Honolulu.

Neller, Earl. 1989. *Archaeology of Hawai'i: Hawaiian heiau with Earl "Buddy" Neller.* Liliha Library.

Novak, Peter. 2002. Division of the Self: Life After Death and the Binary Soul Doctrine. In the *Journal of Near-Death Studies*, Spring 2002. Human Sciences Press. New York.

Nunn, Patrick D. 1999. *Environmental Changes in the Pacific Basin, Chronologies, Causes, Consequences.* John Wiley & Sons. Chichester, England.

Nunn, Patrick D. 2009. *Vanished Islands and Hidden Continents of the Pacific.* University of Hawai'i Press. Honolulu.

O'Brien, Frederick. 1919. *White Shadows in the South Seas.* The Century Co. New York.

O'Brien, Frederick. 1921. *Mystic Isles of the South Seas.* The Century Co. New York.

O'Shaughnessy, D. F. 1990. Globin Genes in Micronesia: Origins and Affinities of Pacific Island Peoples. In the *American Journal of Human Genetics.*

Obeyesekere, Gananath. 1992. *The Apotheosis of Captain Cook: European Mythmaking in the Pacific.* Bishop Museum Press. Honolulu.

Oppenheimer, Stephen and Martin Richards. 2001. *Fast Trains, Slow Boats, and the Ancestry of the Polynesian Islanders.* Science Progress; 84 (3).

Oppenheimer, Stephen. 1999. *Eden in the East: The Drowned Continent of Southeast Asia.* Orion Books, Ltd. London.

Orsmond, Rev. J.M. 1894. The Birth of New Lands, After the Creation of Hawai'i (Raiatea). In the *Journal of the Polynesian Society*, vol. 3, no. 3.

Peirce, Henry A. 1940. *The Spanish Discovery of the Hawaiian Islands.* Hawaiian Printing Co. Honolulu.

Peleioholani, Solomon L.K. Translated by Joseph M. Poepoe. 2004 [18—]. *The Ancient History of Hookumu Ka Lani and Hookumu Ka Honua.* Bernice P. Bishop Museum. Honolulu.

Peterson, Glenn. 1990. *Lost in the Weeds: Theme and Variation in Pohnpei Political Mythology.* Occasional Paper 35. Center for Pacific Islands Studies. University of Hawai'i at Manoa. Honolulu.

Piercy, LaRue W. 1985. *Hawaii—Truth Stranger Than Fiction.* Ficher Printing Co., Inc. Honolulu.

Pogue, John F. (Rev.). *Mooelo of Ancient Hawaii.* Topgallant Publishing Co, Ltd. Honolulu.

Pietrusewsky, M. 1985. The Earliest Lapita Skeleton from the Pacific. In *The Journal of the Polynesian Society*, vol. 94, no. 4.

Pietrusewsky, M., et. al. 1997. A Lapita-associated Skeleton from Waya Island, Fiji. In *Micronesia*, 1997.

Porter, David D., Captain. 1823. *A Voyage in the South Seas in the Years 1812, 1813 and 1814.* Sir Richard Phillips & Co. London.

Porter, David D., Captain. 1986 [1815]. *Journal of a Cruise.* Naval Institute Press. Annapolis, Md.

Pukui, Mary K. 1996. *Hawai'i Island Legends: Pikoi, Pele and Others.* Kamehameha Schools Press. Honolulu.

Pukui, Mary K. and Samuel H. Elbert. 1971 [1957]. *Hawaiian Dictionary.* University of Hawai'i Press. Honolulu.

Pukui, Mary Kawena. 1972. *Nana I Ke Kumu (Look to the Source). Volume II.* Hui Hanai, Queen Lili'uokalani Children's Center. Honolulu.

Rainbird, Paul. 2004. *The Archaeology of Micronesia.* Cambridge University Press. Cambridge.

Rapaport, Moshe (Ed.). 1999. *The Pacific Islands: Environment and Society.* Bess Press. Honolulu.

Razafindrazaka, Harilanto, et al. 2009. Complete mitochondrial DNA sequences provide new insight into the Polynesian motif and the peopling of Madagascar. In the *European Journal of Human Genetics (2010),* vol. 18.

Remy, Jules M. 1979 [1857]. *Contributions of a Venerable Native to the Ancient History of Hawaiian Islands.* Outbooks, Inc. Fayetteville.

Rhys, Ernest (Ed.). 1999. *The Voyages of Captain Cook.* Wordsworth Editions Limited. Hertfordshire. United Kingdom.

Rice, William Hyde. 1923. *Hawaiian Legends.* Bernice P. Museum Bulletin 3, Bishop Museum Press, Honolulu.

Ringgren, Helmer. 1973. *Religions of the Ancient Near East.* Translated by John Sturdy. The Westminster Press. Philadelphia.

Rivers, W.H.R. 1914. *The History of Melanesian Society, Vols. 1 and 2.* Cambridge University Press. Cambridge. United Kingdom.

Rogers, Richard W. 1999. *Shipwrecks of Hawaii: A Maritime History of the Big Island.* Pilialoha Publishing. Haliewa, Hawaii.

Rohl, David M.1995. *Pharaohs and Kings: A Biblical Quest.* Crown Publishers, Inc. New York.

Rutter, Owen. (Ed.). 1935. *Journal of James Morrison, Boatswain's Mate of the Bounty.* Golden Cockered Press. London.

Ryan, William and Walter Pitman. 1998. *Noah's Flood: The New Scientific Discoveries about the Event That Change History.* Simon & Schuster. New York.

Sahlins, Marshall David. 1985. *Islands of History.* University of Chicago Press. Chicago and London.

Sahlins, Marshall D. 1995. *How "Natives" Think; About Captain Cook, For Example.* University of Chicago Press. Chicago and London.

Sahlins, Marshall D. 1981. *Historical Metaphors and Mythical Realities: Structure in the Early History of the Sandwich Islands Kingdom.* University of Michigan Press. Ann Arbor.

Scarr, Deryck. 1984. *Fiji: A Short History.* The Institute for Polynesian Studies. The Polynesian Cultural Center, Brigham Young University, Hawaii Campus. Laie.

Schmitt, Robert C. 1971. New estimates of the Pre-Censal Population of Hawaii. In the *Journal of the Polynesian Society.* vol. 80, no. 2.

Schmitt, Robert C. 1968. *Demographic Statistics of Hawaii: 1778-1965.* University of Hawai'i Press. Honolulu.

Schoch, Robert M. 2003. *Voyages of the Pyramid Builders.* Jeremy P. Tarcher/Putman a member of Penguin Putman Inc. New York

Schutz, Albert J. 1994. *The Voices of Eden: A History of Hawaiian Language Studies.* University of Hawai'i Press. Honolulu.

Serjeantson, Susan W. 1989. S.W. Serjeantson: HLA genes and antigens. In *The Colonization of the Pacific: A Genetic Trail.* Oxford University Press, London.

Sharp, Andrew. 1960. *The Discovery of the Pacific Islands.* Oxford University Press. London.

Shore, Bradd. 1989. Mana and Tapu. In *Developments in Polynesian Ethnology.* University of Hawai'i Press. Honolulu.

Shwartz, Mark. June 16, 2004. *Volcanic Soils Yield New Clues about the Emergence of Powerful Chiefdoms in Hawaii.* Stanford News-Service.

Skinner, H.D. 1933. Three Polynesian Drums. In the *Journal of the Polynesian Society,* vol. 42, no.168.

Smith, Anita. 2002. *An Archaeology of West Polynesian Prehistory.* Pandanus Press. Camberra.

Smith, S Percy. 1899. Hawaiki: The Whence of the Maori: Being an Introduction to Rarotonga History, Part III. In the *Journal of the Polynesian Society,* vol. 8, no. 1.

Smith, S. Percy, (Translator.). 1913. *Lore of the Whare-wananga; Teachings of the Maori College.* T. Avery for the Polynesian Society. New Plymouth.

Soares, Pedro. et al. 2011. Ancient voyaging and Polynesian Origins. In the *American Journal of Human Genetics,* vol. 88, 239-247, February 11, 2011.

Spriggs, Matthew. 1997. *The Island Melanesians.* Blackwell Publishers Limited. Oxford.

Stannard, David. 1989. *Before the Horror: The Population of Hawaii on the Eve of Western Contact.* University of Hawai'i Press. Honolulu.

Stearns, Harold T. 1985. *Geology of the State of Hawaii.* Pacific Books, Palo Alto, California.

Stevenson, Robert Louis. 1973. *Travels in Hawaii.* University of Hawai'i Press. Honolulu.

Stokes, John F. G. 1991. *Heiau of the Island of Hawai'i: A Survey of Native Hawaiian Temple Sites,* Bishop Museum Bulletin in Anthropology, 2. Bishop Museum Press. Honolulu.

Su, Bing. 2000. Polynesian origins: Insights from the Y chromosome. In the *Proceedings of the National Academy of Science of the United States of America.*

Suggs, Robert C. 1960. *The Island Civilizations of Polynesia.* New American Library. New York.

Suggs, Robert C. 1962. *The Hidden Worlds of Polynesia.* Harcourt, Brace and World Inc. New York.

Sykes, B. et al. 1995. The Origin of the Polynesians: An Interpretation from Mitochondrial Lineage Analysis. In the *American Journal of Human Genetics,* vol. 57: 1463-1475.

Sykes, Bryan. 2001. *The Seven Daughters of Eve.* W.W. Norton & Company, Inc. New York.

Tabrah, Ruth M. 1980. *Hawaii, A Bicentennial History.* W.W. Norton and Company Inc. New York.

Tatar, Elizabeth, 1982, *Nineteenth Century Hawaiian Chant,* Pacific Anthropological Records No. 33, Bernice P. Bishop Museum, Honolulu.

Taylor, Albert P. 1922. *Under Hawaiian Skies, a narrative of the romance, adventure and history of the Hawaiian Islands.* Advertiser Publishing Company, Ltd. Honolulu.

Teller, J.T. et al. 2000. *Calcareous Dunes of the United Arab Emirates and Noah's Flood: The Post Glacial Reflooding of the Persian (Arabian) Gulf.* In *Quaternary International 68/71* (2000) 297-308. 2000 Elsevier Science Ltd.

The Holy Bible. King James Version. 1984 [1611]. American Bible Society. New York.

Thomas, Nicholas. 1990. *Marquesan Society; Inequality and Political Transformation in Eastern Polynesia.* Clarendon Press. Oxford.

Thompson, Basil. 1892. The Land of Our Origin (Viti or Fiji). In the *Journal of the Polynesian Society,* vol. 1, no. 3.

Thompson, Laura. 1940. *Southern Lau, Fiji: An Ethnography.* Bernice P. Bishop Museum Bulletin 162. Bishop Museum Press, Honolulu.

Thomson, Basil. 1904. *The Fijians: A Study of the Decay of Custom.* William Heinemann. London.

Thrum, Thomas G. 1893. Ancient Hawaiian Water Rights. In the *Hawaiian Almanac and Annual for 1894.* Press Publishing Co. Honolulu.

Thrum, Thomas G. 1908. Heiaus and Heiau Sites Throughout the Hawaiian Islands. In the *Hawaiian Almanac and Annual for 1908.* Honolulu.

Thrum, Thomas G. 1910. Heiaus: Their Kinds, Construction, Ceremonies, Etc. In the *Hawaiian Almanac and Annual for 1910.* Thos. G. Thrum Publisher. Honolulu.

Thrum, Thomas G. 1919. Ancient Hawaiian Theories as to the Nature and Origin of Things. In the *Hawaiian Almanac and Annual for 1919.* Honolulu, Hawaii.

Thrum, Thomas G. 1979 [1923]. *More Hawaiian Folk Tales.* AMS Press. New York.

Thrum, Thomas G. 1978 [1907]. *Hawaiian Folk Tales, A Collection of Native Legends.* AMS Press. New York.

Torrence, Robin. 2002. What makes a disaster? A long-term view of volcanic eruptions and human responses in Papua New Guinea. In *Natural Disasters and Cultural Change.* R. Torrence and J. Grattan, eds. Routledge. London.

Trejaut, Jean A., et. al. 2014. Taiwan Y- Chromosome DNA variation and its relationship with Island Southeast Asia. In *BMC Genetics* 2014, 15:77

Tregear, Edward. 1893. Asiatic Gods in the Pacific. In the *Journal of the Polynesian Society,* vol. 2, no. 3. September 1893.

Tylor, Edward B. 1871. *Primitive Culture: Research into the Development of Mythology, Philosophy, Religion, Language, Art, and Custom.* Vols. 1 and 2. John Murray, Albemarle Street. London.

Valeri, Valerio. 1985. *Kingship and Sacrifice, Ritual and Society in Ancient Hawaii.* University of Chicago Press. Chicago.

Valeri, Valerio. 1990. Constitutive History: Genelogy and Narrative in the Legitimation of Hawaiian Kingship. In *Culture Through Time.* Ohnuki-Turney, Emiko, Ed.

Wells, Spencer. 2002. *The Journey of Man: A Genetic Odyssey.* Princeton University Press. Princeton.

Westervelt, W. D. 1987. *Myths and Legends of Hawaii.* Mutual Publishing, Honolulu, Hawaii.

Westervelt, W.D. 1998 [1923]. *Hawaiian Historical Legends.* Mutual Publishing. Honolulu.

Westervelt, W.D. 2001 [1915]. *Hawaiian Legends of Gods and Ghosts (Hawaiian Mythology).* Mutual Publishing. Honolulu.

Wheeler, Sir Robert E. Mortimer. 1959. *Early India and Pakistan.* Frederick A. Praeger, Publishers. New York.

Wiens, Herold J. 1962. *Pacific Island Bastions of the United States.* D. Van Nostrand Company Inc. Princeton.

Williams, Thomas. 1982 [1858]. *Fiji and the Fijians: The Islands and Their Inhabitants.* Oceania Printers Ltd. Suva.

Wilson, Ian. 1985. *Exodus: The True Story.* Harper & Row, Publishers, San Francisco.

Wilson, Ian. 2001. *Before the Flood: The Biblical Flood as a Real Event and How It Changed the Course of Civilization.* St. Martin's Press, New York.

Winkler, Jons. 1913. *Der Kalender der Toba-Bataks auf Sumatra.* Translation by Linda Amy Kimball, 1988. In the *Journal of the Center for Archaeoastronomy,* vol. XI 1989-1993, article A. University of Texas Press. Austin.

Woolley, C. Leonard. 1965. *The Sumerians.* W.W. Norton. New York.

Young, J.L. 1919. The Paumotu Concept of the Heavens and of Creation. In the *Journal of the Polynesian Society*, vol. 28, no. 112.

Zerega, Nyree J.C. 2004. Complex Origins of Breadfruit: Implications for Human Migrations in Oceania. In the *American Journal of Botany,* vol. 91. Botanical Society of America Inc.

Zerega, Nyree J.C. December 2003. The Breadfruit Trail. In *Natural History.* 2003:112(10):46-51.

Ziegler, Alan C. 2002. *Hawaiian Natural History, Ecology, and Evolution.* University of Hawai'i Press. Honolulu.

Zimmerman, Elwood C. 1948. *Insects of Hawaii,* vol. 1. University of Hawai'i Press. Honolulu.

INDEX